LIMITS TO DECOLONIZATION

A volume in the series
Cornell Series on Land: New Perspectives in Territory,
Development, and Environment
Edited by Wendy Wolford, Nancy Lee Peluso, and Michael Goldman

A list of titles in this series is available at
cornellpress.cornell.edu.

LIMITS TO DECOLONIZATION

Indigeneity, Territory, and Hydrocarbon
Politics in the Bolivian Chaco

Penelope Anthias

CORNELL UNIVERSITY PRESS   ITHACA AND LONDON

First published 2018 by Cornell University Press

Library of Congress Cataloging-in-Publication Data

Names: Anthias, Penelope, 1980– author.
Title: Limits to decolonization : indigeneity, territory, and hydrocarbon politics in the Bolivian Chaco / Penelope Anthias.
Description: Ithaca : Cornell University Press, 2018. | Includes bibliographical references and index.
Identifiers: LCCN 2017037833 (print) | LCCN 2017039895 (ebook) | ISBN 9781501714283 (epub/mobi) | ISBN 9781501714290 (pdf) | ISBN 9781501714351 (cloth | ISBN 9781501714368

Subjects: LCSH: Guarani Indians—Land tenure—Bolivia—Gran Chaco (Province) | Guarani Indians—Bolivia—Gran Chaco (Province)—Politics and government. | Gas industry—Political aspects—Bolivia—Gran Chaco (Province) | Decolonization—Bolivia—Gran Chaco (Province) | Ethnography—Bolivia—Gran Chaco (Province)
Classification: LCC F3320.1.L35 (ebook) | LCC F3320.1.L35 A58 2018 (print) | DDC 305.800984—dc23
LC record available at https://lccn.loc.gov/2017037833

Contents

Acknowledgments

I am deeply grateful to the many people whose knowledge, support, and hospitality made this book possible. In Tarija, two local NGOs, CERDET and Comunidad de Estudios JAINA, provided office space, logistical support, access to documentation and library resources, and sustained productive dialogue on research questions. Guaraní leaders at the APG IG and the CCGT showed generosity, patience, and courage in their engagements with me, as did non-Guaraní residents of O'Connor Province. Aldo Villena, Hernán Ruíz, Silvia Flores, Erick Aráoz, Juan Carlos Arostegui, Guido Cortez, Pilar Lizárraga, Gonzalo Torrez, Ricardo Gareca, Denise Humphreys Bebbington, Tom Broadhurst, and Judith Van den Bosch were great friends and intellectual allies in Tarija. I am greatly indebted to community members of the community I call Tarairí, particularly Armando, Sandra, and family, who shared their home, food, warmth, and humor under often difficult circumstances. My arrival in Tarairí was facilitated by Bret Gustafson, whose long-standing research with the Guaraní of Bolivia was a source of inspiration. Beyond Tarija, individuals from Oxfam, CEJIS, CEDLA, CEADES, CIPCA, Fundación TIERRA, the APG Nacional, CIDOB, and INRA took time out of busy work agendas to engage in this research.

At the University of Cambridge, Sarah A. Radcliffe was a generous and engaging mentor whose critical insights made this a more rigorous piece of scholarship. Research was funded by a 1+3 Studentship from the Economic and Social Research Council. The Cartographic Unit at the University of Cambridge did an expert job making the maps that appear in this book. The writing of this book was made possible by a Ciriacy-Wantrup Postdoctoral Fellowship at the University of California, Berkeley (2014–2016). At Berkeley, Michael Watts provided guidance and encouragement that enabled my writing to develop in new directions, and I was inspired and challenged by conversations with Donald Moore. Nancy Postero, Bret Gustafson, Sian Lazar, Cheryl McEwan, and Mario Blaser provided invaluable feedback on early versions of this book. Amy Kennemore, Paula Saravia, Jorge Montesinos, Devin Beaulieu, and Andrea Marston gave incisive comments on individual chapters. Tony Bebbington, Fiona Wilson, and Sandip Hazareesingh helped the research for this book get off the ground. During the final stages of editing, I received useful comments from colleagues in the Rule and Rupture Program at the University of Copenhagen. I am especially grateful to the program's director Christian Lund for his patience and generosity during this period. I have been fortunate to have four wonderful editors for this book—Jim Lance at Cornell University Press and series editors Wendy Wolford, Nancy Lee Peluso, and Michael Goldman—who have provided expert guidance and support throughout the publication process.

Finally, I thank my friends and family for all the support they have given me throughout the research and writing process, particularly my parents, Louise and Taf Anthias.

Abbreviations

APG	Asamblea del Pueblo Guaraní (Guaraní People's Assembly, the national Guaraní organization of Bolivia)
APG IG	Asamblea del Pueblo Guaraní Itika Guasu (Guaraní People's Assembly of Itika Guasu)
ASOGAPO	Asociación de Ganaderos de la Provincia O'Connor (Association of Cattle Ranchers of O'Connor Province)
CCGT	Concejo de Capitanes Guaraníes de Tarija (Council of Guaraní Captains of Tarija)
CEADES	Colectivo de Estudios Aplicados y Desarrollo Social Juan XXIII (John XXIII Collective of Applied Studies and Social Development)
CERDET	Centro de Estudios Regionales para el Desarrollo de Tarija (Center for Regional Studies for the Development of Tarija, a regional NGO, also known as Centro de Estudios Regionales de Tarija)
CIDOB	Confederación de Pueblos Indígenas de Bolivia (Confederation of Indigenous Peoples of Bolivia)
CSUTCB	Confederación Sindical Única de Trabajadores Campesinos de Bolivia (Unified Syndical Confederation of Rural Workers of Bolivia)
DANIDA	Danish International Development Agency
EAPG	Equipo de Apoyo al Pueblo Guaraní (Aid Team for the Guaraní People, a local NGO based in Entre Ríos, Tarija)
EINE	estudio de identificación de necesidades espaciales (spatial needs identification study)
FES	función económica social (economic social function, the measure of productive land use under the INRA Law)
INRA	Instituto Nacional de Reforma Agraria (National Institute of Agrarian Reform, the state agency responsible for land titling)
MAS	Movimiento al Socialismo (Movement toward Socialism, the political party headed by Evo Morales and currently in power in Bolivia)
PROSOL	Programa Solidario Comunal (Communal Solidarity Program, a departmental agricultural direct cash transfer program financed by departmental gas rents)

SAN-TCO   saneamiento de TCO (the legal process for titling TCOs)

TAN   Tribunal Agrario Nacional (National Agrarian Tribunal)

TCO   tierra comunitaria de origen (native community land, a category of collective agrarian property that can be claimed by indigenous peoples under the 1996 INRA Law. Also refers to territories subject to such legal claims.)

TIOC   territorio indígena originaria campesina (indigenous originary peasant territory, the official name given to autonomous indigenous jurisdictions under Bolivia's 2009 Constitution and 2010 Autonomies Law)

YPFB   Yacimientos Petrolíferos Fiscales de Bolivianos (Bolivian State Oil Fields, the Bolivian state oil company)

Note on Pseudonyms

In early drafts of this book, I followed the ethnographic tradition of anonymizing all of the people and some of the places that appear in the chapters. I ultimately came to question the ethical validity of this approach, which seemed bizarre and even dishonest to some of my interlocutors. In 2016 and 2017, I contacted those people I was able to reach to ask whether they wished me to use their real name or a pseudonym. All of those consulted opted to use their real name and I have respected their wishes. Nevertheless, owing to the sensitive nature of the conflicts described, I have maintained some pseudonyms, particularly for APG IG leaders and private landowners whose property claims I discuss. I have maintained the pseudonym "Tarairí" for the Guaraní community I lived in, because of the ongoing APG IG leadership struggle and the potential for identifying individuals.[1] Surrounding properties and communities have also been anonymized.

The following names that appear in the book are pseudonyms: Guaraní community members: Fausto, Julio, Bertha, Mabel, Mariana, Hermes, Victoria, Mario, Lorenzo, Rómulo, Jimena, Benita, Jennifer, Alcides, Felix, Alejandro; Guaraní leaders: Celestino, Teodoro, Julio Navarro, Nestor Borrerro, Fabio Montes, Horacio Tarabuko, Angelo, Román, Santiago; state officials: José, Lino, Jorge Campero; non-indigenous land claimants: Beatriz Vaca, Roberto Vaca, Rubén Roble, Winston Mignolo, Oswaldo Cortez, Simón Mendez, Maarten, Franco; técnicos: Freddy Gordillo; Guaraní communities: Tarairí, Yukiporo, Itikirenda, Yumbia; private properties: El Palmar, El Porvenir; Rancho Grande.

LIMITS TO DECOLONIZATION

INTRODUCTION

In March 2009, leaders of the three indigenous peoples of Tarija Department assembled to discuss what they called the "land issue"—their ongoing struggle to acquire collective property titles formalizing their rights to ancestral territories. These territories had gained legal recognition as Tierras Comunitarias de Origen (native community lands, hereafter TCOs) in 1996, following a long history of indigenous dispossession and political exclusion in the Bolivian lowlands. Yet TCO claims in Tarija Department remained fragmented and incompletely titled after a decade of halting and uneven legal progress. The land titling process had recently gained a new sense of urgency: Bolivians had just approved a new constitution recognizing indigenous peoples' rights to territorial autonomy—the implementation of which was contingent on consolidation of their land rights in TCOs.[1]

The two-day meeting was held in a building owned by an agrarian development organization in the city of Tarija—a journey of four to eight hours for most participants, whose territorial claims lie in the remote and semiarid Chaco region (see figure 1). High on the agenda was the issue of how to overcome the lack of funding for land titling procedures, initial titling funds from the World Bank and Danish government having been exhausted.[2] Participants criticized Tarija's departmental government for refusing to contribute additional funds, despite receiving vast revenues from natural gas extraction in TCOs. But even if departmental funds *could* be secured, someone pointed out, local (non-indigenous) cattle ranching organizations would block their use for TCO titling. Another

1

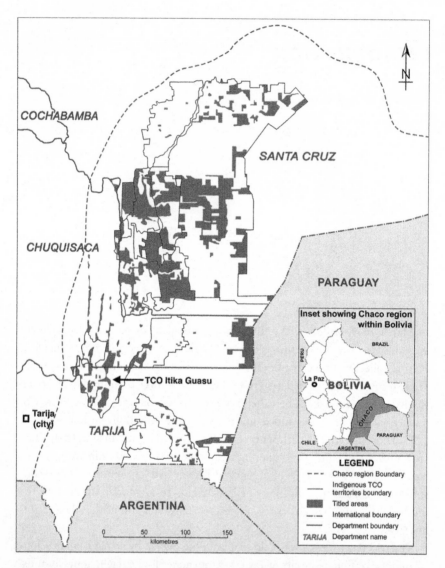

FIGURE 1. Map showing indigenous TCO claims in the Bolivian Chaco (elaborated by Cartographic Unit, Department of Geography, University of Cambridge, adapted from map 5.8 in Fundación TIERRA, 2011: 125)

leader noted that even if the funding issue were overcome, the TCO titling process had so far favored the rights of cattle ranchers—competing claimants for TCO land.

It was now Evo Morales's fourth year in office as president of Bolivia, and indigenous peoples in the Chaco were still, as they often joked, awaiting the arrival of the "plurinational state."[3] Still, many hoped that direct appeals to the central government might enable them to advance with the TCO titling process and circumvent the authority of elite-dominated regional institutions, which had failed to fully implement indigenous land rights over the previous decade. In fact, the objective of this assembly was to meet with national representatives of the Instituto Nacional de Reforma Agraria (National Agrarian Reform Institute, INRA) and the Land Ministry, who had been invited by letter several weeks earlier, following a failed meeting with departmental officials.

To my surprise, on the second day of the assembly, a delegation of state functionaries arrived, including the national director of INRA, Juan Carlos Rojas, and representatives from the Land Ministry and Ministry of Rural Development. Although frequently requested by the indigenous leaders, the presence of such high-level officials at indigenous assemblies in Tarija is rare. Yet this assembly was being held at a critical moment in indigenous-state relations under the Morales government. The state oil company Yacimientos Petrolíferos Fiscales Bolivianos (YPFB) and the Ministry of Hydrocarbons were engaged in tense negotiations with Chaco indigenous peoples over hydrocarbon development in TCOs. The government was also eager to build political alliances with lowland indigenous movements as part of a strategy to undermine departmental autonomy movements led by right-wing elites in Bolivia's eastern lowlands, which had rocked Morales's first term in office.

Despite these incentives for a constructive engagement, Rojas's speech failed to satisfy indigenous participants. Their response owed less to the speech's content—Rojas promised an ambitious target for TCO titling based on funds from the Dutch and Danish embassies—than the fact that many of those present doubted whether this would result in the full legal recognition of their land rights. In a context of intensifying hydrocarbon development within TCOs, many of them believed that funding shortages and local landowner opposition had become a convenient smokescreen for national inaction. As the president of Itika Guasu, a Guaraní TCO claim that overlies Bolivia's biggest gas field, put it the previous day:

> The bottleneck isn't the issue that there are social conflicts. That isn't the fear. The bottleneck that exists here now is that they [the government] have constitutionalized the consultation process, the bottleneck is investment in energy development [to export] abroad—that's the problem of this government. If I were the president, I'd do the same, *compañeros*. Why give them the title if it's going to bring conflicts to fulfill the commitments of energy development overseas? They export gas, oil [from our territories], and without consulting us! *That's* the fear.

> So, better [for the government] to continue delaying with the titling processes, because then they can evade responsibilities and continue doing energy development of all our territory.

As this demonstrates, although land rights and subsoil rights are legally separated—the latter are owned by the Bolivian state—they are intimately connected in practice.

It was this cynicism that ultimately won the day. Following Rojas's speech, the assembly's chair declared an hour's recess, during which participants discussed the "need to take action." After much deliberation, they settled on a resolution declaring a "STATE OF EMERGENCY AND GENERAL MOBILIZATION in all our communities from this date on," granting the government a fixed term to propose "definitive solutions to our land demands" and reserving the "right to take other measures"—that is, direct action such as road blockades and marches to pressure the government to meet their demands.

The preamble to the resolution conveys indigenous peoples' frustration at what they saw as the Morales government's failure to transform a historical trajectory of state-sponsored indigenous dispossession in the Chaco:

Considering

That: The Bolivian State, throughout the course of its history, has snatched the territory from indigenous peoples, with facts like the revolution of 1952 and the Agrarian Reform, which didn't resolve the dispossession, but rather encouraged large estates in indigenous territories of the lowlands.

That: The neoliberal model applied in the country for twenty years has consolidated this dispossession, with a process of land titling that has favored the interests of the groups of economic and political power more than the indigenous peoples.

That: The Process of Change begun in 2005 until now has also failed to show clear signs of resolving our historic demands, given that there is no clear policy and concrete actions to advance with the consolidation of our territories.

That: The work of INRA has not contributed significantly toward resolving the territorial demands and, on the contrary, with its work it has made invisible some of our communities . . . contributing in this way to the disintegration of our ancestral territories.

That: Despite the fact that the wealth that sustains the Bolivian State is in our territories, they tell us that there is no money to conclude with the titling of our land demands.

As the last statement reveals, indigenous peoples' perception that the state's failure to recognize their land rights was connected to the gas being pumped daily from their territories—the economic basis for Morales's "post-neoliberal" project—added to this sense of injustice.

For Guaraní leaders in TCO Itika Guasu, this meeting marked a turning point. Over the previous decade, their struggle for territory had focused primarily on lobbying the government to complete the TCO titling process—an agenda shared by other Chaco indigenous organizations. A few months after the meeting, this strategy took a different course. In June 2009 the Guaraní leadership of Itika Guasu wrote to the Morales government's Land Ministry requesting the indefinite suspension of the TCO titling process in their territory. In December 2010 they signed an agreement with the Spanish oil company Repsol, ending a decade-long conflict over hydrocarbon development in Bolivia's biggest gas field, Campo Margarita.

This agreement has provided the basis for a new vision of territory and autonomy in Itika Guasu. Speaking to communities in 2011, the TCO's president heralded the agreement as granting "full legal recognition of our property rights over the native community territory." By "full legal recognition," he referred to the production of a written agreement, overseen by international lawyers, in which Repsol acknowledged the Guaraní's property rights over TCO Itika Guasu.[4] While this statement of rights had no legal standing under Bolivian law, Guaraní leaders saw the agreement as an alternative to a state land title. They believed it could be used in subsequent private negotiations as evidence of their property rights over the *entire* TCO territory—not only the fragments of land titled to them by the state.

Leaders in Itika Guasu also saw the agreement as offering an alternative pathway to territorial autonomy, in a context where the Morales government's indigenous autonomy process remained unviable. Among the terms of the agreement was the creation of an Itika Guasu Investment Fund totaling $14.8 million, the interest from which was to be managed independently by the Guaraní organization. The TCO president described the Investment Fund as "part of our long-term funding strategy, which will permit us to carry forward our own development [and] guarantees our real autonomy and that of our children." This was a chance to pursue a vision of self-governance that had underpinned their territorial claim but had been eroded by the long and frustrating process of TCO titling. Rather than signaling an abandonment of territory, this vision represents a bold effort to *recapture* territory through a different means and in different idioms. While fraught with ambivalence, this vision has far-reaching implications for sovereignty, autonomy, and governance.

*

This book tells the story of one indigenous group's recent struggle (beginning in the late 1980s) to regain control of their ancestral territory. This struggle followed a century of state-backed dispossession and took place amidst a contemporary boom in hydrocarbon development. The book charts their frustrating engagements with a multicultural indigenous land titling process, their growing disillusionment with a leftist government, and the emergence of a new vision of territorial autonomy based on indigenous control of gas rents.

The people at the center of this story are thirty-six Guaraní communities of the remote and gas-rich Chaco region. These communities organized during the late 1980s to free themselves from a regime of debt peonage on mestizo haciendas.[5] They began by occupying private land and establishing maize-farming cooperatives, a task supported by local NGOs and overshadowed by the threat of violent retribution from landowners. Soon after, they began mapping a territorial claim, which they named Itika Guasu (in Guaraní, Big River) after the Pilcomayo River.[6]

This was part of a wave of indigenous resurgence across Bolivia's eastern lowlands, focused primarily on the demand for "territory." Brought together by a shared history of dispossession and political exclusion, the participating communities in Bolivia's indigenous movement exploited openings in an evolving and contested market-led development agenda. In 1996, a World Bank–sponsored agrarian reform process culminated in the establishment of native community lands (TCOs), a new kind of land title through which indigenous peoples could claim collective rights to their ancestral territories.

The World Bank and European donors argued that TCOs would protect indigenous peoples from the negative impacts of capitalist development, enabling them to practice traditional and environmentally sustainable forms of development (see chapter 1). The Guaraní saw TCOs as a vehicle for a historically grounded project of "reclaiming territory." At the heart of their vision was the notion of becoming *iyambae* (free, without an owner), associated with the recovery of control over their territory and bodies following a century of racialized subjugation and debt peonage.

In practice, TCOs have failed to meet these aspirations. In the Chaco region, TCOs have emerged as legally fragmented and contested territories,[7] interspersed with private cattle ranches, and traversed by a growing network of gas wells, pipelines, and other hydrocarbon infrastructure. Indigenous communities continue to struggle to access land and resources required to sustain their livelihoods, while their leaders have become embroiled in lengthy battles over prior consultation and compensation.

The 2005 election of Evo Morales failed to transform these dynamics. Bolivia's first indigenous president, Morales swept to power amidst a series of mobilizations by peasants, workers, and indigenous movements. His Movimiento al Socialismo party (Movement toward Socialism, MAS) promised an end to "neoliberalism"—two decades of pro-market reform that had benefited transnational companies and elites while impoverishing many Bolivians. Shortly after taking office, Morales nationalized Bolivia's oil and gas fields, the profits from which have been channeled into a range of social programs. Morales also promised to redress the political marginalization faced by indigenous peoples throughout the country's history. He began by convening a Plurinational Constituent Assembly to rewrite Bolivia's constitution. The resulting document, approved by popular referendum in 2009, is probably the most extensive framework of indigenous rights ever recognized by a nation-state.

Despite such constitutional advances, most indigenous peoples have seen little progress on their territorial claims. In the Chaco region of Tarija Department, progress on TCO land titling has remained paralyzed while conflicts over hydrocarbon development in TCOs have intensified. Morales's promise of a "second agrarian revolution" has gradually given way to political accommodations with capitalist and landowning elites, reproducing familiar dynamics of state-formation in the Bolivian lowlands that have long marginalized indigenous peoples.

By exploring these dynamics—and the surprising responses they have given rise to—I rethink common ideas about indigenous territories, cultural politics, and the Bolivian "process of change." It would be easy to dismiss recent events in Itika Guasu as a familiar case of an indigenous leadership "selling out" to a powerful oil company. Instead, I argue that these dynamics have to be understood as a response to the failure of multicultural (or post-multicultural) forms of recognition to transform on-the-ground relations of resource access and control in indigenous territories of the Bolivian Chaco, or to satisfy indigenous demands for "territory."

I highlight how indigenous territorial demands have been undermined by two interlinked sets of dynamics: historical articulations of race, property, and power in the Bolivian Chaco, and the territorial and political dynamics of hydrocarbon development. Following waves of state-backed colonization, the Guaraní of Itika Guasu today share their ancestral territory with a heterogeneous population of non-indigenous land claimants. During the land titling process, these competing claimants mobilized threats of violence, clientelistic networks, and racialized discourses of rights to defend their property claims and obstruct the implementation of indigenous land rights. Their interests were supported by the arrival of oil companies in the territory, which made land use agreements with private land claimants and created incentives to prevent the implementation of indigenous land rights. My analysis sheds light on the enduring collusions between non-indigenous landowners, capitalist resource interests, and state power that have underpinned Bolivia's hydrocarbon boom and the constraints they place on indigenous efforts at "reclaiming territory."

I also place the Itika Guasu leadership's vision of gas-funded autonomy in a more contemporary context: a moment in Bolivia at which unrealized dreams of a plurinational state are giving way to the contradictory dynamics of a hydrocarbon-based development model. Rather than putting an end to struggles around hydrocarbon governance, the nationalization of hydrocarbons under the Morales government has produced a range of competing territorial projects and claims forged in relation to gas rents. I use the concept of *hydrocarbon citizenship* to analyze how notions of recognition, authority, and rights are being rearticulated—and reterritorialized—in relation to the governance of hydrocarbons.

Beyond the Map

Since the 1990s, communal mapping and land titling have emerged as a central focus of indigenous activism in various national and regional contexts.[8] Such initiatives continue to gain support from development institutions and NGOs—more recently as a "win-win" solution to land grabs and carbon emissions from deforestation.[9] This forms part of a renewed focus on land issues and thrust toward formalization within global development policy. Underlying much of the enthusiasm around indigenous land rights is an assumption that legal-cartographic recognition by the state represents "success" for indigenous struggles for territory. This book challenges that assumption.

Combining insights from postcolonial geography and political ecology, I show how racialized inequalities and broader relations of political economy shaped property rights and land control in TCOs, notwithstanding their formal designation as indigenous territories.[10] Moving beyond critiques of neoliberal policy agendas,[11] or the representational limits of maps,[12] this book approaches indigenous territories as a site of articulation and struggle between competing sovereignty claims and territorial projects.

My analysis departs from an understanding of territory as a social relation that is produced and transformed through struggle (Lefebvre 1991; Brenner and Elden 2009). A *postcolonial* account of territory highlights how such struggles are constrained (discursively and materially) by sedimented histories of racialized violence (Said 1978; Wainwright 2008; Sparke 2005). While TCOs had some empowering effects as representations, they did not have the power to override state boundaries, private property, or transnational resource concessions. Rather, their spatial production was shaped by other historical and contemporary processes of territorialization (Vandergeest and Peluso 1995; Peluso and Lund 2013).

Multicultural discourses of indigeneity obscure these complex realities of postcolonial territory. So too do activist countermapping practices, which may airbrush out the inconvenient presence of non-indigenous actors in an effort to conform to global multicultural imaginaries and win national recognition (see chapter 2). Rather than resolving indigenous land claims, processes of indigenous mapping may work to create misleading perceptions of indigenous land control that can be used against indigenous movements. This has already occurred in Bolivia, where TCOs have been attacked by peasant groups as "the new latifundios" and by Morales's vice president Álvaro García Linera as "oversized" in relation to indigenous land needs—accusations that obscure the actual fragmented status of land rights and land control in many TCOs.[13]

I do not mean to suggest that indigenous mapping and land titling *never* serve the agendas of indigenous movements. My point is that we cannot take such gains for granted. Understanding the lasting effects and legacies of indigenous land titling requires ethnographic engagement at a variety of sites and scales, beyond the initial mapping process.

The Politics of Recognition

This book also speaks to broader debates on the possibilities and limits of a politics of recognition for indigenous decolonizing struggles. On one level, indigenous territorial claims challenge left-materialist critiques of identity politics, showing that identity-based claims can be transformative and redistributional rather than simply affirmative in scope (Coulthard 2014). For people who have suffered histories of dispossession that were intimately connected to their status as non-citizens, an analytical separation between recognition and redistribution makes little sense. Nevertheless, this book demonstrates how cultural recognition can become severed from material claims in the process of claiming territorial rights.

In recent Latin Americanist scholarship, recognition politics have been closely associated with the concept of "neoliberal multiculturalism," a term coined by Charles Hale to describe the limited forms of cultural recognition granted by proponents of a market-led development agenda during the 1990s (Hale 2002, 2005, 2006, 2011). Sponsored by the World Bank and implemented during a second wave of structural adjustment in Bolivia, TCOs highlight the ambivalent relationship between cultural rights and capitalist development. Indeed, much of this book is about how TCOs were conditioned by concurrent processes of marketization, in ways that had profound implications for indigenous resource control.

Ultimately, however, this book exposes the limits of this critique. TCOs were not simply the outcome of a governmental project; rather, they emerged from a contingent process of negotiation and struggle involving a heterogeneous set of actors at a moment of political crisis (chapter 1). Labeling TCOs "neoliberal" tells us little about how these territories came into being, and even less about the dynamics of their implementation in the Chaco, where global and national agendas were reworked by local actors deploying their own historically grounded notions of rights and justice (chapter 3).

Most important, by locating the limits of cultural rights in a particular governmental paradigm—a kind of "recognition trap" that indigenous peoples fell blindly into—critiques of neoliberal multiculturalism obscure the deeper structures of coloniality and capitalism that condition indigenous struggles for territory in the present. In doing so, they leave us with few tools to understand why indigenous peoples have *continued* to face similar constraints—alongside an expanding framework of cultural rights—following the election of a self-proclaimed "post-neoliberal" government. Many scholars and activists interpreted the 2005 election of Evo Morales as evidence of indigenous peoples' ability to push beyond a neoliberal politics of recognition in pursuit of more radical systemic change (Postero 2007; Hart 2010). These movements succeeded in bringing into being a more equitable regime of economic distribution. Yet when it comes to indigenous demands for *territory*, the gap between cultural recognition and resource control has persisted.

Understanding these continuities requires situating the multicultural reforms of the 1990s within a longer story of indigenous dispossession, exclusionary citizenship, and resource extraction in the Bolivian lowlands. It also means locating the "neoliberal territorial turn" (Bryan 2012) within a longer history of colonial governmentality and ethnic spatial fixes (Li 2010; Moore 2005). In providing this historical perspective, this book speaks to accounts that interrogate the politics of recognition as a feature of settler colonial and postcolonial governance (Coulthard 2014; Simpson 2014; Rivera Cusicanqui 2012; Povinelli 2002 and 2011; Engle 2010). Such accounts highlight how (post)colonial recognition is *always* conditioned by colonial knowledge-power inequalities and settler interests in indigenous territory and resources. Nevertheless, whereas these accounts focus on indigenous engagements with settler *states*—which sometimes appear as monolithic and all-powerful sovereign actors—this book situates struggles over recognition in a more complex and contested terrain of (post)colonial sovereignty, marked by the presence of *non-state* actors—from local landowners to hydrocarbon companies. Manifestations of "the state" in the Chaco were continually refracted by these "local" and "global" claims to sovereignty. In fact, state authority was produced *through* these localized struggles over property and resources (Lund 2016).

This complicates the idea that indigenous peoples could simply "turn away from" a politics of recognition to focus on constructing their own forms of self-governance (Coulthard 2014; Simpson 2014). It was the presence of these other territorial actors in indigenous territories—and the everyday challenges this posed for indigenous land control—that prompted the Guaraní to turn to the state for recognition in the first place. While the agreement with Repsol can certainly be read as a gesture of turning away from the *state*, the outcome was not a focus on self-recognition but a shift toward hydrocarbon negotiations as the context for achieving recognition. The state did not disappear from the picture; state institutions continued to engage with the Guaraní over hydrocarbon development, as well as supporting local elites seeking to oust them from power. Yet agrarian law was not the only—nor necessarily the most important—forum for achieving territorial recognition.

In sum, this book does not depart from the idea that postcolonial claims to recognition are inherently misguided or limited in scope. Rather, I examine the *conditions under which*, and the *processes through which*, indigenous demands for recognition of territory and sovereignty become severed from their material foundations and rerouted toward empty gestures of cultural affirmation or forms of rent-sharing. These conditions are linked both to the persistence of colonial knowledge-power inequalities and to the limits that a carbon-based capitalist economy places on politics at sites of extraction (see Mitchell 2011).

Indigeneity, Extraction, and New Left Governments

This book provides new insight into the relationship between indigenous peoples, resource extraction, and new left governments in Latin America. In doing so, it raises critical questions about the meaning of decolonization and the role of the state in achieving it. The election of Evo Morales as Bolivia's president in 2005 generated widespread optimism among international leftist observers and indigenous rights advocates. To many, Morales's election represented the possibility of a more equitable and decolonized development model. A 2007 speech by Vice President García Linera encapsulated a "post-neoliberal" vision in which state ownership of Bolivia's natural resources—the "socialization of collective wealth"—would go hand in hand with the construction of a new, unified Bolivian national society, characterized by "varying forms of democratic expression (community-based, territorially-based, direct, and participatory)" (García Linera 2007). Here, García Linera presents the nationalization of hydrocarbons as complementary to, and even necessary for, the thriving of indigenous forms of self-governance.

Since that time, the tensions between indigenous territorial rights and state extractivism have become increasingly visible, and have been subjected to extensive commentary and debate—both in Bolivia and in anglophone academic scholarship.[14] These accounts point to the watering down of indigenous and peasant demands in the 2009 constitution and accompanying laws, the weak implementation of indigenous rights in the context of extractive industry development, and resultant social tensions between the government and its social movement bases. Some authors have interpreted these tensions as reflective of the divergence between the developmentalist and capitalist vision of "New Left" governments, and more radical social movement visions centered on the concept of "vivir bien" (living well) (Escobar 2010; Gudynas 2010).[15] Other scholars have highlighted the policy constraints and "path-dependent" dynamics faced by the MAS government in the context of global capitalism (Kaup 2010; Gustafson and Fabricant 2011) and liberal nation-building (Postero 2017).

In this book I illuminate continuities in the relationships between extraction, territory, and state power in the Bolivian lowlands that are hidden by macro-level institutional or economic analysis. For example, I interrogate the hidden practices and colonial discourses through which non-indigenous property claims have been privileged over indigenous territorial rights in gas-rich lands. I trace how the MAS has consolidated its power in the Bolivian lowlands through political accommodations with landowning elites, who have remade themselves as the unlikely representatives of a plurinational state. In doing so, I show how ethnographic work at indigenous resource frontiers can shed important light on the limits of contemporary resource nationalist projects.

I also reveal how a new discourse of state-led decolonization and national forms of gas rent distribution have shifted the terms of resource conflicts in Bolivia—and not necessarily in indigenous peoples' favor. Groups like the Guaraní of Itika Guasu who demand recognition of their territorial rights—including the right to be consulted on any extraction of resources from their territory—have been framed by the Morales government as "a threat to national development." These dynamics highlight how Latin America's new extraction has pitted the interests of poor and marginalized groups *outside* sites of extraction (who have benefited from gas-funded social programs) against those who suffer the direct social and environmental impacts of extraction—particularly indigenous peoples whose territories overlie key gas reserves.

Recent dynamics in Itika Guasu, however, challenge accounts that construct state extractivism and indigenous territorial projects in purely oppositional terms, revealing how indigenous peoples are participating in struggles over distribution of gas rents under the MAS government. Whereas others have highlighted the intimate relationship between hydrocarbons and nation in Morales's Bolivia

(Perreault 2014; Perreault and Valdivia 2010; Gustafson 2011), my analysis of hydrocarbon citizenship sheds light on how local actors articulate hydrocarbons and citizenship "from the ground up." I draw particular attention to the *territorializing effects* of such articulations in Bolivia, where struggles over distribution of gas rents have produced "competing modes of spatializing practice" (Gustafson 2011). TCOs are emerging as key sites for such articulations.

Indigenous engagements in hydrocarbon citizenship are fraught with ambivalence and disagreement, and produce new inequalities (Humphreys Bebbington and Bebbington 2011). Yet these engagements also represent a bold attempt to recapture the political content of "territory" and its long-standing association with indigenous political autonomy—a dimension that was evacuated from the TCO titling process and "domesticated" by the MAS government (Garcés 2011). A key objective of this book, then, is to situate emergent forms of indigenous hydrocarbon citizenship—which position TCOs as governable spaces within a hydrocarbon economy—in the wake of the frustrated aspirations for territory produced by "multicultural" and "plurinational" governmental projects.

As this reveals, nationalist assertions of resource sovereignty do not imply a spatial containment of sovereignty in practice (Emel, Huber, and Makene 2011). Conversely, efforts to "reclaim the local" (Escobar 2008) may contribute toward—and seek to exploit—the dispersal of sovereignty across multiple scales. Rather than imagining indigenous movements and leftist governments as natural allies in a challenge to neoliberalism "from below," I highlight the shifting alignments of sovereignty—as well as the conflicts—that have emerged between capital, the state, indigenous peoples, and other territorial actors under the Morales government. Following Michael Watts (2009), I show how negotiations (and Faustian bargains) over sovereignty can produce new forms of "governable spaces" that may be at odds with those of the state (chapter 6).

Research at Postcolonial Frontiers

This research deployed an open-ended, multi-sited ethnographic research strategy that combined participant observation, in-depth interviewing, documentary analysis, archival research, participatory mapping, focus groups, institutional ethnography, and a household survey.[16] These methods were selected and refined in context, guided by questions that were also informed by ethnographic engagement—an approach that resembles what Kim Fortun terms "open systems ethnography" (2012). The use of ethnographic methods distinguishes this book from most existing studies of indigenous land titling, which tend to rely on a combination of legal-cartographic data, elite interviews, and institutional and policy analysis to identify statistical progress, procedural shortcomings, and technocratic innovations to overcome these shortcomings (Coombes, Johnson, and Howitt 2011).

I began the research in late 2008, when I worked for ten months as a self-funded volunteer in the NGO CERDET (Centro de Estudios Regionales para el Desarrollo de Tarija).[17] While this provided an important entry point into the politics and history of indigenous land claims in Tarija, I soon realized the limitations of an overt institutional affiliation. Before long, I had discarded my CERDET cap and begun to travel independently or with Guaraní leaders. In addition to CERDET's office, I worked frequently from the Tarija-based Concejo de Capitanes Guaraníes de Tarija (Council of Guaraní Captains of Tarija, CCGT), where political debate and strategy, rather than technical reports and planning meetings, made up the fabric of everyday work. Based on a research proposal elaborated in conversation with both institutions, my first year in Tarija was spent attending multi-day assemblies (political gatherings) of the Asamblea del Pueblo Guaraní (APG), amassing documentation on the Itika Guasu TCO claim, researching regional history, and conducting forty in-depth semi-structured interviews with a variety of actors involved in the titling process.

I returned to Tarija in January 2011 for fourteen months of fieldwork, which took several new directions. First, whereas I had initially focused on the contemporary politics of indigenous land claims, distance prompted me to interrogate the processes through which TCOs had come into being. Back in Tarija, I searched the archives of CERDET and INRA for documentation from the early 1990s. Following leads, I tracked down and interviewed individuals who had been involved in mapping the Itika Guasu TCO claim. Second, I conducted several months of research with non-indigenous land claimants in Itika Guasu—who turned out to be a more diverse bunch than I had envisaged—recording interviews and attending meetings organized by the local cattle ranching association.

Finally, I conducted six months of participant observation in Tarairí (a pseudonym), a Guaraní-speaking community at the heart of TCO Itika Guasu. Just weeks after my arrival, I broke my ankle playing soccer. During my recovery period, I focused on building my relations with Tarairí's thirteen households, improving my Guaraní language skills, and documenting my observations of everyday life and land relations. During January–February 2012, I conducted a series of more structured activities in Tarairí, including interviews, focus groups, participatory mapping exercises, a household survey, and a walk with a GPS device to identify the legal boundaries of TCO land.

Beyond Tarija Department, I conducted several rounds of interviews with indigenous leaders, NGOs, and state officials in Santa Cruz, Camiri, Cochabamba, and La Paz, which provided a broader perspective on indigenous TCO claims, extractive industry conflicts, and the shifting dynamics and tensions of the MAS government's "process of change." Participation in political events and research presentations provided further opportunities for engagement and debate on these broader political and territorial dynamics.

My ability to move in and through these multiple spaces was enabled by the generosity of the people I encountered and the value they placed on critical knowledge production. My multiple engagements did not culminate in a neutral positionality or holistic perspective. But they did open new spaces for critical reflection, which informed my interlocutors' projects as well as my own. In many cases, it was they who engaged me in debates or experiences that addressed, as well as reformulated, my research questions. Interviews and ethnography were not merely processes of data collection but opportunities for knowledge exchange and collective analysis.

Yet working with multiple groups can also generate rivalry and mistrust. Some landowners were careful in how they talked about interethnic relations, in light of my engagement with the Guaraní movement. Some Guaraní leaders were skeptical of my relationship with CERDET and rival factions of the indigenous movement. On some occasions INRA staff engaged enthusiastically with my research; on others I was treated with suspicion and subjected to time-consuming bureaucratic obstacles. Oil companies treated me with suspicion on some occasions, and on others tried to hire me. Working across different groups presents ethical and political dilemmas. Yet it also provided new critical insights that address the limitations of activist research on indigenous land claims (Engle 2010; Bobrow-Strain 2007).

This book is a critical reflection on decolonization rather than a piece of decolonial scholarship by and for indigenous peoples. My position as a white female outsider and temporary visitor radically conditioned my insights. Nevertheless, I seek to make visible indigenous perspectives that are rarely heard in debates on indigenous land rights, extractive industry, or Bolivian politics. As often as possible, I present these insights in the words in which they were offered. By interrogating the functioning of colonial power in its material and discursive manifestations, this book resonates with indigenous projects of decolonizing knowledge and ongoing efforts at decolonizing territory.

Chapter Outline

This book traces the evolution of the Guaraní territorial claim in Itika Guasu from its insurgent origins, through its production in cartography and law, to its growing enmeshment in hydrocarbon politics. While maintaining a roughly chronological progression, the chapters shift between scales, places, and actors to illuminate the distinct but interconnected arenas in which the territory has been produced and contested—from remote communities to national policy negotiations to transnational alliances.

Chapter 1, "Imagining Territory," charts the emergence of a territorial claim in Itika Gausu (1987–1996). I place this narrative in two distinct but interrelated contexts: first, a specific regional history of racialized dispossession, subjugation, and Guaraní ethnic resurgence; and second, the emergence of a global policy consensus around support for indigenous land rights under the rubric of "ethno-development." The chapter then traces the national articulations that led to the integration of indigenous territorial demands into the 1996 INRA Law. It examines the contending actors and visions involved in national policy negotiations, the characteristics of the TCO titling process, the responses it provoked from the indigenous movement, and the creative strategies through which indigenous activists secured state recognition of the first TCO demands. In charting how TCOs moved from indigenous demand to national legal category to recognized territories, I highlight the divergent agendas, unequal negotiations, and uncertain compromises involved in integrating indigenous territorial demands into state law.

Chapter 2, "Mapping Territory," examines the processes of mapping and justifying indigenous territorial claims in Bolivia. While acknowledging the empowering effects of this process, I draw attention to the erasures, concessions, and power dynamics involved in making territory legible to the state. I detail how territorial limits were adjusted to accommodate state and settler geographies, how discourses of ancestral territory gave way to calculations of "indigenous spatial needs," and how indigenous territorial knowledges were silenced in the process. I reflect on the governmental effects of mapping territory, the contradictory development visions invested in TCOs, and the relational geographies that continue to structure indigenous lives "beyond the map."

In chapter 3, "Titling Territory," I examine the dynamics and results of the TCO land titling process in Itika Guasu. Combining insights from postcolonial theory and legal anthropology, I describe how legal norms were reworked in their engagement with local power structures, values, and institutions. Drawing on extensive documentary analysis and in-depth interviews with local landowners, Guaraní, NGOs, and state officials, I chart how racialized power inequalities and colonial discourses of rights and property shaped the application of legal norms in ways that prevented a substantive redistribution of land rights in Itika Guasu. The chapter also examines the experience of poorer non-indigenous residents of Itika Guasu, revealing how the forms of identity production underpinning the titling process produced new forms of exclusion, which fueled interethnic conflict and ultimately bolstered elite-led opposition to the TCO. The chapter concludes with an analysis of the legal results of the titling process and Guaraní responses to them.

Chapter 4, "Inhabiting Territory," shifts scale to the community level to examine what these legal results mean for the everyday lives of Guaraní women, men, and children in Itika Guasu. Drawing on six months of participant observation in the remote community of Tarairí, I examine how Guaraní community members inhabit and imagine the landscape, how they narrate the struggle for "reclaiming territory," and what the results of the titling process mean for their land use practices and livelihood strategies. I highlight the daily challenges that the continuing presence of non-indigenous landowners in the landscape creates for community members. I discuss an intercommunal conflict over access to some nearby palm trees to reveal how the fixing of boundaries in the context of TCO land titling has, paradoxically, undermined Guaraní practices of natural resource use and intercommunal cooperation. I examine how changing climatic conditions and land scarcity present complex dilemmas for Guaraní regarding the staking and policing of territorial boundaries. These ethnographic examples provide the basis for a reflection on the differences between "territory" and "property," and the ways in which indigenous land titling has privileged the latter.

Chapter 5, "Extractive Encounters," analyzes how TCO titling in Itika Guasu has articulated with another territorializing process: hydrocarbon development in Bolivia's biggest gas field (beneath the TCO). I begin by considering the broader policy context that produced an extractive industry boom alongside recognition of indigenous land rights. I then examine in detail how hydrocarbon development in TCO Itika Guasu undermined Guaraní land claims by mapping onto and legitimizing a racialized geography of private property. I detail how, as the Guaraní sought to assert their territorial sovereignty, the status of land rights in the TCO became intimately connected to a conflict over hydrocarbon governance. The second part of the chapter traces the evolution of this resource conflict under the Morales government. I describe the Guaraní's unsuccessful appeals to the "plurinational state," their analysis of the conflicts between state extractivism and indigenous land rights, their shifting negotiating strategies, and their decision to withdraw from the TCO titling process in 2009. Finally, I provide an overview of the scaling up of the Guaraní leadership's negotiations with Repsol and the resulting 2010 agreement, which provided the pretext for new framings of territory and autonomy in Itika Guasu.

These shifting visions of territory and autonomy are the subject of the sixth and final chapter, "Governable Spaces," which examines the emergence of competing forms of "hydrocarbon citizenship" that produce TCO Itika Guasu as an ethnic governable space within a hydrocarbon economy. I begin by exploring the Guaraní leadership's discourse following the 2010 agreement with Repsol, which linked territorial autonomy to their administration of an Itika Guasu Investment Fund. I chart the growing tensions this vision produced, relating to fiscal accountability, political participation, environmental anxieties, and the desire of communities for inclusion in the redistributive politics of the MAS government. I describe how these tensions contributed to the emergence of a rival TCO leadership backed by the MAS and regional elites, and committed to the implementation of gas-funded state-administered development projects in the TCO. I place these shifting forms of hydrocarbon citizenship in the context of the frustrated struggle for territorial control detailed in previous chapters, as well as in the context of the broader territorial and political dynamics of the MAS hydrocarbon state. The conclusion reflects on the limits and legacies of TCOs, the wider significance of the Itika Guasu case, and the shifting relationship between indigeneity, territory, and extractivism in Bolivia.

IMAGINING TERRITORY

Contingent Articulations, Uncertain Compromises

> **First it's necessary to see the situation in which we lived—*empatronados*, in a system of slavery, without rights to land, gripped only by the hand of the *patrón*. It's from there that our ancestors decided to organize themselves [in the late 1980s], first to consolidate or recover their territory, then to recover their freedom, and finally, to recover their cultural identity.**
>
> Guaraní leader from Itika Guasu, April 21, 2009

> **We contend that there needs to be a new relationship among indigenous peoples, scientists, national governments and international organizations . . . This relationship should be a contractual one, whereby indigenous peoples are provided with juridical recognition and control over large areas of forest in exchange for a commitment to conserve the ecosystem and protect biodiversity.**
>
> Shelton H. Davis and Alaka Wali, *Indigenous Territories and Tropical Forest Management in Latin America,* 1993

In October 1996, the Bolivian Congress passed Law 1715 of the Servicio Nacional de Reforma Agraria (National Agrarian Reform Service), commonly known as the INRA Law. Alongside a variety of market-led land reform measures, the INRA Law established a new category of agrarian property: tierras comunitarias de origen (native community lands, TCOs). TCOs were defined as

> the geographical spaces that constitute the habitat of indigenous and originary peoples and communities, to which they have traditionally had access and where they maintain and develop their own forms of economic, social, and cultural organization in a way that guarantees their survival and development. They are inalienable, indivisible, irreversible, and collective, composed of communities or groups of communities, exempt from seizure and imprescriptible. (Article 41.5)

Indigenous groups across the Bolivian lowlands celebrated the INRA Law as marking the first time in history that the Bolivian state had recognized their territorial rights. Following their second national protest march, which coincided with the law's elaboration, they presented the government with thirty-three territorial claims. Among them was the territorial claim of Itika Guasu.

This chapter examines the grassroots, national, and global processes that conjoined to produce TCOs as a new geographical imaginary and category of agrarian property in Bolivia. I explore the divergent imaginaries invested in TCOs, the local practices involved in their construction, and the power-infused negotiations that led to their incorporation in Bolivian law. Neither an indigenous category nor a top-down governmental project, TCOs emerged from contingent articulations between processes unfolding across a variety of sites and scales (Tsing 2005).

I begin by describing the historical configurations of race, nation, and territory that underpinned the Guaraní's dispossession of their ancestral lands. I then move on to the networked relations, insurgent practices, and decolonial imaginaries that undergirded the emergence of a collective land struggle in Itika Guasu. Next, I shift scale to consider the context and rationales for the global "territorial turn"—the emergence of broad support for indigenous land rights among international development institutions during the 1990s. Finally, I examine how these grassroots and global processes conjoined with national dynamics in Bolivia to bring about the creation of TCOs under the 1996 INRA Law.

In tracing these articulated processes, I challenge simplistic accounts of neoliberal governance as a top-down project or coherent rationality of rule. This chapter highlights the agency of diverse actors—including indigenous movements—in shaping national and global policy processes. Nevertheless, I also reveal the constrained circumstances in which indigenous peoples' struggles for territory emerged. In organizing around a territorial claim, Guaraní communities of Itika Guasu faced threats of violent retaliation from local landowners, as well as the prospect of starvation as independent subsistence farmers. In seeking state recognition of their territories, indigenous organizations entered a field of national politics that was infused by colonial power inequalities and capitalist resource interests. The result was that TCOs fell short of indigenous peoples' demands for territory in ways that would have important consequences over subsequent decades. TCOs, however, were more than just a legal category. For the Guaraní, they were a vehicle for a broader project of "reclaiming territory"—a project that would continue to push at the limits of state cartography and agrarian law.

Seating Sovereignty at the Chaco Frontier

It was January 2012 and the midday heat was just beginning to subside in the Guaraní community of Tarairí, nestled in a tight bend of the Pilcomayo River. Sitting on a homemade wooden bench enjoying the shade from the palm-thatched roof of his open-air kitchen, the community's elderly leader (*mburuvicha*), Fausto, described the world of his ancestors. He spoke quietly but confidently in broken Spanish with the occasional Guaraní term, his gaze fixed on the horizon, indicating remembered places with a sweep of his weathered arm:

> Before, *ñande* [us/ours]. They didn't know any Spanish, like that they lived in peace. They took care of their land, from what is now Ivo to the crossroads was all Guaraní land, and the riverbanks, too; everything—up to Ivoca, Ivopeiti, everything, even Puerto Margarita. It was all Guaraní land, land of our grandparents. There weren't any, say, Spanish people. Before, it was pure Guaraní territory; it was *our territory*. We made our fields, they went to that blue hill there; there is still a path of our grandparents, who farmed there . . . And our grandparents walked; they didn't consume any sugar before, it was pure corn, black beans, pumpkin, all our food was like that. They went with the *porongo* [a goard recipient for storing *chicha*], it's called, our grandparents carried *chicha*. *Kaguiye*, they say, don't they? That was our grandparents' food. They went to work in the early morning, they went; returned later, they say. They were intelligent, our grandparents. They were handsome, healthy, they knew neither health clinics nor medicine pills . . . If they got sick, our grandparents would cure themselves. That's what my grandparents told me. As a young boy I knew my grandparents—one of them was a shaman.

He went on to describe the strategies through which *karai* (non-Guaraní) settlers entered the territory and dispossessed his grandparents of their lands. This took the form of a story. His grandparents had plentiful land and their own cattle, as well as other animals. Then one day a *karai* merchant appeared. He brought clothes, cloth, and even hats. "The grandparents before used to wear only a wrap, a piece of cloth, so they were excited to see hats," he recalled. They exchanged some of their cows for clothes, which the merchant delivered on a return visit, at which time he acquired more cattle. "Like that [the *karai* merchant] began to have various cows, and made a fence, made his house," Fausto explained. He described how early settlers like the merchant won the trust of Guaraní communities, telling them, "'I'm going to be your friend, I'll help you'—like that they advanced until they had a house, they started little by little." Before long, settlers had occupied much of the territory, and they began to enlist Guaraní people to work for them, looking after their cattle, putting up fences, or harvesting maize. Then came the 1952 agrarian reform, when "the law appeared—only for the *karai*; it wasn't for the indigenous people . . . Never again could we rescue the land; we couldn't rescue the land."

Pablo, a younger community member, gave another version of this story. He was raised in Tarairí by his grandmother, and described how she used to make clay pots with mud she collected from the bed of the Salado River. She would take the pots all the way to Chiquiacá in the more fertile southern lands of O'Connor Province to trade them for foodstuffs. One day, a *karai* cattle rancher appeared and took ownership of the riverside land where she used to collect her mud. It was because of this, Pablo explained, that he and his grandmother left Tarairí when he was still a young boy. They went to live in Ingavi, where they settled "in a high place with no one bothering them." Then one day when Pablo was fourteen years old, a man from Entre Ríos appeared, claiming to be the owner of the land they lived on. The man informed them that he was going to put cattle on the land and that Pablo and his uncle would work as his cowboys. When his uncle asked to see the man's "papers," he was unable to produce any. Shortly afterwards, the man disappeared. Yet others soon appeared in his place; Guaraní dispossession continued, spaces of refuge became scarce, settlers acquired property titles, and Guaraní people eventually found themselves trapped in exploitative labor contracts with the new *patrones*.

During the course of my research, I heard numerous iterations of this story of territorial dispossession. Such accounts drew on personal memory as well as oral history. They described a lost world that ancestors had inhabited prior to *karai* settlement, the subtle and varied processes through which settlers had gained control of the territory, the regime of debt-bound indigenous labor exploitation this had given rise to, and how parents and grandparents had organized in the late 1980s and 1990s to reclaim territory and free themselves from ties of subordination, dependency, and debt with their *karai patrones*. Julio, whose family had been violently evicted from the land they lived on when he was still a young boy, emphasized the importance of recovering this history, which was erased from official accounts. "Even today, the Bolivian state doesn't recognize this oppression," he complained. "We have an identity that has been trampled on, has been humiliated . . . It's important to remember history, so that it doesn't continue repeating itself and we don't continue being exploited."

Until the late nineteenth century, the Bolivian Chaco—or Chiriguanía—remained an uncolonized frontier of the newly independent Bolivian republic.[1] Having seen centuries of intermittent warfare over the previous three centuries, the Chaco lands continued to be a site of shifting interethnic and intra-ethnic alliances, making state control of them impossible.[2] Early Jesuit efforts to missionize the Chiriguanos (Guaraní) had largely failed, and although the Franciscans had more success (Langer 2009), the Guaraní had largely regained their independence by the mid-nineteenth century, following the chaos of the Independence Wars. Subjecting the Guaraní to the "civilizing" liberal property reforms inflicted on Quechua and Aymara highlanders (Platt 1984) was unthinkable. In fact, Franciscan records suggest that *karai* settlers were paying forms of land tax (usually in cattle) to the Guaraní during this period.

By the end of the nineteenth century, however, the Guaraní had suffered a series of decisive military defeats by Bolivian forces, paving the way for a century of dispossession and racialized subjugation.[3] The 1892 Kuruyuki Massacre is widely seen as marking an effective end of Guaraní anticolonial resistance (Albó 1990: 21; Gustafson 2009: 33–38). The battle took place after a young Guaraní prophet named Apiaguaiki Tüpa gathered Guaraní followers from throughout the region in Kuruyuki, northeast of Itika Guasu, provoking suspicion and fear among the *karai*. Although the Guaraní claimed they had merely gathered to perform religious rites, the rape and murder of a Guaraní woman by a *karai* official provoked them to launch an attack on the Santa Rosa mission. Republican forces pushed them back to Kuruyuki then launched a counterattack, killing eight thousand Guaraní men and boys. In the weeks that followed, the remaining Guaraní fighters were hunted down in their villages, and women and children were captured for distribution among "Christian" settlers. Tüpa, who had managed to escape to the hills, was captured and subjected to gruesome treatment: he was impaled (sodomized) on a long pike, killed, displayed for twenty-four hours in the plaza of Monteagudo, then drawn, quartered, and burned. The indiscriminate killing, hunting down, and enslavement of Guaraní women, men, and children, and the brutal and emasculating tortures enacted on their leader's body, illustrate how the creation of the Chaco as a *karai*, Christian, and Bolivian territory was materially and symbolically predicated on the violent subjugation of its indigenous inhabitants.

The Kuruyuki Massacre was just one milestone in a gradual process of domination and territorial dispossession.[4] Settlement of the Chaco was initially driven by an expanding cattle ranching economy during the late eighteenth century, when the closure of the Pacific trading route during the Pacific War enabled cattle ranchers in Tarija to supply the booming mining economy of Potosí with a range of products. The commercial boom in beef production drew ranchers from other parts of Bolivia, who claimed large areas of indigenous territory, forcing the Guaraní into more marginal lands. The Bolivian state actively promoted frontier settlement, selling off vast tracts of "idle" Chaco lands at rock-bottom prices to any non-indigenous person who promised to settle there,[5] and funding the construction of forts and military outposts near large haciendas. Such policies were underpinned by an imaginary of the Chaco as a savage and mythical land, the conquest of which bound up with the advance of European civilization (Bowman 1915).[6] With a shrinking land base on which to sustain themselves, many Guaraní left the Bolivian Chaco to work on sugar cane plantations in Argentina, sought refuge in missions,[7] or resigned themselves to working on mestizo-owned haciendas.

While Itika Guasu fits within this broader narrative of state territorialization, it also has its own specific history of colonization. Formal legal appropriation of most of these lands occurred shortly after Bolivian independence (1825), when Simón Bolívar awarded them to the Irish-born independence hero Francis Burdett O'Connor (from whom O'Connor Province acquired its name) as a reward for military sacrifice. While Guaraní men were required to contribute annual (unpaid) agricultural labor, work in nearby salt and limestone quarries, and open up roads for their absentee landlord "old man O'Connor,"[8] this initially limited the presence of other *karai* settlers in the territory. This was to change from the 1930s, however, as a consequence of two national events: the 1932–1935 Chaco War and the 1952 agrarian revolution.

The Chaco War with Paraguay, a bloody struggle over the region's oil and gas fields,[9] saw the construction of roads into the Chaco, brought thousands of highlanders to the region to fight, and caused massive Guaraní displacement.[10] Before the war, even the departmental capital, Tarija city, could be reached from La Paz only by donkey via the old Incan road through the Andes. The loss of so many lives at this frontier inscribed the Chaco firmly as "national territory" in the minds of ordinary Bolivians. Even more important, following the war's conclusion, the Bolivian state encouraged ex-combatants—who were largely poor highland farmers—to occupy the Chaco's gas-rich lands, which were seen as vulnerable to future foreign incursions on account of their dispersed and largely indigenous population. Settlement was aided by intensifying hydrocarbon development, which saw the opening up of more roads into formerly inaccessible areas, integrating them into emerging networks of communications, trade, and commerce.[11]

This is the period that Guaraní community members in Itika Guasu most identify with the loss of their communal lands to *karai* settlers. Their accounts often emphasize the gradual and intimate processes through which dispossession unfolded. Pablo recounted his grandmother's tale about how a Chaco War veteran arrived in Tarairí, married a local Guaraní woman, and built his house at the outskirts of the community. "Before long, he had a lot of cattle, everything," he said, "and like that he made himself into a landowner ... He began taking ownership little by little ... [and] in the end they said that he had a title." Julio, who grew up in the mission community of Chimeo, described how "a trickster" had arrived looking for cattle and other animals to purchase, which he would exchange for sugar, rice, and beans. Guaraní community members initially let traders like the man sleep in their homes then gave them permission to build their own houses. Over time, the new settlers acquired property titles and begun to assert their ownership of the territory and of Guaraní bodies. As Julio put it, "Little by little, they went about usurping, usurping, and usurping our territory . . . Different governments did them political favors, gave titles to the gentlemen."

This granting of property titles to new settlers came as a consequence of the 1953 agrarian reform, which emerged from the social and political turmoil of the Chaco War (Klein 1992; Zavaleta 1967). Notwithstanding its revolutionary origins in highland peasant land occupations of the 1940s, the reform was designed and funded by the United States government, which envisioned the modernization of agriculture in the fertile Bolivian lowlands as the basis for an import substitution–based model of economic development.[12] The objective was to keep Bolivia—the site of important strategic resources—on a capitalist development path, following the social upheaval of the preceding decade, and in a context of U.S. fears of the global spread of communism (Murphey 2009).[13] This was to be achieved through the breaking up of highland haciendas to "free up" indigenous labor, the granting of small parcels of land to these "peasants," and an official program to promote lowland colonization. Yet this gateway to citizenship and property rights was not opened to the Guaraní or other lowland groups, who continued to be viewed as "savages," unsuitable candidates for either citizenship or development (Kay and Urioste 2007). Instead, the reform worked to legally consolidate the property claims of settlers, leading to a more aggressive appropriation of Guaraní lands and the exploitation of Guaraní labor, through a system of debt bondage know as *empatronamiento*.

Older community members still recall this period vividly. They describe working long hours for little or no pay, enduring racialized abuse and the prohibition of cultural practices, and incurring unrepayable debts for clothing and other basic necessities. As the Guaraní authors of one document relate:

> We worked day and night, without eating, enduring cold, rain, heat, to be able to survive in these lands, so that our sons began to speak Spanish, our daughters no longer wore the *tipoy*.[14] Some were even obliged to give up the music of the *arête*.[15] We always went around humble and silent because all the *karai* only ever said was "those *chaguancos*, those *ava*, those *cumpa*[16] are too lazy to work," without realizing that, thanks to our labors, they had trucks and knew money, becoming richer and richer. And we, who lived for years working, become poorer and poorer

and we have to die without leaving anything for our children. (APG IG and CERDET 2005: 53–54)

Women and children were recruited as domestic labor and were expected to bring food to male laborers. While relations with *patrones* in Itika Guasu were not uniform,[17] Guaraní people widely associate *empatronamiento* with a loss of control over their lands and bodies. It is this loss of autonomy that gives meaning to the land struggle.

This account highlights how Guaraní dispossession unfolded hand in hand with the production of national territory and the consolidation of a racialized project of citizenship. As the Bolivian state strove to define its geographical and racial boundaries, the Guaraní consistently found themselves placed at its margins, an internal Other against whom the advance of sovereignty and civilization could be measured,[18] a fate shared by many other peoples of the South American lowlands (Sawyer 2004; Valdivia 2005).

The Struggle for Territory in Itika Guasu

In the mid-1980s, a group of Guaraní men began having secret nighttime conversations about how to end their situation of virtual enslavement on *karai* haciendas.[19] Soon, the group began traveling through the zone, spreading their dream of living *iyambae* (free, without an owner). *Patrones*, including the descendants of O'Connor, pursued them with threats of violence. Community members gave them shelter. These early leaders were inspired and supported by a wave of indigenous resurgence unfolding across the Bolivian lowlands. Some of them had come from the neighboring departments of Santa Cruz and Chuquisaca, which had organized to found the Asamblea del Pueblo Guaraní (Assembly of the Guaraní People) in 1987. Others had returned from sugarcane plantations in Argentina, bringing stories of Guaraní organizing they had witnessed there. Leaders of the lowland indigenous umbrella organization CIDOB (Confederation of Indigenous Peoples of Bolivia), founded in 1982, also participated in these early assemblies. In March 1989, representatives of Guaraní communities from throughout the region gathered in Ñaurenda community to form their own indigenous organization, the Asamblea del Pueblo Guaraní de Itika Guasu (APG IG).

Also present at early Guaraní assemblies were an array of nongovernmental, civic, syndicalist, and religious institutions—from local NGOs to Catholic nuns to international human rights organizations.[20] The presence of such actors is typical of region-wide processes that brought marginalized ethnic groups into contact with transnationally articulated networks of development actors during the 1980s and 1990s.[21] Less recognized is the role of local agrarian actors in shaping these processes. In Itika Guasu, these included "Comunidades en Marcha," a militant campaign of land occupation led by the peasant federation CSUTCB (Unified Syndical Confederation of Rural Workers of Bolivia). Shortly after the founding of the APG IG, members of this group helped the Guaraní carry out the first land occupation to clear a communal plot in Ñaurenda—a community that was trapped within the hacienda of the local *patrón*. As one source recounts: "A line of 300–500 entered with axes, machetes, and pots; playing flute and drum with great happiness 'in the face' of the *patrón*. They made the first clearing of ten hectares, and with the show of unity of the people, the *patrones* didn't put up a direct resistance" (EAPG and APG IG 2013: 13).

Notwithstanding the APG IG's diverse allies and bold actions, engaging thirty-six dispersed communities over an area of around three thousand square kilometers in a struggle to transform the existing racial-spatial order required work. Following the first assemblies of 1987–1989, held in what would become zone 1 of the TCO, leaders of APG IG and their NGO allies went from community to community, often on foot, informing people of the process under way. In accordance with an established APG organizational structure, a *mburuvicha*, or community leader, was elected in each community, as well as representatives for production, infrastructure, health, education, and land/territory.[22] If this might make Guaraní "resurgence" in Itika Guasu appear a somewhat top-down affair, then it is clear that the process acquired its own organic momentum. As CERDET's former director Miguel Castro described it:

> It was *incredible*. A community would organize and afterwards it spread like wildfire, the news started to spread. And every week it was a matter of going to a new community and electing a new *mburuvicha comunal* and they came out very [quickly]—thirty-six communities in two or three years organized, the executive committee of the APG, the three zones. That is, it was *incredible*.

Despite this dynamism, the Guaraní faced major challenges. First and foremost, in order to become and remain *iyambae*—independent of the *patrones*—communities had to reestablish independent subsistence livelihoods. The immediate challenge they faced in doing so was a lack of land. It was in this context that land rights were quickly identified as a central objective of the newly formed organization. At an assembly in 1989 in Ñaurenda, participants agreed to research the legal situation of land rights in the area and take steps toward constructing a territorial demand (CERDET 1989), a commitment that was reaffirmed at subsequent assemblies. This gave rise to the first attempts at mapping territory, detailed in the next chapter.

Yet more immediate steps had to be taken to free communities from their ties to *patrones* and to meet their subsistence needs. This involved negotiations with *patrones* over the annulment of debts and reduction of labor hours, in which NGO staff played a mediating role. In parallel with such negotiations (and a pretext for them), Guaraní communities embarked on further land occupations, establishing communal plots in privately claimed but uncultivated lands and forming work groups to farm them. They did so with support from local NGOs, which provided coca, tools, barbed wire, and food. These communal plots acted as important symbols of Guaraní independence and organizing capacity. They were also a way of staking out and justifying Guaraní land claims, in anticipation of a formal land titling process. As Miguel explained:

> Even if there was also a legal struggle, on the other hand, they were in the process of taking lands. Because when I arrived in Itika in '89 there wasn't a person, a community, that had land. By '95–'96 almost every-one had land. And that wasn't the fruit of legal work; it was occupa-tion of lands . . . We went occupying lands, occupying—the idea was to occupy the largest quantity [possible] so that, when the declaration of the territory came, we would already have possession; we would be able to demonstrate that we are already in possession of the land.

This logic of "redistribution before recognition" echoes the highland peasant land occupations of the 1940s (Zavaleta 2008), as well as the more recent tactics of the Movimiento sin Tierra (Landless Peasants' Movement). It also resonated with the established logic of Bolivian agrarian reform. As the legal name for land titling, *saneamiento* (literally "sanitizing" or "cleaning up") suggests, Boliv-ian land reform has historically been oriented toward the regularization of land rights, making possession an important basis for property ownership. Further-more, since the 1953 agrarian reform, agrarian law has been premised on the social function of property, captured in the popular mantra "la tierra es para quien la trabaja" (land is for those who work it). In this context, Guaraní coop-erative work groups served a dual function: as well as providing an alternative source of food necessary to break economic dependency on *patrones*, they served as a visual symbol of Guaraní productive capacity, challenging racialized stereo-types of indigenous peoples as lazy, unproductive, and therefore undeserving of land rights. More broadly, this illustrates how Guaraní engagements with car-tography and law were accompanied, and preceded, by material acts of claiming territory, which took place at multiple sites across the territory-in-the-making of Itika Guasu.

If all this constituted something of a micro–agrarian revolution, then it did not go unchallenged. Guaraní organizing efforts provoked strong, and sometimes violent, resistance from local landowners, many of whom relied on unpaid Guaraní labor to make their haciendas economically viable. As the Guaraní movement spread and became more visible, landowners extended their attacks and threats to NGO staff, who they assumed to be responsible for "stirring up" the Guaraní. Noe, an employee of EAPG (Aid Team for the Guaraní People, a local NGO), remembered how one local rancher had told him outright to stop the NGO's work. Guaraní leaders also faced threats of violence (APDHT 1990), as well as a local state that was overtly aligned with landowner resistance. In 1989 a local official, who was also a local landowner, appeared at an assembly to reproach Guaraní participants for attending without his permission (CERDET, n.d. 1). Various Guaraní men were held by the police, or in jail, both for their organizing activities and for the ensuing confrontations with landowners, which in a few cases ended in a landowner's death (APDHT 1990). Aware that physical force and the law were not on their side, the Guaraní and their allies sought to overcome this resistance through informal negotiation and moral argument. They managed to persuade some *patrones* to sign informal agreements stating that they would not oppose Guaraní organization, reminding them of the Guaraní's ancestral ownership of the territory.

Despite the remarkable achievements of the land occupations and work groups, Guaraní communities continued to face major challenges in sustaining independent livelihoods. The years 1995–96 saw a particularly acute food crisis, which threatened to undermine the entire process, motivating people to return to work on haciendas, which had previously guaranteed them food. It was in response to this that CERDET began to orient its assistance toward agricultural production, under the slogan "How to make freedom sustainable." While the world of formal *empatronamiento* had been dismantled in Itika Guasu,[23] the dream of reestablishing autonomous subsistence livelihoods would remain an ongoing struggle.

Territorial Counternarratives

Alongside political organization, the breaking of labor contracts, and land occupations, Guaraní communities were engaged in a process of epistemic resurgence—of retelling history, regaining cultural pride, and mapping identity to place. As APG IG leaders and NGOs went from community to community spreading news of the organizing process under way, they spoke of the construction of a territorial claim through which the Guaraní would once again be owners of their territory. A booklet titled "Solidarity with the Guaraní People,"[24] used to educate communities about the land struggle during this period, is illustrative. It opens with a picture of a small crowd of Guaraní men, women, and children in traditional costume, who proclaim (as depicted in speech bubbles), "Five hundred years of resistance,"[25] "We will reclaim again . . . ," ". . . territory" ". . . and power" (figure 2a). On the next page, a Guaraní man declares, "We, the Guaraní, should recover our history because . . . knowing our history helps us to understand our current problems," and "We Guaraní men and women have a past that we should feel proud of." The remainder of the booklet offers an alternative narrative of Guaraní history, which charts the Guaraní's arrival in the region in search of the "Land without Evil,"[26] their long anticolonial resistance, and their eventual domination and subjugation by "the Spanish" who "wanted their lands to raise cattle." Another page depicts Guaraní ancestral territory in Tarija, shown to cover the entire Chaco region, under which is written: "Our fathers had their own territory . . . We, the sons, should reconquer it!" (figure 2b). These territorial counternarratives aimed to help community members regain self-esteem and cultural identity eroded by a regime of *empatronamiento*, in which their *patrones* had addressed them with racialized insults that made them "[go] around humble and silent" for half a century (APG IG and CERDET 2005: 53–54).

If this points to the role of NGOs in shaping and articulating the meaning of the land struggle, then community members also had their own orally transmitted historical counternarratives, which shaped as well as reflected broader movement discourses. As one community member from Tentaguasu put it: "Our grandfathers fought so that they could leave territory for our children [but] the Spanish came . . . fifty years ago and occupied a lot of land, our territory . . . and for that motive we, as the Guaraní people, have to organize ourselves, so that we can defend our land, our territory." Community members contrasted stories told by elders about a world of material abundance and free movement with the restrictions placed on their own movements. As one elderly man from Ñaurenda told me:

> Reclaiming territory is . . . that is, the old great grandfathers lived from that, the grandfathers, the great-great-grandfathers lived from that—from the forest, from land, from hunting, and looking for honey, and making their products. In contrast, when it's private property, you can't even go to look for some little animal to eat. When one already has his own land, one is happy—you go to walk, you go to hunt, you can already plan. But when there isn't any [land] it's difficult to enter a property—the owner gets angry.

FIGURES 2A AND 2B. Illustrations from booklet "Solidaridad con el Pueblo Guaraní" (CERDET, n.d. 1), found in archives of CERDET's central office in Tarija city. Courtesy of CERDET.

3. EL TERRITORIO GUARANI-CHIRIGUANO DEL SUR.

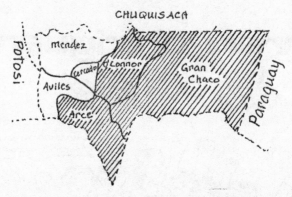

Los Chiriguanos ocupaban un gran territorio en nuestra región en lo que hoy se conoce como las provincias O'Connor, Gran Chaco y Arce.

Mientras tanto otros Chiriguanos ocupaban un extenso territorio que abarcaba la zona de Cordillera hasta llegar al río Grande en lo que hoy son los departamentos de Chuquisaca y Santa Cruz.

¡Nuestros padres tenían su propio territorio.........

¡NOSOTROS LOS HIJOS DEBEMOS RECONQUISTARLO!

=4

FIGURES 2A AND 2B.   (Continued)

Remembering this history enabled community members to imagine a future in which land access was the basis for autonomy and well-being. As Pablo from Tarairí put it, "When we speak of the TCO, our hope is . . . to live better, to live better, without anyone being able to tell us, 'Hey, that's my land; you have to work for free.'"

The APG IG and CERDET also produced historical and territorial counternarratives directed at a broader regional audience. One such document observes:

> According to the official history of our region, the Guaraní are beings who existed a long time ago and live only in the yellowed pages of the chronicles written by Franciscan missions and conquistadores . . . On the contrary, the true history, which is made through struggle and doesn't aspire to be crowned with official reports, is different. According to this, the Guaraní are a people who, from remote times until the present, inhabit an extensive territory.

The authors go on to describe the Guaraní as "the most fitting metaphor of what our country is: victims of a neocolonial system that has always insisted on denying them [their rights]" (CERDET 1993). In doing so, they locate the Guaraní land struggle in Itika Guasu within a broader national indigenous project of re-founding citizenship in Bolivia. I observed the continuing power and erasures of this "official history" during the course of my research. In early 2011 I was attending Guaraní language classes with my friend Hernán Ruíz, a non-Guaraní activist working within the Guaraní organization CCGT. The other students were schoolteachers and public officials, who were now required under the 2009 constitution to learn an indigenous language. Our teacher was from Itika Guasu but resided in Tarija city, where the classes took place. For the final session of the course, Hernán brought with him a video about the struggle to end *empatronamiento* and reclaim territory in Guaraní communities of the Chaco. The students were shocked by what they saw and expressed indignation that they had never before been told the "true history" of Tarija. After weeks of studying the Guaraní language, they had no idea about the Guaraní's history or ongoing political struggle. Nevertheless, the fact that they were watching a video about it—and being taught compulsory classes by a Guaraní teacher—is evidence of the broader political effects of the Guaraní movement and its counternarratives in Tarija.

The Territorial Turn

While Guaraní communities of Itika Guasu were busy organizing, occupying land, and retelling history, other changes were afoot at a global level that would help pave the way for legal recognition of their territorial claim. A broad consensus was emerging among global development institutions regarding the importance of legally recognizing indigenous land rights. In what follows, I explore the discursive framings of indigeneity, nature, and territory associated with the "territorial turn" (Offen 2003a) and consider the political, economic, and historical contexts for its emergence. I argue that the territorial turn must be placed in the context of a market-led development agenda and efforts to mitigate the crises it produced. But it must also be understood in relation to a longer history of "ethnic spatial fixes" (Moore 2005) through which colonial rulers sought to manage colonized peoples' continuing presence in territories of conquest.

As will become clear, there was no single coherent vision of what indigenous territories would look like or what governmental objectives they would serve. Rather, indigenous territories were subject to multiple and contradictory imaginaries, all of which differed from Guaraní community members' aspirations for "reclaiming territory." An exploration of these contradictions provides important insights into the possibilities and limits of indigenous land rights as an instrument for decolonizing territory—insights that will be developed in subsequent chapters.

From Assimilation to Ethnodevelopment

During the 1970s, indigenous rights advocates began to challenge the until then dominant assimilationist paradigm of indigenous development. Exposing the violence enacted on indigenous peoples throughout the world in the name of development, they called for alternative models of development that would allow indigenous peoples to develop in culturally appropriate ways according to their own priorities (Engle 2010: 190). This activism contributed to a paradigm shift within global development policy toward what is often referred to as "ethnodevelopment."[27] This shift was both reflected and advanced by the International Labour Organization (ILO) Convention 169, passed in 1989. Explicitly rejecting the assimilationist philosophy of its predecessor, Convention 169 called for respect for the cultural integrity of indigenous peoples, their co-participation in national society and development decision making, and recognition of their territorial rights. During the 1990s, leading global development institutions began promoting indigenous land rights as a precondition for achieving successful ethnodevelopment.[28] This occurred against a backdrop of indigenous activism throughout the Americas, which gained momentum and international attention around the 1992 quincentennial of Columbus's landing. In voicing their demands—first and foremost for territorial rights—indigenous peoples (like those in Itika Guasu) drew support from emergent transnational networks of development actors, funded as key advocates of the new ethnodevelopment paradigm.[29]

Ethnodevelopment gained traction in the context of a broader crisis of legitimacy of "development" following the devastating social impacts of pro-market "neoliberal" reforms implemented in much of the global South since the 1980s.[30] The World Bank and International Monitory Fund in particular faced a barrage of critiques from activists, social movements, indigenous organizations, and academics, who pointed to the damaging social impacts of their policy prescriptions. Such critiques contributed to bringing about a shift toward a more socially oriented, participatory, and preemptive development agenda.[31] Along with "participation" and "empowerment," "social capital" was one of the buzzwords of this new approach. Used to refer to the positive role played by social networks and cooperation in development, the concept was taken up in discussions of ethnodevelopment in ways that emphasized how "traditional values and structures," including collective control of natural resources, could enhance economic security for indigenous peoples.[32]

The Ethno-Environmental Fix

A pervasive argument was that indigenous land rights would help strengthen indigenous peoples' role in biodiversity conservation. While the discourse of Amerindians as "guardians of nature" has a long history (Wade 2004), it gained force in the 1970s, in the context of growing environmental concerns and on-the-ground engagements between conservationists and indigenous movements.[33] The late 1980s and 1990s saw an explosion of policy and academic discourse on the links between indigenous peoples and biodiversity. The 1987 Brundtland Commission's report *Our Common Future* connected indigenous peoples with the earth's sustainability owing to their unique environmental knowledge. The UN's 1992 Earth Summit in Rio recognized indigenous peoples as a "Major Group" that should participate in sustainable development (Colchester 2004: 148). The 1992 Global Biodiversity Strategy highlighted the link between cultural diversity and biodiversity (World Resources Institute 1992: 21). The following year, the World Bank declared that "environmentally sustainable development will not come about unless indigenous and other traditional peoples are brought into the effort to solve the world's urgent environmental problem" (Davis 1993: 14). This led to the establishment of a new Social Policy and Resettlement Division tasked with developing guidelines for increasing indigenous participation in natural resource management and biodiversity conservation (Marquette 1996).

The links between culture and conservation were elaborated in an extensive literature on "ethnoecology" (Toledo 2002: 7), while a variety of mapping projects highlighted the "striking spatial overlap" between indigenous peoples and biodiversity (Marquette 1996). Collective land rights were identified as a prerequisite for realizing indigenous peoples' potential as natural resource managers (Davis and Wali 1993: 11). Conservation organizations supported these moves, with the added incentive that land rights were often a prerequisite in market-based conservation and development schemes. Such schemes, and their celebration of indigenous environmental knowledge, reflect a broader shift away from the "fortress conservation" approach toward community-based natural resource management during this period.[34]

While environmental arguments lent legitimacy to indigenous land claims, it is important to recognize the power relations implicit in this framing. Rather than being based on indigenous peoples' sovereignty over their ancestral territories, this discourse vests the moral authority to evaluate indigenous land claims in an ambiguously defined and homogeneously conceived global society, implying potential restrictions on indigenous land use (Engle 2010). As will become clear, the imaginary of indigenous territories as bounded spaces of ethno-environmental difference is unrealistic for many indigenous peoples, who live not in pristine forests but rather in environmentally precarious conditions alongside settler populations, and embedded in unequal relations of capitalist political economy.

Securitizing Capital

Global support for indigenous land rights also had another, even more ambivalent context. Some of the earliest global policy statements on indigenous land rights emerged against a backdrop of efforts to mitigate the effects of large-scale capitalist projects on indigenous populations, projects in which global development institutions were deeply implicated. The World Bank's 1982 operational policy statement OMS 2.34 recommended "the recognition, demarcation and protection of tribal areas containing those resources required to sustain the tribal people's traditional means of livelihood" (Davis, Salman, and Bermudez 1998: 5–6) as one of a number of "safeguards" to protect "tribal people" in the context of World Bank–financed development projects. Operational Directive 4.20 of 1991 strengthened this commitment to indigenous land rights, recommending that, where World Bank–funded projects affected the lands and resources of indigenous peoples, "regularization of customary rights" could be used "to avoid, minimize or mitigate such impacts" (Davis, Salman, and Bermudez 1998: 7–8). Moreover, all World Bank–funded projects that affected indigenous peoples should contain a special Indigenous Peoples' Development Plan, with a land tenure component to establish indigenous titles to ancestral lands and resources.

The directive indicates the bank's intention to provide funding and technical assistance to borrower countries in the process of indigenous land regularization.

The fact that indigenous land rights were advocated by multilateral agencies that were aggressively promoting capitalist investments in indigenous territories is a source of profound ambivalence (Bryan 2012; Hale 2002 and 2006). During the 1980s and 1990s, the World Bank provided substantial loans for extractive industry projects in Latin America, as well as applying loan conditionalities that forced privatization of hydrocarbon and mining industries, opening the way for transnational investment in extraction (Griffiths 2000; Hindery 2013). While the notion of "safeguards" might appear to stem from a concern about indigenous peoples' well-being, what was being safeguarded here was the security of capital investments. In addition to providing legal security, the World Bank argued that clarifying the boundaries of indigenous claims would "reduce the risk that tribal people will suffer from the project's consequences *or disrupt its implementation*" (OD2.34, cited in Davis 1993: 5; emphasis added).

Weaponizing Maps

Efforts to "make legible" indigenous land claims (Scott 1998) can also serve broader military-strategic objectives. The genealogy of indigenous mapping projects (particularly in Central America) is deeply implicated with U.S. counterinsurgency strategies since the end of the cold war, and reflects a growing emphasis on understanding the "human terrain" of warfare (Bryan and Wood 2015). This "weaponization of maps" has accelerated over the past decade or so, with the American Geographical Society's controversial Bowman Expeditions Program—a $500,000 indigenous mapping project funded by the U.S. Army's Foreign Military Studies Office that began in 2009. The first of these "expeditions" mapped indigenous lands in Mexico for a nationwide GIS (geographic information system) database, without informing participating communities of the U.S. military's role in the project.[35] In a related mapping project in Panama, principal investigator and U.S. academic Peter Herlihy (who also led the Bowman expeditions) was accused of taking ownership of the completed maps (Chapin and Threlkeld 2001: 83) and admitted to sharing data with the Panamanian National Geographic Institute (Herlihy 2003: 326). These examples raise important questions about whose interests indigenous mapping projects ultimately serve.

Interrogating these double-edged governmental agendas complicates celebratory accounts of indigenous countermapping as a tool of resistance. It does not mean, however, that indigenous peoples were merely dupes of a global conspiracy. As the rest of this chapter shows, Bolivia's TCOs emerged at a moment when a neoliberal reform agenda was being challenged and transformed by growing social and political activism. Indigenous peoples' historic struggle for territory was part of this picture.

It is also important to place today's indigenous territories in a broader historical context. Ethnic communal territories played an important role in colonial governmentality in many parts of the world—from Africa (Moore 2005; Mandami 1996; Chanock 1991; Hodgson and Schroeder 2002) to Asia (Li 2010) and North America (Simpson 2014). Ethnic territories were instrumental to settler projects of territorial appropriation, erasing existing tenure regimes, suppressing land markets, and restricting the mobility of colonized peoples. Spanish colonialism in the Andes also rested on an ethnic spatial division; a Republic of Spaniards coexisted with a Republic of Indians, subject to separate laws and communal land titles, as well as extraction of labor and tribute (Rivera Cusicanqui 2010). At this point the Guaraní remained unconquered, their presence marked on colonial maps by the sprawling inscription "Chiriguanos." Yet their long-standing exclusion from Bolivian citizenship forms part of a complex and uneven (post)colonial geography in which processes of racial classification and territorial appropriation were intimately connected.

Ethnic territories also functioned as sites for interruptive assertions of indigenous sovereignty in the face of colonial rule. In Africa, local populations looked to reserves as a defense against further land loss to white settlement or expropriation (Li 2010). In the Andes, indigenous peoples fiercely defended their communal territories against liberal reforms that sought to dissolve their lands for private redistribution (Gotkowitz 2007). In the United States, Indian reservations constitute the basis for contemporary indigenous assertions of sovereignty that interrupt settler states' territorial projects (Simpson 2014). After long histories of dispossession, ethnic territories may represent the spaces indigenous peoples can fight *for* and *from*. Thus, whatever double-edged governmental agendas underpinned the recent "territorial turn," we should not underestimate indigenous peoples' ability to critically engage processes of postcolonial governmentality in defense of their own decolonial projects. As Audra Simpson argues, indigenous struggles for sovereignty and self-determination take place "in the teeth of Empire" (2014: 158). I now return to Bolivia to examine how such engagements shaped the elaboration of the 1996 INRA Law.

National Articulations: The Making of Agrarian Law

Parallel to the local and global processes just described, a national indigenous movement was gaining force in Bolivia, with "territory" as its central unifying demand. In 1987—the same year that saw the founding of the APG IG and the publication of the Brundtland Commission's report *Our Common Future*—the lowland indigenous umbrella organization CIDOB drafted a proposed Indigenous Law. Drawing on ILO Convention 169, the document called for recognition of the legal personhood of indigenous peoples and protection of their collective rights,[36] including the right to hold land collectively and their right to "cultural, political and administrative autonomy within their territorial jurisdiction" (Van de Cott 2000: 136). While the proposed law was an important unifying document for the nascent lowland indigenous movement (Paredes and Canedo 2008: 35), translating it into state law was no simple matter. When the draft proposal was formally presented to the Bolivian National Congress in 1992, it was quickly dismissed.

Alongside this legal advocacy, lowland indigenous peoples staged a series of national mobilizations, beginning with the forty-day March for Territory and Dignity of June 1990. Catalyzed by logging concessions in the Amazon and led by the Mojeño people of Beni Department,[37] the march demanded recognition of indigenous territorial claims, respect for their traditional uses and customs, and intercultural bilingual education. This played an important role in making lowland indigenous peoples visible to a national audience. Following the march, President Jaime Paz Zamora signed presidential decrees recognizing nine indigenous territorial claims—although without any legal instrument for titling this land to indigenous claimants.[38] In 1991 the government ratified ILO Convention 169, which calls on governments to recognize indigenous territorial rights under state law (articles 7 and 13–19).

This was followed by the 1992 "500 Years of Resistance" campaign, when indigenous peoples from across Latin America staged events and mobilizations to mark five centuries of indigenous resistance to Spanish colonial rule. The event fortuitously coincided with the one-hundred-year anniversary of the Kuruyuki Massacre, which saw more than seven thousand Guaraní delegates march through the ancient battlefield (Gustafson 2009: 38). These mobilizations led to a further eight presidential decrees recognizing indigenous territorial claims (Deere and León 2002: 65). In 1993 the Bolivian constitution was revised to recognize the "pluri-cultural and multi-ethnic" character of the Bolivian state (Article 1) and the territorial and cultural rights of indigenous peoples (Article 171). This was followed in 1994 by a new education law that included intercultural bilingual education (Gustafson 2009) and the Law of Popular Participation, which opened space for indigenous participation in municipal governance (Postero 2007).

Even at this multicultural moment, indigenous claims to *territory* proved highly contentious. When President Gonzalo Sánchez de Lozada took office in 1993, he rejected the presidential decrees signed by his predecessor Paz Zamora, declaring them "unconstitutional" (Paredes and Canedo 2008: 35). Fortunately, by this point a new political space had emerged for pursuing indigenous land claims. Under pressure from the World Bank to restructure its defunct agrarian institutions in line with a market-led development agenda, Paz Zamora's government had opened a four-year national debate (1992–1996) on the content of a new agrarian reform law. This process was overseen and financed by the World Bank through its National Project for Land Administration (World Bank 2001).[39] Indigenous movements seized on the process as an opportunity to gain legal recognition of their territories.

The national debate over what would become the INRA Law highlights the conflicting visions of agrarian rights and development articulated by global development institutions, the Bolivian state, and Bolivian social movements during this period. Despite its market-led reform agenda, the World Bank was well aware of the need to respond to the land demands of an increasingly restive peasant and indigenous population (World Bank 2001: 2). The bank also argued that TCOs would put "limits on the expansion of un-managed, illegal extraction of forest resources" (World Bank 2001: 5)—an agenda that coalesced with its parallel investment in protected areas. The Danish development agency DANIDA, which emerged as the major funder of TCO mapping and titling procedures in eastern Bolivia, similarly argued that "the titling of TCOs permits indigenous peoples and communities to police and denounce social, cultural, or environmental impacts that the exploitation of resources in their environment could give rise to" (DANIDA 2005: 23–24). Both institutions also stressed the importance of a more transparent and efficient system of property rights for transnational companies investing in oil and gas exploitation in Bolivia (DANIDA 2005: 15). In this way, global support for TCOs was distinctly double-edged, reflecting the contradictory agendas discussed in the previous section. As we will see, these agendas shaped the legal attributes of TCOs in important ways.

State officials tended to be far less sympathetic to indigenous land claims, viewing them as a threat to state sovereignty and to the integrity of the nation. This was affirmed by Tomy Crespo, a long-time indigenous rights advocate from Tarija who worked in the newly created INRA during the mid-1990s. He claimed that the U.S.-educated president Gonzalo ("Goni") Sánchez de Lozada and members of his government were particularly nervous regarding the Guaraní's national territorial claim, which combined nineteen TCO claims and covered 81.3 percent of the Bolivian Chaco. According to Tomy, critics within the government argued:

> "All this Chaco is Guaraní; you could see the dismemberment of the country as such," and that gave rise to a lot of fear . . . Don't forget that the INRA Law came out under a neoliberal government, and there was a lot of fear. It fell to us, a group of around thirty young employees,

to fight for it. We met with the president [Sánchez de Lozada], and he always said [putting on a heavy gringo accent]: "Isn't there a danger that the country will divide? Because the Guaranís are still going to be down there [in Argentina and Paraguay] and what will happen?" Because they already had information that there are hydrocarbons here [in Tarija], so it was like, the Guaraní [could] ask for a territory, and then they [could] end up with the hydrocarbons and they make another country . . . Based on this internal political argument, of maintaining national sovereignty, they said, "They're asking us for a lot."

His remarks powerfully illustrate how national interests in the Chaco's hydrocarbon wealth, combined with colonial discourses that placed the Guaraní on the fringes of the Bolivian nation-state, combined to construct their territorial claim as a threat to the nation's integrity. Instead of inscribing state sovereignty over indigenous lands, Sánchez de Lozada feared that titling Guaraní territory would have the effect of *unmaking* the Bolivian nation. Tomy's account also points to an underlying (and not unfounded) fear that behind indigenous demands for land rights lay far-reaching aspirations for political autonomy.

Still, as Tomy's presence within INRA demonstrates, state actors were far from unified in their stance on indigenous territorial demands. Nor was "the state" always distinguishable from global donors and social movements. The "thirty young employees" of INRA to whom he refers were a product of institutional and financial support from the Danish development agency DANIDA, which had overseen the hiring of a young and politically radical staff—many of whom, like Tomy (previously an intern with the rural development NGO Fundación ACLO and an employee of the Instituto Indigenista Boliviano[40]), had worked in NGOs or indigenous organizations. This gave rise to ideological conflicts within the state. As Tomy explained:

In INRA there were technical teams with a very . . . neoliberal vision . . . of creating a land market in Bolivia. And there were those of us who were frowned upon within the process, who were the counterweight to that, those of us who had a vision that the indigenous peoples should have TCOs. They called us bad names . . . At one point we were a majority . . . because Denmark gave money to *us*. Of course, [it was] for the indigenous peoples, wasn't it? It was much more interesting to finance the indigenous populations, wasn't it? So there were more of us. Later, [the government] started to introduce other teams with other criteria.

Despite contrasting TCOs with this "neoliberal vision," Tomy suggested that the two positions were in fact intimately connected. TCOs were justified as a protective measure to prevent indigenous peoples' dispossession in the context of the neolib-eral thrust of the INRA Law:

> We invented a law, a regulation, and in that regulation you can see the legal terms of the system, of the neoliberals, who were in favor of open-ing a land market, and also a lot of fuss: "Listen, we have to see how the indigenous people will access that, respecting for them one class of property ... so that the system doesn't end up buying [their land] from them." So they designed what ended up being native community lands, with the characteristics of being irreversible, unseizable, etcetera.

A range of other Bolivian social actors also weighed in on the 1992–1996 national debate in defense of their own interests and visions of agrarian develop-ment. These included lowland indigenous peoples; highland indigenous peas-ants; individual "colonist" peasants; small, medium, and large entrepreneurs; and the private owners of large idle estates (Urioste and Pacheco 1999). Highland peasants and colonists demanded a range of tenure options (communal and household), the redistribution of unproductive large estates in the east, and the rejection of a market-based model of agrarian development. Large landowners argued for a "free land market" based on private property, legal security, access to credit, and productive investment, and fiercely rejected the state's right to expropriate and redistribute unproductive large estates. All these agrarian actors expressed their demands through social mobilization and activism, as well as through participation in the formal debate.[41]

Fearing that the state would accede to pressure from powerful landowner organizations, the indigenous movement stepped up its own mobilizing efforts. In August 1996, as the INRA Law was being debated in Congress, indigenous groups staged a national March for Territory, Land, Political Participation, and Development (often referred to simply as the March for Land and Territory). More than two thousand lowland indigenous people participated, includ-ing leaders from Itika Guasu. Alongside them were representatives of peasant organizations—an overlooked precursor to the peasant-indigenous alliances that led up to Evo Morales's 2005 election. The marchers demanded the titling of indigenous territories already recognized by presidential decree and the rapid promulgation of the INRA Law. They stipulated that the law include procedures for the titling of new indigenous territories, a guarantee of indigenous claim-ants' exclusive rights over natural resources, and mechanisms of social control over land distribution (CERDET 2004b: 20–21). Following the march, CIDOB presented the government with thirty-three territorial claims (Almaraz 2002), which included the feared nineteen claims from the Guaraní. Among them was the territorial claim of Itika Guasu, the result of early mapping efforts by the APG IG and local NGOs (discussed earlier, and in more detail in chapter 2).

An Ambivalent Resolution

Reflecting these competing agendas and social pressures, the INRA Law combined contradictory logics. It has been described as a "transitory and ambivalent resolution" (Almaraz 2002), the result of an "unstable equilibrium" between conflicting sectoral interests (Urioste and Pacheco 1999), and "an unusual combination of neoliberal and social justice measures" (Deere and León, quoted in Gustafson 2002: 17). Ismael Guzmán and colleagues identify three main currents (Guzmán et al. 2007: 12). First, responding to the demands of Andean peasant organizations, the law reaffirms central principles of the 1953 agrarian reform: the social function of property, the state's obligation to support smallholdings (including those of new settlers), and the state's right to expropriate unproductive lands for redistribution to landless groups. Second is a "neoliberal" current, which promotes the commodification of land and the consolidation of private property as the basis for a market-driven model of agrarian development.[42] Finally, the INRA Law recognized indigenous claims for land rights through the creation of a new form of agrarian property: native community lands. In addition to defining TCOs as indigenous peoples' "habitat" and emphasizing their collective, indivisible, and inalienable character (see quoted passage at the beginning of this chapter), the INRA Law declares its conformity with the concept of "indigenous territories" in ILO Convention 169 and stipulates that "the titles of native community lands will be awarded in favor of indigenous and native peoples and communities, recognizing the right to participate in the use and sustainable exploitation of the renewable natural resources existing therein" (Article 3).

The indigenous movement celebrated the INRA Law as the first time in history that the Bolivian state had recognized indigenous territories (Paredes and Canedo 2008: 36). Guaraní people in Itika Guasu remember the festive atmosphere that surrounded its promulgation. Yet critics were quick to point out the numerous ways in which TCOs fell short of indigenous peoples' demands for territory.

First, there was the question of private property claims within TCOs. Responding to pressure from landowner organizations, the INRA Law stipulates that all private property claims within TCOs will be recognized and titled, provided they fulfill an "economic social function," that is, provided the land is used productively.[43] This applies not only to third parties already in possession of a land title but also to those who did not previously have land rights, provided they have possessed the land claimed for more than two years. The INRA Law thus puts indigenous claimants in a position of *inferior* right compared to private claimants (Almaraz 2002). In theory, indigenous peoples are to be compensated for these territorial losses through the allocation of state lands adjacent to the TCO or, where no such lands are available, through forced sale of private properties. This has not happened in practice, however (see also Paredes and Canedo 2008: 36–37). Beyond its practical implications, this prioritization of private land claims violated the principle, established in ILO Convention 169, of indigenous peoples' *preexisting* (pre-colonial) rights to their territories. As two authors from CIDOB put it:

> By not recognizing the preexisting indigenous rights to areas subject to SAN-TCO [saneamiento de TCO, the legal process for titling TCOs], the indigenous claimants remain, in the titling of their own territories, in a position of inferior rights to any legal possessor. In this way, the commitment of the Bolivian state to recognize the right of indigenous peoples to their TCOs, incorporated in the constitution, in [the state's] subscription to and ratification of ILO Convention 169, and in the adoption of the INRA Law itself, loses all effectiveness. (Martínez 2000: 21)

Another issue of contention was the creation of estudios de identificación de necesidades espaciales (spatial needs identification studies, EINEs), which enabled the state to redefine the area of TCO claims. In practice, such judgments were often influenced by state and private economic interests within TCO claims (Paredes and Canedo 2008). EINEs quickly came to be seen by indigenous organizations as an "instrument of amputation" (Almaraz 2002: 33). CIDOB complained that by enabling the state to determine how much land to award indigenous peoples, they undermined the basic purpose of TCOs: recognizing indigenous peoples' ancestral land rights (Martínez 2000: 42). EINEs were also seen as a waste of scarce funding for TCO land titling and a tactic for delaying recognition of indigenous land rights (Martínez 2000: 43). These critiques culminated in a 1998 CIDOB-led mobilization demanding the annulment of EINEs, which eventually removed their power to determine TCO boundaries (see chapter 2).

A third important way in which TCOs fell short of indigenous demands for territory was their exclusion of indigenous rights to the subsoil—an explicit demand of CIDOB's 1991 proposed Indigenous Law. The subsoil remained the patrimony of the Bolivian state, as stipulated in the Bolivian constitution, giving the state rights to exploit (or award as concessions) mineral and hydrocarbon resources within TCOs. In severing the soil from the subsoil, TCOs reflected a modern capitalist view of nature as "a unique object that can be atomized into bits to be owned" (Mansfield 2007: 401). In practice, the complex land-based infrastructure and synergistic effects of hydrocarbon development belied such a neat separation (see chapters 5 and 6). In TCO Itika Guasu, conflicts over land rights and subsoil rights would become intimately, and explosively, intertwined.

The foregoing critiques converged around the assertion that TCOs offered indigenous peoples "land and not territory" (García Hierro 2005; Paredes and Canedo 2008: 36)—a phrase repeated regularly by Guaraní leaders. "Territory" here is understood as "the ensemble of resources that corresponds to [indigenous] strategies of survival" (CERDET 2004: 24,)—a vision articulated in CIDOB's 1991 proposed Indigenous Law.[44] As one female indigenous leader put it: "We're not asking the government for lands, we're asking that they give us papers—titles— recognizing our rights to our territory, where our ancestors lived, where we currently live, and where our children will live" (cited in Martínez 2000: 12).

Activists and NGO staff in Tarija tended to be pragmatic about these limitations, arguing that the INRA Law represented "the limits of possibility" of a particular political moment. As Miguel Castro put it: "[The TCO titling process] has many, many limitations, but it's what is possible. If I learned anything in all this process it's that you have to play with what's possible. Don't you? So, it's what's possible and you have to keep on advancing." Tomy emphasized the urgency of moving ahead within these limits, in a context of new territorial incursions: "The strategy was: grab what they could now, and from that point afterwards, fight, but that they would already have something."

Yet many Guaraní leaders and community members in Itika Guasu claimed they were unaware of the implications of these political-legal compromises. As one leader reflected, "We didn't have our own direct advisors; we had advisors from friend institutions but these institutions, for all their good will, have their own work policy." The APG IG's president Nestor Borrero argued that leaders entered the TCO titling process with a limited understanding of legal norms and procedures.

Yet the inherent legal limitations of TCOs were not the only obstacle indigenous peoples faced. The broader social, political, and economic context continued to play a central role in defining territorial outcomes, beyond—and sometimes against—what legal norms stipulated. Legal norms were themselves subject to continuing contestation and modification in the context of ongoing political struggles. As a preliminary example, I turn to the surprising story of Bolivia's first TCOs, where the investment safeguards of a World Bank–funded hydrocarbon project proved more influential—and more useful for indigenous claimants—than the historic new INRA Law.

Extracting Recognition

In 1997, just a year after the INRA Law was passed, the future of TCOs was suddenly thrown into doubt by the election of a new president: the seventy-one-year-old right-wing ex-president (1971–1978) and former dictator Hugo Banzer Suárez. As Tomy Crespo explained:

> [Banzer] came with clear intentions . . . of overturning the whole process that had been initiated with the issue of the native community land claims. For [Banzer's government], the concept was very clear: native community lands shouldn't be titled, they should be reverted . . . [We should] do a reevaluation of how much land the communities *really* need, and if a community is productive, award [land], but they weren't going to give land to a load of lazy people who don't do anything . . . As many of Banzer's ministers in the seventies said: "We should put the highland Indians in overalls and boots so they look cleaner." There wasn't any respect for cosmovision, culture—nothing; it was a concept of production, work, and "Why do they need land?"

This observation reveals the precariousness of indigenous gains in a context of chronic political instability, institutionalized racism, and elite rule in Bolivia. Despite the state's official adoption of multiculturalism, Banzer embodied the sedimented effects of an assimilationist paradigm of citizenship, which framed agrarian reform as a tool for transforming savage Indians into civilized and productive peasants worthy of inclusion in the national community. In this context, Tomy described how indigenous organizations were faced with "a kind of emergency," in which the formal recognition of the first TCO seemed a matter of utmost urgency:

> It was a moment of risk—*truly*, of risk. And we decided to get a title. And many . . . technicians or whatever, we met up in Santa Cruz and we chose [the territorial claim] of the Tapietes . . . because it was the first process completed. So the government knew that the Tapietes were on the point of being titled—a tiny territory [65,132 square miles]. They were reconciled with the cattle ranchers, there was no trouble, there was nothing—it had to be titled.

Despite the strategic selection of a well-advanced and relatively noncontentious TCO demand, activists' efforts were soon thwarted when Banzer's government invented a new process of "quality control" whereby the Geographical Military Institute was required to verify all of the measurements created by civil topographers. Faced with this laborious monitoring process, Tomy and his colleagues changed tack, focusing instead on a TCO claimed by the Ayoreo people of Santa Cruz Department. The reason for their choice, he explained, was that this territory was already the site of a hydrocarbon project, financed by the World Bank, to build a gas pipeline from Bolivia to Brazil.[45] The project involved a $7 million compensation plan, which included a land program that obliged the government to move ahead with indigenous land titling. With this in mind, Tomy and his colleagues at the Indigenous Institute worked with the Ayoreo organization to rapidly elaborate a TCO claim:

> Six months later we presented [four TCO demands] of the Ayoreos to the [Presidential] Palace. Banzer refused to sign them, and the Ayoreos marched to La Paz and carried out marches and blockades in Santa Cruz . . . But in addition to this, the oil company demanded that the World Bank get involved, because it was a [World Bank] loan, and [the bank] said [to Banzer], "You're obliged [to sign the title]," so Banzer says, "What should I do?" He signed two, two of the four Ayoreo titles, and the other two we kept in reserve. And that's his strategy; he says, "We'll sign two and then later we'll annul them," because he hadn't signed four.

In practice, under continuing indigenous pressure, recognition of other TCO claims was quick to follow:

> After signing those, the first TCO titles in Bolivia, that was what opened the way—with the most . . . let's say, *complicated* government . . . The other two [Ayoreo titles] were demanded under pressure from the Ayoreos themselves—the indigenous peoples rose up once again, they demanded [the government] sign the other two [titles], and because of those two, another seventy-four titles with the Chiquitanos. At that point [the government] forgot about that Tapiete quality control process and titled the Tapietes five new titles . . . and they started to abandon the ideology of denying land to the indigenous peoples, because someone said [to Banzer], "It's strategic for your image before the World Bank and the international community" . . . And look at that, the dictator is the one who ends up awarding the first TCO titles.

This little-known story of how the first TCO titles in Bolivia came to be recognized demonstrates that extractive industry was not just a backdrop to global discussions on indigenous land rights; it was also an on-the-ground reality that shaped the law's implementation. Moreover, rather than being duped into occupying double-edged neoliberal spaces, indigenous peoples and their advisers knowingly exploited transnational capitalist agendas in order to overcome resistance from a hostile elite-led government. This is emblematic of the "boomerang" strategy through which indigenous movements bring international pressure to bear on domestic elites (Keck and Sikkink 1998; Brysk 2000). Yet rather than simply scaling up its demands, Bolivia's indigenous movement took advantage of the fact that the global—in the guise of transnational oil companies—was already present in the local. What Charles Hale fails to note when he asserts that indigenous peoples accepting World Bank funding for land titling gave "implicit endorsement" to a neoliberal agenda (2006: 110) is that World Bank–financed extraction was already under way in indigenous territories—with or without indigenous peoples' endorsement, and with or without their territorial rights.

This story also shows that transnational companies and international financial institutions *preceded* the Bolivian state in recognizing indigenous land rights in Bolivia. From the outset, indigenous land rights surpassed the arena of indigenous-state relations, demonstrating the power of non-state actors in governing territory. This provides an important precursor to recent events in TCO Itika Guasu, where an agreement with the Spanish oil company Repsol has been framed as an alternative route to territorial recognition and autonomy beyond the power-infused arena of state land titling.

MAPPING TERRITORY
The Limits of Postcolonial Geography

In early 2012, I borrowed a GPS device and set off on a trek with twelve women, men, and children from Tarairí, a riverside community at the heart of Itika Guasu where I had been living for the past six months. The objective was to identify the legal boundaries of Guaraní land—that is, of the fragment of titled TCO land within which Tarairí community members' homes were located. I'd been on a practice run with the device the day before. Spurred on by the false security of GPS coordinates, I'd strayed off navigable paths and ended up getting disoriented and horribly scratched amidst the variety of thorny plants that make up the dense Chaco forest. In contrast, my Guaraní companions moved nimbly through the landscape, sauntering up steep rocky hillsides in rubber flip-flops, stepping effortlessly through tangled foliage, and clearing obstacles with machetes. Meandering on and off barely visible paths, they paused to remark on familiar and forgotten places. They knew the territory—its natural features, its plants and animals, spirits and stories—in a way that I never would. And yet here I was: a visitor from a faraway place, prepared with GIS references from digital state maps to show them difinitively where the legal boundaries of "their territory" lay. Boundaries that had been established two decades earlier, whose only physical evidence was a few weathered posts, marked with a splash of yellow paint and a carved inscription of Roman letters and numbers (figure 3). The posts were relics of "translations" made during the 1990s between the Guaraní's ancestral territory and the abstract space of the state, expressed in the form of a numeric code whose reference point lay in Europe.

FIGURE 3.   Community members locate a boundary post marking the legal limits of TCO Itika Guasu (photo by author).

There was a kind of ironic inversion in the activity I had instigated. Walks with GPS devices and indigenous community members were normally associated with the early stages of countermapping projects, when optimism about the benefits of putting indigenous places "on the map" remained high. In this case, however, my intention was to translate the abstract lines of state maps—a reflection of an ambivalent and power-infused titling process—onto the lived landscape. It was not that I imagined doing so would "empower" community members or resolve their everyday land problems (discussed in detail in chapter 4). Rather, my intention was to interrogate what I had already observed about the disjunctures between the legal-cartographic constructions of the TCO and the ways in which community members imagined and inhabited their territory.

This chapter offers ethnographic insights into these disjunctures based on my experiences in Tarairí. I also seek to contextualize these epistemological conflicts through an account of the discursive and cartographic processes through which TCOs came into being. The processes I describe took place in parallel, and in articulation, with the national-level negotiations leading up to the promulgation of the INRA Law, described in chapter 1. In scrutinizing them in this chapter, I highlight the erasures and power relations involved in making indigenous territories legible to the state. I show how, even before they gained official recognition, indigenous territorial claims were conditioned by state and settler geographies, (post)colonial knowledge hierarches, and the power asymmetries of NGO and activist networks.

Reconstructing this mapping story was not a simple task. As critical geographers have observed, part of the power of maps lies in their capacity to obscure the conditions of their own production. When I began my fieldwork in the Bolivian Chaco, TCOs seemed like such a naturalized geographical category among NGOs, indigenous peoples, and state institutions that it took me some time to inquire into how they came into being. When I eventually did so, it was unclear where I might turn for an account of these processes. Guaraní accounts of this period tend to recall assemblies and marches rather than mapping methodologies. While yellowing documents from NGO archives provided some clues, only one current employee had been present in the 1990s. Through a process of snowballing, I did eventually track down four individuals who were intimately involved in mapping Itika Guasu and other TCOs. Although heavy reliance on these informants makes this account a partial one, it also reflects the exclusions and power asymmetries that underwrote the mapping of TCOs. I provincialize these activist narratives by juxtaposing them with ethnographic insights from community life.

The chapter is structured as follows. Part one, "Translations," describes early efforts at identifying and mapping ancestral territory in Itika Guasu, and charts the modifications that were made as the Guaraní and their NGO allies encountered the "logics of the state"—the nonnegotiable boundaries of state and settler geographies, as well as the requirement for bounded and "viable" territories. I explore how non-indigenous activists saw themselves as "translators" in this process, and how indigenous territorial knowledges were silenced even as they were enlisted in the production of maps. Part two, "Calculations," describes the emergence of a new methodology for establishing and justifying territorial limits: indigenous spatial needs. I show how this evolved from an activist discourse for justifying indigenous territories, to an official (and highly contested) "instrument of amputation," and finally to a means of rationalizing indigenous territories within established grids of intelligibility and broader discourses of development. On the basis of an analysis of the official Spatial Needs Identification Study for Itika Guasu, I reflect on the governmental effects of mapping territory and highlight the contradictory development visions invested in TCOs. I conclude both sections with ethnographic interludes based on everyday life in Tarairí, which explore what—and who—was excluded from the mapping process, the enduring power effects of the TCO's legal-cartographic construction, and the fluid, relational, and racialized geographies that continue to structure indigenous lives beyond the map.

Translations

> **The cartographic and legal "representation" of indigenous clients is always already conditioned by unequal relations of social power: property, citizenship, territoriality, legal norms, the nation-state system, and so forth.**
>
> Joel Wainwright and Joe Bryan, "Cartography, Territory, Property," 2009

> **It's about translating elements of the people so that the state can process them . . . One has to do all this work of seeing what will do, and what will not do.**
>
> Sarela Paz, Bolivian anthropologist and indigenous rights activist, interview with author, February 14, 2012

Mapping Ancestral Territory

During the first Guaraní assemblies held in Ñaurenda in the late 1980s, participants reflected on the importance of secure land rights for achieving lasting independence from the *patrones*. Without such security, they realized, families would simply go hungry and be forced to return to exploitative labor contracts. With Bolivia's ratification in 1991 of ILO Convention 169, legal recognition of indigenous land rights seemed like a tangible possibility for the first time in the country's history. It was in this context that the APG IG and its NGO allies began work on the construction of a territorial claim. As CERDET's former director Miguel Castro remembers, early mapping efforts in Itika Guasu were oriented toward the reconstruction of ancestral territory:

> The most important criterion was historical, that is, where did their [i.e., the Guaraní's] territory extend to? . . . Because at that time—and this was to change later—the future of the communities was the past . . . There was a mythic dream of freedom, of abundance, where they emerge as owners of their lands, so you say: what we want isn't to go forward, we want to reclaim what we had . . . What did we have? We had all this territory.

At this stage, he emphasized, the Guaraní were not thinking about the legal sphere, or even about territory as a concept; rather, they simply wanted to "reclaim the lands they've always had." In order to identify these, communities began a process of consultation with older people about where their ancestral lands had extended to.

Miguel's account points to the agency of Guaraní communities and the role of oral memories of land occupation in shaping early mapping efforts in Itika Guasu. Yet "ancestral territory" was not just an indigenous concept. According to

Sarela Paz, an anthropologist who worked with the national indigenous organization CIDOB on numerous indigenous territorial demands during the 1990s, the focus on ancestral territory was informed by the language of ILO Convention 169, which defined indigenous territory as indigenous peoples' "traditional habitat." This gave rise to the question "How do you identify this traditional habitat?"—a question that had animated earlier indigenous mapping efforts by cultural ecologists in Canada and Central America.[1] As Sarela explained:

> Place names were a central element. I remember that I fought hard for this issue—that to approach a historical dimension of what is territory, traditional habitat, place names helped enormously . . . When you speak of historical territory, the people say: "Over there, for example, that place, of course we don't live there anymore but that's what it's called, in my language. The grandparents were there."

Sarela was so committed to this idea that she completed a sociology master's dissertation on indigenous place names and their utility in mapping indigenous territories.[2] The methodology she developed, and promoted among Bolivian activists and NGOs during the 1990s, involved triangulating information gathered from oral interviews with state and colonial maps:

> I said to the [indigenous people]: "What is your territory?" "I don't know"—the first response is "I don't know." Delving deeper, trying to understand, this "I don't know" isn't true. "Where are you settled? Where do you go?" . . . When you see that—where their relatives are, and you look on the map—what you see are [indigenous] place names.

Indigenous peoples are framed here as incapable of representing their own territorial imaginaries or claims in a language comprehensible to the state, requiring the presence of a non-indigenous intermediary, whose task was to establish "chains of equivalence" (Blaser 2010: 216) between indigenous and postcolonial geographies. Relying on indigenous place names to provide this link, however, made indigenous territory contingent on its past legibility to Spanish-speaking settlers and the Bolivian state. Sarela drew on colonial and missionary archives for evidence of historic land occupation, which helped add legitimacy to the indigenous territories she mapped:

> The archives of the Franciscans, Jesuits, the governors . . . officials of the colonial empire also left their registers and that was also a documentation we started to use to formulate the territorial demand . . . So many demands started to have, let's say, a package of documents, of archives, which said, which proved, what was the historical territory.

This recourse to colonial documentation is not unusual for indigenous territorial claims, and raises questions about the decolonial potential of maps produced.[3] Nonetheless, maps of ancestral territory did pose a semiotic challenge to contemporary postcolonial geography. As Miguel described, in Itika Guasu historical references were combined with oral histories of community members to produce a map of ancestral territory that covered an area far exceeding that currently occupied by Guaraní communities, incorporating cities and villages, and traversing provincial and departmental boundaries:

> The first map they made was *huge*. It included cities . . . everything. And that was on the basis of the old people, what they remembered. One said, "I, for example, before the hacienda came, I used to go to hunt up to that place." Well, that's part of the territory. "I used to go to fish up to that place." "I remember that with my father I traveled . . ." So there is an element of historical memory, you see?

Some APG IG and NGO materials produced in this period depict Guaraní ancestral territory as covering the entire Chaco region. By making visible the Guaraní's pre-colonial occupation of territory, these maps contributed to the territorial counternarratives discussed in chapter 1. They also had a strategic function in ongoing negotiations with the state; in Sarela's words, they were "a discourse that we're going to spread . . . in such a way that the state understands that our habitat was much bigger, but that, for the sake of this dialogue, we're reducing it—so that the state understands the fact that we're accepting *its* logic." Whether indigenous people viewed such representations as merely a precursor to vastly reduced claims is doubtful. What is clear is that maps of ancestral territory were not just an inscription of a preexisting indigenous territoriality; rather, they represent the first iteration of NGOs', activists', and indigenous organizations' efforts to map bounded indigenous territories legible to the state.

The role of non-indigenous interlocutors in mapping ancestral territory in Itika Guasu was ready acknowledged by Miguel, who described how, when he began working with the Guaraní in the late 1980s,

> they didn't talk about their territory; they talked about their land. But when they entered into this [mapping] process, they started to change. This ancestral notion of land started to change. First because of the influence of the theoreticians [of], let's say, of "indigeneity," who said, "What you need is a territory, and territory is this, that and the other." The concept they now have of territory isn't an indigenous concept; it's a very well-meaning interpretation of the *técnicos*.[4] So there is a change, you see? There is a change in the idea of territory.

As this makes clear, although some accounts distinguish between indigenous visions of "territory" and state visions of "property," the notion of "territory" as a bounded, mappable space is itself a construct, reflecting the global imaginaries associated with the "territorial turn" (discussed in chapter 1)—and, more broadly, European notions of property and abstract space (Blomley 2010). In order to become visible, indigenous territories had to meet a set of predefined expectations that eclipsed alternative indigenous territorial imaginaries and practices. Tomy, who worked in Itika Guasu in the late 1980s as an intern of the NGO Fundación ACLO, put it more starkly:

> If I'm honest, beyond whether anyone is annoyed, there wasn't even contact between some communities, and that's important to say, because we have to understand that Itika is also . . . an entelechy (*una entelequia*, a pipe dream).[5] Entelechies are creations of the brain; they're images that you create to help you with comprehension . . . Itika Guasu as such, as a whole territory, *never existed*, as you must understand; it *never existed*.

These statements resonate with my ethnographic engagements in Itika Guasu, where the TCO, as a bounded space, did not feature prominently (if at all) in community members' imaginative geographies (discussed later in this chapter). As Xavier Albó notes (1990: 33, 43), Guaraní migration patterns mean that the quest to identify a timeless ancestral territory can only be an act of imagination and political claim. Indigenous territory was thus from the outset a discursive and cartographic construction, and one that non-indigenous interlocutors played a key role in producing. In fact, as I now elaborate, the mapping of a bounded territory constituted the first step in a gradual process of *limiting* the Guaraní's territorial claim.

The Logic of the State

Even if maps of indigenous ancestral territories had a political-strategic function in negotiations with the state, they were not something the state could easily process. As Sarela explained:

> With the place names and the identification of historical territory, there was this debate with the state itself, with state functionaries; they said: "Yes, that's the *historic* territory, but they [indigenous peoples] don't live there anymore; there are already third parties [non-indigenous land claimants] there. And we, as the state, can't deny the presence of third parties." So that's the logic of the state.

The presence of non-indigenous settlers within these ancestral areas was not the only issue; these territories also traversed, and threatened, the internal spatial order of the state, represented by municipal, provincial, and departmental boundaries. In this context, NGOs and APG IG leaders began to make pragmatic decisions about what to include in, and what to exclude from, indigenous territorial claims. As Miguel described the situation in Itika Guasu:

> There was a judgment that, well, [the Guaraní] themselves realized that [what they were demanding] was a lot; . . . that no one will believe it . . . So after that—[after] saying, "Well . . . this is what we wanted, this is what we *were*," [the question is] now, *What is possible*? And [the territorial demand] began to be reduced. A first judgment was to remove the cities. For example, Entre Ríos. "Why are we going to go and fight with the residents of Entre Ríos?" They took out Entre Ríos. Another judgment was [to take out] the main roads.

As this implies, such decisions responded not only to the national political context but also to perceptions of what would be politically viable in the regional context, where the Guaraní remained a politically and geographically marginalized minority. Nor was there much to be gained by indigenous peoples claiming territories they could never hope to control politically; according to Sarela, the Guaraní speculated that "the *karai* are never going to accept a government of ours, and all [such claims are] going to do is limit our possibility of government." Put simply, indigenous territorial claims could not ignore the hegemony of settler geographies; they unfolded "in an already-mapped world where one cannot elect to live outside of sovereignty, territory, or the law" (Wainwright and Bryan 2009: 156).

Concessions were also made to the administrative boundaries of the state. By excluding communities east of Palos Blancos, the Guaraní and their allies confined the Itika Guasu territorial claim within the administrative limits of O'Connor Province. As noted in chapter 1, these provincial limits were based on the boundaries of the hacienda of Irish-born independence hero Francis Burdett O'Connor; the Guaraní thus located their claim within a colonial geography of rights (established through violence) that underwrote the state's own territoriality. Similarly, the administrative limit of Tarija Department was used as the TCO's northern boundary, despite the fact that lands to the north of it are occupied by Guaraní communities. The shrinking territorial limits of Itika Guasu were also informed by the uneven geographies of NGO intervention. As Tomy recounted:

> Why aren't the communities on the other side of Palos Blancos part of Itika Guasu? Because I decided, as an organization,[6] to [exclude

them] . . . because the [fiscal] resources were only enough to last up to here [Palos Blancos] . . . so [the exclusions] are also the result of situations of access, opportunities of access—that's the issue. Because I always asked myself, I always looked at the whole process—even after twenty years, I always asked myself: *Why didn't we go into these communities?* Sincerely, why did we strengthen here, strengthen there, while other zones were left out?

This provides a compelling example of how non-indigenous actors, rather than indigenous peoples, shaped the production of indigenous territorial claims, enacting exclusions that would have profound consequences for the communities in question. EAPG director Renán Sánchez described how some communities were also excluded from the Itika Guasu territorial claim because they hadn't yet acquired legal personhood. As this reveals, collective territorial recognition was also predicated on uneven processes of multicultural recognition enacted at a community level under the 1994 Popular Participation Law.

The shrinking boundaries that accompanied these adjustments are made visible by comparing a 1992 map of Itika Guasu produced by CERDET to the final TCO limits established in 1997 (figure 4), although this was but one stage in a series of more substantial reductions; documentation and interview accounts point to an original territorial claim of 310,000 hectares—an area 70 percent larger than the TCO area recognized by INRA.[7] The document attached to the 1992 map (CERDET, n.d. 2) reveals that both the area of the territorial demand and the mode of presentation to the state were still being worked out between 1992 and 1996, as indigenous peoples and their *técnicos* awaited the results of the ongoing national debate about the future of agrarian law. Yet ordinary women and men of Itika Guasu were largely excluded from these pragmatic adjustments—as were those who, owing to a series of contingencies, ended up outside the territorial demand.

In his analysis of indigenous development programs in the Paraguayan Chaco, Mario Blaser describes how NGOs acted as "translators," who worked to construct a "chain of equivalences" between local indigenous realities and state visions of development (2010: 216). When I proposed to Sarela that her work had been one of translation, she reflected:

It's a role of mediation, or of translation, as you say—there's no doubt about it. And most of the *técnicos* are doing that role of mediation and of translation. In one case the *técnicos* can be *técnicos* who form part of these institutions, NGOs, that support the issue of the indigenous peoples, but for another part, we're also talking about indigenous intellectuals, who are educated, who have already been professionalized,

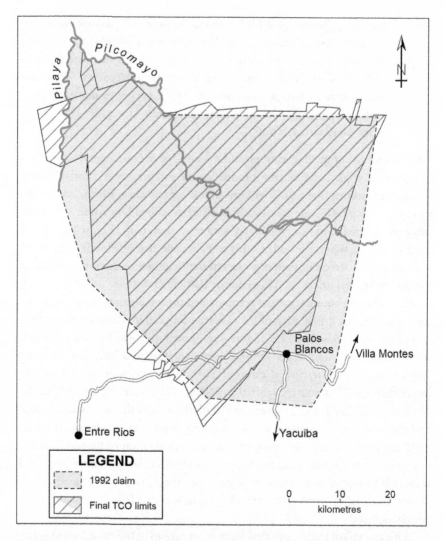

FIGURE 4.   Map showing 1992 Itika Guasu territorial claim and final TCO limits (elaborated by Cartographic Unit, Department of Geography, University of Cambridge)

who also perform this role of translation and mediation in this whole thematic. So it's about translating elements of the people so that the state can process them ... One has to do all this work of seeing what will do and what will not do.

While some indigenous leaders had a central role in this process—particularly those at CIDOB and the APG's national office in Camiri—in Itika Guasu the task of translation fell largely to non-indigenous activists and NGOs.[8]

Toward a Discourse of Indigenous Spatial Needs

As the APG IG and its allies—along with other indigenous organizations—adjusted the boundaries of their territorial claims, the question reemerged about how these territorial boundaries could be justified and made legible to the state, consistent with its own spatial production. Historical archives and indigenous place names were of limited use in rationalizing territories that, by the mid-1990s, represented only a fraction of these ancestral areas. It was in this context that the logic of "indigenous spatial needs" came to the fore as a means of establishing and justifying territorial limits. As I go on to elaborate, this logic ultimately became associated with the state's efforts to *reduce* indigenous territories through the creation of official spatial needs identification studies (EINEs). Yet it was the indigenous movement—and more specifically its *técnicos*—that first proposed the concept of indigenous spatial needs. Sarela claims the concept stemmed from indigenous peoples' realization that, although they aspired to regain control of larger territories, legally securing the lands they already occupied was a matter of "life or death." Indigenous spatial needs were also a means of justifying indigenous territories to the state and society, in a context of strong opposition from landowner organizations:

> Why spatial needs? Precisely to find the boundaries . . . Don't forget that the discussion wasn't only with state functionaries. I remember that, for example, in CORDECRUZ [Regional Development Corporation of Santa Cruz] we debated this issue a lot with the people from CAINCO [Chamber of Industry, Commerce, Services, and Tourism of Santa Cruz (Department)], with the cattle ranchers, the Civic Committee . . . That was the context we were working in.

The notion of indigenous spatial needs resonates with the social function of property, the guiding principle of Bolivia's 1953 agrarian reform, which establishes the automatic right of persons to legally own land they occupy and use productively, in the absence of competing claimants. Just as the communal plots in Itika Guasu functioned as visible symbols of Guaraní productive capacity, spatial needs analysis reframed indigenous land claims within an established discourse of rights. It was hoped that indigenous spatial needs would prevent the state from rejecting indigenous territorial claims or redefining them to cover an even smaller area (CIDOB-CPTI 2000). As I go on to elaborate, some of the key proponents of this discourse saw it as a challenge to prevailing racist visions of productive land use (and racialized stereotypes of indigenous peoples as unproductive).

Above all, indigenous spatial needs provided indigenous organizations and their allies with a means of rationalizing territorial boundaries that emerged from a rapid, improvised, and highly politicized process of mapping. Although NGOs and APG leaders in Itika Guasu began mapping a territorial claim during the early 1990s, other lowland groups were less prepared by the time of the INRA Law's promulgation in 1996. Wendy Townsend, a North American ecologist who worked at CIDOB during this period, described how, as the legal creation of TCOs became an imminent possibility, indigenous organizations and NGOs scrambled to put together territorial demands:

> It was like, there's a space: Goni [President Gonzalo Sánchez de Lozada]'s going to be leaving [office] and he's going to sign this [INRA Law] before he goes, and in [CIDOB's] office all these lines were drawn of what would be *territorios*. By CEJIS [the NGO Centro de Estudios Jurídicos e Investigación Social], by whoever was the technical person working then; they weren't demands that were necessarily, "We want this because my territory was . . . you know, my grandfather planted whatever tree there"—there was no real . . . *grounding*. They just had a chance to get land and they drew lines . . . It was like, "Okay, you're demanding what?" If you know what, then BOOM!—there had been no maps made, it was all more of an intuitive territorial . . . *right* feeling.

This statement again illustrates how the mapping of indigenous territorial claims proceeded through arbitrary and highly politicized processes from which indigenous community members were largely excluded. As Wendy went on to explain, this improvised and office-based process of mapping territories was accompanied by incessant pressure from the state to provide a convincing rationale for these rapidly constructed territorial demands. State officials even sought to interrogate indigenous leaders independently of their technical advisers, asking them:

> "Why do you need a million hectares, why do you need this?" So all of that argument drew the government to come to, "Well, okay, you're going to have to establish how much you need," which is an absurd concept! Absolutely absurd, because, one, we don't even know what they use, and, "What do you mean it has nothing to do with how much you *need*?" It's really your *right*.

While this would seem to suggest that the idea of indigenous spatial needs came from the state, this was not in fact the case. Several years prior to such discussions, Wendy completed a doctoral dissertation addressing the question of how much land the members of an indigenous group required to sustain themselves—a study that sought to justify indigenous territorial claims and was used by CIDOB to *counter* state efforts to reduce indigenous territories.

Thus the logic of indigenous spatial needs was neither merely a state ploy to reduce indigenous territorial demands nor an indigenous-activist strategy to justify them. Rather, in a context in which "ancestral territory" was losing its political value, indigenous spatial needs emerged as a new discursive terrain of struggle, providing a crucial link in a "chain of equivalence" between established notions of productive land use, indigenous territorial claims, and global discourses of ethnodevelopment. Although the displacement of a discourse of ancestral rights proved to be a risky move, indigenous leaders and their allies clearly believed they could mobilize this discourse toward their own ends, portraying bounded collective territories as a material basis for the traditional, sustainable livelihoods that global development actors had envisaged for indigenous peoples. In doing so, they showed how the project of making indigenous territories visible to the state involved not only locating them within postcolonial geographies but also framing them within dominant discourses of indigeneity, rights, and development.

In this broader context, Guaraní leaders and NGOs working on the Itika Guasu territorial claim gradually abandoned the contentious discourse of ancestral territory in favor of a more mundane claim for land as a basis for livelihood. As Miguel described this shift:

> There was a communal notion of ancestral territory, which is what came out at first. But then the [Guaraní] realized that, well, it wasn't viable ... So, well, first of all they had to change; we can't aspire to our ancestral territory anymore; instead we have to try for a quantity of land that's viable in legal terms, but that at the same time is enough to be able to live. You see? So I remember that we did a lot of exercises, of how much land a family, a community needs to live—taking into account productive use, symbolic, religious use, population growth—and we made a demand. The first thing they changed was the issue of the [territory's] size.

Rather than presenting this as a strategic reframing, a way to justify claiming *more* land—the thrust of Wendy's account of her work on indigenous spatial needs—Miguel suggests that, at least in Itika Guasu, the shift was more of a pragmatic concession, signaling the abandonment of politically unviable aspirations of reclaiming ancestral territory in favor of a claim for a more limited area of land necessary for indigenous survival. In fact, this is precisely what the shrinking boundaries discussed earlier signal: the transition from a claim of recovering land control to one of recognition of areas indigenous peoples already occupied. While Miguel uses the collective pronoun "we" to refer to this pragmatic shift, I would question the extent to which Guaraní community members abandoned their dreams of "reclaiming territory"—dreams that were fueled by CERDET's earlier community-level organizing efforts.

Spatial needs analysis involved the compilation of an array of data about indigenous land use practices—an early indication of the calculative techniques that would accompany state recognition of indigenous territorial claims (discussed later in this chapter). As Sarela remembered:

> I would arrive at a community: "How do we make our boundaries?" Well, in this community, talking maps—that's how we started to work. "You, sir, where do you make your *chacos* [agricultural plots]?" "Here, here, here." Well, we have to mark up all of that. "Now, you, sir, where do you go to fish?" "To the river, in my lagoon, along the road" . . . So we started to establish a new, very contemporary version [of territorial demands] . . . You could later identify all that [information] on a cartographic chart . . . We went from community to community . . . The work of the [formal territorial] demands started like that—that's how we did it when they [the Bolivian Congress] were about to approve the INRA Law . . . In the heat of the march [of 1996] they [the Guaraní and their *técnicos*] elaborated eighteen [territorial] demands; with the [APG] leadership we did them all . . . [and in each case] we ended up commanding an area with boundaries.

The objective was not to create a territorial representation meaningful to indigenous community members but to "command an area with boundaries" legible and acceptable to the state. Moreover, "talking maps" produced their own exclusions. Given that few (if any) activists or NGO employees speak Guaraní, they relied on the accounts of those who spoke Spanish—usually male leaders—to provide information about land use and territorial limits. Women were largely excluded from this process. Given the different ways in which Guaraní people use and value territory on the basis of age, gender, location, and livelihood strategies (discussed in the next section and in chapter 4), we can speculate that alternative limits might have emerged had informants or knowledge practices been different.

Interlude: The Power of Maps

The distance from the field to the map and back again, from the village to the computing office, would come to mark what seemed an absolute gap: the divide between reality and its representation, between an image-world and its object

Timothy Mitchell, *Rule of Experts*, 2002

It was late August 2011 and I had had just returned to Tarairí community with my lower leg in a cast after breaking my ankle playing soccer with the community's women and children, just two weeks into my six-month stay in the community. In an attempt to dispel the initial shock and guilt my injury had provoked among community members, I had brought paints and was sitting in the crumbling adobe edifice of the former school (now used as a preschool center) while the children painted my cast with colorful representations of community life. As usual, I had with me a notebook I used for my Guaraní language study. Two teenagers, curious about the gathering, had picked it up and were marveling over the columns of Guaraní and Spanish words (being bilingual themselves and unused to seeing their native language written) when a large folded sheet of paper fell out. It was a map of the TCO, divided into polygons, which I had photocopied and highlighted in different colors to show the land awarded to the Guaraní in two separate titles. The map became the subject of intense scrutiny by the young woman and man, who were able to identify some place names and rivers. I asked them if they had ever seen a similar map before, and they said they hadn't. In the conversation that followed, it became clear that they did not know what "TCO" meant, although they were aware that they lived in "zone 2."[9]

Having spent my previous years of fieldwork immersed in APG IG assemblies and NGO activities, where the TCO was a central political and geographical category, I was surprised by these young people's lack of familiarity with the term. I soon discovered that they were not the only ones to whom "TCO" meant nothing. One day soon after, I accompanied Hermes, the brother-in-law of Armando, the father of my host family, en route to an agricultural day job on a *karai* hacienda. When I asked him about the TCO, he dismissed it as "something of the APG IG" that was of no importance to ordinary community members. Over subsequent months, I observed that the TCO did not crop up in everyday conversations in the community, even when people where talking explicitly about problems of land rights or access. Toward the end of my stay, in January 2016, I conducted two separate focus groups with men and women, where I used participatory mapping to explore the disjunctures between the legal-cartographic construction of the TCO and the ways in which they imagined their territory.[10]

Despite what I had learned in previous months, the results of the activities surprised me. About half of the participants in the men's focus group claimed they did not know what the TCO was. None of them knew whether land where they lived and worked had been titled to the TCO. Nor did they have any idea what was currently happening with the land titling process. The men blamed the APG IG for not providing adequate "training" or sharing information and noted that many communal leaders who had participated in the titling process had either died (as in the case of Tarairí's former *mburuvicha*, Armando's father) or been replaced in their positions. The men clearly felt ashamed of their lack of knowledge about the titling process. In a concluding remark, Pablo, the community's nurse, who knew more than most people as a result of his frequent visits to the APG IG, lamented:

> We too, as the interested party, we have to be up to speed, because it's always useful. It's always useful. People come here to ask, and we have to know something to answer, you see? Even me, I know nothing! Look at Kuñati.[11] It's not long ago that she came and she already knows everything. And we, the interested party, we don't know anything! Above all, young people . . . and she comes to ask and we don't know how to respond.

The younger men in the group seemed to accept Pablo's chastisement, admitting that they hadn't always paid attention in APG meetings:

> PABLO: Because we need to know [*porque nos falta*]. Now Kuñati herself is asking you.
> PARTICIPANT 2: True—and we don't know anything.
> PABLO: And now you can feel bad: how bad that we don't know.
> PARTICIPANT 2: Sometimes one goes to the meeting and . . .
> PARTICIPANT 3: Doesn't pay attention.
> PABLO: They don't pay attention.

Uncomfortable with this dynamic—that the young men should feel humiliated by my interrogation of their knowledge of the legal-cartographic constructions of the TCO—I moved on to a brief presentation about the history of the land struggle, the TCO titling process, and the current status of land rights, using a series of maps produced by INRA and NGOs—information that was immediately taken up in relation to an ongoing boundary dispute with a neighboring community (discussed in chapter 4). Pablo also provided his own "translation" of what the TCO meant—in part based on a series of discussions we had had about it over the previous six months:

> Where the limit to Tarairí is—that's what the TCO means for us. So, the TCO, we now have the TCO. I don't know where it extends to, but we have the TCO. We are inside the TCO . . . because there is a map—I believe Kuñati has it—there is a map [showing] where the TCO extends to, where it extends to toward the east, toward the north, toward the south, toward the west . . . and the zone Itika Guasu is also where we live. The TCO is very . . . that is, it's recognized by the state; inside the TCO is where a landowner can't sell the land. Also where other landowners

can't come there because it's inside the TCO, inside the demanded land. You see? That's what the TCO means ... If some *karai* want to come and live here, are you going to let them build their house here in the middle of the soccer field? Are you going to let them? No. That's the TCO. That's how I understand what the TCO is.

As this illustrates, men in Tarairí appeared more embarrassed by the fact that a (female) outsider should know more than they did about a "Guaraní" political matter than they were convinced of the practical use of this knowledge. Yet this is precisely the point: with its digitized maps, legal complexities, and technical procedures, TCO titling does not simply appear distant from the realities of community members' lives; it also *disempowers* them, making them feel excluded from, and ignorant about, what was once conceived as a Guaraní struggle. In the case of the focus groups (in contrast to everyday conversations), my methodology and line of questioning served to perpetuate the disempowering effects of the legal-cartographic process while obscuring what people *do* know about territory—both their lived relationship with it and the broader meanings of the land struggle.[12]

It is worth considering how maps appeared in these discussions. In Pablo's assertion that "there is a map [showing] where the TCO extends to," maps appear as a distant, inaccessible form of knowledge marking the legal-cartographic limits of Guaraní territory. When he goes on to note that "the zone Itika Guasu is also where we live," the gap between reality and representation is clear. While his assertion that landowners could not build their house on Tarairí's soccer field (or *oka*) gestures at a tenuous connection between the two, everyone was well aware that this scrubby patch of land would be of little interest to *karai* settlers, who already occupied the best surrounding land. Maps also appeared in the community in the form of crumpled photocopies I carried around with me. Yet the effect of such maps, I discovered, was to introduce new power-knowledge asymmetries between myself and community members, unsettling relations built over previous months of participating in everyday tasks and conversing in Guaraní.

I don't mean to suggest here that no community members knew or cared about the TCO. As will become clear in subsequent chapters, knowledge and opinions were varied, on both the history of the land struggle and the legal titling process. Yet what is notable is that some people who felt unable to talk about the TCO, or the legal-cartographic processes surrounding its production, talked passionately about the broader struggle for "reclaiming territory." For example, in the course of an unstructured interview, Tarairí's oldest man, Katuire, talked at length about the past: the days of *empatronamiento*, the loss of territory to the *karai*, the early days of the APG IG, and the ongoing inconvenience of having to deal with "stingy" landowners. Yet when I finally raised the issue of TCO titling, the conversation suddenly dried up:

> PA: Can you explain to me what hopes you had for the TCO, for land titling?
>
> KATUIRE: I hardly understand that; I don't understand it.
>
> PA: Do you know what the TCO is?
>
> KATUIRE: No.
>
> PA: Or the Guaraní territory of Itika Guasu . . . the titling of the land?
>
> KATUIRE: I hardly understand it.
>
> PA: When INRA came here to measure properties?
>
> KATUIRE: I knew, but there was Armando's father [the previous *mburuvicha*, now deceased]. They took measurements over there, there's a post . . . but I wasn't here.
>
> PA: So you never knew much about what it was?
>
> KATUIRE: No, I don't know, I don't know.

This passage, in the context of the discussion that preceded it, illustrates the disjuncture between Guaraní knowledge of territory and the legal-cartographic knowledge of the TCO mapping and titling processes. It also illustrates the capacity of the latter to silence the former, making people feel unable to say anything beyond "aikuaä" "I don't know"—a common response to my inquiries about the TCO in Tarairí.[13] Katuire's shift from impassioned dialogue to silence reflects how the titling process has, quite literally, taken the land struggle out of the hands of ordinary Guaraní community members.

If men in Tarairí felt unable to talk about the TCO, then this was even more the case with women. The TCO and titling process were certainly not topics that cropped up in everyday conversation (although problems accessing land and other natural resources did). When I asked direct questions about the TCO in a women's focus group, almost all the women (who ranged in age from their teens to their sixties) claimed they knew nothing about it. Even framing a question about the TCO or land titling in Guaraní was difficult—not only for me with my limited language skills, but also for bilingual women present in the group. These seemed to be concepts far removed from daily life, with no obvious translation. Some older women vaguely remembered "INRA," but no one had much to say about a fleeting visit of some state officials twelve years ago.

This is not to say that women knew nothing of the land struggle; older women had lived through and participated in the process of early Guaraní organization and had vivid memories of these events. Benita, Armando's older sister and the community's *kuña mburuvicha* (female communal leader), remembered her father (the former mburuvicha) going to meetings where they talked about land

and the TCO. When I asked about the TCO, however, she quickly went from admitting she knew "michiraimi" (a little bit) to declaring apologetically, "Mbaeti aikua" (I don't know). The TCO was not something she felt able to talk about. Other women in the group claimed to know nothing at all about the TCO, with two exceptions. First, Jimena (Pablo's partner, who had been present in some of our previous discussions) explained to the others that it means "ñande ɨvɨ" (our land or territory).[14] This did not seem to clarify matters for the other women. The term ɨvɨ conjured up images of fields and forests, not of state maps. Nor did the imaginary of a collective Guaraní territory correspond with the material realities of land control in Tarairí (discussed in chapter 4). Second, Rosalia, an older woman, reported that she had heard a prominent Guaraní leader talking about the TCO on the radio, arguing that the *empresas* (companies) were not respecting it. That a Guaraní woman should learn of the TCO through a Tarija-based radio station reporting on extractive industry conflicts is indicative of how the land struggle's displacement from community life to state cartography and law paved the way for its eventual regrounding in broader conflicts over hydrocarbon governance (discussed in chapters 5–6). Neither Jimena nor Rosalia could say whether they lived inside the TCO or where it was located.

Most young people claimed they didn't know what the TCO was, nor had they been told about the history of the land struggle. While some older community members blamed this on a lack of interest among young people, who they claimed had not endured the same hardships they had, younger people contradicted this, accusing their elders of not teaching them. As one sixteen-year-old, already engaged in wage labor outside the community, told me somewhat ashamedly:

> I don't know about land; my grandparents didn't tell me . . . I almost don't know. But I *want* to know. The older people haven't told me so that I also know . . . They haven't told me anything. Here generally there isn't much . . . that is, the older people don't teach, or one goes to ask and they don't like it that you ask . . . It's stupid [*una huevada*] . . . The old people don't tell the young people; that's how it is.

Other young people in Tarairí shared this sense that the land struggle was something they didn't know about but ought to. By the time I left the community, and following the focus groups, some young men were asking me for *capacitación* (training) on the TCO titling process.

As John Brian Harley notes (1989), maps are not just an instrument of the powerful but also a form of power in their own right. Part of this lies in their capacity to naturalize and universalize the subjective, selective gaze of the cartographer. Yet this rhetorical power is only one dimension of the power of maps.

For those who *cannot* read maps, their power also lies in their ability to mystify, to confuse; to invalidate and silence alternative forms of geographical knowledge and, in doing so, to disempower the owners of that knowledge. Even with my privileged access to information, literacy, language skills, mobility, extensive research time, and other resources, I often experienced bewilderment when trying to make sense of the mass of legal and cartographic data I collected. The generation of Guaraní people who participated in the land struggle during the 1990s are largely illiterate and speak limited or no Spanish. Even if they had been able to read or interpret cartographic data, they do not have access to this information, which is spread between the departmental and national offices of INRA (in digital and documentary form), APG offices in Entre Ríos and Tarija, and local NGOs. Meetings with INRA officials that I witnessed generally did more to baffle and silence the audience than to answer their legitimate questions about land rights. Of course, by this point the TCO claim had progressed well beyond early activist and APG IG mapping efforts, becoming mired in legal and bureaucratic complexities that exacerbated the inaccessibility of the resulting legal-cartographic construction. Nevertheless, the "translations" described in the previous section (and in the remainder of this chapter) represent the opening of a gap between reality and representation (Mitchell 2002) that would continue to widen after official recognition of the TCO claim.

Besides the epistemic asymmetries and exclusions of the territory's mapping, there was also another explanation for why people in Tarairí knew and talked so little about the TCO. Quite simply, it was not the only, or the most significant, geographical category they encountered in their everyday lives. This was illustrated in a focus group activity, in which—having already produced a map of "Tarairí and its surroundings"—men and women (in separate groups) were asked to add to a second map, showing "other important places." The maps produced were strikingly different, revealing gendered geographies of work, travel, and kinship relations.[15] Yet both maps challenged the primacy of the TCO as a spatial category. The women's map depicted strong relations with some other Guaraní communities (both within and beyond the TCO) but few relations with others, while the men's map illustrated how livelihoods are forged across multiple spaces that transcend TCO boundaries—from nearby urban centers to farms outside Buenos Aires. As chapter 4 elaborates, it is these networked relations that constitute Tarairí as a place.

Community members were also well aware of the dominance of other geographical imaginaries within the broader regional context. As Pablo noted, "I think, talking of the TCO, the people of Entre Ríos *don't know what it means...* they don't know what the TCO *is*." For this reason, men said that they were unlikely to refer to the TCO in describing their home to outsiders, referring instead to O'Connor Province, Entre Ríos, or the Pilcomayo River. The relative marginality of the TCO within dominant (*karai*) geographies was demonstrated by my own experiences traveling within Tarija Department. On trips between Tarija and Entre Ríos, on a dirt road that passes through several mountain ranges and sees frequent accidents, I would usually opt to take a shared taxi, which takes an hour less than the bus and is marginally safer. My fellow passengers were generally non-Guaraní people from O'Connor Province, whose lives involved frequent trips to Tarija for business, schooling, or family visits. During these journeys, my traveling companions would often inquire what I was doing in the region and where I was headed. I soon discovered that, if I mentioned the TCO, most people had no idea what I was talking about; they were much more likely to know Guaraní communities by name. On several occasions, I was surprised to learn that someone was heading to a place inside the TCO yet was unaware of its existence. This is not to say that no one had heard of TCO Itika Guasu. But the TCO was far from being a dominant spatial category in a landscape overlaid with numerous other boundaries and geographical markers—municipalities, cantons, communities, urban settlements, haciendas, rivers, roads, and gas fields, to name but a few.

As I discuss at the end of this chapter, the legal-cartographic construction of the TCO—premised on a world of subjects and objects located in Cartesian abstract space—also effaced the relational geographies of Guaraní relations with non-human inhabitants of the territory. I now return to my mapping story by tracing how the activist mapping "translations" described in the previous section fed into official procedures for mapping TCOs. I highlight how, as they moved into the realm of state knowledge, mapping efforts exceeded their original mandate—of fixing indigenous territorial boundaries—and became vehicles for broader techniques of calculability, involving the compilation of an array of geographical, statistical, economic, cultural, and demographic data on indigenous populations and territories.

Calculations

A technology of government . . . is an assemblage of forms of practical knowledge, with modes of perception, practices of calculation, vocabularies, types of authority, forms of judgement, architectural forms, human capacities, non-human objects and devices, inscription techniques and so forth, traversed and transected by aspirations to achieve certain outcomes in terms of the conduct of the governed.

Nikolas Rose, *Powers of Freedom*, 1999

Indigenous peoples during the past three years have been the most studied people on the same subject [Characterisation Studies, Preliminary Identification and Spatial Needs Studies], with results that distort their reality.

CIDOB-CPTI, "Atlas Territorios Indígenas en Bolivia," 2000

Instruments of Amputation

So far we have seen how, in the period leading up to the INRA Law's promulgation (1992–1996), indigenous leaders and technical advisers began to deploy a discourse of indigenous spatial needs to justify the limits of pragmatically constructed (and vastly diminished) territorial claims. Notwithstanding the ambivalences and exclusions I have noted, activists like Wendy did set out to challenge hegemonic (and fundamentally racist) ideas of productive land use by making visible and validating indigenous land use practices. Yet this strategic shift from ancestral rights to productive land use arguments ultimately backfired; with the creation of official spatial needs identification studies (EINEs), the Bolivian state co-opted the discourse of indigenous spatial needs and used it to reduce the spatial extent of indigenous territories.

EINEs were created under the 1996 INRA Law as a means of determining TCO limits, in a context in which a discourse of spatial needs analysis was already being used by the indigenous movement. With funds from the Danish development agency DANIDA, the completion of these official studies was contracted to anthropologists and sociologists—many of whom, like Sarela Paz and Tomy Crespo, were already involved in indigenous mapping as employees of NGOs, CIDOB, or the Instituto Indígena Boliviano. Once again, indigenous peoples were assumed to be incapable of representing their own territorial claims, requiring the deployment of educated non-indigenous "experts." As Wendy, a passionate advocate of indigenous ownership of knowledge, observed, "Basically [the state] handed [the process] over to anthropologists, instead of the [indigenous] people themselves coming up with information." While giving non-indigenous actors the power to determine indigenous territorial limits flew in the face of indigenous assertions of territorial sovereignty, this delicate task at least fell to individuals who were supportive of indigenous land claims.

The limits of state-sanctioned mapping quickly became evident, however. When the anthropologist consultants produced studies that justified large indigenous territories, the state intervened, rewriting EINEs according to its own vision and methodology. As Wendy explained:

> [The anthropologists] went out and gathered all this information, and then [the EINEs] were taken and they were reworked [by the state] with

this [alternative] model. So somebody else [from the government] went in afterward and put in all the economic stuff and made up the model . . . There was like two bursts: these first studies were done [by anthropologists], and then [the state] didn't like them, the government *did not like them*, and so they rewrote them and put this new model in—this economic model.

As I go on to elaborate, this "economic model" of indigenous spatial needs reproduced colonial discourses that framed indigenous land use practices as illegitimate. In an echo of assimilationist discourses of the 1950s, indigenous peoples' enjoyment of citizenship rights was predicated on their abandonment of indigenous subsistence strategies in favor of peasant agriculture oriented toward the market. For example, ignoring Wendy's meticulously researched models of indigenous land use, the government model excluded indigenous hunting practices—which would have implied a need for more expansive territories—on the basis that these were "backward" practices that would soon be phased out by indigenous peoples' incorporation in "development." In Wendy's words:

> The government made the statement . . . , "We really don't have to consider wildlife in this, because in another 5 or 10 years [indigenous peoples] won't have to hunt because of the pace of development." So they were trying to *limit indigenous territories* by these studies, when the studies [as conducted by anthropologists] were actually *expanding* their territory. So that's when [the state] came in, and when I showed them my models, that's when they had to come in with a competing model, and the model that they chose was done by an economist and it was based on economically maintaining them [indigenous peoples] as a little bit above poverty level, but using their resources and their territory—selling them. So that model was kind of built in, trying to . . . *counteract* the fact that we had a model; the indigenous people had a model showing how much they needed for land—not for money, just for subsistence. So the government came in with another model, but it was based on maintaining them just above poverty level and selling off everything they have.

As this implies, the state's vision of indigenous spatial needs was oriented toward the commodification of land and resources within indigenous territories, a vision that diverged from the ethnodevelopment discourse of the World Bank and DANIDA, which funded the implementation of TCOs.[16] Moreover, this economistic methodology of spatial needs was deployed by the state as a means of *reducing* indigenous territorial claims. In this way the state asserted its sovereign power to define the size and status of indigenous territories, undermining the claims of indigenous peoples to pre-colonial rights over their ancestral lands.

Indigenous peoples did not respond lightly to this effort to reduce their territorial claims. Such was the tense atmosphere around EINEs that indigenous claimants in one case held government ministers and INRA technicians hostage until they changed recommendations that decreased the claimants' TCO area. In 1998 CIDOB organized a national indigenous mobilization demanding the dissolution of EINEs, which it denounced as an "instrument of amputation" (Almaraz 2002: 33) and a "trap for indigenous peoples" (CIDOB-CPTI 2000: 42). Wendy claims she actively sought to raise indigenous leaders' awareness of "how [EINEs] were being manipulated against them" so they would "have the force to do a march to make [the government] stop those stupid, stupid reports having the power to cut their territory size." As a result of this march, the government finally conceded to indigenous pressure and agreed that EINEs would not have the power to determine the size of indigenous territories. This is a reminder of the fact that, however exclusionary mapping processes might have been, indigenous community members remained key protagonists of their territorial claims throughout the 1990s by way of their participation in national mobilizations. This political activism was a backdrop for ongoing negotiations with the state, which had tangible consequences for indigenous territorial demands—in this case, succeeding in overturning state efforts to redraw and reduce indigenous territorial boundaries.

The politics of indigenous activism challenged the technocratic framing of indigenous spatial needs. As Donald S. Moore notes, the "lens of social function" plays an important role in postcolonial agrarian governmentality precisely because it makes spatial orders appear "controlled by natural, mechanical or organic laws" (2005: 77), thus obscuring the agency of those governing. Activists used indigenous spatial needs to play down the political content of indigenous land claims (making them appear naturalized), while the state appropriated this discourse to mask its own political agenda of reducing indigenous territories. Yet the debate over indigenous spatial needs ultimately failed to mask the political nature of struggles over indigenous territorial boundaries. This did not, however, mean that EINEs were completely abandoned. Given that funds from DANIDA had already been allocated for their completion—providing employment and revenue for both state employees and activist consultants like Tomy—the studies went ahead. As the experience of Itika Guasu illustrates, the neoliberal and colonial logics of the EINEs remained firmly in place, despite the more limited influence of these studies. In fact, the retraction of their power to fix territorial boundaries made visible their broader mandate: that of rationalizing indigenous territories within existing national grids of intelligibility.

Rationalizing Territory: The EINE for Itika Guasu

The spatial needs identification study for Itika Guasu (VAIO and MACPIO 2000) reveals the contradictory effects of the political struggles I have detailed, as well as the shifting orientation of spatial needs analysis after the promulgation of the INRA Law. Despite the denunciation of EINEs as "instruments of amputation," the Itika Guasu study does not recommend a reduction of the TCO area; rather it recommends that the Guaraní should be titled 293,000 hectares, that is, 77,000 hectares *more* than the 216,000 hectares area recognized by INRA in 1997. This reflects the fact that some EINEs remained in the hands of indigenous rights activists or pro-indigenous anthropologists, without significant central state intervention. Tomy was one such individual, having moved from the peasant NGO Fundación ACLO to the Instituto Indigenista Boliviano before being contracted by INRA to conduct EINEs. In fact, the recommendation of 293,000 hectares had no legal effect, given that the power of EINEs to define TCO boundaries had by 2000 been overturned by indigenous mobilization. Nevertheless, it has served as a discursive reference point for the APG IG in its ongoing struggle for the legal consolidation of its land rights to the TCO.

It is noteworthy that the EINE for Itika Guasu was not conducted until 2000—that is, three years *after* the TCO had been legally recognized and "immobilized" for land titling.[17] This was not unusual, and reflects a temporal disjuncture between the politically urgent task of *recognizing* indigenous land claims (which occurred in the heat of the 1996 march) and the bureaucratically laborious process of elaborating regulations for their full legal consolidation. Indigenous opposition to EINEs caused further delay. As Tomy explained:

> Most of the time, the spatial needs reports were done *after* [INRA's] fieldwork, when you already had results regarding how much land was left [i.e., not titled to third parties], so if 24,000 [hectares] was left, I would do a report for 24,000; if 100,000 was left, I would do a report for 100,000—so I tell you, it wasn't scientific.

As a result, the TCO land area recommended by EINEs was often a mere post hoc justification of limits already established by INRA (or an activist critique in the case of Itika Guasu)—limits identified on the basis of private property claims. Arguably, EINEs ultimately served to rationalize and inscribe state sovereignty over the messy, contingent, and highly politicized process of demarcating and justifying indigenous territories rather than assessing indigenous land needs according to supposedly objective scientific criteria. This is indicated by the rapid and improvised manner in which the EINE for Itika Guasu was produced; as Tomy recounted:

> Given that there was a limited time—there [in Itika] they [i.e., the team of consultants hired by INRA] did it in one week . . . In many cases those teams couldn't easily reach thirty-six indigenous peoples or, in the case of the Guaraní, thirty-three—that is, from only one indigenous people—so what they [the teams] did is, to speed up the process, they took general considerations and tried to invent a formula. Where you said, [the indigenous people] have this many fenced agricultural plots, they have this many resources; they need 100,000 hectares . . . It was a very fast, *very* fast process of negotiation.

The reference to an "invented formula" and a "process of negotiation" points to the primacy of political rather than scientific considerations in determining results. Wendy, the North American ecologist, lamented the lack of scientific rigor that went into the elaboration of EINEs, describing them as "a lot of made-up numbers" and a waste of valuable resources:

> They [INRA] had all this money from the Danish and they just hired all these young consultants to go out there and gather information, and what most of them did was [they consulted] the literature—they were just packed full of information, very poorly cited, mainly, because most of the citations were taken out [subsequently, by the state, in order to insert its own logics], which to me is a total crime.

In her view, the politicized context of the EINEs' elaboration undermined their potential utility as sources of historical, social, economic, or ecological data—data that she believed could have been an invaluable tool for autonomous indigenous territorial management (a key motivation for her Ph.D. research). Clearly most individuals involved in the completion of EINEs did not share either Wendy's belief in scientific rigor or her vision of empowering indigenous organizations as the owners and beneficiaries of these data. What, then, was the purpose of EINEs? Given that the battle over indigenous territorial boundaries had moved elsewhere, and largely been concluded, what was the purpose of compiling lengthy studies packed with historical, geographical, and sociocultural data on indigenous land use, the accuracy of which seemed of little concern to the authors of EINEs or the state? Was this simply an epistemological performance enacted for the benefit of Danish funders?

Rather than being read as an explanation for TCO limits, a scientific indication of indigenous land needs, or even a futile exercise to justify a now redundant funding stream, EINEs provide a window into how the mapping of indigenous territories initiates, and forms part of, broader processes of rationalizing indigenous territories within existing grids of intelligibility. These grids relate not only to the state's knowledge of territory but also to its knowledge of population. Just as Sarela and her colleagues sought to construct equivalences between indigenous geographies and official cartographies, EINEs—which are but one of a whole host of studies of indigenous territories conducted during this period—sought to *know* indigenous populations in order to situate them within an established governmental and epistemological apparatus. Specifically, the EINE for Itika Guasu can be read as an effort to construct "chains of equivalence" (Blaser 2010: 216) between newly created indigenous territories, national development priorities, and global discourses of indigeneity and environmental management. As we will see, the results were highly contradictory.

The EINE for Itika Guasu (VAIO and MACPIO 2000) is 150 pages long (not including seven appendices) and is organized in eight chapters. The first six provide information on, respectively, the legal framework and methodology for the territorial demand; the pre-colonial presence of the Guaraní in the zone and subsequent shifts in their spatial occupation; current spatial occupation and socio-demographic characteristics; the basic needs of this population (relating to nutrition, health, education, and other aspects); the biophysical aspects of the zone, its renewable natural resources, their productive potential, and the environmental sustainability issues; and the productive system and livelihoods strategies of the Guaraní population and the infrastructure that supports them. The seventh chapter puts these data into a mathematical model to arrive at a figure (293,000 hectares) that purportedly expresses the "spatial needs of the Guaraní population of Itika Guasu." This calculation rests on a series of assumptions and prescriptions regarding the forms of territorial governance and development that will take place in the TCO. Following a "Methodology Guide" elaborated by the government agency MACPIO (Ministry of Peasant, Indigenous, and Originary Peoples' Affairs), the authors of the study divide the territory into three areas, categorized as follows:

> *Sociocultural Area,* [later referred to as "historic-cultural area"] consists of spaces that the indigenous peoples traditionally occupy, in which the man-land-nature relation that indigenous people have with their environment is demonstrated, and in which they carry out reproductive activities (hunting, fishing, gathering), achieving an integral use of space. This is the area identified to strengthen the cultural identity of the claimant people.

> *Economic-Productive Area,* spaces or areas where the action of man *over* nature allows the establishment of a productive process (agricultural, forestry, pastoral, and others). Areas that should provide the necessary natural resources, which, if exploited sustainably, guarantee social and economic growth of the claimants and their future generations.

> *Conservation Area,* which may or may not be circumscribed as a
> Protected Area . . . The Conservation area has as its objective to secure
> the presence of resources provided by biological diversity (flora, fauna,
> ecosystems, etc.) necessary for the cultural and biological reproduction
> of the claimant indigenous people . . . As is logical, economic manage-
> ment of these areas of a commercial nature is not anticipated, although
> the exploitation of the natural resources under a system of sustainable
> management oriented at subsistence consumption is permitted. (140)

Together these three areas reflect, and seek to reconcile, the multiple and competing logics underpinning TCOs' discursive and legal construction, described
in chapter 1. The first, the sociocultural (or historical-cultural) area, echoes the
discourses of ancestral (pre-colonial) rights and "traditional habitat" enshrined
in ILO Convention 169—what Karen Engle terms "territory as culture" (2010).
The second, the "economic-productive area," rests on a Western ontological separation between nature and culture (enshrined in the gendered phrase "man over
nature"), and overlays a racialized discourse of productive land use with a neoliberal preoccupation with economic growth. The third, the "conservation area,"
echoes global concerns with biodiversity conservation and its assumed compat-
ibility with indigenous "traditional" livelihoods under the rubric of ethnodevelopment. The attempt to reconcile these potentially contradictory visions of territory through the demarcation of different "zones" is emblematic of neoliberal
zoning practices, wherein the social and environmental destruction wrought by
marketization is thought to be remediable through the designation of particular
natures and populations as "outside the market." The spatialized governmental
logics within which indigenous territories were embedded (chapter 1) were thus
replicated within indigenous territories in ways that sought to preserve an envi-
ronmentalist discourse while broaching the unresolved question of indigenous
livelihoods.

As well as demonstrating how state employees adapted, and struggled to reconcile, competing discourses of indigenous development, this raises an important question: In the process of gaining state recognition, did indigenous peoples
unwittingly subject themselves to the governmental designs of the state and other
governance actors? Certainly EINEs created a "technical grid of intelligibility"
(Scott 1998: 76) and reflected a "will to improve" (Li 2007) on the part of the governmental agencies (the Ministry of Peasant, Indigenous, and Originary Peoples'
Affairs, or MACPIO, and the Ministry of Indigenous and Originary Affairs, or
VAIO) and individuals involved in their elaboration. As the foregoing excerpt
makes clear, EINEs went well beyond their initial mandate of defining territorial
limits, making a series of prescriptive recommendations for indigenous territorial

governance, which reflected state and global agendas with little reference to indigenous development priorities or demands for autonomous self-governance. These studies demonstrate how territory functions as a "political technology," involving not just the recognition of a preexisting socio-spatial order but also "its production through the application of an array of calculative practices used to define territories, the rights associated with them, and enumerate their qualities" (Bryan 2012: 217).

Yet rather than a coherent model for indigenous development, what emerged was a series of contradictory expectations for indigenous peoples' livelihoods and land use practices. On the one hand, this EINE reproduces a global discourse of ethnodevelopment and indigenous social capital, suggesting that "indigenous cosmovision" and "ancestral knowledge" of natural resource management will serve to buffer indigenous peoples from "the negative effects of globalization of the economic system" and "permit cultural, social, and economic strengthening of the claimants, which is ultimately what the State looks for through its development policies" (VAIO and MACPIO 2000: 134, quoting the official MACPIO EINE "Methodology Guide"). At the same time, the calculation of Guaraní spatial needs in Itika Guasu is based on a statistical model taken from peasant agriculture, which identifies how much income individual *households* will need "to cover their necessities of the food basket and other basic goods and services for the maintenance of their family," factoring in the need for "sustainable economic growth" (136). In fact, 88 percent of the recommended area for the TCO is justified with reference to households' required monetary income.[18]

The remainder of the territory is earmarked for the *combined* purposes of conservation and "sociocultural" activities. Although the spatial overlap between these activities is justified with reference to a discourse of indigenous environmentalism, the conclusion contradicts this, stating that restrictions may need to be placed on indigenous communities' activities in order to meet conservation objectives.[19] The authors further suggest "promoting and training the beneficiary population in the integral management and sustainable use of natural resources, with the objective of guaranteeing the perpetuity of the productive processes" (148). Such recommendations are illustrative of what Engle calls the "invisible asterisk" of cultural rights, whereby "in achieving land or development rights based on the protection of their traditional practices, indigenous peoples are often restricted in their ability to make autonomous decisions" (2010: 7). In fact, the conclusion is peppered with further recommendations about what kinds of activities, projects, and forms of natural resource use should take place in the TCO.[20] These proposals in some case correspond with NGO projects implemented in the TCO.

FIGURE 5.   Guaraní boy returns home with firewood, Tarairí community (photo by author)

The EINE of Itika Guasu thus demonstrates how the engagement of indigenous peoples in processes designed to recognize their territorial rights can also work to reinforce the power of the state or NGOs (rather than indigenous peoples) to govern territory.[21] Above all, it reveals the propensity for knowledge practices designed to identify and make legible indigenous territories to become a form of governmentality in their own right. Yet the contradictory and entangled logics of this study—and the contingent processes that surrounded its production—diverge from James Scott's depiction of "legibility" as a basis for "large-scale social engineering" (1988: 5). The state certainly does not appear here as a unitary, all-powerful entity acting under a coherent logic of rule; rather it was represented by largely foreign-funded staff, which included indigenous rights activists, who patched together knowledges and methodologies developed over a previous decade of political activism, which included sedimented traces of an ancestral rights discourse.[22]

The EINE was in this way more of an attempt to inscribe national sovereignty over highly contingent processes than a reflection of the state's actual power to govern indigenous territories. If anything, it was *non-state* actors whose role in territorial governance is made apparent by these processes. Indigenous territories were thus subject to "shifting alignments and contingent constellations of power" rather than "a single ruling rationality" or "coherent regime of intelligibility" (Moore 2005: 7–8). Yet, without reading EINEs as an inscription of some top-down governmental master plan, we should not lose sight of what they obscure with their spatial representations and statistical projections: forms of indigenous territoriality that were illegible to the state; assertions of pre-colonial sovereignty; the presence of non-indigenous landowners; and demands for autonomous territorial governance. By filling in, or overwriting, the Itika Guasu territorial claim with a tangled array of *karai* textual and numerical inscriptions, the EINE continued the effacement of the decolonial knowledges that had animated the Guaraní land struggle beyond the realm of cartographic translation. I conclude this chapter by returning to Tarairí community to reflect on a further dimension of what was excluded from and made invisible by these mapping processes.

Interlude: Spirit Sovereignties

It was late January 2012, and community life in Tarairí was gradually settling back to normal after the excitement of a five-day visit by a group of evangelists from Santa Cruz. People treated the evangelists with a mixture of curiosity, amusement, and pragmatism; few identified with their Christian beliefs, but most were quite happy to participate in communal meals, watching films about Jesus, and the distribution of secondhand clothing. They had even agreed to the building of a church in the community. During the evangelists' visit, I made several attempts to inquire into community members' spiritual beliefs and practices. Was God different from Tüpa, the supreme God in the Guaraní creation myth? How were Guaraní beliefs different from those of Christians? But no one wanted to answer my difficult questions, and I soon gave up.

Several days later I informed Armando that I was thinking of accompanying a group of men to the *toma de agua* (the community's water source, a natural spring) on a maintenance mission. The community had had no drinking water for the past week after taps suddenly ran dry. After speculating that the municipal ecotourism project had used all the water, people eventually began to suspect a leak in the now decades-old piping and remembered that it was years since the men had organized to conduct repairs. This seemed like an ideal opportunity to spend time with the men collectively, which was usually impossible, given that so many were away for wage labor, fishing, or working on their separate *potreros* (agricultural plots). Yet when I raised the idea, Armando immediately warned me against going, telling me that the *dueño del agua* (Spanish: owner of the water) wouldn't recognize me and something bad could happen (he didn't specify what). I had read about *iyareta* (Guaraní: *iya*, meaning owner, and *-reta,* a suffix indicating plural), the non-human owners of particular natural resources with whom the Guaraní share their territory, but knew little of their characteristics or dangers. Armando went on to describe how he'd once taken a *karai* engineer to the spring and the man had nearly died, although he didn't provide details. And the APG already blamed him for my broken ankle, he complained, mentioning it regularly (though I knew this to be an ongoing joke rather than a serious accusation); if anything happened to me, it was Armando who would be held accountable. By transgressing the territorial boundaries of the *iiya* (Guaraní: owner of water), Armando implied, I would be endangering not only myself but also him—and, by implication, his family.

I asked if there was anything I could do to appease or greet the spirit, but he answered no, it wouldn't work because I was from another country. Eventually he conceded that I could still go on the expedition with the men; I would just have to stop a certain distance from the spring and wait. This implied that others would be able to advise me about where precisely this boundary lay. In fact, I suspected that Armando's warnings were only partially about spirit relations and partly an attempt to prevent me from strengthening my relationships with other men in the community, some of whom he clearly had rivalries with. Nevertheless, I continued to wonder about the *iiya* and pursued the subject in subsequent conversations.

When I told Pablo about Armando's warning, he quickly dismissed it. He agreed that of course I couldn't approach the spring and touch the water "just like that" (*así no más*); I would have to chew coca and pour alcohol on my head, and only then could I sit down to rest near the spring. Only when I'd been there a good while should I approach the water, he advised. But this was the same for everyone, he emphasized; unlike Armando, he made no special distinction because I was from outside the territory and not Guaraní. He told me that he'd also been warned about the *iiya* when he first went to the spring, because he hadn't lived his whole life in the community (although his grandmother was from there), making him something of an outsider. Given the evident rivalry between the two men, it struck me that warnings about the *iiya* and whom it would or wouldn't recognize acted as a trope for articulating belonging and, by proxy (in the case of my proposed trip), authority. That is, although Pablo had previously experienced the same warnings as me, the current issue at stake was who had the territorial knowledge and authority to instruct or permit me regarding my own interaction with the *iiya*.

Several days later I was at Fausto's house looking for eggs, having just returned from collecting palm for handicrafts (an activity that fit within the EINE's definition of sustainable resource use). The women offered me a plate of beans, rice, and *muïti* (corn bread). As I ate, I chatted to the *mburuvicha* and he asked me about my trip to the *toma* the previous day, when I'd accompanied the men to dig up water pipes. I recounted how I hadn't made it to the spring because we'd stopped to work en route, but I planned to go another day. He encouraged me to do so, and I asked him about the *iiya*. Like Pablo, he reassured me that, as long as I poured alcohol on my head and showed respect, then I could go. Nevertheless, he reinforced Armando's warning that the *iiya* could be dangerous, emphasizing "ipochi, ipochi" (Guaraní: it's bad-tempered/angry). He said that he'd once experienced this himself when he'd gone to bathe in and drink the water and had been sick afterwards. If you approached the *iiya* the wrong way, you could freeze up and start shaking, he warned me, performing the possible effects. He then told me his own version of the story of a *karai* engineer, which I'd heard from Armando. Fausto recounted that he himself had warned the engineer not to approach the spring's crystalline water, which was so clear that the *iiya* guarded it jealously (*mezquina*).[23] The engineer had paid no heed and had proceeded to wash his feet and lower legs in the water. By the time they'd got back along the route to the first house, the engineer could hardly walk. Yes, the *iiya* was *pochi* and powerful, he concluded; even as you approached the *toma* you could feel gusts of wind. He wrapped his arms around his wiry body to illustrate.

My final discussion about the *iiya* was with Felipe, a young man whom I accompanied on the several-hour trek to complete more piping repairs the next day. I'd noticed that every time we stopped to begin the arduous task of digging up the hard earth in search of old water pipes with a possible leak, the men would first sit down for some time, chewing coca and sharing cigarettes rolled from corn husk. In fact, I had had to donate my own entire coca supply—which I normally kept for interviewees or to exchange for fish for my household—to the expedition. I soon realized that this familiar activity was also a form of offering to the *iiya*, similar to the *challa* ritual practiced throughout the Andean region.[24] Of course, this was why fishermen accepted coca in exchange for fish. When I asked Felipe about the *iiya*, telling him about my conversation with Fausto, he seemed reluctant to elaborate, as if not wanting to commit himself to such beliefs. He did, however, confirm that it would also be important to make an offering to the *iiya* once we approached the spring.

In the event, I never made it as far as the *toma* to experience the *iiya*'s power for myself; after another full day of digging—something I had not managed to find an appropriate tool for—we traipsed back to the community. The two-hour walk took us through a series of private properties. Our narrow path, through dry Chaco forest packed with thorny bushes and cactus-like trees, was lined on one side with a barbed wire fence. As we approached the community, we passed fields where well-fed cattle grazed on patches of green pasture belonging to *karai* landowners. During the expedition, I learned from the men that the *iiya* was not the only "owner" of water with whom the Guaraní had had to contend to secure their own drinking water supply; there had also been a conflict with the cattle rancher on whose property the spring was located. The landowner had complained about not being "consulted" when the water infrastructure was installed a decade ago and had erected the barbed wire fence along the piping route in his own effort to *mezquinar* the water. In the end, a meeting was held in Entre Ríos, where the landowner resides, to reach agreement on the water access. The matter was settled when the APG IG and state engineers (who included the *iiya*'s reckless victim) had proposed giving the landowner his own private tap. Nevertheless, the barbed wire fence remained as a material reminder of this resource conflict and a manmade obstacle to the men's diligent repair work before they had even entered the treacherous terrain of the *iiya*'s sovereign rule.

This story is just one example of what was effaced by the cartographic and calculative practices described in this chapter, through which indigenous leaders, activists, NGOs, and eventually state officials sought to make indigenous territories legible to the state. Underlying their efforts was a concern with the *fixing of boundaries*. While this began with a quest to find and justify external territorial limits, these lines were soon replicated by various internal boundaries. NGOs divided Itika Guasu into three separate zones, based on the expanding geographies of their projects, cross-cutting relations of kinship and intercommunal cooperation. The EINE's complex zoning practices provide a compelling illustration of the impulse to divide these newly mapped territories into discrete and governable units. Such "bright lines" (Blomley 2010) were to multiply and solidify during the official titling process, when the TCO was divided into over a hundred separate GIS-located polygons, which imprisoned communities within fragments of the territory they already occupied (see chapter 3). It was as a result of these divisions that the Guaraní were forced to appease a *karai* landowner as well as a spirit sovereign, the *iiya*, in their quest to secure a supply of drinking water.

In contrast to these cartographic knowledges—which depicted a reality composed of subjects and objects located in Cartesian space—the *iiya* belongs to a world in which human–non-human relations unfold across space, respecting limits shaped by expansive and shifting resource geographies, and cross-cutting boundaries established by cartography and law. We saw in chapter 1 how Guaraní territorial narratives depicted territory as an unbounded space of free movement and unrestricted access to abundant resources and dispersed ancestral places. Whereas such narratives included *iyareta* and promoted the freedom of movement necessary to retain relations with them and access to their resources, state cartographers paid no heed to their power, geographies, or relations with the Guaraní.

Interestingly, there is one exception to this: the EINE contains one sentence recommending that the Guaraní be given "unrestricted access" to the Pilcomayo River, owing to the "very important link of cultural union between riverside families and the mythic possessors of these resources" (VAIPO and MACPIO 2000: 147). Yet, as subsequent chapters show, this recommendation was not followed by INRA in cases where there were competing private property claims. In being "translated," the *iiya* was inserted into a postcolonial hierarchy within which it was subordinate to *karai* notions of land use and property. Nor does this statement reflect the dominant logic of the EINE, which privileged notions of abstract space and passive nature, calculating the hectares per household required for Guaraní economic survival—"spatial needs" that would remain unfulfilled by the titling process.

This chapter has examined the complex and previously undocumented processes involved in the mapping of indigenous territories in Bolivia. Challenging celebratory accounts of countermapping as a liberating practice, it has exposed the relations of knowledge and power involved in making indigenous territories legible, and politically acceptable, to the state. This entailed subordinating indigenous territorial claims to established limits of state and settler geographies. In an effort to justify shrinking territories and combat racist ideas of land use, indigenous and activist mappers gradually abandoned a discourse of ancestral rights in favor of one of indigenous spatial needs.

These processes demonstrate the impossibility of subalterns' achieving recognition within the dominant discourses of colonial society.[25] Maps were predicated on a notion of abstract space that delegitimized indigenous knowledges and erased indigenous sovereignties. Non-indigenous activists saw themselves as "translators" of indigenous territories, while the participation of indigenous community members was limited to the provision of ethnographic and land use data. Mapping also subjected indigenous peoples to new forms of governmentality. What started as an effort to determine indigenous territorial limits rapidly evolved into a whole series of calculations and prescriptions regarding indigenous land use. An examination of these processes helps explain why, more than a decade later, many Guaraní community members felt distant from, and disempowered by, the legal-cartographic knowledges of the TCO.

It was not just indigenous geographies and knowledges that were effaced by the mapping of indigenous territorial claims. These maps also obscured a geography of non-indigenous settlement and property rights *within* TCO boundaries. Like most Chaco TCO claims, most of the land—and the most productive land—in Itika Guasu is taken up by private cattle ranches and small peasant properties. These "other" territorial claimants were absent from maps of indigenous territorial claims elaborated by activists and presented to the state in 1996. Only once the legal land titling process got under way (see chapter 3) would the consequences of this erasure become fully apparent.

TITLING TERRITORY

Race, Space, and Law at an Indigenous Frontier

"When INRA awarded the paper [recognizing the TCO], I have photos of that day. [We thought,] 'The APG will have a title' . . . We were happy—what great happiness! There was a party . . . but it hasn't been like that." It was 2009 and I was chatting with Alejandro, a leader from Mokomokal community in Itika Guasu, about the progress and outcomes of the now decade-long TCO titling process. The festive day he referred to was January 10, 1997, when INRA formally recognized TCO Itika Guasu, setting in motion the official TCO titling process.[1] Like many leaders, Alejandro emphasized the gap between Guaraní expectations for TCO recognition and the actual outcomes of the titling process. He noted that only one or two communities in zone 1 of the TCO, where he lived, had actually gained land from the process. Above all, he highlighted the fragmenting effects of the titling process and their implications for indigenous sovereignty: "The APG [IG] doesn't carry papers. [The TCO]'s arriving one bit at a time, but not all. It's a single big TCO, but it's only arriving bit by bit."

Alejandro's observations are borne out by an analysis of the legal results of the TCO titling process in Itika Guasu. The TCO area recognized by INRA in 1997, 216,002 hectares (later remeasured at 235,949 hectares), was already a reduction of the APG IG's original territorial claim and fell short of the 293,584 hectares recommended by the EINE. Thus, even if *all* land in the TCO had been titled to the Guaraní, this would have fallen short of the state's analysis of their "spatial needs." In fact, the area titled to them was much smaller. By 2012, the Guaraní of Itika Guasu had been awarded legal title to 90,540 hectares, or 38.4 percent of the total TCO area (see figure 6).[2] This area is discontinuous, interspersed with

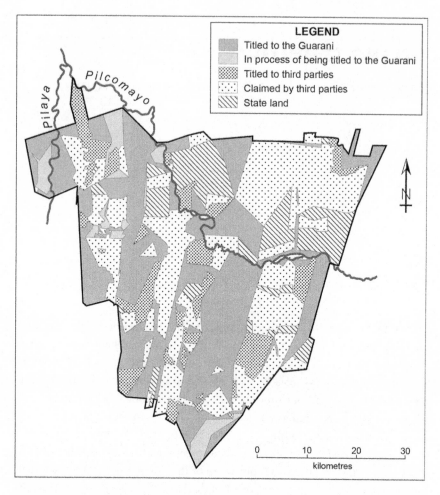

FIGURE 6. Map showing legal results of TCO titling in Itika Guasu (elaborated by Cartographic Unit, Department of Geography, University of Cambridge, adapted from map 1 in Fundación TIERRA, 2011: 308).

properties that are titled to private claimants ("third parties") or that have not completed the titling process, which together make up 42 percent of the TCO's total area. Some 25,452 hectares (10.8 percent) of the TCO land has been titled to third party claimants, distributed among 136 properties. A further 74,696 hectares (31.7 percent), distributed among 198 properties, are privately claimed but remain in a state of legal limbo. Of the remaining TCO land, 27,969 hectares (11.9 percent) are identified as state land and 8,563 (3.6 percent) are designated "untitled."

As another APG IG leader summarized the situation:

> Our hope was that [the government] would title the whole [TCO] demand that the APG [IG] had made. The demand is 216,000 hectares, and that wasn't sufficient for the people; they needed 293,000 hectares, that's what the study, EINE, said ... Our hope was that everything would already be titled [by now]. But the government hasn't done that.

This chapter draws on legal-cartographic, ethnographic, and interview data to examine the social relations and political dynamics that produced these results.[3] Given what we already know about the INRA Law, these results might not seem surprising. What follows is partly the story of how compromises forged in the arena of national politics—such as the state's recognition of private property claims within TCOs—played out in practice. The application of legal norms in Itika Guasu was not merely a technical process, however; it was a contested set of practices underwritten by historical configurations of property, race, and citizenship. Some third parties who could legally justify their claims failed to participate in the titling process. Others who should have been targets for legal expropriation used clientelistic networks and covert strategies to defend their property. This chapter reveals how legal norms were adapted, negotiated, and reworked in the course of their implementation. Combining insights from postcolonial theory and legal anthropology, I show how historically sedimented networks of racialized power and colonial discourses of rights shaped the application of law in ways that prevented a substantive redistribution of land rights in Itika Guasu and frustrated Guaraní communities' aspirations for "reclaiming territory."

My account moves beyond the technocratic analyses of land titling offered by global development policy literature to situate TCO titling within broader postcolonial struggles over territory, sovereignty, and citizenship.[4] My analysis builds on work by legal ethnographers, who have shown how international legal norms and discourses become reworked in their engagement with local power structures, values, and institutions (Merry 2006; Eckert et al. 2012). This perspective is highly relevant to TCOs, which were framed by global discourses of ethnodevelopment, institutionalized in national law, then implemented in local contexts marginal to central state power. Until the 1930s, the Chaco region of Tarija was accessible from the highland capital La Paz only via a donkey track built by the Inca. National governmental projects become "fragmented by the topography, translated, broken down, and reworked through local voices" (Gustafson 2009: 64). For indigenous TCO claims in the Chaco, the people responsible for adapting and applying national legal norms were local officials who often had personal and political ties to private landowners. Even without such clientelistic obligations, local officials lacked the capacity to enforce the law in the face of landowners who threatened to defend their land with violence. In this way the process of vernacularizing law (Merry 2006) worked to preserve the existing racial and spatial order in the face of indigenous efforts to "remap" the nation.

While acknowledging in this chapter how racialized power inequalities shaped titling outcomes in Itika Guasu, I challenge stereotyped representations of non-indigenous landowning elites (see Bobrow-Strain 2007). As will become clear, TCO Itika Guasu is home to a heterogeneous non-Guaraní population, who are diversely situated along axes of class, ethnicity, and belonging. Such differences were highly consequential for non-Guaraní claimants' engagements with, and treatment by, the law. A key objective in this chapter is to explain how, *despite* this heterogeneity, non-indigenous land claimants ended up forming an effective and coordinated movement in opposition to the TCO titling process. Part of the answer, I suggest, lies in the exclusions produced by the titling process and the way it functioned to foreground ethnicity as an axis of difference, weakening the potential for an interethnic alliance in favor of land redistribution.

I begin the chapter by introducing five non-indigenous individuals who claim land in Itika Guasu, in order to give a sense of the heterogeneity of this group. I then turn to the covert strategies, clientelistic networks, and collective mobilizations through which landowners sought to defend their property claims during the TCO titling process. I highlight how the de facto exclusion of many poorer non-indigenous TCO residents from that process ultimately served to bolster an elite-led non-indigenous opposition movement. The third section examines the discourses of race, rights, and citizenship that underpinned these actions. I then detail how the threat of violent conflict served as a justification for the flexible application of legal norms—including through the recourse to informal agreements—in ways that ultimately undermined the Guaraní's project of "reclaiming territory." The chapter concludes with some Guaraní responses to the results of the TCO titling process in Itika Guasu.

(Re)presenting Landowners

In his ethnography of landowners in Chiapas, Aaron Bobrow-Strain critiques a dominant academic and popular discourse that "collapses the diversity of landowners, glosses their historical mutability, and invests them with almost superhuman powers of class unity, political domination, and resistance to change" (2007: 18). Rather than a homogeneous group with unified identities and interests, he shows Chiapan landowners to be a diverse population that defies simple classification along axes of class, race, and gender. As he makes clear, recognizing this complexity does not diminish the importance of such differences; rather it necessitates inquiry into how they are understood and mobilized in particular ways, in particular contexts.

If Chiapan landowners are a diverse bunch, then this is perhaps even more the case in Itika Guasu, where non-indigenous land claimants range from wealthy urban-based professionals hailing from traditional elite landowning families to small farmers settled illegally on marginal land and living in conditions comparable to those in Guaraní communities. This diversity was obscured by the activist narratives of the APG IG and CERDET—which tended to acknowledge rival land claimants only through the oppositional figure of the *patrón*—and by the official legal category of *tercero* (third party), which applies to all non-Guaraní claimants to TCO land. Of course, the Guaraní term *karai* is also a homogenizing category.

The diversity of people living in Itika Guasu is a product of the processes of nation building, frontier settlement, and agrarian reform detailed in chapter 1. As noted, non-indigenous settlement of the Chaco began in the late nineteenth century, in the context of an expanding ranching economy and liberal land reforms, and intensified after the 1930s Chaco War, when many ex-combatants opted to try their luck as *chaqueño* ranchers instead of returning to precarious highland livelihoods. The closure of state mines following the neoliberal reforms of the 1980s brought a further wave of highland migrants, who were joined by a steady trickle of land-poor farmers from Tarija's central valley. These diverse migration histories account for differences not only in ethnic and class status but also in notions of rights, feelings of belonging, political affiliations, repertoires of struggle, and responses to Guaraní land claims. To give a better sense of this heterogeneity, I begin by introducing five non-indigenous land claimants, whose accounts I draw from (among others) in the remainder of this chapter.

Simón Mendez

I first met Simón Mendez in the Guaraní community of Tarairí, which lies at the center of the TCO, sandwiched between two large properties he owns. For community members, negotiations with Mendez regarding access to farmland and forest resources are an inconvenient fact of life (see chapter 4). Guaraní women peered out of palm-thatched kitchens, and children rushed over excitedly as his shiny red 4x4 swerved into the community's central *oka* (Guaraní: courtyard, the communal area around which houses are situated), coming to a halt outside the next-door house of my host Armando's sister Rosa. Although people in Tarairí claimed that land and labor relations with the Mendez family had always been less exploitative that with many other local *patrones*, relations remained starkly asymmetrical. Armando told me that his father, the community's previous *mbu-ruvicha* (now deceased), was once offered work as a *vaquero* (cowboy) for Mendez, although Armando's mother forbade him to accept the offer. As Armando reflected with a hint of regret, "He could have been a cattle rancher."

While I lived in Tarairí, only two (male) community members still worked regularly on the Mendez estate. One of them was Armando's brother-in-law, Jesús. His payment—part of which was in kind—was the reason for Mendez's visit. Armando's sister Rosa accepted the sacks of sugar, rice, and pasta and placed them in her storeroom. As I timidly approached the house, Mendez was telling her how much cash he'd given her partner "so he didn't drink it." I was invited to sit on a bed in the porch, where I awaited my opportunity. As he was leaving, I accosted Mendez and succeeded in getting his cell phone number as well as some details on the history of his property. Members of my household snickered in the background, amused and impressed to see me conversing in Spanish with a powerful *karai* landowner. The two properties in Mendez's name form part of a large hacienda owned by his father, the son of a general who settled in the region prior to the Chaco War. As I learned on this occasion, the land was purchased from another local landowner, who apparently bought it from "a Turk." The Mendez family hacienda is today subdivided between Mendez and his siblings.

My next encounter with Mendez took place in a quite different setting: the large house where he lives in an elite neighborhood of Tarija city, where he is a practicing medical doctor. The house was well kept and adorned with artifacts from the family's military and agricultural past, including a sugar mill from a liquor distillery they previously owned. Although he was nostalgic about rural life, as for many of the wealthier landowners of Itika Guasu, land was no longer a significant source of income for Simón and his family. Only his younger brother lives in Itika Guasu and makes his living as a cattle rancher. His children, who study in Tarija city, have little interest in ranching or agriculture. Mendez stressed that it was the same for many landowners of Itika Guasu:

> For those of us who have studied and . . . *overcome* a bit, it's no longer the place to live. It's only the place to . . . to have, to . . . to try to keep some kind of extra income. That's it. For example, my sons aren't going to go back there. They don't have good possibilities for employment there—there is nothing, you see? They're not going to go anymore.

He explained that those who do live in Itika Guasu also gain additional income as drivers, teachers, professionals, or traders—as well as from family members who live outside the territory in locations ranging from Tarija to La Paz to Spain.

Mendez does not participate in the local cattle ranching federation ASOGAPO (Cattle Ranchers' Association of O'Connor Province) and certainly not the peasant union CSUTCB (Unified Syndical Confederation of Rural Workers of Bolivia), the two main non-indigenous organizations in Itika Guasu. Although he acknowledged that he'd lost out on some state benefits because of this—such as animal feed during serious droughts—he claimed it was not worth his time to sit through so many long meetings; besides, ASOGAPO was barely functioning anymore. He seemed proud as well as vaguely aggrieved to proclaim, "We don't receive anything from the state." As this brief introduction highlights, although Mendez is an absentee landlord for whom land in Itika Guasu is not a significant source of livelihood, his inheritance of part of a large family estate and his ongoing labor relations with Guaraní community members mean that—at least in Tarairí—he remains an important presence in the landscape, although not in the broader political struggles surrounding the TCO titling process.

Beatriz Vaca

I met Beatriz Vaca in 2011, when she was the acting president of the (supposedly nonfunctioning) cattle ranchers' federation ASOGAPO. She spends most of her time in her veterinary shop, which is located just off the central square of Entre Ríos. In addition to animal vaccines, the shop sells an assortment of cattle-related equipment, cowboy hats, and other items required by people from nearby rural communities. When I first entered the shop and introduced myself, Beatriz—a robust and charismatic woman in her thirties—ushered me hospitably to a plastic chair and launched into an impassioned speech about the injustices of the TCO titling process (which we will hear more of later). Our first conversation stretched over the course of several hours. At intervals, Beatriz would rise from her chair—she was at the time heavily pregnant—to dispense veterinary advice over a crackly radio and to serve a motley assortment of customers, all of whom she seemed to be on intimate terms with. As people came and went, she helpfully enlisted them in our discussion; in this way our interview evolved into a kind of revolving focus group in which Beatriz acted as convenor. She made sure to inform each customer about a forthcoming meeting with INRA that she had organized in her role as acting president of ASOGAPO. My visit was thus rather timely.

The name of Beatriz's shop, El Porvenir (a pseudonym), mirrors that of the property where she grew up, which is located just across the Pilcomayo River from Tarairí and claimed by her father under the TCO titling process. Beatriz has taken a leading role in contesting the legal outcome of the property claim, which was earmarked for reduction by INRA (discussed later in this chapter). Despite her important professional and political roles, as Beatriz herself stressed, her family is from much humbler origins than the likes of the Mendezes. In fact, her father arrived in the region as Mendez's *vaquero*. Only after working for Mendez for many years, and being paid partly in calves, did Roberto Vaca manage to amass a large enough herd to set himself up as an independent rancher. His ability to do so was also enabled by Mendez's leasing then selling him part of the estate, at a moment when the impending TCO titling process encouraged such arrangements. Owing to the fact that private land claims are evaluated on the basis of their "economic social function"—which, in theory, means that claimants must work the land themselves—*vaqueros* have been among the beneficiaries of the titling process, in part because it encouraged absentee landlords to sell or award them land. As we will see, however, this advantageous position has been counterbalanced by their more limited ability to pay administrative fees and land tax, or to influence legal outcomes through personal and political contacts.

Distinguishing her family from wealthier absentee landlords, Beatriz emphasized the difficult conditions of drought, isolation, and poor land quality that her family had in common with Guaraní communities. She recounted how she had once challenged an INRA official with an invitation to spend a week living on the property, farming and ranching in temperatures over 120 degrees Fahrenheit. She concluded: "But that's where we all *live, mamita,* and we *produce* there—that is, in the *least apt lands.* I'm telling you, I live *inside an indigenous village,* and that's the land [INRA] has given us too."[5] Beatriz emphasized the intimacy of her relations with the Guaraní, how she had grown up "hearing their drums," and felt this was part of her cultural identity as someone "from Itika." (Unlike some other private claimants, she referred to the TCO by its name.) As I later learned while living in Tarairí, despite long-standing conflict between Guaraní communities and the Vaca family over land control (discussed later in this chapter), her father is godfather (*padrino*) to a number of Guaraní children in Tarairí, whom he visits during Carnival. As we will see, Beatriz's indignation at the TCO titling process combines ethnic and class dimensions; it is directed *both* at the different treatment of Guaraní and non-Guaraní claimants, *and* at the greater capacity of wealthier claimants like Mendez to defend their property claims.

Winston Mignolo

I don't recall when I first came across Winston Mignolo—his reputation probably preceded him—but our first proper interview took place in an elite café in central Tarija in early 2009. He was an affable man in his forties with a clean-cut appearance, only his broad-rimmed leather hat denoting his identity as a *chaqueño* cattle rancher. Mignolo is the son of one of Itika Guasu's most infamous *patrones*, renowned for his harsh treatment of Guaraní *peones* during the days of *empatronamiento*. Yet whereas some *patrones* hailed from families settled in the region since the late nineteenth century, Mignolo's grandfather was a Chaco War veteran. Like other land claimants who shared this heritage, he talked proudly of his ancestor's sacrifice for the nation. At the time of our meeting, he was president of ASOGAPO (Beatriz's predecessor). This was back when the association was still going strong, acting as the primary organizing axis and mouthpiece for local opposition to the Guaraní TCO claim.

In our interview, Mignolo glossed over themes of *empatronamiento* and racialized land conflict, offering a romanticized picture of paternalistic interethnic relations and differentiating local ranchers from the wealthier landowning elite of Santa Cruz Department. He also expounded at length on climate change, sustainable ranching practices, his respect for the APG, and the undervalued role of cattle ranching within the regional and national economy. As I began to suspect at the time, Mignolo's position as ASOGAPO president was merely a stepping-stone in his political career. (He was in the city that day for a media interview.) By the time I returned to Tarija in 2011, he had assumed the position of provincial governor (*ejecutivo seccional*) of O'Connor Province, which comprises TCO Itika Guasu, Entre Ríos, and surrounding peasant communities. I ran into him on numerous occasions that year, including at the APG IG's anniversary celebrations (see chapter 6) and at the public meeting with INRA that Beatriz had organized (discussed later in this chapter).

Mignolo has been at the forefront of local non-indigenous opposition to the TCO titling process in Itika Guasu. As we will see, this role has involved not only mobilizing clientelistic networks of landowning power at a variety of scales but also constructing a local oppositional movement that transcends differences of class, race, and gender. Despite Mignolo's leading role in local opposition to the TCO titling process, he in fact benefited from the process, gaining title to his entire property claim—an outcome that is contested not only by the Guaraní but also by less influential or successful private claimants, among them Beatriz Vaca. As we will see in later chapters, Mignolo's interventions in Guaraní politics have not been limited to the TCO titling process. In the context of struggles over hydrocarbon development in the TCO, he has been instrumental in the formation of new gas-fueled alliances between the MAS government, landowning elites, and Guaraní communities, designed to undermine the APG IG leadership's own vision of hydrocarbon-based autonomy (discussed in chapter 6).

Oswaldo Cortez

I met Oswaldo in CERDET's central offices in Tarija city, where I worked as a volunteer in 2008–9. Oswaldo was employed by CERDET as a vet, and we often traveled to communities and meetings together. For a long time I saw him as just another *técnico* in a large and almost exclusively male staff. It was only during a trip to Itika Guasu that I learned Oswaldo had grown up in a remote community inside the TCO. He thus fell into the category of "third parties" subject to the TCO titling process—which was, of course, one of CERDET's major priorities. Oswaldo's unique position as a CERDET employee and local land claimant—and his long-standing relations with Guaraní people and non-indigenous TCO residents—gave him a unique, if conflicted, perspective on the titling process.

It was not until 2011 that I broached the subject of Oswaldo's family history and personal experience of the titling process. Our first rather uncomfortable shouted conversation took place in the back of a dusty pickup truck bumping and swerving along the dirt roads of Itika Guasu en route to the APG IG's anniversary celebration in Ñaurenda. We talked at greater length a few weeks later sitting on rickety chairs in a hidden corner of the patio of the Plaza Hotel in Entre Ríos. Although hardly private, it seemed to be the only place out of earshot of CERDET technicians, local landowners, and Guaraní leaders, which accounted for most of the town's inhabitants. For Oswaldo, this was not an easy conversation. He knew that I was immersed in Guaraní politics. Yet he also knew I was talking to landowners about their experiences. As for other landowners, his initial reluctance to broach a sensitive topic was overshadowed by a desire to make his voice heard—or, rather, to make visible truths he knew were eclipsed in APG IG and CERDET narratives of the land struggle.

If Oswaldo's positionality was unique, then his background was less unusual. His parents had migrated to Itika Guasu from a highland peasant community during the 1950s, a decade before he was born. He described how, as a child, he had traveled all over the region with his father, who worked as a cattle trader. These journeys and interactions made him aware of the social, cultural, and economic differences between highland migrants like his family and the region's established cattle ranching families like the Mendezes. In fact, he suggested that both more established settler families and Guaraní communities discriminated against people like his family on the basis of their *colla* origins—a term that has strong ethnic as well as regional connotations.[6] As we will see, Oswaldo offered important insights into how such differences have played out vis-à-vis the land struggle and the difficult choices faced by people who were "neither *patrones* nor Guaraní." Yet his account also reveals how widespread discontent and colonial discourses of rights ultimately worked to privilege a binary (Guaraní/*karai*) racialized understanding of difference. When I attended Beatriz's meeting with INRA, Oswaldo was among a diverse audience of local claimants who signed a resolution demanding an audit of the entire TCO titling process.

Rubén Roble

I met Rubén Roble only twice. The first time was in March 2011, when Beatriz gave me his cell phone number. I finally managed to track him down at an agricultural development center near Entre Ríos, where we recorded an interview at the edge of a maize field, shouting over the noise of a tractor. The second occasion was at the ASOGAPO meeting later that month, where he sat on a panel facing the audience alongside Beatriz and Winston Mignolo. Rubén's prominent position at the meeting reflected his high-profile role in the peasant federation CSUTCB, where he held the title national secretary for justice and conflicts. Although his position gave him a certain status, enabling him to rub shoulders with the likes of Winston Mignolo, the TCO residents Rubén sought to represent were largely small farmers and recent migrants from Tarija's central valley. He began our interview by proclaiming:

> INRA Tarija came and did titling in Itika Guasu for the . . . the indigenous people, but they didn't inform us well, so there has been discontent among the *campesino* people . . . The Guaraní call us the whites . . . but the truth is that we're *campesinos* who have the same needs; the truth is that here the *compañeros* don't even have lands either.

In fact, he complained bitterly of the Guaraní's failure to distinguish between poor *campesino* families like his own and the *patrones*, against whom the land struggle had initially been directed:

> [The Guaraní] think that our fathers were those who discriminated against *them*, but it wasn't like that. That is, even my father also served— worked—for the *patrones*. Before, this was the land of the *patrones*, there were *patrones*, so they thought that the *patrones* were our fathers, but no. My father suffered a lot, so we were also slaves, and they think that we are the ones who enslaved them, and it isn't like that.

While Rubén's account echoes Oswaldo's in revealing the forms of discrimination (ethnic as well as class-based) faced by poorer and more recent migrants in Itika Guasu, Oswaldo's father's position as a cattle trader afforded him a certain independence, whereas Rubén's family appears to have been subject to forms of labor exploitation that characterized ethnic land relations in the territory prior to the Guaraní land struggle. While my engagement with Rubén was limited, his account—like Oswaldo's—revealed how these shared discourses of rights and grievances around land titling have bound together a broad spectrum of non-indigenous land claimants in Itika Guasu in opposition to the TCO claim.

These introductions serve to highlight the multiple axes on which land claimants' diversity mapped out, as well as the relational positionalities of these individuals. Beatriz Vaca's leadership of a flailing ASOGAPO positioned her as a cattle ranching leader alongside Winston Mignolo, yet her family's humbler origins—as cowboys rather than landowners—situated them quite differently vis-à-vis regional institutions and the law, as we will see. For Tarairí community members, Roberto Vaca and Simón Mendez were both *karai* landowners who restricted their land access but also served as godparents to their children. Yet the elite circles in which Mendez moved in Tarija city were a different world from that of the disheveled visitors to Beatriz's shop, who wore agricultural work clothes. Oswaldo's participation in APG assemblies as a CERDET *técnico* gave him a different positionality from the others, and his highland indigenous origins marked him as different from Mignolo, Mendez, or Vaca. Yet, as we will see, he shared many of their grievances. While Mignolo and Mendez might seem to have in common the same elite status, Mendez had no time for Mignolo's meetings or political projects, having made his life and career in the city. Finally, while Rubén Roble sought to distinguish his origins from those of "*patrón*" families like Mignolo and Mendez, his and other *campesinos'* grievances about the TCO titling process resulted in their eventual participation in an opposition movement led by traditional landowning elites.

Of course, these individuals do not cover the full spectrum of non-Guaraní land claimants in Itika Guasu. I have not mentioned, for example, the former cowboy Pedro and his wife, who live in a remote house a few hours' walk from Tarairí community, who participate in a Guaraní water committee, and whose son lives with a Guaraní woman in Tarairí—one of numerous "mixed" households in Itika Guasu. Nor did I mention Maarten, an eccentric and racist Dutch landowner who had grand plans of establishing an eco-forestry reserve but became embroiled in legal disputes with his Guaraní laborers, as well as with state authorities. Nor my Quechua-speaking friend Franco, whom I'd often run into over breakfast at Entre Ríos market, and whose experiences of discrimination as a Bolivian migrant in Argentina had transformed his view of local interethnic conflict, if not his racially inflected discourses of productive land use. These characters may or may not crop up later on. Either way, it is important to keep them all in mind as I trace how the TCO titling process articulated with existing ethnic and class cleavages in ways that culminated in a coordinated movement in opposition to the Guaraní's TCO claim.

Defending Property

Covert Strategies and Clientelistic Networks

As noted in chapter 1, early processes of indigenous organization in Itika Guasu provoked a strong, and sometimes violent, reaction from the *patrones*, who had previously relied on debt-bound Guaraní labor to make their estates economically viable. As EAPG director Renán Sánchez put it: "The first reaction was that those of us who weren't from the zone, the NGOs, were going to violate the intimacy of the property of the third party, so there were many threats. These threats didn't end with the process of titling." As this implies, the legal TCO titling process entered what was already a scene of heightened interethnic tension in Itika Guasu. In this context, landowners' responses were informed not by an analysis of the legal particularities of the INRA Law but rather by deep-seated fears of losing control of land and indigenous labor. When INRA personnel entered the territory in 2000 to conduct preliminary fieldwork, they were met with many violent threats. As former director of INRA Tarija (2000–2004) Jorge Campero (a pseudonym) explained:

> It was very difficult for people to understand you. Because we had to verify a property, measure a property, count cows, verify the work, and tell you whether or not the whole property will remain yours. It was very difficult to make them understand this issue. We had to have a lot of explanatory meetings to avoid, one, that they don't let you enter and attack personnel; and two, that they don't let the other parties [i.e., INRA staff and APG IG representatives] enter.

CERDET staff described receiving written threats from landowners at their Entre Ríos office, as well as verbal threats during trips to Guaraní communities. As I discuss later in this chapter, the threat of violence has been a continuous presence in the land titling process, which has underpinned both the implementation of the law and extralegal negotiations at its margins.

Despite this initial hostility, many landowners ultimately cooperated in the titling process but deployed a range of irregular and fraudulent practices to influence the outcomes of their property claims. CERDET and the APG IG were well aware of the challenges involved in implementing indigenous land titling in a regional context marked by racialized (and institutionalized) power inequalities, and went to considerable lengths to prepare for INRA's fieldwork. Conducted in 2000–2001, this fieldwork involved cadastral measurement, the drawing up of plans, and the collection of legal documentation and on-site observations relating to the "economic social function" (*función económica social*, FES) of properties.[7] Over the preceding two years, CERDET and the APG IG conducted a capacity-building program for communal, zonal, and regional (TCO-level) APG leaders, in addition to community training sessions, regular land assemblies, the formation of monitoring teams, and the establishment of a radio communications network (CERDET 2004a: 83–84). They demanded that INRA brigades be accompanied by an APG IG representative for all property measurements, and insisted on the marking of cattle to combat the practice of cattle lending.[8] These efforts were seen as exemplary by NGOs I spoke to that worked on TCO titling in other regions of Bolivia and undoubtedly curbed many distortions to the titling process that might otherwise have occurred.

Despite these efforts, documentation and interviews indicate that fraudulent practices were widespread during the course of INRA's fieldwork. Landowners presented false immunization certificates in an effort to exaggerate the size of their herds, which directly affected the number of hectares they could justify as fulfilling the FES. False property titles were also presented, even though they did not determine titling outcomes. According to CERDET, "the falsified information that third parties . . . presented delayed the fieldwork of the [INRA] brigades in charge of this activity," compounding delays caused by "permanent conflicts waged by third parties . . . to prevent [INRA from] conducting fieldwork" (2000: 5). Some landowners also attempted to bribe or influence INRA officials, either with money or by throwing lavish feasts during their visits. As Beatriz Vaca related:

> There's a team responsible for land surveying. They come with all their equipment; they go to the forest, create points. There are people who *buy* this team, do you understand me? . . . I didn't buy them, I didn't throw them a party . . . I didn't give them daughters, so I'm not going to be all right. But the others . . . they bought them directly and they gave them [money], so . . . the information that those responsible [INRA] produced is not trustworthy.

One elderly community *mburuvicha* I spoke to in Ñaurenda in 2009 described how landowners had pressured, and offered payments to, him and other APG representatives to sign documents that increased the number of cattle registered on a property.

Such irregularities were partly enabled by the ambiguity of the process through which INRA evaluated property claims. While the methodology for assessing the FES of properties varies from region to region, in Itika Guasu this generally came down to the counting of cattle, according to the controversial equation that five head of cattle "justify" one hectare of land (known as the *carga animal*, the animal carrying capacity). This equation is challenged both by local cattle ranchers, who argue that the area is insufficient for ranching in the arid lands of the Chaco, and by the Guaraní, who frequently complain that "a cow is worth more than a Guaraní person" under the INRA Law. More important, given the semi-extensive nature of ranching in Itika Guasu, the task of rounding up all of a claimant's cattle on a given day proved challenging, with INRA officials often running out of time, energy, or patience before the task could be completed. These difficulties were recounted in detail by former APG land promoter and

CCGT president Celestino—who himself walked many miles during the titling process—as well as by Erick Aráoz, a former INRA technician who led one of three fieldwork teams in Itika Guasu. Landowners' post-fieldwork complaints that not all cattle had been counted were often impossible to verify, as was the ownership of cattle presented—ambiguities that are reflected in INRA documentation. Furthermore, despite the APG IG and CERDET's insistence on the introduction of cattle marking, they were unable to prevent the borrowing, renting, or sale of cattle between neighboring ranchers for the purpose of justifying property claims (CERDET 2004a). For those claiming more land than they could legally justify, the partitioning of large estates between family members, as well as the awarding of less fertile areas to cowboys and long-term tenants of absentee landowners, were additional strategies for avoiding property reduction. As noted earlier, this appears to have been the pretext for Beatriz's father, Roberto Vaca's, property claim, which makes up part of the original Mendez estate.

Such irregular practices were not neutral in either class or ethnic terms. It was private landowners rather than the Guaraní who could afford to bribe or indulge INRA technicians—many of whom (including departmental director Jorge Campero) were themselves from local landowning families and sympathetic to the interests of private claimants (discussed later on). It was also wealthier, better-connected landowners who were most adept at ensuring their claims were recognized through irregular means—whether direct bribes, political favors, or the renting of cattle. Such class inequalities added to the sense of injustice for land claimants who faced property reductions during the titling process, as revealed by Beatriz's comment "I didn't buy this team . . . so I'm not going to be all right." Beatriz went on to complain that Winston Mignolo—ASOGAPO's former president—had "benefited from the process," as had his successor, a wealthy individual who lives in Tarija city and is married to the sister of Simón Mendez. She claimed that both had done so by "mak[ing] cows appear"—that is, renting cattle from other landowners. She decried the injustice that "there are people who shouldn't have title who managed to have title," when "people who work and live [in Itika] don't have the right to title." This led into a lengthy discussion of her father's property claim.

The influence of racialized and class-based power inequalities on titling outcomes was even more apparent in the post-fieldwork stages of the titling process. Termed the "legal technical evaluation," this office-based work consists of INRA officials (in Tarija and La Paz) analyzing data collected during fieldwork to determine the legal status of property claims, including their justification of the FES, and the identification of any resulting property reductions. During this phase, which began in 2001, many private claimants used personal or family connections within INRA Tarija to influence the outcome of the evaluation of their property rights. As CERDET employee Alipio explained:

The INRA technicians had connections with the cattle ranchers. What's more, we came to know also that they received money from the cattle ranchers. And as part of that favor, they made some files disappear. And afterwards, they resigned from INRA; they left, and of course the file had disappeared . . . so the new technician found neither the file nor the information and they said, "It isn't here; we have to do it again."

These accusations are supported by the findings of a second internal quality control conducted by INRA Tarija in 2008, which reported the loss of various documents and files by INRA technicians, among other irregularities (CERDET 2008: 6). By this point, CERDET had begun making its own copies of all official documents, and so was able to provide INRA with replacements for some of the missing paperwork.

Guaraní leaders and community members identified corruption, nepotism, and racialized power inequalities as key obstacles to the consolidation of their land rights. APG IG leader Teodoro, who accompanied INRA's fieldwork as a CERDET-trained "land promoter," emphasized the Guaraní's inability to monitor post-fieldwork bureaucratic processes that happened behind closed doors:

One goes and does an on-site verification in which you have to count the animals that a landowner has, you have to see the improvements he has made, the issue of infrastructure, fill out a file . . . Later, when they [INRA officials] take the information away, it turns out that they're changing information . . . I think they should respect only that report and not invent other subsequent reports.

Celestino, who was also an active participant in fieldwork monitoring efforts, made a similar point: "[INRA technicians] always make mistakes in the figures; they change everything, them and the cattle ranchers as well . . . They listen more to them than to us . . . . There are cattle rancher functionaries in INRA, too, and they make negotiations." Alejandro, an APG IG leader from Mokomokal community, blamed kinship relations between landowners and state officials for the lack of titling progress:

ALEJANDRO: Of course, [the cattle ranchers] went to fight this law; that's why [the process] is still frozen . . . . The cattle rancher himself is the director of INRA—before, that is [he names two previous directors].
PA: Are they allies of the cattle ranchers?
ALEJANDRO: They *are* cattle ranchers—they're their cousin, or their nephew. That's why it's kept on being obstructed.

Julio Navarro, who was president of the CCGT when I interviewed him in 2009, put it even more starkly, proclaiming: "The people from INRA . . . are the sons of the *patrón*! That's what they are, and they still don't know the truth about the indigenous peoples."

Other Guaraní people emphasized money as the crucial factor that allowed private claimants to shape the legal process in their interests. As one community member from Cumandaroti whom I spoke to after a 2009 assembly explained:

> Silently, that's how they do it—a paper over there; [land rights are awarded] to whoever has money . . . They put down money and INRA has to do it [recognize their claim]; grabbing money like that, we've seen the little face of [Jorge Campero, the former director of INRA Tarija]; he's lied a lot to the [Guaraní] people and that's how it is—bribe and continue.

A Guaraní man from Mokomokal told me: "The biggest problem for us is trusting in [INRA], that they're really going to do the work . . . because here there are many cattle ranchers and that's why everything is obstructed, as they have money . . . They have money and more influence."

While many state officials in Tarija Department come from local landowning families, some individuals actively sought employment in INRA's departmental office during the titling process with the intention of influencing their family's property claim. An informal discussion with Lino, a plump man in his thirties whom I met by chance outside his small legal office in Entre Ríos, shed light on this strategy. From a landowning family of Itika Guasu, Lino described how he had gained employment in INRA Tarija when his "intimate *compadre*,"[9] Jorge Campero, took over as the agency's director in 2000. While at INRA, Lino worked on the evaluation of the FES of private properties—something in which he had a personal interest, given that his father and several other family members claimed properties within the TCO. While not directly implicating himself, he admitted: "There are *ganadero* [cattle rancher] people who . . . put money in INRA itself . . . We too, as we're the state, we look the other way; we don't get involved much, but if they ask for help, we sometimes intervene." Lino's involvement in the TCO titling process continued when he was contracted as a lawyer by ASOGAPO during a series of controversial roundtable negotiations in 2003 (discussed later in this chapter).

The role of social and family networks in allocating privileges and rights in Tarija Department is both routine and widely acknowledged (Lizárraga and Vacaflores 2007). Such networks both *reflect* and *reproduce* racialized and class-based inequalities in political power and land control—inequalities rooted in a history of colonial frontier settlement, nation building, and indigenous dispossession that left state institutions dominated by non-indigenous landowning families.[10] In the context of TCO titling, these entrenched ethnic power inequalities created micro-level opportunities for the obstruction or reorientation of legal norms, in ways that favored the interests of non-indigenous land claimants.[11]

As already noted, not all private claimants had the same capacity to influence the legal process through family and social networks, just as not all of them were able to pay for the renting of cattle or the bribing of INRA officials. Indeed, as Beatriz's account suggests, such practices attracted criticism from private claimants who felt that regional power inequalities did not work in their favor. Moreover, landowners' attempts to defend their properties through irregular means were not always successful. In this context, individual actions to defend property claims soon evolved into a series of coordinated actions to obstruct the implementation of the legal process. Before we turn to these more coordinated acts of opposition, however, it is important to highlight the experience of another group of non-Guaraní residents of TCO Itika Guasu. This group did not present private land claims to INRA but instead opted to assimilate into the Guaraní organization and collective TCO claim—a decision that many subsequently came to regret.

Racializing Space: The Erasures of Ethnic Land Claims

As should by now be clear, the local non-indigenous population of Itika Guasu was far from homogeneous. Locally this diversity is often expressed through a distinction between the categories *ganadero* (cattle rancher)—a term closely associated with *hacendado* (hacienda owner)—and *campesino* (peasant farmer).[12] As former CERDET director Miguel Castro explained, "The third parties are basically two groups; the *hacendados*, who have a lot of land—sometimes they don't even live there, they live in Tarija and administer the land they have here—and the poor *campesinos* [who] are also third parties." Nolberto Gallado—former CERDET lawyer, CCGT affiliate, and 2009 director of INRA Tarija, who is from a local *karai* landowning family—claimed: "The *campesino* doesn't rear cows, he doesn't have property, he lives in a poor community and, even more, the *campesino* is a low social class. The cattle rancher is an elite." Of course, such identities are constructed and subject to varying interpretations; many poorer residents of Itika Guasu combine agriculture and rearing animals, while even wealthier landowners may strategically locate themselves in the category *campesino*, as will become clear. Nevertheless, these labels highlight differences in class positioning, property ownership, and social status that were both obscured and accentuated by the titling process.

The existence of poorer non-Guaraní residents of Itika Guasu—many of whom are more recent migrants and live in "mixed" communities alongside Guaraní families—was not acknowledged in the territorial claim the APG IG presented to the Bolivian state in 1996. Nor was this group provided with information about the TCO titling process under way and their rights within it.

While CERDET focused its training initiatives exclusively on the Guaraní, INRA focused its fieldwork on larger landowners, many of whom already possessed property titles that made their land claims (and identities) legible on state maps. As Oswaldo put it:

> On the side of the sector of the APG, yes, there was training, there was guidance, and . . . they were on top of this information about the issue of the titling of the TCO—everything. But the *campesino* sector . . . they were *orphans*, let's say; they didn't have anyone to help them, anyone to guide them.

INRA's 2000 public information campaign failed to reach many smaller land claimants living in more remote areas of the TCO, reportedly holding a single meeting for ten or more dispersed communities. Without information about their legal rights—which were in fact given priority by the INRA Law—many *campesinos* simply assumed that they would be evicted from the TCO.[13] As Oswaldo explained:

> When the cattle ranchers found out [about the TCO claim], when the *campesinos* found out—that is, those who live in the region—it was like a bucket of cold water. There was uncertainty about . . . that is, they also had wrong information: some Guaraní *compañeros* said that once they started titling, then everyone would have to leave. That it was *theirs*, the territory was theirs, and the people have to *leave*.

This suggests that such fears were fueled by the bravado of some Guaraní leaders, who viewed the TCO claim as a means of realizing their broader project of "reclaiming territory." According to Miguel, they were also a result of fear-mongering by more powerful *patrones*, who "scared [the *campesinos*] into being their allies." These fears of eviction reflect the precarious position of poorer land claimants and more recent migrants in Itika Guasu, who—unlike the *patrones*—lacked property titles, capital, or political influence within regional institutions.

In this context, many poorer non-indigenous residents of Itika Guasu did not declare property claims to the land reform agency. Instead, they opted to join the APG IG, effectively occupying the "indigenous slot" (Li 2000) in an effort to secure continuing access to TCO land. Former INRA technician Erick Aráoz described how this was a last resort for claimants who had failed to present property claims to INRA:

> In some cases, clearly they didn't participate in the [titling] process . . . and also they lost out because of poor information. And when they

finally realized they were making a mistake, it was already too late . . .
the [fieldwork] process had already finished, so it was going to be hard
for them to consolidate [their rights], so the only [option] left to them
was to belong to the indigenous organization.

Some accounts suggest that CERDET and EAPG staff and APG IG leaders actively
encouraged small farmers to join the APG IG during the initial stages of the titling
process instead of presenting individual claims. They apparently did so in an
attempt to smooth the path of the TCO claim and gain support for their ongoing
struggle against the *patrones*. While some—particularly those living alongside
the Guaraní in "mixed communities"—may have felt genuine solidarity with the
Guaraní land struggle, decisions to join the APG IG were also underwritten by
this group's marginality and fears of eviction. According to Oswaldo:

It was . . . due to their fear of [eviction] that many people—based on
what they tell me, because I walked to many places—they, the *karai*
people, those who are Christian people, who aren't Guaraní, entered
the [Guaraní] organization. Because, according to them, there they felt
secure—that [the Guaraní] weren't going to remove them from the territory . . . Many people entered the organization in that way.

Such efforts to "pass" as Guaraní must be placed in the context of an ethnic
politics that deliberately played down the heterogeneity of non-indigenous land
claimants within the TCO. Keen to appeal to global and national imaginaries of
indigenous territories (discussed in chapter 1), as well as to negative stereotypes
of non-indigenous landowning elites, the Guaraní and their NGO allies had little interest in making visible the existence of poorer non-Guaraní people living
inside the TCO. As Oswaldo commented, drawing on his experience as both a
CERDET employee and the son of Andean migrants settled in Itika Guasu:

When [the APG IG and NGOs] presented the [TCO] demand to the government, then *no one knew* [about the *campesinos*]. And according to what
the people who entered to work there—those from INRA—told me, when
they presented the demand, they said that there were no [non-Guaraní]
people . . . there were just a few cattle ranchers, *hacendados*; there weren't
any other people. That is, they didn't talk much of the *campesinos* . . . They
had, in some way, to argue the demand. I think that one of the . . . [reasons]
why in the end [the government] approved the TCO demand was that
they presented some false information—at least that's what people tell me.

The discursive erasure of the heterogeneity of Itika Guasu as a multiethnic territory was thus viewed as a precondition for gaining state recognition, in ways

that had lasting repercussions for ethnic political representation and interethnic relations within the TCO.

Ultimately this move backfired, for several reasons. First, despite being assured of equal participation in the Guaraní organization, many non-Guaraní people felt marginalized in the context of APG IG assemblies, where they were (as I myself observed) often treated with suspicion. As Rubén Roble, the local CSUTCB representative, told me:

> I have many friends there [in the APG IG], but they're not well treated. That is, they're always discriminated against. I've seen in some meetings in Itika Guasu—I've gone and I've seen that . . . they have to abide by the rules of the community because, as you know, every community has its statutes and regulations . . . For [the Guaraní] to let them enter with their animals to . . . to Itika Guasu, the communal terrain that they have, they now have to be submissive [*doblegados*] to them. Various times I've been in [an APG] meeting and *even I* feel discriminated against by them: "You, what are you doing here? You're not one of the Guaraní; you, the white people, in so many meetings" . . . So sometimes one has to remain silent because we can't start fighting with them over that.

As this suggests, differences centered not only on political participation but also on access to collective TCO land—in particular, the rights of non-Guaraní people to graze their animals on it. On several occasions, non-indigenous TCO residents—including APG IG affiliates—complained to me about being subject to a form of land taxation by Guaraní communities. As one man complained:

> MAN: I have some ten or twenty cattle. What do they do? They charge 10 percent per year. If I have ten calves, obligatorily I have to give them a calf; if I have one hundred calves, I have to give them ten.
>
> PA: To have use of the communal land?
>
> MAN: Of the land. And what's more, I believe they make them pay; they oblige them to pay as well, a salary.

Such "taxation" practices must be read in the context of Guaraní communities' frustrated aspirations for regaining control of ancestral lands occupied by non-indigenous landowners, as well as the annoyance created by the presence of their cattle on TCO land (discussed in chapter 4). The fact that *campesinos* often maintained membership to the peasant federation CSUTCB, viewed as politically hostile to indigenous land claims, exacerbated their tendency to be viewed as "spies" or potential traitors. It is worth noting that the strategic decision to encourage non-indigenous membership of the APG IG was made by NGOs and

APG IG leaders rather than communities. From the *campesinos'* perspective, APG IG membership was also a largely pragmatic move; most expressed a clear preference for individual, rather than communal, property rights. As Rubén put it:

> RUBÉN: I tell you, for us, the *campesinos*, communal [land] doesn't suit us.
>
> PA: Why not?
>
> RUBÉN: Because it restricts us . . . you can't sell that property, you can't take out credit from any bank. But if I buy this plot, it's mine, you see—to be communal I have to renounce it. Renounce it and give it to the community. For selling my land, I can't get money, nothing. In contrast, if it's individual . . . I have my title and I'm the owner of this plot and I can sell it, I can give it to my sons; I can do anything, and I don't have to ask permission from . . . from the community.

For all these reasons, this conjunctural interethnic alliance failed to withstand the test of time. Ultimately, many of those who initially joined the APG IG—often in a climate of misinformation, fear, and uncertainty—came to regret their decision, not least when they belatedly learned that the INRA Law recognized small property claims, irrespective of previous legal status. As Oswaldo described their frustration: "For the cattle ranchers, they've been measured—that is, now they don't have difficulties . . . [But] for the *campesino* sector, who only have their plot and a few animals . . . they entered the [Guaraní] organization, so they've lost all that." As I describe next, this sense of regret, misrecognition, and even deception has served to facilitate the emergence of a broad-based and elite-led non-indigenous opposition to the TCO titling process.

Collective Mobilization and the Coloniality of State Power

In spite of the creative strategies through which landowners sought to defend their property claims, when INRA began publicizing the official legal results of the titling process (from March 2003), it became clear that numerous properties in the TCO had failed to demonstrate fulfillment of the economic social function and had been earmarked for "reductions," totaling over forty thousand hectares—land to be awarded to the Guaraní. This catalyzed a series of coordinated actions by landowners, who organized around two local cattle ranching groups, ASOGAPO (the Cattle Ranchers' Association of O'Connor Province) and FEGATAR (Federación de Ganaderos de Tarija, which has a cantonal subsidiary based in Entre Ríos). Between 2003 and 2008, numerous public meetings were held for private claimants to discuss the titling process and voice complaints. These meetings resulted in a series of collective resolutions addressed to INRA's regional and national offices and to other state authorities.[14]

Individuals from elite landowning families were at the helm of these collective mobilizing efforts, as illustrated by the leadership of ASOGAPO, which passed from Jorge Sabat, a traditional landowner who resides in Tarija city and owns several properties in zone 3 leased to the oil company Repsol (see chapter 5), to Winston Mignolo, and then to Simón Mendez's brother-in-law (Beatriz's predecessor). Nevertheless, documentation produced at these meetings (obtained from CERDET) reveals that participants were diverse and included many of those who had failed to register their property claims. A letter sent to the Vice Ministry of Land on March 28, 2008, declares that "approximately 70 percent [of the TCO's population] . . . are not Guaraní, they are *campesinos* who speak Spanish and dedicate themselves to agriculture and raising a small number of animals in terrible conditions." The letter goes on to list numerous complaints about the TCO titling process, one of which is the high titling price, stated as up to $300 or $400, which is described as "blackmail so that these families come to belong to the Asamblea del Pueblo Guaraní [APG] and renounce their property right." The letter also complains, "The Guaraní are extorting [money from the landowners] for the grazing of their animals and for occupying lands that have always been theirs."

Another letter addressed to the Vice Ministry of Land in December 2007, accompanying a collection of forty-one individual handwritten complaints, denounces the mismeasurement or non-measurement of properties, as well as the high price of titling. These complaints were not unrelated, given that some claimants acknowledged having intentionally minimized the number of "points" recorded for their properties—resulting in the exclusion of some land areas they used—in an effort to keep costs down, only to learn later that costs were calculated on a "per hectare" rather than a "per point" basis. According to Erick, the high titling fee was partly a result of INRA's inefficiency: "They repeated many of the fieldwork processes; they spent a lot of money on paying technicians who were there scratching their asses; they delayed, they went again, they returned to do the same—then they calculated the expenses that INRA incurred and divided them among the quantity of hectares titled." The inability of some claimants to meet titling costs again illustrates how class-based inequalities in access to property rights (and to information on legal norms) added to the sense of injustice of many land claimants, ironically serving to bolster elite-led opposition to the TCO titling process.

For members of traditional landowning families like Mignolo—who later came to occupy the position of provincial governor, running as a MAS candidate—the presence of *campesinos* at such meetings provided a politically expedient means of distancing the defense of settler property from negative images of lowland landowning elites. At the same time, the effectiveness of local opposition to the TCO titling process hinged on the ability of wealthier landowners to draw on racialized and class-based networks of regional power to amplify these collective demands. For example, the 2007 letter to the Land Ministry that accompanies the forty-one individual complaints was authored by the then provincial deputy of O'Connor Province—a member of a prominent landowning family—giving these private claims the added legitimacy of support from a democratically elected official. As I describe later on, Winston Mignolo has similarly used his position as provincial governor to amplify the demands of non-indigenous landowners in TCO Itika Guasu. For individuals like Mignolo—who himself benefited from the titling process—such mobilizations transcended individual property interests, and were driven by a deep-rooted political and ideological opposition to Guaraní land claims.

Crucially, the cattle ranching sector's mobilizing capacity and articulations with regional authorities allowed them to consistently block the allocation of financial resources available for the TCO titling process in Itika Guasu. Fiscal problems began in 2007, after Jorge Campero (the 1999–2004 director of INRA Tarija) diverted funds provided exclusively for TCO titling by the Danish development agency DANIDA (see chapter 1) and used these to finance individual titling processes in other parts of Tarija—something he openly admitted in a 2009 interview. In April 2007, INRA Tarija formally announced that it did not have sufficient funds to continue the titling process, and had lacked sufficient personnel since 2006. After hearing this, the APG IG sought to secure funding from the departmental government, which was at the time unable to spend its staggering annual share of hydrocarbon royalties. A small amount of funding was secured in September 2007, but only a month later, the APG IG's proposal was blocked by the presence of cattle ranchers within municipal and departmental authorities (CERDET 2008). APG IG efforts to secure funding from INRA's national office and from the Vice Ministry of Land were also unsuccessful. By 2009, APG IG leaders were heatedly debating a proposal to apply for money from the Indigenous Fund financed by a national indirect hydrocarbon tax.[15]

Private land claimants from Itika Guasu also joined forces with landowner groups from other lowland regions to obstruct TCO titling at a national level. In 2004, ASOGAPO affiliates participated in a national mobilization led by the more powerful cattle ranchers of Santa Cruz Department. Among the protesters' key demands was a fivefold increase in the *carga animal*—the amount of land that could be justified per head of cattle, on which the FES of properties is calculated. Although the protest did not succeed in changing the legal norm, it delayed the progress of TCO titling processes nationally—not least because, as former INRA employee Tomy Crespo explained, ranchers from Santa Cruz Department "had a strong presence in the ministries, in the state institutions."

Landowners also sought to avoid property reductions by presenting legal complaints before the National Agrarian Tribunal (TAN), an institution created under the INRA Law to resolve land disputes, which was widely seen by NGOs and Guaraní leaders as partial to landowner interests. Then CCGT president Julio Navarro, expressing a view shared by many Guaraní people, argued in 2009 that the TAN was yet another bureaucratic obstacle created by the state to block the consolidation of indigenous land rights: "The Bolivian state wants to . . . keep bureaucratizing. What does the Bolivian state do? It creates various administrative stages, various obstacles. For that reason the National [Agrarian] Tribunal appeared. But who is the National Tribunal open to?"[16]

This flood of legal challenges effectively paralyzed the TCO titling process. As one CERDET document declares: "[INRA] lost time, resources, hopes, and documents . . . These years [2004–5] can be considered LOST years" (CERDET 2008: 3). The Guaraní's inability to break this deadlock led them to agree to participate in a series of controversial roundtable negotiations in 2003. This deadlock also persuaded them to opt for a "partial titling" strategy—a strategy that focused resources on titling uncontested areas of TCO land and indefinitely deferred the contestation of land claimed by third parties. As I discuss in more detail later on, both these pragmatic decisions have contributed toward the failure of the titling process to achieve a significant redistribution of land in the TCO.

Despite having support from local NGOs, the Guaraní lacked representation, or allies, within municipal, provincial, or departmental government during the first decade of the titling process (1997–2007). Accordingly, they lacked their own networks of political influence through which to counter landowners' efforts to block legal progress. As APG IG president Nestor Borrero explained in 2009:

> We are organized, the indigenous peoples, well-organized, maybe we're strong, but the issue is that we don't always have political representation, at least not in the arena where they make decisions. In contrast, the cattle ranchers *have been* represented—they've had senators, they've had deputies, they've been in the prefecture all the time, so that is . . . I think they obstructed us. Whereas we, at no time have we had that arena where someone is going to defend us or take a position where they make important decisions.

While the Guaraní had taken important steps toward addressing their historical exclusion from regional institutions in Tarija,[17] they continued to face marginalization and discrimination throughout the titling process.

This was illustrated during INRA's fieldwork of 2000, when field teams in zones 2 and 3 of the TCO measured private property claims *before* Guaraní communities—a strategy that made Guaraní communities located within private estates invisible. This erasure was denounced by the APG IG, which demanded that the measurements be repeated. Erick, who led the fieldwork team in zone 1, described how many of his colleagues had "the classic vision of the public servant: they're there for a job, for an economic remuneration, but they don't understand the social context and, worse, they are ignorant of the cultures . . . [and] the rights of indigenous peoples; that this was a process of claim, a historic part of this long struggle for territory." What's more, "according to their mentality, the indigenous person is [worth] less and the cattle ranchers and *campesinos* are worth more, and so they tried to favor them."

Angelo, who in 2008 became the first Guaraní to assume a position within the departmental government when he was appointed to head an underfunded Departmental Unit for Indigenous Affairs and Native Peoples, described how he faced discrimination and derision, and wasn't even provided with a desk. As he summed up his experience:

> It was like making a new settlement in a community so far out in the countryside . . . you don't have a house, you don't have food to eat, you have to start to work, building your house . . . No one remembered the indigenous peoples—Guaraní, Tapiete . . . . In other words, we had to build a house.

State authorities' disregard for Guaraní demands was also illustrated in Guaraní assemblies at which the APG IG had requested the attendance of responsible authorities—usually from either INRA Tarija or the Land Ministry. In many cases, officials did not appear at all, citing transportation problems or prior engagements. When they did come, their brief contribution often consisted of the delivery of incomprehensible statistics from an official report and excuses about the lack of funds available to continue the titling process. APG demands for photocopies of official documentation were routinely ignored.

In the foregoing account, I have detailed how entrenched racialized power inequalities in Tarija Department worked in tandem with a double-edged legal process to protect non-indigenous private property claims at the expense of Guaraní land rights. This was not simply a case of a powerful and homogeneous landowning class obstructing the progress of an indigenous land claim. Non-indigenous residents of Itika Guasu were diversely situated vis-à-vis legal norms, state institutions, and ethnic organizing processes. *In spite of this diversity,* however, non-Guaraní opposition to TCO titling ultimately became widespread, coordinated, and highly effective. This reveals how indigenous territorial claims can serve to accentuate ethnicity as an axis of difference, precluding the possibility for class-based and trans-ethnic alliances in favor of land redistribution. Although some poorer non-indigenous residents of Itika Guasu were initially sympathetic to the Guaraní territorial claim, they also found themselves subject to new exclusions: they were overlooked by INRA officials and CERDET training programs, marginalized within APG IG assemblies, disadvantaged by expensive titling procedures, and denied free access to TCO land. In this context, many ultimately opted for inclusion in an elite-led movement in opposition to the TCO titling process. Sedimented structures of racialized power thus worked in tandem with the erasures of activist (and state) cartography in ways that ultimately jeopardized the progress of the Guaraní TCO claim. I now offer a more ethnographic portrayal of these dynamics and their continuing evolution during my fieldwork, based on the ASOGAPO meeting I attended in March 2011.

Interlude: Defending Property as Culture

As I concluded my first afternoon at Beatriz's shop, she urged me to attend the forthcoming meeting with INRA, which was scheduled for the following Friday (March 18, 2011). Given what I'd heard from other people about the inactivity of ASOGAPO (some even claimed the organization no longer existed), I assumed that this was the first such meeting for some time. The meeting took place above Entre Ríos' central market, in the largest of various rooms occupied by the municipal government. As I downed a watery coffee and ascended the grimy stairs, I reflected that there was something rather comical about the juxtaposition of state bureaucracy with fruit sellers and stands serving *criollo* chicken soup. On other visits, municipal employees complained about their unwanted proximity to the chaos and scruffiness of the market. Yet for the local cattle ranchers and farmers affiliated with ASOGAPO, this was an ideal venue—official yet accessible—for the much-awaited meeting with the national director of INRA. Although the meeting was open to all ASOGAPO affiliates, some of whom lived outside of Itika Guasu, Beatriz's own concern was clearly with the TCO. The meeting's objective—to request an audit of all land titling in O'Connor Province—brought together those dissatisfied with TCO titling with people from other parts of the province, who had their own complaints about INRA.

Although Beatriz had informed me the meeting would begin at 8 a.m., there were only a couple of people hanging around the municipal offices when I arrived. Someone reminded me that there had been torrential rain the night before, making the dirt roads connecting Entre Ríos to rural communities and farms even more treacherous than usual. People began to arrive gradually over the course of the morning, and stood around speculating about whether the meeting would go ahead. I took the opportunity to chat with a few people, who related a variety of complaints regarding their experiences of state land titling, both within and outside the TCO. These brief encounters highlighted the complexity of problems relating to land titling in the province, which went well beyond the TCO titling process.[18] Nevertheless, the TCO would remain a focal point of the meeting, and acted as a kind of unifying symbol of the injustices of state land titling in general. Conversely, a more generalized dissatisfaction with INRA served to bolster support for established opposition to the TCO titling process.

Around 11 a.m. the doors of the meeting room opened, and those waiting in the corridors filed inside. The national director of INRA still hadn't shown up, so we stood around chatting for another hour or so while Beatriz made some inquiries. A man from Itika Guasu complained to me about the lack of information and training given to local people regarding the SAN-TCO process, which had discouraged him and many of his neighbors from participating. Another man was more overtly hostile to the TCO; he complained that the Guaraní didn't want to "help" the cattle ranchers, were envious of their land, and didn't know how to work. He claimed to have sent six letters to INRA (two of which he showed me, dated 2006 and 2010) complaining about the results of his property claim. A third rancher, also from Itika Guasu, described how he had been persuaded by local NGOs to "stay inside the TCO" in order to speed up the titling process, and had therefore lost out on the chance to gain individual title. Emphasizing that "there are *many* of us who are inside the TCO," he complained that he felt trapped, unable to "develop" as a rancher, owing to his obligation to consult the Guaraní before he could "do anything."

Just before the meeting began, Oswaldo Cortez turned up. He greeted me warmly, expressed his approval that I was attending the meeting, and informed me that he was no longer working for CERDET. Eventually, following numerous phone calls, Beatriz announced that the national director of INRA would not be coming. She apologized but suggested that they use the opportunity to produce a joint statement (*voto resolutivo*) to present to the land reform agency. As people took their seats in rows of chairs, Beatriz ushered me into an uncomfortably prominent position alongside her and the *campesino* leader Rubén Roble at a long table facing the audience. At least I had a good view of participants from where I was sitting; I counted around thirty-five people, the majority of whom were men. A minority wore smart urban attire; most had come from the countryside and wore rough clothes used for rural work. Some looked visibly poorer than others, wearing cheap peasant sandals and worn garments. I noticed a mixture of baseball caps and cowboy hats. Some women wore Western clothes; others wore the traditional *chapaca* skirts, plaits, and broad-brimmed hats used by rural women in Tarija's central valley.

Following Beatriz's introduction, the meeting commenced with a few participants expressing doubts as to whether INRA would respond to a demand for an audit. Rubén Roble spoke out in favor of such a demand, arguing: "You have to ask the authorities. At any moment there [could] be a death and who will be responsible? We requested [INRA's] presence. INRA has to fulfill its duties." Beatriz suggested elaborating a resolution and waiting to see how INRA responded. The audience agreed to follow this familiar course of action. One man in the audience recalled that a year earlier the vice minister of land had attended a meeting and they had made a written agreement, which he suggested using as a reference point for the new statement.

At that moment the discussion was interrupted by the arrival of Winston Mignolo, former ASOGAPO president and now provincial governor, who confidently took his place at the table (see figure 7). I attempted to use his arrival as an excuse to sneak off into the audience, but Beatriz was just launching into an enthusiastic presentation of my research and called me back. With a mixture of gratitude and embarrassment, I returned to my seat, edging discreetly to one side to try and distance myself from the authority of the panel.

FIGURE 7.   Winston Mignolo speaks at ASOGAPO meeting, March 18, 2011 (photo by author)

Mignolo took up where Beatriz left off, giving a lengthy formal speech that established his leadership of the meeting:

> Well, first, good morning to all present: leaders, also community members from all zones of the province, [here] for this issue of the land problem; Dr. Beatriz Vaca, as president of ASOGAPO; comrade Rubén Roble as officer of . . . land and territory—of conflicts, isn't it?—of the Unified Syndical Confederation of Peasants of Bolivia; and also to Penelope. I think we met once when I was president of the cattle ranchers two or three years ago, didn't we? We spoke about precisely this problem . . . It seemed to me very valuable, the work that she's doing, a study of the issue of the land situation, especially in Itika Guasu, and I broadly explained to Penelope what today I'm going to hear from the people: in reality, what is the situation in Itika, the problem of the bad land titling [and] how it affects people . . . We talk so much of development, we talk of production, but if we don't have our property rights consolidated, we *can't* speak of development, we can't speak of the productive issue; it's *so fundamental,* this issue, *compañeros,* and I'm going to deal with the matter beyond whether INRA comes or not. I wanted to be in this meeting today because this issue is really, really important, *compañeros.* Look; they've done a land titling in the northern zone . . . there is the TCO of Itika Guasu . . . They've also done land titling in the southern zone . . . Today they're doing land titling in . . . the northeastern zone. But where INRA has entered, there are conflicts. *That's* the problem—that is, that's the *result* of the land titling: conflicts remain, and precisely once they've done titling, there shouldn't be a single conflict! What has been left? Left are native people [*gente orionda*], who were born here, in these communities since their ancestors, who today don't even have a plot of land to *work.*

He went on to attribute these results to claimants' ignorance of legal norms and INRA's failure to conduct a proper public information campaign (*socialización*). He declared: "We're a peasant class [*una clase campesina*], which perhaps doesn't have many possibilities of being able to understand the law," thus masking the differences in wealth, power, and status that separated him (and other wealthy landowners) from the poorer participants he was addressing – differences that had enabled him to consolidate rights to his own property claim where they had failed to do so. His words are illustrative of how the term *campesino* has enabled a reframing of rural identities in the Bolivian Chaco under the Morales government, an era of politics in which the power of traditional landowning elites was being called into question. For Mignolo, who, like many traditional elites in

Tarija Department, had recently switched his political allegiance to the MAS (following a long history of affiliation with right-wing parties), this was a politically strategic act of self-identification. In a revealing twist, this obscuring of class difference was rapidly followed by an articulation of *ethnic* difference as the central problem of land titling. Suggesting there were whole peasant communities that hadn't been recognized by INRA, Mignolo asked:

> What is the problem? *That they're inside a territory.* Now, clearly we have to put this thing in context because it isn't good perhaps to suggest—and I believe it isn't the feeling or the spirit of *anyone* here, of *none* of us who are here—to go against the rights that the Guaraní friends legitimately have, as a community, as the Guaraní people . . . If you just look there at the wall of this room of the municipality [see figure 8], it's expressed, it's painted—their . . . their customs, their culture. That means that O'Connor Province is *characterized* by, *identifies* with, Guaraní culture, so one can't go against that culture from any point of view. But, however, . . . there are problems that aren't the failure to recognize[19] the rights of the Guaraní brothers; rather it relates to the failure to recognize the rights of the community members who *are not* Guaraní. So

FIGURE 8. The mural to which Mignolo refers, painted on the back wall of the Entre Ríos municipal hall, combines colonial representations of the Guaraní with Christian settler iconography, local topography, and hydrocarbon infrastructure (photo by author).

in this context, I believe that that situation has to have a solution. Unfortunately, up till now there are many *campesinos* who have been affected; some haven't been recognized; others have had their properties reduced without any justification—50 percent, 70 percent of their private plot.

There followed a discussion of broader concerns about land titling in O'Connor Province, focused on a critique of INRA's growing preference for "internal land titling" in conflictive areas like the Chaco Tarijeño—specifically about how the agency was pressuring claimants to title grazing areas communally.[20] One man used a play on the word *sanear* (to title land; also to clean up or sanitize), suggesting that INRA's job should be "to heal" (*sanar*), but in reality INRA had created more conflicts. He drew a comparison between the "bad titling" in Itika Guasu and the creation of the Tariquía Flora and Fauna National Reserve, a protected area to the south, where people faced restrictions on access to land and forest resources.[21] He concluded:

> [In both cases] it could arrive at extremes and there could be deaths, so in my humble opinion, all the titling should stop and INRA Nacional in coordination with [INRA] Departamental and the work teams should come to an agreement because, as our president of the republic says, governance should be by the people—that's why they [public officials] are "servants" [*servidores*].

The conflation of national parks (managed by a separate state parks agency) and TCO land titling illustrates how critiques of INRA are informed by a broader set of (shifting) relations with state power in the Bolivian Chaco. His proposal—that ordinary people should determine the course of land titling—ironically resonated with the logic behind, if not the practical application of, INRA's "internal titling" approach. It did not, however, address the conflicting understandings of sovereignty and rights of indigenous and non-indigenous land claimants in Itika Guasu.

Following this more generalized tirade against INRA, Winston Mignolo took the floor once again. Taking up the discourse of other audience members, he referred to the mixed and spatially variegated land use practices of the region as local *usos y costumbres* (uses and customs), suggesting, "We have to ask [INRA] to freeze the titling issue in O'Connor Province until we have defined well what are our *usos y costumbres*." This should be the basis, he suggested, for defining land titling practices "according to the reality of every zone." He proposed working through the peasant union CSUTCB to encourage communities to form "titling committees," determine *usos y costumbres*, and conduct their own "internal titling" to define property limits—again, a proposal seemingly in line with the principles of INRA's "internal titling," if not its prescriptive mode of application.

Once again, however, a discourse of local ownership of land titling obscured the competing sovereignties and land claims of indigenous and non-indigenous actors in the province. It seemed to me doubtful that the Guaraní would accept a form of community-led titling that enabled their *karai* neighbors to determine their land rights, or that "agreement" would ever be reached if they did.

As if responding to my thoughts, an audience member proposed the formation of a "titling commission" in Itika Guasu that included both indigenous people and cattle ranchers. He recalled that, at the time of INRA's original fieldwork in the TCO, "there was only a group of INRA and the . . . the . . . ["originarios" (natives), Beatriz chipped in] . . . that is, there wasn't a group of us, and the cattle ranchers were all on their own [*solitos*]."

Taking up this suggestion, Winston Mignolo proposed the formation of a "Provincial Agrarian Commission" including representatives from the Central Campesino (CSUTCB), APG, cattle ranchers, other productive sectors, and state institutions. He suggested they elaborate the joint statement demanding an immediate freeze on land titling in the province; the formation of an INRA commission to investigate local *usos y costumbres*; and the formation of a provincial, zonal, and communal entity to deal with land issues. The audience members expressed their agreement. The fundamentally *restitutive* logic of indigenous land claims remained unacknowledged in this discussion, which—for all the critique of INRA—remained framed by the state's technocratic logic of rationalization and regularization.

The fact that non-indigenous land claimants should frame their demands for local ownership of land titling through a discourse of *usos y costumbres* is telling. Under the MAS government, *usos y costumbres* has emerged as an important trope—in both state law and everyday discourse—through which to revalorize and legitimize indigenous norms and institutions, in ways that challenge a long history of racialized discrimination and assimilationist nationalism. This recognition of *usos y costumbres* is intimately connected to indigenous demands for self-governance, on the basis of forms of cultural and political organization that preceded the imposition of colonial and state rule. *Usos y costumbres* can thus act as a profoundly *decolonizing* discourse. Yet as this meeting shows, this discourse is also open to multiple uses by differently situated groups—in this case, non-indigenous land claimants defending the sanctity of settler property against the threat of an indigenous territorial claim. While indigenous land claims have since the 1980s rested on the notion of "land as culture" (Engle 2010), participants in this meeting articulated a notion of "property as culture" that located private and indigenous land claims on an equal discursive and moral terrain.

Following Mignolo's suggestion, the meeting concluded with the elaboration of this joint resolution, which Beatriz transcribed and then read out to the audience.

Participants crowded around the table to sign their names. In addition to the demands noted earlier, the statement proposed an alternative date for a meeting with the national director of INRA and, as a final point, demanded "an audit of the previous land titling process, especially in Iticaguazu." This meeting gives an insight into how shared discourses of rights—in this case, the representation of private land claimants as a disadvantaged group, private property as a cultural right, and the state as a servant of the people—have played a critical role in mobilizing diversely situated TCO residents in collective efforts to contest, obstruct, and even reverse the TCO titling process. In the next section, I provide a more detailed interrogation of the discourses of race, rights, and citizenship that animated the individual and collective actions I have detailed, interpellating a broad range of non-Guaraní TCO residents in an ideological rejection of the Guaraní's territorial claim.

Articulating Race, Rights, and Citizenship

> **As it evolves, a white settler society continues to be structured by a racial hierarchy. In the national mythologies of such societies, it is believed that white people came first and that it is they who principally developed the land . . . European settlers thus *become* the original inhabitants and the group most entitled to the fruits of citizenship. A quintessential feature of white settler mythologies is, therefore, the disavowal of conquest, genocide, slavery, and the exploitation of the labour of peoples of colour . . . [A]t each stage, the story installs Europeans as entitled to the land, a claim that is codified in law.**
>
> Sherene Razack, ed., *Race, Space, and the Law,* 2002

As I detailed in chapter 1, the colonization of the Chaco rested on colonial imaginaries of indigenous peoples as uncivilized savages and their lands as unused and unproductive. I described how the Guaraní sought to contest these colonial knowledges through "territorial counternarratives" that made visible their pre-colonial occupation of the Chaco and the violent processes of dispossession inflicted on them by settlers and the Bolivian state. This process of decolonizing knowledge did not, however, engage non-Guaraní residents of Itika Guasu, who saw only its visible effects—endless APG assemblies, Guaraní land occupations, and, finally, the arrival of INRA. In what follows, I seek to understand local opposition to TCO titling in relation to the discourses of race, rights, and citizenship that defined *karai* society on this (post)colonial frontier. These discourses played a central role in how legal norms were contested, translated, and "vernacularized" in Itika Guasu. Responding to calls for a "rematerialized postcolonialism"

(McEwan 2003), I reveal how racialized identities, geographical imaginaries, and discourses of rights are mobilized around property claims in ways that reproduce material inequalities in the present.

In what follows, I highlight four interrelated discourses that resurfaced in the context of interviews, informal discussions, and cattle ranchers' meetings I attended: productive land use and economic citizenship; liberal discourses of equal rights; nation building and native status; and outsider intervention versus local sovereignty.

Productive Land Use and Economic Citizenship

One way in which non-indigenous claimants defended their land claims—both in interviews and in correspondence with state institutions—was by arguing that land should be awarded to those who use it productively. This did not, in their view, include the Guaraní; as Rubén Roble argued, in an interview conducted in March 2011:

> One can't take [land] away from [private land claimants] if they're fulfilling a social function. Also, the Guaranís *aren't* fulfilling a social function. They only say, "It's my territory"; they don't sow, they . . . don't have a hacienda, so I believe that the land should be for people who . . . fulfill the social function. So that's my proposal to INRA's national office.

This discourse draws on the liberal idea of the "social function of property,"[22] enshrined in Bolivian law since the 1953 agrarian reform. As noted earlier, this idea resurfaces in the INRA Law as the economic social function (applicable to medium and large properties) and social function (applicable to smallholdings and indigenous communal land). The remark just quoted thus reveals how entrenched national discourses of agrarian rights were deployed by private claimants to counter multicultural recognition of indigenous land rights. Yet this discourse also has deeper roots. As in many settler colonial contexts, regional identities in the Chaco are constructed around the idea that settlers legitimately earned their rights to land through a combination of hard work and enterprise (Razack 2002). As Roble's comments make clear, this rests on the notion of indigenous lands as empty or unused, awaiting conversion into civilized and productive spaces by *criollo* or mestizo farmers (Sundberg 2008; Wainwright, 2008). Although the "social function of property" has historically lent moral weight to the claims of dispossessed rural populations in Bolivia (for example, during the 1952 Agrarian Revolution), it can also serve as a vehicle for colonial discourses that delegitimize indigenous land claims vis-à-vis those of non-indigenous settlers.

This colonial stereotype of the Guaraní as unproductive, and therefore unde-serving of property rights, also informed local state officials' views on the TCO titling process. José, a local government official whom I met in Entre Ríos in 2009, provided the following reflection:

> JOSÉ: This [INRA] law, it seems that it doesn't have influence, because a cattle rancher comes and says, "I have so many cows, so I'm going to take [the land] away from [the indigenous peo-ple]"; [the cattle ranchers] say, "You don't have cows . . . you don't have agriculture." It's because the same indigenous per-son five years ago did nothing; "lazy" is the word. [Indigenous people] have the idea that they can stay sitting on their asses and everyone gives them everything. Life's not like that—no; one has to work.
>
> PA: So if [indigenous peoples] were producing, they would earn more respect?
>
> JOSÉ: From the government and from the cattle ranchers, the whites. The cattle ranchers say that they're not using the land—that's the problem.

This conversation is revealing in several respects. First, it is suggestive of how racialized discourses of productive land use underpin everyday forms of indig-enous dispossession in Itika Guasu. Second, it reveals how the forms of socioeco-nomic dependency and labor exploitation that accompanied Guaraní disposses-sion are used to shore up racist depictions of the Guaraní as lazy, rent-seeking, and unproductive. Third, in slipping from apparently disinterested description to personal judgment, José's remarks reveal how these colonial discourses of rights are shared by state officials in the Chaco. While José did not have a direct involve-ment in the TCO titling process, he was the director of a controversial municipal agrarian development program that provided free barbed wire fencing to private claimants of TCO land. As the Guaraní complained, this not only restricted their land access but also helped claimants justify the economic social function of their properties by providing evidence of property "improvements" (mejoramiento).

A Dutch landowner whom I met by chance in an elite café in central Tarija—the only non-Bolivian claimant of land in Itika Guasu that I have ever encountered—revealed himself to be surprisingly well versed in these local dis-courses, proclaiming: "The [titling] process is misguided . . . [The Guaraní] don't want to work; they want to continue their life as it was before, using up every-thing . . . They don't think about tomorrow, they don't want to work, they want to get everything from the patrón." Emphasizing the Guaraní's own responsibility for their poverty, he claimed he "would live like a king" in their situation, whereas they couldn't even be bothered to maintain basic standards of hygiene. His reference to "using up everything" reflects a widespread (inaccurate) popular belief that the Guaraní did not farm prior to their contact with non-indigenous settlers, and lived solely through hunting and gathering. As José argued:

> The native [*el originario*][23] wants land for nothing; he doesn't work—that's the problem. And the natives are only fishermen.
> PA: They also farm.
> JOSÉ: But very little. They don't work. They're not farmers, nor are they cattle ranchers; they're fishermen and gatherers . . . but now the influence of the whites has arrived and they've changed.

Several private claimants linked this racialized stereotype to the limited achievements of indigenous development projects in the TCO, arguing that—despite receiving disproportionate help with their productive activities—the Guaraní have *still* proved incapable of development. As Simón Mendez put it, drawing on his own long-standing labor relations with the Guaraní: "They have a different vision—a vision of living in a community and not having obligations; they like freedom . . . It seems their culture was like that. So now they have to learn . . . to be employees, to have obligations—they're going to learn it, for sure."

While most informants, when pushed, acknowledged that Guaraní communities practice subsistence farming, the superiority of *karai* land claims was often justified on the basis of the greater integration of *karai* in local and regional markets. As Roble complained:

> Sometimes it hurts . . . that they take away your land, and you being the person . . . who produces, who provides meat here in the town, so [the titling process] wasn't good, no. I also expected the Guaraní to produce because they're also human beings and they can produce. They also have hands, they can produce and sell—they could farm, but no . . . they don't even sell a couple of cows; until now they don't sell. I don't know . . . to have land for free and not make them raise other . . . We say in local dialect, "You neither eat nor let [others] eat."

He implies here that the Guaraní have not *earned* the land they claim through commercial production; rather, it is "for free." In contrast, *karai* claimants' ability to sell their produce, and the status of meat as a preferred foodstuff for the expanding urban middle class, serve to bolster the legitimacy of non-indigenous land claims.

Market integration in turn served to link *karai* land occupation to broader discourses of regional development. As Winston Mignolo proudly pointed out, lamenting the central government's declining support for cattle ranching: "The productive agro-pastoral sector here in the province is the main driver of development. We're not an industrial province, even less so an industrial department, so everything is sustained by agriculture, cattle ranching." This frames private land claimants in Itika Guasu—most of whom are cattle ranchers—as not just defending private interests but serving the interests of broader Tarijeño society by providing meat to urban centers and fueling the regional economy. The implication is that indigenous land rights could potentially undermine the reciprocal networks of production and exchange on which society depends. Of course, this depiction of a "neutral" market obscures the colonial history that robbed indigenous peoples of their land base and rendered them an exploited labor reserve for, rather than equal participants in, regional markets. Such discourses of economic citizenship use indigenous peoples' disadvantaged status within a (post)colonial economy to undermine their present claims for land rights. In other words, they defend a colonial regime of citizenship (Quijano 2000; Taylor 2013; Soruco 2011).

As noted earlier, these links between race, nation, and economy are sustained by a particular *spatial* order. Elite landowning families tend to reside and work in Tarija city and (like Mendez) view rural landholdings in Itika Guasu as a source of secondary income—a spatial configuration that offers access to political power alongside economic security. Even poorer *karai* claimants tend to have economic links with urban centers, many of them working as *transportistas* (commercial drivers) or *comerciantes* (petty traders). As Simón Mendez put it in an interview in his large family home in one of central Tarija's elite neighborhoods:

> [Non-indigenous residents of TCO Itika Guasu] have other sources of income—many who are there [in Itika Guasu] are old, or part of their family is also in the city, or outside. For example, in Tarupayo, there are some who have gone to Spain; they send money from Spain. Others live here in Tarija; they send money from here to their family. When the buses arrive . . . it's with that [money] that they maintain themselves, because their children who live here [in Tarija city] send money so the peasants there can maintain themselves.

In contrast, although Guaraní men (and some women) do travel to urban centers for wage labor, the inability of most communities to produce agricultural surplus in a context of land scarcity, drought, poverty, and poor transportation infrastructure prevents them from participating in these regional circuits of production and exchange. In this context, market integration symbolizes a spatial relationship that links *karai* landowners to the nation via urban centers—sites of state power and economic opportunity—a relationship from which the Guaraní have been historically excluded. Racialized land inequality is of course fundamental to this exclusion.

In the context of demands addressed to national government, landowners also stressed the importance of cattle ranching to the nation's "food security." As Tomy recalled, referring to national landowner mobilizations of 2004:

> The cattle ranchers organized through their Cattle Ranching Federation and they started to work on the issue of how they would defend [their claims] and what their position was before the government . . . [They said:] "We're producers and we're connected to the food security of this country. So they're not going to give all the land to the indigenous peoples while we're giving food to eat to the whole country."

The discourse of "food security"—when couched in nationalist terms—serves to legitimize *state* sovereignty over territory, highlighting the need for rational management of the nation's land and resources.[24] Appealing to the Bolivian state's long-standing support for large-scale commercial agriculture, as well as to colonial discourses of indigenous peoples as unproductive, national landowner organizations framed TCOs as a threat to the well-being of the entire nation. As I have noted, these lobbying efforts—which combined moral argument with political mobilization—succeeded in obstructing the TCO titling process across the Bolivian lowlands.

Liberal Equal Rights

In conjunction with the discourses of productive land use, private land claimants used a liberal discourse of equal rights to challenge the fact that the Guaraní enjoy "special" rights under the SAN-TCO process and, specifically, are *not* required to demonstrate productive land use. The following conversation, recorded prior to the ASOGAPO meeting on March 18, 2011, is illustrative:

> MAN 1: The problem is that the law demands that the land possessor fulfills the FES—economic social function. And it doesn't demand that of the *originarios* [natives] . . . that is, they justify [their land claim] by being *originarios*. So that's a disadvantage, because it says that if we don't fulfill [the FES] . . . then we're going to face a [property] reduction. Imagine a plague: you have one hundred head [of cattle], a plague comes, the plague kills fifty, and when they come to do a census after two years, you're not going to have the one hundred, so they're going to reduce [your property].
>
> PA: So the law doesn't seem fair to you in the sense that there is one treatment for the Guaraní and another treatment for the cattle ranchers?
>
> MAN 1: Of course [not].

MAN 2: They [the cattle ranchers] already demanded that—that if something is demanded of the cattle ranching producer who's there . . . that the same should be demanded also of the [Guaraní] community, that they make use of the land, because they have it without using it.

The two men went on to reiterate this argument with reference to a specific piece of TCO land the Guaraní had fenced with assistance from CERDET:

MAN 1: They've fenced a big area now . . . They can work, they can sow maize, they can sow pasture, and in the end . . . no one does anything. Over there they've closed it for no reason [*de ganas*]. If someone goes to work over there—[like] the clearing I do to sow pasture—they're there looking at what this person is doing.
MAN 2: Just standing there [*parados*].
MAN 1: They don't progress, so you can't . . . a problem is . . .
MAN 2: That is, they demand the FES from us—obligatorily [*sí o sí*]—and not from them. And it's a big disadvantage. We're all Bolivians, aren't we, so we should get treatment that is . . . [equal].

Here, liberal concepts of equality before the law are interwoven with racialized depictions of the Guaraní as idle and uncivilized. By demanding equal treatment on the basis that "we're all Bolivians," this discourse obscures the state's historically *unequal* treatment of indigenous and settler populations, and the history of violent dispossession this gave rise to.

What made these discourses so powerful in the context of TCO titling in Itika Guasu was that they were shared by many of those responsible for implementing the titling process. Jorge Campero, the former departmental director of INRA who held the post in the crucial years 1999–2004, openly admitted, in a 2009 interview in his small private law firm in central Tarija, that he did not agree with differential treatment given to indigenous land rights in the SAN-TCO process:

You have the rule that work is the fundamental source of retaining the right [to property]; if you don't work the land, [the state] can expropriate it. *For one sector* [non-indigenous claimants]. But for another sector [indigenous peoples], you have a large quantity of land and you don't do anything, so it's not right, is it? I think that all the sectors without distinction should be required to use the land . . . all should fulfill the social economic function . . . You can't justify that a people have so much unproductive land . . . It doesn't serve any purpose; they're going to be a threat to society.

This statement echoes those of private claimants in obscuring the colonial foundations of the current ethnic spatial order, suggesting indigenous and non-indigenous production can be assessed on an equal basis, as a reflection of industry and merit. Indigenous peoples are located here on the margins of national belonging, their unwarranted "special rights" posing a threat to Bolivian society. It is noteworthy that many of the events I have described—such as the diversion of Danish funds allocated for TCO titling and the disappearances of INRA files—occurred under Campero's watch. Competing discourses of rights are thus intrinsic to the processes and dynamics described earlier in this chapter.

Some non-indigenous land claimants went further, claiming they had suffered a form of (reverse) ethnic discrimination. During my afternoon visit to Beatriz Vaca's veterinary shop in March 2011, she related to me her long struggle to overturn INRA's decision to reduce her father's property. Formerly a cowhand for the Mendez family, by the time of INRA's fieldwork, Roberto Vaca had managed to amass his own herd, establish himself as an independent rancher, and negotiate occupation of a sizable piece of the Mendezes' land—a property coveted by Guaraní residents of Tarairí community (see chapter 4). During the titling process, however, Vaca failed to demonstrate fulfillment of the FES and received notification from INRA that his property would face reduction. He challenged this decision before the National Agrarian Tribunal, during the brief period when its judges were not systematically ruling against indigenous land claims.[25] Beatriz described her experience accompanying her father to Sucre to present the unsuccessful legal challenge:

> [It's] discrimination because, like I told you before, when I went to make the legal challenge . . . the judge said to me: "Understand, madam," she said, "that we're doing a favor by giving you a piece of the TCO. You know very well that the indigenous sector are the natives and they are owners of the land." And this, for me, is *total discrimination* . . . So in a rage, I tell you, I grabbed her arm like this [she grabs my bicep and squeezes till it hurts] [and said]: "Would you happen to know that I was *also* born there, that I am *just as* native [*originario*] as the indigenous people? Or do you need me to put on a *tipoy* [traditional Guaraní garment] and paint my face so that you recognize me?" I said that to her, with the irony of the anger that I felt at that moment, because I felt *so bad*—after having worked . . . my father born, having worked, my grandfather too, as an old man in an indigenous territory—that they tell me now that there's no land left over for them! And when we, the cattle ranchers of the zone of Itika Guasu, are the ones who contribute more to the mar-

ket . . . for me, that's discrimination—*total discrimination*—because it can't be that because we're not indigenous they want to remove us from the indigenous territory, can it? We don't deserve any blame for not being indigenous. I tell you, we're just as native as [the Guaraní] are, and there [in Itika] they respect us.

In this passage, Beatriz appropriates and adapts two of the key concepts underpinning indigenous land claims. First, the Guaraní claim for preferential rights as a redress for historic discrimination is subverted to claim that it is *non-Guaraní* people who now face ethnic discrimination. (Winston Mignolo made a similar argument at the 2011 ASOGAPO meeting.) Second, indigenous claims for territory on a basis of ancestral occupation are countered by rival claims to *originario* (native) status—a status earned, in Beatriz's eyes, by the embodied labor of two generations of her family in Itika Guasu.

Nation Building and Native Status

Beatriz's counterdiscourse of ancestral rights was echoed in other accounts. In an interview conducted in Tarija in 2009, Winston Mignolo, who was at the time president of ASOGAPO, provided some reflections on the term *originario*:

> Now, looking a bit farther back at what we are, that is to say, as non-Guaraní people . . . I think it's difficult to understand when they speak of *originarios*; at least I very much disagree with the interpretation that this word implies. *Originario* . . . Evidently history tells us that the ancestors—the Guaraní ethnic groups—lived on the banks of the Pilcomayo River, but I find myself in a dilemma; for example, the majority of the [non-Guaraní] families who live inside the TCO Itika Guasu have always lived in this zone. *Always.*

For Winston, a third-generation immigrant to the area, the birth of one's parents in the territory was sufficient to claim native status. Significantly, this claim to native status was reinforced by the conditions under which his grandfather arrived in Itika Guasu. He continued:

> And on the other hand, there is another factor that must be taken into account: for example, my grandfather was an ex-combatant in the Chaco War; he fought in the Chaco War. He went to war when he was seventeen years old . . . He returned missing an eye, with a bullet in the lung, which thirty years ago cost him his life. I, as a grandson, believe that I also consider myself *originario*, don't you think? That is, beyond the estate and when we [acquired it], I believe that in the end we're

originarios—we *are originarios;* we were born there, even the grandparents were there. So I think we have to begin to understand this issue
there. We are *just as much* owners of this territory . . . The Guaranís, they
deserve all the respect, valuation, and we do as well. When we understand that, I believe that we're going to come to understand each other
more. So, in relation to the issue of our identity: our identity is being
from the place, we're from the place, we're also *originarios* of the place.

As Thomas Perreault and Gabriela Valdivia (2010) relate, the Chaco War—
popularly remembered as a heroic struggle in defense of the nation's hydrocarbon wealth—retains a central role in the construction of an imagined national
community in Bolivia. Under the Morales government, memories of the
war—which was fought largely by poor indigenous highlanders, many of whom
perished—have been strategically deployed to reassert national sovereignty over
the Chaco's hydrocarbon reserves.[26] The 2006 "Heroes of the Chaco" decree that
"nationalized" Bolivia's hydrocarbon reserves—announced by Morales at the site
of a Chaco War memorial in Camiri—provides one illustration. Yet as Mignolo's
discourse reveals, the Chaco War is equally important for *local* non-indigenous
territorial sovereignty claims. As detailed in chapter 1, after the Chaco War ended
in 1935, many ex-combatants decided (with the encouragement of state land
awards) to stay and make their lives as ranchers or cowboys in the Chaco. For
the numerous descendants of these war veterans who currently claim land in
Itika Guasu, their ancestors' sacrifice in the war effort provides an important
moral basis for their claims. The imaginary of land as a prize for sacrifice in
battle has a long genealogy in Bolivia, where, since the time of the Independence
Wars, ex-combatants have been awarded frontier lands (and indigenous laborers) as a reward for military service. This was the context for the creation of
the O'Connor estate, which later became O'Connor Province. Mignolo's reference to his grandfather's sacrifice thus reproduced a sedimented discourse that
links property rights to participation in nation building—a violent process from
which indigenous peoples were of course excluded, and which was predicated on
their dispossession.

The Chaco War was also an important reference point for claimants whose
families had settled in the region earlier on. Simón Mendez emphasized the sac-
rifices that his and other local landowning families had made during the war. Not
only did they "send all their sons, all their family to war," but also, he claimed,
they were forced to hand over all their animals and other goods to the war effort,
and were "left impoverished" as a result:

> Many of the cattle ranchers lost everything. They lost everything
> because in the war all goods were common property. That is, no one

could say, "This is my cow" or "This is my horse," because they declared goods common property in service of the war . . . My family, they say that they had cattle, a good quantity of cattle, but after [the war] they were left with some ten or twenty head of cattle . . . because they had used all of them in the war.

In contrast, he claimed that the Guaraní had not participated in the war at all:

The Tarijeños [and] those from La Paz went to war, but the Guaraní declared themselves impartial. They declared themselves impartial. Also they didn't go to war—no Guaraní person went to war . . . they were declared impartial, [saying] that we're not in any war with Paraguay, because Paraguay also had Guaraní, so . . . they didn't participate in the war; people only came from the north of La Paz, from Potosí, from Tarija.

Here, Mendez reproduces a wartime discourse according to which the Guaraní could not be trusted as allies owing to their spatial mobility and transnational kinship ties in Paraguay. In the context of TCO titling, private claimants' patriotic histories are frequently juxtaposed with Guaraní's purported indifference to (or betrayal of) this nation-building effort—framed by Mendez as their "impartiality." As Guaraní leader Julio Navarro argued, speaking at an APG assembly in Karaparí (the most recent Guaraní TCO claim) in 2008, *karai* opponents to TCO claims "say that Guaranís didn't fight in the Chaco War" when in reality "they were made invisible for belonging to the *patrones*." In fact, the Guaraní suffered huge losses and massive displacement during the Chaco War, in which they served as foot soldiers, guides, and messengers for both Bolivian and Paraguayan forces (Pifarré 1999). According to the Guaraní authors of one publication, they also suffered conscription and military raids on their animals:

During the Chaco War many [Guaraní] men were taken to Villamontes and enrolled in the forces of the Bolivian army, or to work on the construction of the Tarija-Villamontes road . . . According to what the old people of the region say, during the war, the army entered the communities to take not only men but also the few cattle that the indigenous families had left. (APG IG and CERDET 2005: 6)

Yet, as Mendez's account demonstrates, the Guaraní's erasure from nationalist historiography continues, in ways that work to delegitimize their claims to sovereignty over their ancestral lands vis-à-vis those of non-indigenous settlers.

As well as articulating their own rival claims to native status, non-indigenous land claimants argued that some Guaraní residents of Itika Guasu were *not* native to the area. This is implicit in Mendez's reference (quoted earlier) to "Guaraní ethnic groups" who lived "on the banks of the Pilcomayo River"—a statement suggestive of the Guaraní's historic mobility and decentralized forms of organization. This subtly questions the Guaraní's current claim to a fixed and bounded territory, demonstrating a common (post)colonial conflation of property and settlement (Wainwright 2008: chap. 5). References are also made to the fact that some current residents of Itika Guasu migrated during the last half century from the neighboring department of Chuquisaca, where they faced a more widespread and extreme regime of *empatronamiento*. José, the local state official quoted earlier, weighed the claims of Chaco War veterans against those of these Guaraní "newcomers," finding the former more deserving of land:

> The leaders—that is, the old Guaraní leaders who fought for the TCO demand, all that—they're not . . . they weren't *native* to here, from *Itika*. They're people who came from Chuquisaca. So . . . they're people who came from another department and, well, . . . because they married women from here, they've stayed in the place. So perhaps there are people, let's say, ex-combatants of the Chaco War, who were born in the place, and they feel they have much *more* right than people who've come, than the Guaraní who've come from the Chuquisaca side . . . So they complain; they say, "Why don't we have the same rights as them?"—as the Guaraní, the Guaraní who weren't from there—that is, who came after . . . precisely for motives of the slavery that there was on the Chuquisaca side . . . they say that there the *empatronamiento* was worse.

Ironically, in moving within their ancestral territory to seek refuge from racialized labor exploitation, the Guaraní have found themselves accused of being strangers in their own lands. As this remark reveals, the pragmatic process of territorial reduction and boundary fixing involved in the mapping of TCO claims, although a precondition for state recognition, leaves indigenous claimants open to accusations of inauthenticity, owing to their failure to live up to the incarcerating spatial logic of their land claims.

Outsider Intervention versus Local Sovereignty

By questioning the geographical origins of APG IG leaders, the statement just quoted suggests that the TCO claim was the product of intervention by "outsiders" rather than an organic process of indigenous organizing.[27] This denial of local Guaraní agency in claiming territory was further elaborated through references to the role of NGOs in ethnic mobilization and the construction of a territorial claim. The following passage from my 2009 interview with Winston Mignolo is illustrative:

> MIGNOLO: I want to tell you something in relation to the conflict—and I can back this up in any debate. These are *created* conflicts, Penelope.
>
> PA: Before the [titling] process, was the relation [between Guaraní and non-Guaraní] good?
>
> MIGNOLO: Before the process, the relation was fine, before the TCO the relation . . . there have always been—not only in the Guaraní zone but in all the country—there were problems between workers and *patrones*; there's always been that. That's a reality; we're not going to deny it. [There was] a certain kind of imposition by some landowners, that's true . . . but what I want to get at is that there are *interests*, and who manages those interests? It's the same people who have obtained a lot of resources—millions and millions of resources from international cooperation to improve the life of those people [the Guaraní]. And how have they improved the life of the Guaraní after more than twenty years in the zone?
>
> PA: Are you talking about the NGOs [*instituciones de apoyo*]?
>
> MIGNOLO: About some NGOs, some *instituciones de apoyo*, specifically in O'Connor Province. That's like an open secret, which one can't complain about, because Tarija lacks documentary evidence of many things . . . but it's popular knowledge; many families who are beneficiaries [of NGO salaries] have got rich on the money that came for them [the Guaraní]—that's not fair. So what suits them? It suits them to have us divided . . . For me, those [organizations] are to blame for the bad [i.e., unfair] titling, because it was with their resources that they paid for the land titling.

In this passage, a measured acknowledgment of the master-slave relations that prevailed in Itika Guasu prior to Guaraní resurgence (forced by my question) is quickly masked by the depiction of interethnic conflict as a product of the self-serving activities of NGOs. Rather than being agents of their own history, the Guaraní appear as passive victims of manipulation by outside interests. Private claimants, by contrast, are framed not as self-interested actors but as the defenders of a harmonious *chaqueño* social order in the face of these foreign interventions (by both local NGOs and the global sponsors of SAN-TCO, which are conflated in Mignolo's account). The effect is to displace the Guaraní's territorial claim from the realm of citizenship (as a response to a long history of non-recognition), reframing it as emanating from *outside* the territory and the nation.

This denial of Guaraní political agency and citizenship claims was even more explicit in the account of Beatriz, who speculated:

> I think they [the NGOs] have trained [the Guaraní] like that, with the idea that the land belongs to the indigenous sector. And this is something I've felt and I've heard and I've seen various times—that no, the indigenous person has rights, the indigenous people are *originarios*, that they have rights and the *terceros* (third parties) don't, and some people have transmitted that in the minds of the indigenous people, but the thing is . . . it made us [feel] a bit like this: that they wanted to do us *harm* . . . but they didn't succeed because at the end of the day we live on the same piece of ground [*terreno*], and we have to live as a community, always united.

Once again the implication is that NGOs unsettled otherwise stable and harmonious interethnic relations within the territory. As Oswaldo Cortez acknowledged, reflecting on his delicate positionality as a non-indigenous land claimant and CERDET employee: "CERDET is the wolf of the cattle ranchers, just like the Equipo de Apoyo, like INRA—it's the wolf of the cattle ranchers . . . [They think] it's the fault of the NGOs that now the Guaranís are . . . a strengthened organization and everything." Underlying this imaginary (in which the Guaraní are analogous to lambs or calves) is a settler claim to sovereignty, which implies not only rights to land but also ownership of Guaraní bodies.

A similar argument was presented in a newspaper article published in the elite-owned Tarijeño newspaper *El País* on July 1, 2006. Based on an interview with Winston Mignolo, the article reads as follows:

In Tacuarandi, O'Connor
Two NGOs Promote Conflict over Land
Community members from Tacuarandi hold responsible a few NGOs, like CERDET and the Equipo de Apoyo al Pueblo Guaraní, for bringing to this zone a confrontation between *campesinos* and indigenous people over land, through a bad titling process implemented by INRA in 2000.

"Through the intervention of a few NGOs they've created discrimination, these money-grabbing Machiavellians employ the principle of "divide and rule," denounced the representative of some *campesinos*, [Winston Mignolo], not ruling out a kind of war for land. The complainant, indicating that the NGOs do whatever they want without any oversight, has acquired substantial documentation which he intends to send to the embassies of the countries that finance this type of organization.

Capable of Anything

"They should find out what they are donating money to and what they do with this money," he emphasized, warning that the *campesinos* are capable of anything in order to make people respect their land rights, which is a highly sensitive issue, concerning their whole life's work.

INRA carried out a land titling process, establishing a Native Community Land (TCO) for the indigenous people with an area of 216,000 hectares; however, 80 percent of this plot is occupied by *campesino* families.

Land Titling

As a consequence, the indigenous people, with the argument of the TCO and the support of the NGOs, tried to evict the *campesinos* from the land which, according to them, they have occupied since their ancestors, and [they claim] the land titling was very badly undertaken.

"We're on the brink of a new Pananti," [Mignolo] again warned. In Pananti, Gran Chaco, there was a bloody confrontation between the landless settlers [from the Landless Peasants Movement] and cattle ranchers over this issue, with the tragic toll of eight people dead at the beginning of this decade.

Violating Their Rights

The *campesina* [name removed] said that the indigenous people are starting to violate their rights with the argument of being owners of the land and that the *campesinos* are tenants, they expect payment in calves, "no one gives [help] to us like the NGOs give to them," she said.

"We lived here before the Chaco War, we feel like natives from here, a year ago the NGOs took away four families from Tacuarandi, where we live, that started the conflict, they're committing violations," complained the *campesino* [a relative of Beatriz, name removed].

This article powerfully illustrates how local elites like Mignolo used the notion of NGOs as self-serving "outsiders" with links to shady foreign interests, who are seeking to undermine the agrarian social order of the Chaco, as a way to bolster an emergent alliance with peasant communities excluded from the titling process owing to misinformation and economic disadvantage. Landowners' connections with the owners of regional news media facilitated the wide dissemination of such discourses.

Relational Histories, Selective Sovereignties

The foregoing examples demonstrate how non-indigenous land claimants in Itika Guasu justify their claims by drawing on a repertoire of discourses of rights, rooted in a history of colonial settlement, nation building, and agrarian reform. These discourses do not operate in isolation. As I have shown, arguments about the productive function of property are interwoven with liberal discourses of equal rights; competing claims to native status are bound up with past experiences of nation building; critiques of NGO intervention mask racialized claims to sovereignty over indigenous lands and bodies. Together, these discourses reveal how "localized land rights became articulated through relational histories of nation" (Moore 2005: 4). As Tomy Crespo observed:

> Who gave [settlers] lands there? . . . It's the state that gave them that right . . . A fact: there was legal slavery in Bolivia until 1952.[28] And you had the right to exploit the indigenous slaves [*pongos*] according to the law, and no slave could leave your property without punishment. If you didn't punish him, national justice would punish him. Why? Because the Indian didn't have the right to *citizenship*.

Whereas Guaraní claims to citizenship are fundamentally revisionist—based on making visible this historical violence and exclusion—private property claims rest on a defense of the racialized citizenship project from which settlers historically gained rights to indigenous land and labor. Rather than acknowledging that Guaraní speak from *within* the nation, or for a sovereignty that predates the nation, indigenous claims were situated *outside* the nation, as a product of self-serving interventions by foreign-funded NGOs. Furthermore, Guaraní land claims are framed as *a threat* to the nation—its economic productivity, liberal justice system, geographical borders, and origin myths of frontier conquest. The Guaraní's true relationship with the nation, this discourse implies, is through their bonds to their *patrones*, whose discipline and tutelage is required to transform them into civilized and productive subjects. Guaraní efforts to transform land relations by drawing on multicultural discourses of indigenous rights were thus thwarted by "previous sedimentations," which "remained consequential" for local enactments of rights in the Bolivian Chaco. State recognition of indigenous rights did not prove decisive in a frontier region where "selective sovereignties" continued to "compete with state assertions of absolute authority"—and where state officials themselves questioned the legitimacy of indigenous land claims (Moore 2005: 3).

As the 2011 ASOGAPO meeting highlights, shared discourses of rights have played a crucial role in mobilizing a heterogeneous local non-indigenous population in collective actions to obstruct and contest the TCO titling process in Itika Guasu. Despite the fact that these private claimants themselves embodied divergent "relational histories" of nation, they found common ground as non-Guaraní settlers in a region long defined by the "right of conquest" (Soruco 2011). This conjunctural alliance served the interests of both elite and poorer land claimants, allowing the former (many of whom are absentee landlords) to appropriate discourses of productive land use and place-based *campesino* identity, and enabling the latter to access elitist networks of non-indigenous power within the regional context. Shared discourses of rights underpinned concrete actions to block or distort the application of legal norms, adding moral argument to personal connections and political clout.

In the final section of this chapter, I turn my attention to a factor that played a crucial role in how racialized discourses of rights shaped the application of law in Itika Guasu, the ever present threat of violence. Strategically mobilized by land claimants and instinctively felt by Guaraní communities, this threat of violence had the effect of producing a continual recourse to informal negotiation—an approach that worked to contain Guaraní aspirations of "reclaiming territory" through the TCO titling process.

Vernacularizing Law in the Shadow of Violence

Anticipating that TCO titling would be a conflictive process, the INRA Law promotes the use of informal negotiations between indigenous claimants and "third parties"—specifically to determine the boundaries of indigenous communal spaces and private properties during INRA's fieldwork. In Itika Guasu, official documentation suggests that such agreements occurred in seventeen of twenty-seven Guaraní communities initially measured within the TCO area (INRA, n.d.: 18). Yet the use of informal negotiations in Itika Guasu went far beyond this initial mapping work. These informal negotiations—conducted at the margins of the law and in spaces conditioned by racialized inequality—emerged as a key mechanism through which private landowners (with INRA Tarija's and CERDET's collusion) neutralized the redistributive potential of the TCO titling process.

In 2003, following the first significant wave of collective landowner mobilization (discussed earlier), INRA Tarija instigated thirty-four "roundtable negotiations" (*mesas de concertación*) in an effort to defuse tensions and prevent landowners from presenting further legal complaints before the National Agrarian Tribunal. As one CERDET report describes the context for these agreements: "The cattle ranchers gained strength and made claims but now in an organized manner, and for that reason INRA was obliged to instigate CONCILIATION acts between communities and cattle ranchers with the objective of avoiding greater social conflicts" (CERDET 2008: 5). Another internal CERDET document (no title, n.d. [2010?]) reports that forty-three such informal agreements were made between cattle ranchers and Guaraní communities, in order "to make the process viable and avoid legal challenges" to the legal results of titling. These roundtable negotiations succeeded in this immediate goal, reducing the number of legal challenges by third parties from one hundred to seven. This achievement came at a cost, however; in most cases, "the APG IG ceded spaces in favor of third parties" (CERDET 2008: 5). This is confirmed by INRA documentation of the "conciliation acts" (*actas de conciliación*) that resulted from these negotiations, photocopies of which I obtained from CERDET. These documents show that in twenty-one of thirty-four properties subject to *mesas de concertación*, indigenous representatives agreed to an increase in the number of cattle recorded by INRA officials during fieldwork, thereby enabling the private claimant to justify land that would otherwise have been reverted to the TCO (Actas de Concertación 2003; INRA 2008b).[29] Interviews with Guaraní leaders involved in these negotiations shed light on how such agreements were reached. Celestino described how, typically, Guaraní leaders agreed to halve the area of a planned property reduction:

> [Third parties] accepted the reductions, but through a process of negotiation. If they had a reduction of 50 percent, well, there they entered into the *mesas de concertación*, there we arrived: "Look, we don't want that, what can we do? That reduces a lot." [And so we agreed to] half and half [i.e., to halve the proposed property reduction]. They had 50 [percent of the original reduction] for each party—50 for the TCO and 50 for them . . . That isn't in the law, but that's what we call informal agreement.

As CERDET noted, such agreements constituted "a flexible application of the [legal] norm and adjusted fieldwork documents, that is, they modified the FES files and these constitute UNTOUCHABLE documents . . . violat[ing] the rights of the communities," although, the author adds, "at the time it was a measure that [INRA] considered the most appropriate for avoiding bigger confrontations and conflicts in the zone" (2008: 5). In light of this doctoring of official legal documents—and despite INRA Tarija's role in instigating and overseeing these agreements—in June 2008 INRA pronounced them illegal and demanded the revision of all affected property files, which it referred to the National Agrarian Tribunal (CERDET 2008). Thus, while the Guaraní participated in these irregular and unfavorable negotiations (under pressure from both CERDET and INRA) in a bid to advance with the legal consolidation of their TCO claim, these agreements ended up bringing further delays to the titling process and generating an additional layer of legal confusion.

In light of these events, it is unsurprising that some Guaraní leaders in Itika Guasu reflected critically on the *mesas de concertación*. As Teodoro lamented, "Everything was an error . . . we ceded a lot." He complained, "[INRA] pressured us a lot to sign the agreements . . . because they had to finish the titling as soon as possible." This again points to the state's collusion in the containment of Guaraní territorial rights—in part owing to INRA's target-driven culture and concern with "making territory legible" (as opposed to decolonizing territory).[30] APG IG president Nestor Borrero criticized the roundtable agreements as just another delaying tactic of the Bolivian state:

> It's part of the strategy of the structure of this state to block [titling progress]; it's been the clearest strategy of delay, delay, delay, intensify, pacify, and not reach a conclusion . . . We had a clear idea that the agreements were to accelerate the process when in the end they told us that making agreements had no legal value . . . These were clear strategies for not arriving at the central objective that we, the indigenous peoples, had: concluding the titling.

Despite these critical reflections, most Guaraní leaders and NGO staff I interviewed continued to argue that the informal agreements were necessary *at the time*. This was partly because, as noted earlier, they saw no alternative means of overcoming the legal paralysis resulting from third parties' complaints before the TAN. As one CERDET employee put it: "What would have happened if we hadn't arrived at agreements? All the third parties would have challenged the titling process; they would have blocked the possibility of the process advancing . . . We would have waited much longer with this process."

Yet interviews also point to another factor underlying the decision to enter into these agreements. As the Guaraní leader Angelo explained in 2009:

> The law is the theoretical part, you see? In practice, it's another thing, isn't it? It's not applied; if the law had to be applied, it would start to generate many conflicts. Following the law, there is an internal negotia-

tion. One can negotiate the law internally [that is, in informal negotiations between interested parties] beyond the [official norms of] law . . . You can't generate conflicts there. We have to look after the integrity of the communities, where they live, the Guaraní people, the peasant farmers . . . We can't start a fire. If we allow a fire to start, how are you going to put it out?

As this observation reveals, the recourse to informal negotiations responded not only to the cattle ranchers' ability to obstruct the titling progress but also to their willingness to defend their property claims with violence. Through his metaphorical reference to "starting a fire" (by refusing to cede ground to landowners), Angelo expresses his fear that interethnic conflict resulting from confrontations over land rights in the TCO could quickly spread. For Guaraní communities that, unlike many private claimants, have literally nowhere else to go, the implications could be severe. Reading between the lines of Angelo's remarks, we could reflect that the "integrity of communities" involves not only protection from violence but also (asymmetrical) interethnic relations of labor, property access, exchange of goods, and co-parentage—relations whose breakdown could exacerbate vulnerable Guaraní households' existing difficulties in accessing land or sustaining precarious livelihoods (see chapter 4).

If Angelo's view of the law as a flexible instrument might appear divergent from a statist vision, this was not generally the case in Tarija Department. INRA employees I spoke to—whether ideologically opposed or sympathetic to indigenous land rights—also seemed to take for granted the impossibility of applying "the dead letter of the law" in the face of local landowner opposition. As former INRA employee, CCGT affiliate, and certified lawyer Erick told me:

> Of course, beyond what you can apply as the dead letter [of the law], I think that everything is done according to . . . to how you see it *socially*, because even if the law is rather complex . . . if you have this experience on the ground, you realize that you're fucking up people's lives. So you realize that the law was elaborated not by people who have lived the reality of the zone, but rather by bureaucrats who had a different vision . . . Obviously, if you applied the law inflexibly, it would generate more conflicts.

Nolberto Gallado, who was director of INRA Tarija in 2009, took a similar view: "Regarding the flexible application [*flexibilización*], well, it's obvious, isn't it? One thing is what is written in law; another thing is what one does on the ground—in practice, let's say, isn't it? So you have to apply the law flexibly [*flexibilizar*]." Jorge Campero, who headed the agency from 2000 to 2004 and oversaw the *mesas de concertación*, justified them in the following manner:

The Guaraní sector recognized certain limits with the landowners in such a way that they also gained a certain space. And they did it through agreement [*conciliando*]. You know that in the agrarian issue, conciliation is the best way to solve a conflict because . . . if you just impose the law in favor of one party, the other is going to be in an injured position; they're going to continue making problems.

These statements convey a pragmatic acceptance of the impossibility of implementing indigenous land rights in practice in the Chaco as outlined in national and international law. Underlying this acceptance, as these statements make explicit, is the de facto sovereignty of non-indigenous landowners within the territory, and their willingness to use violence against those who challenge that power—including state officials.

This threat of violence was not just a reality experienced by INRA, APG IG leaders, and NGO staff; it also constitutes a central element of third parties' discourse, used to pressure regional and national institutions into responding to their demands. As Winston Mignolo warned in a 2009 interview:

I feel that this issue is a time bomb . . . Because you can't come and say to a non-Guaraní producer of the zone: . . . "You know what, sir? It turns out you're in this TCO. You don't belong here, it's a legally indigenous territory of the Guaranís, so you have to pick up your little house, your things, and go." You can't do it! I think many people are going to prefer to stay there until the bitter end [*hasta las últimas consecuencias*]; if they have to die there, they will do it . . . We've already seen it; there have been deaths over this issue. So it's the responsibility of the leaders, of the authorities, not to politicize this issue.

This statement echoes the 2007 newspaper article cited earlier, in which Mignolo is quoted as predicting "a kind of war for land" if third-party complaints were not addressed, and warns that "we're on the brink of a new Pananti"—a reference to a bloody massacre of members of the Movimiento sin Tierra (Landless Peasants' Movement, MST) by a local landowning militia that took place on October 24, 2001, in the neighboring province of Gran Chaco.[31] These warnings were reiterated in ASOGAPO affiliates' correspondence with state authorities, as these examples illustrate:

The *campesinos* have made the decision that they will defend their properties with their own lives . . . If in the future there should be a loss of human life due to this conflict, it will be the responsibility of the relevant authorities who are denying the right of the *campesinos* to be listened to. (letter from the provincial deputy of O'Connor Province to Land Ministry, March 28, 2008, accompanying forty-one individual complaints from cattle ranchers of Itika Guasu)

We don't want to spill blood among *campesinos* and Guaranís; that's why we want them to attend to our demands as soon as possible. (complaint to INRA, November 15, 2007)

The affected parties resolve to make everyone respect their lands and their ownership of these until the last consequences and they will not be responsible for events that could occur in the zone of Itika Guasu. (act from meeting of cattle ranchers, December 22, 2007)

Relations are tense, with a possible emergence of a new Pananti, like that which happened in the Chaco. (letter from third-party resident of Itika Guasu to President Evo Morales, December 28, 2007)

Despite their vivid references to blood being spilled and lives lost, the authors absolve themselves of responsibility for potential violence instigated by them or their allies, on the grounds that violence is an *inevitable* and *justifiable* outcome of the violation of private property—presented here not as a legal right granted by the state, but as an expression of the inviolability of settler sovereignty over "territories of conquest" (Soruco 2011). This sheds important light on the nature and limits of state power in postcolonial frontier regions, where many indigenous people live (Das and Poole 2004). Contravening Max Weber's (1919) characterization of the modern nation-state as "the sole source of the 'right' to use violence," private claimants in Itika Guasu "reserved the right" to use violence *against* the state to defend their own sovereignty claims. Once again, this must be seen as rooted in a history in which state sovereignty in the Chaco has been predicated on, and functioned through, settler control of indigenous territory and bodies (see chapter 1). It was this hitherto unshaken alliance between state and settler sovereignty claims that the TCO titling process called into question.

As I have shown, these "selective sovereignties" (Moore 2005) had profound consequences for the implementation of indigenous land rights. Beyond adapting, or vernacularizing, global and national norms to fit local meanings (Merry 2006), private claimants raised the more fundamental questions "Who has the right to have rights?" and "Who has the right to allocate land?" While the rights of settlers were presented as preceding and transcending state law, the Guaraní's rights—although framed by the Guaraní as prior to those of the state or settlers—are eclipsed altogether. By denying the Guaraní "the right to have rights," this discourse returns them to their colonial status as "non-persons with respect to justice" (Fraser 2005).

It is worth reflecting on what made the Guaraní TCO claim so unsettling for local landowners. Describing Guaraní Tüpaist messianic movements during the colonial period, Bret Gustafson argues that what made these so subversive was the fact that they involved "mimicking or appropriating symbols of colonial authority." Such performances were "invariably met with excesses of colonial violence that pursued order through terror." As Gustafson notes, a century later the Guaraní "again questioned the racial and political order . . . now in a language of NGO development projects, the intercultural reforms of the state, and global visions of indigenous rights (2009: 34, 38; see also Bhabha 1994: 85–92). Their appropriation of state cartography and law—the epistemological basis of settler land claims—toward these ends unsettled the very foundations of *karai* identity at the Chaco frontier.

In this context, informal negotiations constituted a space at the margins of the law within which legal norms could be renegotiated, taking into account these selective sovereignties and their propensity to be defended through violence. For the Guaraní, whose legal-cartographic strategy relied on the scaling down of nationally recognized rights, this opened the way for the sacrifice of their own historically grounded territorial sovereignty claims. Informal agreements made recognition of indigenous land rights contingent on the compliance of actors with whom the Guaraní were engaged in intimate and asymmetrical relationships of dependency, patronage, and land competition. Local NGOs' (as well as INRA Tarija's) endorsement of these agreements reinforced the idea that indigenous rights were subject to negotiation. As some critics pointed out, NGOs were themselves embedded in relations with state and landowner interests, and faced pressure to report titling "success" to international donors (Ferguson 1990).

Informal agreements with landowners were not the only way in which the Guaraní responded to this climate of mobilized opposition, legal paralysis, and threats of violent conflict. In 2002, encouraged by both CERDET and INRA, APG IG leaders made the decision to opt for what is called "partial titling." While the regular procedure for SAN-TCO is to complete the legal technical evaluation for *all land claims* within the TCO, then proceed to the awarding of individual and communal titles, a "partial titling" strategy implies focusing resources in the first instance on issuing titles to communal areas that are uncontested by individual claimants. The result was that the Guaraní were awarded title to much of the land that Guaraní communities already controlled sooner than they might otherwise have been (through the two awards issued in 2002 and 2008); but the more contentious task of reclaiming land occupied by private landowners who failed to fulfill the FES was put on hold—for what turned out to be an indefinite period.[32] Guaraní and NGO staff had mixed views on this decision; although it did give rise to a first title in 2002—enabling the APG IG, as well as NGOs and

INRA, to show "progress" (to communities, donors, and national authorities, respectively)—this amounted to "paper progress" in so far as it brought no real change in land occupation. As the national president of the APG explained to me in 2009, many Guaraní TCO claims have followed a similar legal pathway:

> Legally, [in Itika Guasu] we have 68,000 hectares. So that's been happening . . . at a national level, all [TCOs] are in this process: there's a title, but they haven't finished; they haven't arrived at the reallocation of the [private] property reductions . . . In reality, I believe that the land that's been titled . . . was *our own land*. The state hasn't awarded land to the indigenous peoples.

As this leader astutely observes, the "partial titling" strategy transformed a process that had initially promised a redistribution of TCO land in favor of indigenous claimants into a mere process of recognition of rights to areas indigenous communities already occupied. By focusing on "uncontested areas," INRA and the APG IG may have avoided violent conflict, but they also disappointed communities' aspirations for "reclaiming territory."

Just as the process of mapping indigenous territorial demands had squeezed these into spaces between urban centers and state boundaries, TCO titling slotted indigenous land rights into an established geography of private non-indigenous land claims. As this chapter has detailed, this was a product of both legal norms (shaped by pressure from landowner organizations) and the law's flexible and incomplete application in a context of entrenched colonial discourses, racialized power inequalities, and "selective sovereignties" that challenged the state's authority to allocate land. In so far as it mainly gave the Guaraní rights to uncontested land they already occupied, TCO titling resonates with critiques of state multiculturalism as offering indigenous peoples limited forms of cultural recognition that fail to challenge dominant power relations in society (Hale 2002; Rivera Cusicanqui 2012: 99–100).

An important consequence is that—reflecting the geography of *karai* settlement—the areas titled to the Guaraní tend to be the least productive lands in the TCO, consisting largely of slopes in the foothills of the TCO's three mountain ranges, or arid lands along the banks of rivers. As one female Guaraní community member from Tentaguasu complained:

> We don't have flat land . . . the only part that belongs to us is peaks, roads . . . The private properties have land for growing: the large ones are twenty hectares, forty hectares. In contrast, we don't have [flat, productive land], so that is what we also want to have, you see: land, but like that—flat.

Her complaints are supported by this map (figure 9), which demonstrates that the areas of the TCO titled to the Guaraní are predominantly those with the greatest incline. This becomes even more striking if we bear in mind that the largest flat area titled to the Guaraní (just north of the Pilcomayo River) was purchased privately by the Swiss-funded NGO EAPG.

This tendency to award indigenous claimants the least productive lands was exacerbated by the fact that—in the context of informal agreements and landowner-state collusions—third parties facing property reductions have in

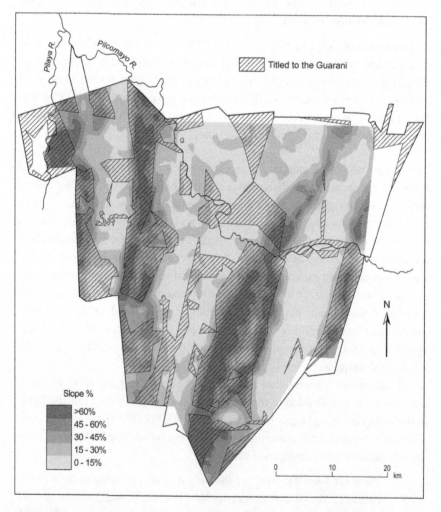

FIGURE 9. Map of Itika Guasu showing land incline and TCO titling results (elaborated by Cartographic Unit, Department of Geography, University of Cambridge, based on incline map elaborated by CERDET employee Ángelo Lozano)

many cases been able to *choose* which part of their property will be reduced and reallocated.

In light of this, many Guaraní complain that the TCO titling process benefited third parties more than it benefited them. As one APG IG representative from Mokomakal complained in 2011: "It's only recognized land for the cattle ranchers; above all, it's giving more to them, but not to the claimants like us." It is not only the results of TCO titling that have favored third-party claimants but also its lack of conclusion. Because of a failure to implement property reductions, many private claimants continue to occupy, work, and fence land despite their claims' having been assessed as illegitimate by INRA. Had SAN-TCO advanced through all its legal stages, the state would have been (at least according to legal norms) obliged to compensate indigenous claimants with any lands "deducted" from the TCO as private property, either by adding adjacent state lands to the TCO or, if no such lands were available, by the state's purchase (through forced sale) of third-party properties. In Itika Guasu, these final redistributive procedures—in addition to the reallocation of property reductions—have failed to materialize.

Reflecting on these ambivalent outcomes, another APG IG leader, Román (who will appear in later chapters), concluded that TCO titling had proved to be a "double-edged sword." Articulating perhaps the most common complaint of all, he lamented that Itika Guasu was being titled "in little pieces" instead of as a single continuous territory.[33] He emphasized that this ran contrary to the Guaraní's territorial vision and land use practices. Using a popular metaphor, he complained that TCO titling "shuts you in a room," when the Guaraní "live in a single house, a single patio." Although he used the Spanish *patio* (courtyard), the reference here is to the Guaraní *oka*, a shared communal space (see chapter 4) that in this context symbolizes cultural differences in how land is imagined and inhabited. The implication was that TCO titling had failed to recognize or accommodate Guaraní ways of life (*ñande reko*). While the Guaraní had demanded "territory," TCO titling offered only "land." For many Guaraní, the failure to achieve rights to a single contiguous territory is interpreted as a failure of the legal-cartographic strategy in general. As another man put it: "We began thinking of reclaiming and consolidating the territory, but it hasn't been easy. Up till now we haven't managed to consolidate 100 percent; TCO Itika Gausu still hasn't been achieved." Nor did there seem to be any prospect of further legal progress. On August 27, 2009, the APG IG wrote to the Vice Ministry of Land demanding an indefinite suspension of the TCO titling process in Itika Guasu. As chapter 5 details, this decision was catalyzed by escalating conflict over the governance of hydrocarbons in the TCO. Yet the letter also denounces the fragmentary outcomes of TCO titling, insisting on the Guaraní's desire to maintain "the INTEGRITY of the TCO."

The dynamics that produced these results were subject to in-depth analysis and debate in APG assemblies I attended in 2008–9. Many APG IG leaders were able to expound at length on how landowners' political maneuvers, institutionalized power inequalities, and hydrocarbon interests (see chapter 5) had obstructed their territorial claim. Yet for many Guaraní community members, the titling process and its dynamics remained opaque. As one elderly *mburuvicha* from Ñaurenda put it in 2009:

> The government isn't fulfilling; it hasn't given us the territory that it had to give us. I don't know what exactly [is the problem], but there is no solution for us as the Guaraní people. And we have many; we have the family that is suffering from not having land to work; that's why we, as leaders, are fighting for our territory . . . I don't know why, and we continue the fight and we continue waiting . . . We're waiting for results from government to government; I don't know, it isn't a decision where I can say, "Well, we should [get land]."

This sense of powerlessness, of simply "waiting for results," stands in stark contrast to the sense of agency and empowerment that many Guaraní experienced during the early years of the land struggle (see chapter 1).

This is not to suggest that all Guaraní expressed the same view about the titling process, which has had uneven effects; while some communities remain hemmed in by private properties, others have significantly improved their land access. As the next chapter demonstrates, such inequalities have themselves created conflict between neighboring communities, undermining the vision of a single shared territory. Nor do I wish to suggest that the TCO titling process has had no positive effects in general. As many Guaraní emphasize, as part of a broader process of making visible their territorial claims and challenging ethnic power inequalities within the regional context, the process has had a profound and lasting importance. TCO titling provided a central agglutinating force for the Guaraní movement for two decades, both in Itika Guasu and nationally (Albó 2012). As chapter 5 details, the Guaraní have also used TCO status—irrespective of titling outcomes—to make far-reaching claims for territorial control in the context of hydrocarbon development. Nevertheless, in terms of historically grounded material aspirations for "reclaiming territory"—understood as a collectively owned and internally contiguous Guaraní space—the legal-cartographic strategy of TCO titling has failed to deliver. In communities of Itika Guasu, people experience these results not in legal or cartographic terms but in everyday life—as ongoing land scarcity, restricted mobility, malnutrition, labor migration, and resource competition with *karai* (and Guaraní) neighbors. The next chapter takes us to Tarairí community, in the heart of Itika Guasu, to explore these lived realities and their relationship to the TCO titling process.

INHABITING TERRITORY

Land and Livelihoods in Tarairí

I first met Armando in the context of a medical emergency that brought him to Tarija city in late June 2011.¹ During our initial meeting, he generously agreed to host me for six months in his home in Tarairí (a pseudonym), one of the more remote communities of Itika Guasu, located on the southern bank of the Pilcomayo River at the heart of the TCO. We'd arranged that I would contact him over a radio connection installed at Tarairí's health clinic to confirm the timing of my arrival in Entre Ríos several weeks later. There he would meet me and accompany me to Tarairí for an initial visit, in which I would seek consent from other community members regarding my proposed stay. This plan proved easier in theory than in practice. I made several journeys to the APG IG office in Entre Ríos in early July, only to discover that the radio connection with Tarairí's health clinic—the community's only means of communication with the outside world—was broken.² With no other means of reaching Armando, I finally resorted to announcing my arrival over a Tarija-based radio station, Radio ACLO Tarija. Although he got the message, my next arrival in Entre Ríos (from an APG assembly in Villamontes) was not until the evening, by which time he had returned to the community.

It was with great relief that I finally found Armando in Entre Ríos on APG business several days later. After stocking up with provisions, we boarded a cramped and battered bus for Tarairí that same afternoon. The journey took us eastward along the cliff-edge dirt road toward Villamontes, then turned north into TCO Itika Guasu along another, even bumpier dirt road. A flat tire extended the journey slightly beyond its usual three and a half hours. As we bumped along sharing coca and pure alcohol, Armando told me more about the community. He talked about the newly completed road that had, for the first time in history, made Tarairí accessible by vehicle, claiming credit for relentlessly lobbying the Guaraní municipal representative to secure its construction. He talked proudly about his roles in the APG IG, as zonal education representative and health and infrastructure officer for Tarairí. Although the latter two roles were self-designated, he claimed to be well qualified for both, having learned traditional medicine from his mother and worked in numerous casual construction jobs.

When we finally arrived at *el cruce* (the crossroads), it was already dark. The walk to the community, along the newly graveled (but now largely invisible) road through dense Chaco forest, took us nearly two hours owing to the large amount of baggage we were carrying. I lugged a backpack, a rucksack, bedding, and a five-liter container of sunflower oil, while Armando hauled a huge backpack containing rice, potatoes, pasta, batteries, fruit, candles, coca, yerba mate (a caffeine-rich herb used for tea), onions, and other items unavailable in the community. He was drunk by the time we began walking and struggled to bear his load. By the time we arrived in Tarairí, it was 10:30 and most of the community were already asleep, their beds strewn casually across the ground in front of identical plastered adobe houses, which stood clustered around a large central courtyard. Given that Armando had told me that he lived "on his own," I was somewhat relieved to meet his partner, Sandra, and three children.[3]

The assembly regarding my stay took place the following afternoon. Around twenty people came, representing all of Tarairí's thirteen households. All were Guaraní and most were women, many of the men being away for casual jobs in Entre Ríos or beyond. They sat in a rough circle on makeshift benches outside the house of the elderly *mburuvicha*, Fausto. Following an introduction by Armando (in Guaraní), a speech by me (in very poor Guaraní), and Armando's reiteration (at my request) that I was not doing either an agricultural development project or a statistical survey, community members spoke in turn endorsing my visit. In the discussion that followed, I received a warm welcome and a new name: Kuñati.[4]

In this chapter, I draw on my experiences in Tarairí and surrounding communities to explore the lived realities of land and livelihoods in Itika Guasu, both beyond and in relation to the TCO titling process.[5] Existing literature on indigenous land titling has tended to focus on procedural obstacles and legal-cartographic outcomes, ignoring the implications of these processes for ordinary indigenous community members. Yet such an analysis is imperative if we are to measure the potential of land titling against "the political struggles it derives from and is intended to advance" (Wainwright and Bryan 2009: 169). As chapter 1 revealed, it is at a local level that indigenous land claims acquire meaning, in relation to lived experiences of racialized dispossession and continuing problems of land inequality. This chapter makes two key arguments. First, I expose how the legal consolidation—and unresolved status—of private land claims in the TCO presents severe restrictions on Guaraní communities' access to land and resources, making subsistence livelihoods increasingly unviable. Second, I show how the fragmentary effects and boundary-fixing logic of the titling process have served to exacerbate resource conflict between Guaraní communities, undermining traditional notions of shared use and negotiated access. Together these dynamics reveal how the titling process failed to meet community members' aspirations for "reclaiming territory," instead further entrenching an exclusionary postcolonial regime of property.

Part one of this chapter, "Enduring Exclusions," describes the location and spatial organization of the community, the hybrid forms of land use and tenure that have emerged from a recent history of dispossession, TCO titling outcomes and their implications for land access and livelihoods, and how community members evaluate the achievements of the land struggle in this context. Part two, "Fixing Boundaries," examines a resource conflict with a neighboring Guaraní community to highlight how the "bright lines" of state land titling—combined with an acute land and resource squeeze—have worked to undermine the fluid relations that characterize Guaraní land use practices, provoking communities to enact their own exclusions. The chapter concludes with a reflection on the lived effects of propertizing territory and the limited capacity of state land titling to redress the legacies—and ongoing processes—of indigenous dispossession.

Enduring Exclusions

Fluid Boundaries

Located on a flat, dry plateau overlooking the Pilcomayo River to the northeast and the Salado River to the south, Tarairí is one of a string of riverside communities that, despite being surrounded by water, inhabit some of the most arid lands of the TCO. To the west, the terrain drops down to several hectares of cleared communal land used for household plots, followed by miles of dense dry forest, cut through by a dirt road. This road, made passable to vehicles following the recent municipal project, now enables regular access to the community by NGOs, the municipal government, and *karai* traders, who come intermittently to buy fish or sell provisions. As noted earlier, the road connects Tarairí to a bus route an hour and a half's walk away, where a bus to Entre Ríos (a three-and-a-half-hour journey) passes every morning.[6] Community members—especially men—frequently make this journey to buy household provisions, attend APG IG meetings, or get to jobs on nearby *karai* haciendas, in the town of Entre Ríos or farther afield.

During my stay, Tarairí had ninety-six residents, distributed among thirteen households, making it an average-sized Guaraní community in Itika Guasu.[7] All households contain members of four generations of one family, generally women, reflecting the uxorilocal structure of traditional Guaraní communities (Gustafson 2011: 110; Albó 1990). Tarairí thus constitutes a traditional *tëtami*, the basic unit of social organization for the Guaraní, in which a group of family members live close together and share a single *oka* (patio) (Gustafson 2011: 88). Houses were spaced a good five to ten meters apart around the periphery of this central communal space, which first became known to me as *la cancha* (the soccer field) and was quickly the cause of a broken ankle. People told me they had insisted on maintaining this distance between homes in the context of a housing project implemented by the NGO EAPG and a local group of Catholic nuns during the 1990s—something that was especially important, given that almost all households kept some chickens, goats, sheep, or pigs. As a legacy of this project, houses shared the same design—wooden beams, plastered adobe walls, ceramic-tiled roof, and a front porch supported by four large pillars. In most cases, part of the previous palm-thatched adobe structure had been maintained for use as a kitchen.

Although indistinguishable from the dirt area beyond it, the space in front of each house was very much part of people's homes, regularly swept and, for those households that enjoyed the shade of a tree,[8] the place where families spent most of their time at home, eating, receiving visitors, drinking maté, doing handicrafts, weaving fishing nets, doing school homework, or sleeping in the heat of the afternoon. As noted earlier, *okape* was also where families slept at night, on *guirapembireta*—wooden bedframes cross-woven with strips of leather. Indoor rooms were essentially used only for storage and for sleeping during the rainy season. I observed the frequency of people's visits to other households, as well as the wide berth they gave those homes not being visited in their walks around the community—an indication of the coexistence of, and fluid boundaries between, private and communal space (discussed later in this chapter). Aside from the houses, the community also contains a basic health clinic and (Spanish-language) primary school, completing the circle of buildings around the central *oka/cancha*.

This uxorilocal family structure, the absence of *karai* households,[9] older women's continuing use of the *mandu*,[10] and the fact that Guaraní was still preferred over Spanish were some of the factors that conjoined to designate Tarairí, at least in the minds of NGO and state employees, as one of Itika Guasu's more "traditional" Guaraní communities. Combined with the community's relatively enthusiastic embrace of NGO projects, this also led one CERDET employee to award Tarairí the dubious title of "a model community."[11] Perhaps reflecting this perception, during my six-month stay, Tarairí was the site of agricultural development projects by both CERDET and the EAPG, as well as a municipal "ecotourism project,"[12] and a weeklong visit by some evangelists, who selected the community as the site for a church. Reflecting a less romantic reality, there were also visits by anti-Chagas fumigators,[13] and a food aid program sponsored by the World Health Organization. As I elaborate later on, this is indicative of the multiple and multi-scalar relations through which community life in Tarairí is reproduced, "traditional" characteristics notwithstanding.

Having provided some brief context regarding Tarairí's spatial location and organization, I now turn to the land situation. I begin with a brief description of land relations prior to the creation of the TCO as context for the discussion that follows on the impacts of the titling process.

Entangled Tenures

Traditionally, Guaraní land tenancy is characterized by individual household plots, managed under a system that combines shifting and continuous cultivation. In the days before *karai* settlement, people recounted that parents and grandparents would walk a long way from the community to find the best land for cultivation, sometimes leaving for a week at a time and constructing a makeshift house so they could "look after the maize." Following the 1930s Chaco War and 1952 agrarian reform, community members in Tarairí saw their land base gradually eroded by *karai* settlement. As noted in chapter 1, people were able to describe in detail how specific areas of land used by their grandparents had been lost to settlers—a process that usually involved a combination of coercion and *engaño* (trickery). Increasingly, subsistence farming required negotiation with *karai* landowners.[14]

The spread of *empatronamiento* practices brought further challenges to Guaraní subsistence farming. This was most dramatic in the case of "captive communities"—those located within the hacienda of the *patrón* for whom community members worked unpaid. Tarairí's situation was slightly different: although the community did come to be located inside a private property (owned by the Mendez family, discussed later in this chapter), the community's men—sometimes accompanied by women and children—worked for *patrones* in the more fertile lands around Timboy (to the west) and Tarupayo (to the south), earning either no wage at all or a pittance. As Tarairí's oldest man, Katuire, recounted, the arrival of the *patrones* signaled both a loss of autonomy for community members and a rupture in the history of land relations in Guaraní territory:

KATUIRE: At that time [before the arrival of the *karai*], there was none of this *tierra mezquina* [restricting access to land]—nothing! . . . All the land had only one owner . . . Then the *karai* appeared, they restricted access [*mezquinaban*], and then [the Guaraní] worked for the *patrón*.

PA: Did you work for the *patrón*?

KATUIRE: Yes, when I was young I worked for the *patrón*. In Timboy . . . he would say, "Come here!" "Okay." "Help me for a day." "Okay." We helped him, even though he didn't pay us anything—he paid two and a half bolivianos [about thirty-six cents according to the 2017 exchange rate].

PA: Two and a half per day?

KATUIRE: Per day we earned, per day—two and a half . . . We sowed like thirty, sixty hectares, and with that he bought a truck; we remained poor . . . We sowed, he sold, and only then would we see the money, but it wasn't enough . . . He had a truck and he sold [maize] in Tarija for a high price. That's why, in time, the *karai* got rich, got *oikokatu* [Guaraní: rich]; he already had money, already had a truck, had a tractor—already had everything. We stayed just like that [*así no más*, i.e., poor].

Accounts differ as to the degree of agency the Guaraní exercised in these labor arrangements; some people (such as Armando's brother-in-law Hermes) suggested they were entered into voluntarily and not everyone in Tarairí worked for the *patrones*, while others (including Fausto) claimed that work was "obligatory" and *patrones* exercised "total control" over their workers. In the context of APG IG efforts to distance themselves from NGOs amidst hydrocarbon negotiations (see chapters 5 and 6), such debates have become highly politicized. By 2011, some APG IG leaders (such as Román) strongly rejected the victimized position constructed by NGO narratives of *empatronamiento*, insisting that the Guaraní "have always been autonomous" and denouncing NGOs as the "new *patrones*." My ethnographic engagements have led me to view *empatronamiento* as a set of complex and heterogeneous relationships that were not devoid of indigenous agency (see also Killick 2008), but were, in most cases, highly exploitative and culturally degrading. As chapter 1 details, memories of "suffering" under *empatronamiento* give meaning to the recent land struggle for many community members. As Alcides, *mburuvicha* of the neighboring community of Itikirenda, recounted:

[A *karai* landowner] took ownership of everything, so then they, our grandfathers, worked as employees, but he didn't pay them. He ordered them around, said what they had to do, so they suffered more than us . . . and then our captains met, the *mburuvicha guasu*, those who are highest; they saw that . . . that we always suffered—so they said: "Enough! Enough working, enough!" . . . We started then to work on our own.

As this highlights, *empatronamiento* marked the Guaraní's loss of control over their land and labor, preventing them from producing territory according to their own cultural practices and needs. It is in this context that "reclaiming territory" gains meaning for many Guaraní people.

Yet even in the days of *empatronamiento*, households in Tarairí continued to practice some subsistence farming—something they achieved through a combination of stealth and informal negotiation with the Mendez family (introduced in the previous chapter), whose estate (now partitioned) surrounds the community. According to Armando's elderly mother, it was women who took charge of growing maize during this period. If this illustrates Guaraní resilience in the face of racialized dispossession, then the situation was hardly ideal. Not only were many community members forced, whether by coercion or circumstance, to work long hours for no wage far from their homes, but also their community itself was the property of a *karai* landowner. In this context, it is easy to see why the idea of "reclaiming territory" resonated with community members in Tarairí. As Pablo, the community's nurse, put it, "When we speak of the TCO, our hope is . . . to live better, without anyone being able to tell us, 'Hey, that's my land, you have to work for free.'"

Today, land use practices in Tarairí combine traditional norms with more recent influences. As in the past, household plots remain an important form of informal land tenancy, although, as I will elaborate, not all households have their own plot, owing to the limited land available. With some caveats and nuances (discussed later), land allocation follows this principle:

> [Community members] have the right to use any unoccupied part of the territory to establish their house, their crops, and the grazing area of their animals . . . When someone has established a determined place for their crops, this usufruct is respected . . . This right also extends to arrivals from other communities, provided they fulfill communal obligations in the new place and have received the approval of the authority and assembly. (Albó 1990: 84–85)

This notion of labor as a basis of property resonates with many indigenous tenure systems (Li, 2014), although it challenges global imaginaries of indigenous territories as "collective" spaces. Ironically, it also resonates with the slogan of Bolivia's 1953 agrarian reform: "la tierra es para quien la trabaja" (land is for those who work it)—a reform that proved instrumental to Guaraní dispossession. As Xavier Albó notes, this Guaraní system of provisional land rights is "completely different from that of the *patrones* that surround them" (Albó 1990: 65). As we will see, however, its exercise in practice is severely curtailed by landowners' continuing presence in the surrounding landscape.

In Tarairí, most household plots were located a short walk from the houses, although others were half an hour away. Despite the general principle outlined earlier, land was also passed down through families. Some discussions pointed to a patriarchal system of land inheritance: five of ten households reported that they had acquired their *potrero* (plot) from an older male relative. Others emphasized that daughters and sisters had equal rights to inherit land, although it is normally men who do farming; for example, although Armando had inherited a plot from his father, he stressed that it also belonged to his sister Rosa, who received an equal share of the harvest. Armando's mother, an elderly widow, also had her own plot, which was being worked on her behalf by one of her male grandchildren who formed part of her household. Pablo emphasized that although men normally inherit land, allocation "depends on need," and if a woman—for example, a single mother—requires land to feed her family, she will be awarded land "by the community." This was demonstrated by Armando's cousin Victoria's all-female household (consisting of Victoria, her young daughter, her older sister, and her elderly mother), who farmed their own plot.

As this reference to "by the community" suggests, individual land use rights and inheritance exist alongside a notion of communal land ownership whereby permission to farm a new plot is granted by the community—or, in some accounts, by the *mburuvicha*. Accounts differed as to the importance of the *mburuvicha*'s role in land allocation. One household reported that they had been "given permission" to farm by Fausto (this was also sometimes referred to as permission "by the APG"); another household said they had requested a plot from the *mburuvicha* but had been told none was available. Armando—who is the son of the former *mburuvicha* and often challenged Fausto's authority—insisted that all community members can make their *potrero* where they want, provided they consult the community. As Victoria elaborated, in some communities the *mburuvicha*'s role in land allocation has been subject to abuses of power (see also Albó 1990; Postero 2007). In Tarairí, the *mburuvicha*'s role in land allocation was both limited and contested.

In fact, a simple dichotomy between individual and community rights breaks down in a context in which land use is subject to flexible negotiation between community members who are all members of one extended family. The continuous reciprocal exchange of food, produce, and labor between households further blurs these boundaries. In the past, Armando's mother told me, labor on household *potreros* was organized communally, and the community used to eat from an *olla común* (common pot). While this no longer happens, the exchange of food between households is still common. Small children could be seen constantly scurrying from house to house bearing dripping fish, jugs of *kaguiye,* or other foodstuffs as part of a perpetual but carefully monitored exchange. I soon learned to participate in these reciprocal food relations, bringing food from Entre Ríos to households that sometimes fed me (often by unexpectedly sending a plate of fish to my host household), providing biscuits when I visited other households to drink mate, and providing fishermen with coca to obtain fish for my own household. My research engagements were sometimes factored into these exchanges.

The Guaraní land struggle and contact with NGOs during the 1990s added a further layer of complexity to these land relations by introducing communal plots. Although initially communal plots were farmed collectively by men, as a means of establishing autonomy from *patrones* (see chapter 1), Tarairí's communal plot is now farmed exclusively by a "women's work group," which receives support from both CERDET and the EAPG, which provide seed, advice, and irrigation infrastructure. This shift in the gendered division of agricultural labor resulted both from male labor migration and from the inability of NGOs to persuade men to dedicate themselves to communal production, in the context of customary individual household production. Produce from Tarairí's communal plot—known as the *koo comunal,* an apt mixture of Guaraní and Spanish—is shared among women who participate in agricultural work, complementing produce from family plots and occasionally providing a small amount of income. This income is quite significant in more fertile communities like Mokomokal, although less so in Tarairí.

As this description illustrates, the impacts of TCO titling overlie a complex and hybrid reality of land relations, an "entangled landscape" (Moore 2005) in which traditional Guaraní tenure arrangements and land use practices have endured colonial dispossession and now coexist in awkward articulation with a racialized regime of property rights, as well as with NGO projects that imagine indigenous peoples as "collective" resource users. I now turn to a description of the legal results of TCO titling in and around Tarairí and what they have meant for everyday practices of land use and land relations in the community.

Titling Outcomes

Tarairí was recognized and measured as a Guaraní communal area during INRA's fieldwork of 2000 and appears on subsequent TCO maps and documentation.[15] As chapter 3 makes clear, this did not mean that this land was automatically awarded to the Guaraní. In fact, because of its location within the Mendez property, Tarairí was excluded from the first TCO land award of 2002—an award that included only "undisputed" TCO land, according to NGOs' and INRA's "partial titling" strategy. Although the Mendezes had gained title to this property following the 1953 agrarian reform, their failure to demonstrate its economic social function resulted in a property reduction. INRA documentation (2008a; 2008b) and my informal discussions with Tarairí community members suggest that the Mendez family initially disputed this reduction but eventually reached an informal agreement with the Tarairí community regarding the size of the reduction. The agreed-upon area was titled to the APG IG on January 25, 2008, as part of the second and more recent TCO award of 27,007 hectares.

This collectively titled area, which contains all Tarairí's thirteen households, in addition to the neighboring community of Yukiporo, leaves Tarairí surrounded on three sides by three private properties (figure 10). Only one of these properties, El Palmar (owned by Simón Mendez), has been recognized and titled under the SAN-TCO process. Yet all three continue to be occupied by private claimants. El Porvenir, the property on the opposite shore of the Pilcomayo River (*la banda*)—which is particularly coveted by people in Tarairí—remains occupied by Roberto Vaca (Beatriz Vaca's father), the former cowhand for the Mendez family, from whom he acquired the property. As related by Beatriz in chapter 3, Vaca has pursued a long, and ultimately unsuccessful, struggle to gain legal rights to his property. He comes into frequent conflict with Guaraní communities over the grazing of his cattle on TCO land and has also come to blows with NGO staff on more than one occasion.

TCO titling has not resulted in a substantial restructuring of land rights in this part of the TCO. Owing to the recognition of private property claims, and a failure to implement property reductions in cases where these were not legally justified, community members of Tarairí enjoy legal rights (as TCO members) to only a small area containing their houses, school, health clinic, communal plot, and several household plots of one to two hectares each, located nearby.[16] While they are *legally* entitled to use any other part of TCO land, as I discuss later, geographical obstacles, customary norms, and intercommunal competition for resources place restrictions on their ability to do so in practice, demonstrating the difference between the state's vision of "land" as an abstract resource and the richly variegated and subjectively experienced "territory" that the Guaraní inhabit.

In fact, Guaraní women and men in Tarairí did not base their evaluation of the gains of TCO titling on a legal-cartographic analysis of the official results. As discussed in chapter 2 and elaborated later in this chapter, most people were unaware of the legal status of property rights or the location of legal boundaries. What was clear to them, however, was that in almost every direction they

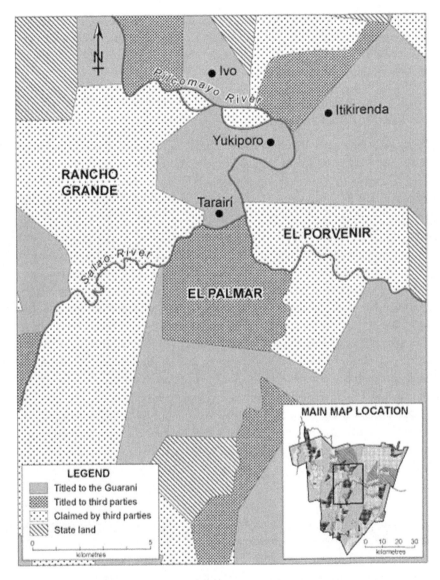

FIGURE 10.   Status of property rights in and around Tarairí in 2017 (elaborated by Cartographic Unit, Department of Geography, University of Cambridge, based on figure 6). Names of private properties and communities have been changed.

walked, they encountered *karai* landowners, many of whom who had erected barbed wire fences around their properties. The use of barbed wire fencing was exacerbated by TCO land titling, whereby property "improvements" are factored into calculations of economic social function. The provision of barbed wire by regional development programs—such as that overseen by José, the state official we met in chapter 3—has also played a role in this. The presence of fenced private properties in the landscape places severe restrictions on Guaraní people's movements and their ability to access land and other natural resources required for their livelihoods, as I now describe.

No Land for the Children

It was early January, and despite scarce rainfall and uncertain climate prospects following a series of recent droughts, most households in Tarairí were busy sowing their *potreros* with maize, squash, black beans, yucca, and watermelon. Armando left for his *potrero* immediately after lunch, at around 11 a.m., and I waited behind with his fifteen-year-old daughter Mabel, who was bringing the seed. While most agricultural work (clearing land, plowing, fencing, and so on) is done by men and boys, as in many Andean indigenous societies it is women who sprinkle seed. Mabel and I watched as her mother, Sandra, prepared three varieties of maize, as well as squash, picking some of it off dried corncobs, scooping some out of food sacks or makeshift containers. She sifted through the seed in a palm-woven bowl, searching for weevils and throwing these to the chickens, then placed a measured quantity of each variety into a small plastic pot, which she gave to Mabel. I followed Mabel over the hill behind the house and down a steep dirt path to a circular *potrero*—several hectares of stick-fenced land, some of which was being farmed by other relatives for their households.

Armando was already hard at work, swinging a hoe from over his head in deft movements to complete a row of shallow trenches in the dry earth. Mabel filled a small rectangular cloth bag with seed, slung this across her shoulder, and then walked slowly along the rows, sprinkling the seed imprecisely into the trenches, a single squash seed for every four or five seeds of maize. I soon found a role for myself, kicking the mounds of loose earth to cover the seed. After an hour or so, we stopped to rest under the shade of a large tree (figure 11). As we chewed coca, I took the opportunity to broach the subject of the land situation in the community. While it was not the first time we had discussed this—Armando frequently told me that land was the community's number one problem—now, sitting contemplating his half-sown *potrero*, he conveyed to me more emphatically than ever before his frustration. The community was growing, and there simply wasn't enough land to go around for the children, he complained. His anxiety was perhaps exacerbated by the fact that his partner, Sandra, was at the time pregnant with twins, in addition to his three existing children.

Contemplating the prospect of growing land scarcity and food insecurity, he articulated a specific aspiration I had not heard before: that all of the land on this side of the Salado River—that is, the entire property of Rancho Grande—be

FIGURE 11. Armando (with Mabel) contemplates his *potrero* (the visible part is cleared but unsown) (photo by author)

confiscated from Mendez and awarded to the community. (His use of "the community" and not "the TCO" here is significant, reflecting the persistence of informal notions of community usufruct rights, the collective nature of TCO titling notwithstanding—a point I return to later on.) He justified the claim by noting that Mendez doesn't even work the land himself but employs people from the community to do so. These people include Armando's brother-in-law Jesús, whom Mendez employs casually as an agricultural laborer. Armando's complaints not only expressed the frustration community members feel regarding the limited land available for farming but also called into question the legitimacy of *karai* landowners' control over the surrounding landscape. Although based on the Guaraní's historically grounded demands for "reclaiming territory," this questioning was framed within a national discourse of the "social function of property," enshrined in refracted terms in the SAN-TCO process.

This concrete demand for a reallocation of private property in the surrounding area was echoed by other community members. The most common target of such discussions was Vaca's property, El Porvenir (which was formerly part of the Mendez estate). As Fausto explained, this owed less to the property's unjustified legal status, of which not everyone was aware, than to the fact that the community had until recently enjoyed unrestricted access to this land. Indeed, many households are in a more precarious situation than Armando's. In the household survey, nine of the community's thirteen households complained they had insufficient land to meet their livelihood needs. Four households claimed to possess no land at all, with three of these reporting that they actively desired land but none was available. A further four households farm plots of land located within Mendez's property, an arrangement negotiated through informal agreement.[17] While views about the acceptability of this last situation were mixed—some people reported that there was no problem because "Mendez no mezquina" (Mendez isn't stingy with his land), while others complained about having to ask permission—such arrangements provided little security for Guaraní community members. This was illustrated on at least one occasion when the property changed hands and the community was denied access altogether.

The restrictions on subsistence (let alone commercial) production caused by the lack of land available for farming are compounded by the poor quality of this land—a result of the continuing monopolization of the most fertile areas by *karai* landowners, combined with worsening drought conditions in the Chaco, which have been exacerbated by extensive cattle ranching over the last half century. During the period of my fieldwork, my host household and many others were purchasing maize from *karai* landowners or merchants, having used up supplies from the previous year's harvest. As this demonstrates, contrary to the state's construction of land as abstract space, for communities, the location and ecological qualities of land are of prime importance. As many community members emphasize, it is the unequal distribution of environmental risks and benefits among Guaraní and *karai* claimants, as much as the quantity of land titled to them, that presents the gravest threat to Guaraní livelihoods, requiring community members to increasingly forge non-subsistence livelihood strategies beyond the TCO. As one sixteen-year-old put it: "When it rains a lot, we don't leave, we can make our *potrero;* now that it doesn't rain much, we sometimes sow and it dries up, so there's no point being here. That's why we leave to work."

During my stay, eleven of the community's thirteen households had at least one member engaged in wage labor outside the community and contributing to household income. These jobs included agricultural labor, cattle ranching, construction, driving, and domestic work; were temporary, seasonal, or semi-permanent; and took place in a range of locations, from neighboring private properties, to Tarija's urban centers, to farms outside Buenos Aires. In early 2012, the first Tarairí community member began work in the rapidly expanding nearby Margarita-Huacaya gas field. The semi-proletariat status of even the most "traditional" Guaraní communities of Itika Guasu contrasts with the visions of indigenous land-based subsistence livelihoods underpinning policy discussions of indigenous land titling (see chapter 1). As Tarairí's predicament shows, this trend is exacerbated by the failure of TCO titling to resolve long-standing problems of indigenous land access. It is also a result of growing environmental pressure from non-indigenous land users within and beyond the TCO—from local cattle ranchers to nearby hydrocarbon operations, agro-industrialists diverting the Pilcomayo River in Argentina and Paraguay, upstream contamination from highland mining operations, and global anthropocentric climate change.[18]

Given that it is women who undertake the labor of cooking and caring for children, and who remain in the community while men migrate for work, it is they who most feel the everyday effects of land scarcity, diminishing fish supplies, and resultant food insecurity. During my stay, the community renewed a food aid project targeting pregnant women and children under five. Despite these present-day difficulties, the primary concern of most women regarding the land situation related to their children's future. When asked about the land situation in the context of a focus group in early 2012, women's responses included "jeta sambiaɨreta, mbaetɨ ɨvɨ" (Guaraní: there are lots of children, there is no land) and "mbaetɨ espacio sambiaɨretare" (Guaraní/Spanish: there is no space for the children).

Community members also complained frequently about the problems they confronted accessing other natural resources. Perhaps the biggest challenge is faced by women, who rely on the collection of palm and twigs for making their handicrafts, the sale of which provides an important supplement to meager household incomes.[19] In order to collect palm, women frequently have to enter private property, risking confrontation with *karai* landowners, a situation compounded by a boundary dispute with a neighboring Guaraní community (discussed later in this chapter). For Victoria's all-female household, for whom handicrafts were the main source of income, the situation was particularly difficult—one factor precipitating Victoria's eventual departure from the community in 2012 for a low-paid job cooking for hydrocarbon workers in the nearby village of Palos Blancos. Men also complained of problems accessing forest products, including timber and other materials used for house construction, some of which can be found only inside private property. Supplies of firewood—the sole source of fuel—within communal land are also diminishing, requiring increasingly long trips for collection, usually undertaken by women and children.

The Elusive Promise of Territory

The foregoing discussion reveals how the INRA Law's prioritization of private property claims in TCOs, combined with its incomplete and flexible application (detailed in chapter 3), has served to consolidate the existing spatial order—an order predicated on indigenous dispossession. Despite the cartographic representation of the TCO as a contiguous and collectively owned territory, in practice indigenous land rights have been squeezed into the spaces left between privately claimed areas; a geography of absence. In Itika Guasu, such free spaces were few and far between. Around Tarairí, land recovered by the Guaraní is little more than the areas already occupied by communities. As I have shown, this situation limits the Guaraní's ability to practice the "traditional" livelihoods imagined for them by global and national policy makers—livelihoods predicated on spatial mobility and access to land and resources from a wide geographical area.

In fact, by fixing boundaries and materializing boundaries, the titling process *exacerbated* the community's problems accessing land and resources. This was made clear to me one day by Fausto, as we sat chewing coca by a toilet block he was building for the municipal ecotourism project, which had employed a handful of the community's men. Gazing across the Pilcomayo River at the coveted property of Roberto Vaca (figure 12), he complained that, whereas "before it was free, you could go anywhere," TCO titling meant that the *karai* had started fencing their land, limiting Guaraní people's movements. As noted earlier, the Guaraní have historically relied on negotiations with landowners and covert access to survive the onslaught of formal dispossession. Although this scenario was far from ideal, to materialize boundaries without significant land redistribution arguably leaves communities like Tarairí more squeezed than ever.

Fausto's comments resonate with APG IG leader Román's complaints of people's being "shut in a room" by the fragmentary effects of TCO titling when they wanted to live in a "single courtyard" (see chapter 3). They illustrate the differences between "territory" and "property" (Blomley 2010; Wainwright and Bryan 2009), and the limitations of the latter for achieving decolonization. Whereas traditional Guaraní land use practices were based on fluid boundaries and networked relationships across space the territorialization of property required "conscious 'cuts' in the processual networks through which social spaces are produced." This "zero-sum categorical logic" is encapsulated in the notion of "trespassing," whereby "mere physical presence, even absent any damage to a resource, constitutes an offence" (Blomley 2010: 203, 208). If community members in Tarairí are routinely faced with this logic, then they also contest it. By accusing *karai* landowners of *mezquinando* (being stingy, restricting others' access to land), community members articulate an alternative "agrarian moral economy" (Wolford 2005), in which the failure to enter into flexible negotiations over land use constitutes a hostile act that disrupts "normal" neighborly relations. As community members often reminded me, it was their ancestors' willingness to "share" their territory with *karai* settlers that enabled landowners to establish themselves in the first place.

FIGURE 12.   Roberto Vaca's disputed property claim on *la banda* (photo by author)

As I have noted, however, not all *karai* neighbors *mezquinan*; Tarairí community members remain dependent on informal negotiations over land and resource
access with Simón Mendez. From a positive perspective, these agreements attest
to the Guaraní's agency in shaping land relations even in a constraining context
of postcolonial dispossession. When I asked what the community would do if
Mendez denied them access to his land, one person told me that the community would "kick him out." This defiant statement clearly underplays the power
relations involved in such negotiations. The fact that communities like Tarairí
continue to have to *ask permission* from a *karai* landowner to farm or collect
natural resources provides a stark illustration of the failure of TCO land titling
to significantly transform ethnic land relations in the TCO. This is not to suggest that nothing has changed since the days of *empatronamiento*; as community
members acknowledge, the TCO—as part of a broader Guaraní decolonizing
struggle—has forced *karai* landowners to recognize and "respect" the Guaraní as
subjects of rights. The failure to match recognition with redistribution, however,
places continuing constraints on their lives and livelihoods. One result is that
they are forced to negotiate land access, purchase produce, and seek employment
from *karai* landowners, who are in some cases their former *patrones*.

In this context, it is little surprise that some community members in Tarairí conclude that, as a route toward "reclaiming territory," TCO titling has failed to deliver. As Fausto reflected:

> Of course, if I think about it... [I want] to reclaim [territory]. But... as they say, to reclaim [territory] is going to be a bit difficult. It's already like that—a piece here, a piece there. Everything already... because before it was... there weren't any *karai*; we went to sow all the way to... where there's a bridge, on the Salao River, beyond that there was a *potrero*... From here our grandparents went to sow over there... I myself also went to sow; for a week I went to sow there, from there I came back here... I made my house there to look after the maize. Not anymore—there's a landowner there.
>
> PA: And do you remember, when they presented the TCO demand in 1996, what hopes people had?
>
> > FAUSTO: Of course, people had the hope of being able to rescue everything, so they could live peacefully. But... it continues like this, with nothing.

Pablo similarly evaluated TCO titling according to the contrast between the territory described to him by his grandmother and the present realities of land access in Tarairí, marked by the continuing presence of property:

> In reality, what my grandmother told me [is that] years ago everything was freedom, there was freedom: where to live, where to make your house, everything. But now... For example, why can't the people of Tarairí make their *potrero* there in *la banda*? Because it's private property. Because I know that if they make it there, [the landowner is] going to say, "Hey, who gave you permission?" You see?

In a passage that resonates strikingly with Nicholas Blomley's (2010) description of the making of liberal property, he went on:

> Before, there wasn't this... keeping land separate. Everything was... for everyone, everyone did everything, we had land and nothing had an owner. Now it's already... the *karai* are here and they have land, separate; it's already fenced... that's how it is now. Before it wasn't like that—everyone went to their *chaco* to make a little *potrero*... Anywhere you went you could put up a fence, make your house. Look, I would go to make my house in Timboy; from there I went to Tomatirenda and made my house. From there I returned to Timboy, then I returned here. So there wasn't this... *tierra mezquina*—nothing! Now they don't let

you; before I could go to Salao, make my house; now they're not going to let me make my house over there.

Yet even as Guaraní community members dreamed of recovering a world of free movement and fluid boundaries, even as they denounced the exclusions of liberal property as *mezquinando*, they were not exempt from the regimes of exclusion that Tania Li (2014) identifies as intrinsic to the politics of land. In a context of growing land and resource scarcity, Guaraní communities were becoming increasingly implicated in the fixing and policing of boundaries—endeavors that brought communities into conflict not only with *karai* landowners but also with one another. Such intercommunal conflicts articulated in complex ways with the TCO titling process, as I now describe.

Fixing Boundaries

Yukiporo's New Fence

During the time I lived in Tarairí, community members did not complain only about neighboring landowners fencing land. An equally frequent complaint was directed at a neighboring Guaraní community, Yukiporo, which in 2010 fenced an area of forested TCO land between the two communities (figure 13). This fence runs parallel to the newly graveled road, extending from the Pilcomayo River to the boundary of this fragment of TCO land, where it cuts into the forest, tracing the boundary line southward. It is Tarairí's women who have been most directly affected by the new fence, as the area of forest inside it is one of the main places where they collect palm and twigs for handicrafts. As noted earlier, almost all women engage in this time-consuming work, which requires frequent (weekly or fortnightly) trips to gather raw materials. Even the oldest women embark on these trips, moving nimbly through dense forest, using specially selected sticks in a scissor action to break off palm leaves high above them, then trekking home along the road with neatly bound bundles of palm tied to their backs. Over recent years, a combination of drought and plagues has made palm increasingly scarce, and the area fenced by Yukiporo is one of the few remaining places within walking distance where they can find it, the other being within Mendez's property.

In practice, the barbed wire presents no material obstacle to accessing the palm, given that there is a wooden gate at the beginning of the dirt road to Yukiporo. The women's main complaint is that they feel that their right to do so has been called into question. As Victoria's sister, whose all-female household relies primarily on handicrafts for income, put it, "We have to take it clandestinely" [*ocultita*]. Beyond the inconvenience it caused them, women and men

FIGURE 13. A section of Yukiporo's new fence (photo by author)

in Tarairí objected to what the fence represented: Yukiporo's claim of exclusive rights to a portion of territory to which they had traditionally had access. They routinely complained that their neighbors were *mezquinando* palm, something they asserted went against Guaraní customs.

I discussed the issue with Pablo one afternoon in November as we sat together on the patio of his house, sipping mate from a hollow gourd. Pablo had just returned from a health visit to Yukiporo, and while seeing to a patient there, he had overheard a quarrel between a local woman and some women from Itikirenda (the community on the other side of the Pilcomayo) who had crossed the river to collect palm from the forest. He described how the local woman had chastised the visitors for helping themselves to the palm without consultation, arguing that it belonged to Yukiporo and that there was scarcely enough to meet the community's own needs. Pablo lamented that, after such a long battle with the *karai* for land rights, the Guaraní now seemed to be "fighting among brothers," all because of Yukiporo's attempt to *mezquinar* resources. It was all the more insulting, he complained, when they did nothing to prevent the *karai* landowners from grazing cattle on communal TCO land. His complaints were echoed by other community members; as Fausto declared: "The Guaraní himself is fencing! There is Yukiporo, they're already restricting other communities' access to [*mezquinando*] land, palm . . . the women go for palm, and they restrict access [*mezquinan*]."

There is nothing new about resource conflict between neighboring Guaraní communities (Albó 1990), and informal accounts suggest a long history of resource competition between Tarairí and Yukiporo. Yet some people in Tarairí blamed the TCO titling process for *exacerbating* these tensions by fixing informal boundaries between communities that had once been fluid and negotiated. As Pablo explained:

> INRA came here and said, "This part, this belongs to the community; this belongs to the community of Tarairí," and this is what Guaraní people went for [*es a esto que va la tetarareta*].[20] And they don't want . . . they don't want another brother to go to build his house, to go to do his work, and that's what they think. But, however, the organization isn't like that.
>
> PA: So maybe the titling process . . . had the effect of dividing the communities? Is it because of the land titling that they think like that?
>
> PABLO: Because of titling. But I think that INRA said: "Well now, we're going to title land. Now, this [piece of land]; what is it called? Right, this for a *karai*, this for a *karai*, this is for the Guaraní." But among the Guaraní you can't be *mezquinando* like that.

Here Pablo refers to the process through which INRA went about its fieldwork, measuring the informal or negotiated boundaries of individual Guaraní communities, as well as those of private properties. He suggests that, in measuring communities as separate and bounded entities, INRA created a notion of fixed boundaries among Guaraní people where none had formerly existed. As noted earlier, the boundaries of "communal areas" were a function of those of adjacent private properties, the presence of which INRA's measurements legitimized.[21] More broadly, the mapping of community boundaries reflected the entrenched logic of the agrarian reform agency, whose technicians viewed their task as recording clear, GIS-located lines between one property claim and the next. Such is the logic of liberal property. These were the "bright lines" to which Blomley (2010) refers; this was the task of "cleaning up" from which *saneamiento* takes its name.

Paradoxically, then, in its preliminary attempts to make Itika Guasu "legible" to the state (Scott 1998)—a precursor to any possible reallocation of land—INRA reinforced the fragmenting effects of *karai* settlement, segmenting territory into discontinuous areas and leaving communities isolated in existing "regions of refuge" (Albó 1990: 48). While the Guaraní demanded *territory*, the state translated this as *property*, a notion premised on "the production of bounded, coherent spaces, through which . . . individuated subjects and objects . . . can be rendered legible" (Blomley 2010: 203). This logic was inscribed not only on state maps (which represent TCO Itika Guasu as 517 separate polygons) but also on the landscape (where faded yellow fence posts still mark supposed community limits), and—most important—in the minds of community members, who came to view such boundaries as consequential for everyday struggles with their neighbors over resource access.

This is not to suggest that communal boundaries were merely a creation of INRA. Conversations highlighted the existence of Guaraní notions of community entitlements over particular areas of land. This passage from an interview with Felix, the *mburuvicha* of Yukiporo, is illustrative. After he told me about conflicts with neighboring *karai* landowners, I asked if there were also problems with neighboring Guaraní communities. He responded:

> FELIX: Yes, yes, yes … yes. That happens, it happens a lot because … in my community that doesn't happen, [because] we've built a fence so we can make them [other Guaraní communities] respect [boundaries].
>
> PA: So for you [plural], the resources that lie in Yukiporo belong to the community and the others shouldn't come just like that [*así no más*], but they sometimes do?
>
> FELIX: Here in my community, no; first they have to . . . to take [resources], they have to . . . they have to . . . they have to enter with *permission*.
>
> PA: So with the land issue, it isn't that it all belongs to everyone; every community has its space and has to respect other communities—their space?
>
> FELIX: That's it. That's it, because of course they have to respect. That is, with the issue of Tarairí they're not doing that.

The existence of such informal "environmental entitlements" (Leach Mearns, and Scoones 1999; Ostrom 1990) was supported by other accounts; for example, Alcides, the *mburuvicha* of the nearby community of Itikirenda, argued that, while any Guaraní person had the right to come and live in his community, resource usufruct rights were contingent on residency: "If they've been living [here] a month, a year, they have the right to take their product [natural resources from the surrounding area], but on the other hand, if they come directly from another place to take, it isn't fair either."

Further evidence of community entitlements, as well as their contested nature, was provided by a focus group I held with Tarairí's men in January 2012. The men were asked to draw a map of the community and its surroundings, which then provided the basis for this discussion of legal and informal boundaries:

PA: Is there a limit with Yukiporo? Or not—is it not very clear?

> PABLO: The thing is that I can't say because I don't know every-
> thing. [Asks the others,] Do we share with Yukiporo or not?
>
> FAUSTO: There are limits.
>
> PABLO: There are limits.
>
> [The other men discuss and agree, but do not seem very sure.]

PA: Do they [Yukiporo] want to establish limits?

> PABLO: They want to establish limits.

PA: But for you there aren't any?

> PABLO: But the thing is that they don't understand that—that's
> why they've put up fencing.
>
> LORENZO: There is already fencing. They're already separated.
>
> PABLO: I think that if Tarairí wants to do work there, they would
> say no.

PA: So if I ask them if there's a limit, they would say yes?

> PABLO: Of course they're going to say yes.
>
> JULIO: They would say yes.
>
> FAUSTO: Definitely. I think that they want [limits], that's why they
> fence—there's a fence. And us, what are we going to do?
>
> MARIO: We tend to understand that there aren't any limits.
>
> LORENZO: But they don't understand it that way; they want to be
> like the *karai*.
>
> [PAUSE]

PA: Because a long time ago, there were no limits?

> MEN: No.
>
> YOUNGER MAN: Before, what was it like then? Didn't they even have
> [limits]?
>
> OTHER MEN: Of course not.
>
> YOUNGER MAN: [Jokingly, to me,] You could live over there, or over
> there [he points to the mountains behind us].

In this passage, the men both affirm the existence of a boundary with Yukiporo and call this into question by referring to a past in which no clear boundary existed. In the discussion that preceded this, the men implied that boundaries were, at least in part, a creation of INRA; as one participant put it, "When INRA came they said there were limits—there are posts—but the thing is that we, given that we're Guaraní, we don't . . . that is, one doesn't locate oneself." This last phrase, "one doesn't locate oneself" (*no se ubica*) is sometimes used figuratively to denote confusion in the face of complex information. Consequently, its usage here may refer to the Guaraní's inability to navigate the complex legal-cartographic knowledges of the state, as much as their wholesale rejection of boundaries. Although Lorenzo's reference to his neighbors in Yukiporo wanting to "be like the *karai*" represents such boundary policing as un-Guaraní behavior, the notion that someone from Tarairí would have to seek permission from Yukiporo to "do work there" seems equally taken for granted. Moreover, the younger man's satirical portrayal of the remembered limitless world, in which you could live wherever you wanted, makes clear that this is a distant reality from the world he inhabits. My argument, then, is not that communal boundaries were a fiction created by INRA, but rather that the *fixing* of these boundaries, in both cartographic and material terms (via a barbed wire fence), had important effects, preventing communities' consensual renegotiation of temporary entitlements to land and resources in light of evolving social and environmental conditions.

The importance of such negotiations over resource access was illustrated in a discussion with Alcides, the *mburuvicha* of Itikirenda, whom I visited at his home one day in early 2012, accompanied by Armando's niece Jennifer. After we were ferried across the Pilcomayo River by a local fisherman, the hour-long walk to the community took us along a sandy track lined with *karapari* cacti, which skirted the perimeter of Roberto Vaca's land, where we glimpsed a large area of pasture through a barbed wire fence. En route, we passed Jennifer's uncle José, who, she informed me, was working for Vaca as a cowhand—Vaca's previous job on this same land (formally Mendez's property) before he became an independent rancher. When we arrived in Itikirenda—my first visit owing to my broken ankle, which had restricted my movements in previous months—I was surprised to see that community members still lived in traditional palm-thatched adobe houses, not having benefited from NGO housing projects, owing to their isolated location. My discussions confirmed that the community is more self-sufficient than many in Itika Guasu, with lower levels of labor migration. If this was partly the result of poor transport links, it also reflected the community's access to a large and relatively fertile fragment of TCO land, purchased by the EAPG in 2000 with funds raised in Switzerland.[22] Unlike in Tarairí, households in Itikirenda were not purchasing maize from *karai* farmers or merchants, having saved enough from the previous year's harvest.

Despite the relative availability of land in Itikirenda, Alcides emphasized the importance of informal negotiations over land and resource access with the neighboring community, Yumbia, with which he claimed they maintained cordial relations:

> Here we are the community of Itikirenda, and we have also the community Yumbia. And here we don't have conflicts—that is, fighting over land. We also can't fight over land because we're the Guaraní people,

we're the same brothers, and we can't be fighting. So to be able to get some products, or do some work, such as a road, to do our work, we have a meeting, the two communities meet, to be able to reach a clearer conclusion, to be able to see what work we can do, and also to help each other.

It is precisely these kinds of flexible negotiations, framed by Alcides as intrinsic to Guaraní collective resource management, that are precluded by Yukiporo's erection of a barbed wire fence. People in Tarairí saw Yukiporo's fence as an infringement of their rights to renegotiate rules and boundaries and to maintain their former permeability. They thus accused their neighbors of *mezquinando*, deploying the same moral discourse they directed at *karai* landowners who denied them access to land and resources. Although Fausto admitted to having signed a written agreement permitting the fence's erection several years previously—a crumpled scrap of paper he once showed me—as Felix, the *mburuvicha* of Yukiporo, observed, "the problem is [that] only now are we fencing it."

Ironically, although some people in Tarairí implicated INRA in the fixing of boundaries, my affirmation of the TCO's collective legal status was quickly seized on by both men and women in support of their claims to access the disputed palm reserves. That is, they argued that, as equal members of the TCO, they had *just as much right* to collect these resources as their neighbors. Following my presentation of the results of TCO titling in a concluding session of the men's focus group, Pablo turned to the group and exclaimed: "In that case, look, *compañeros*! If there is a title here, Tarairí together with Yukiporo, then at no point can they *mezquinar* land from us. So why are they doing this fencing?" The group readily agreed, a reflection of how the collective nature of the TCO title lent legitimacy to their claims.

This scene was repeated the next day. I had just finished informing households about a forthcoming focus group for women and returned home to find Rómulo, one of Armando's many nephews, sitting in the kitchen—as usual, slightly drunk. Since being left with a limp after a road accident a few years previously, Rómulo worked mainly in the community as a fisherman and was therefore around more than most men of his generation. He had brought us fish, which Sandra was busy cooking, binding it between split sticks that leaned over a smoking wood fire. The real reason for Rómulo's visit, it emerged, was that he had missed the focus group the previous day and wanted information on the TCO titling process. He also felt that he should have participated in the map-drawing exercise on the basis of his experience having once rowed a brigade of officials downstream to Puerto Margarita as part of a hydrocarbon map–making mission. I began apologizing until I remembered that I had invited him in person the day before the activity.

We sat on my leather-woven bedframe in the porch and sifted through the materials I'd prepared for the previous day on the history and current status of land titling in the TCO. Like Pablo, Rómulo took the uniformly colored polygon of collectively titled TCO land (which included Tarairí and Yukiporo) as ammunition in the community's battle with its neighbors. It soon became clear that Rómulo had a personal interest in the legal status of this boundary; as he went on to explain, his father, Hermes, along with him and his brothers, has been engaged in a long-standing dispute with Yukiporo over the grazing of cattle in the area between the two communities. Hermes, who owns a small herd of cattle acquired while working as Mendez's cowhand, had grown accustomed to grazing his cattle in this area. A decade earlier, Yukiporo had informed him that he should take them to graze elsewhere. In Rómulo's account, his father did transfer his cattle to a different area, but they made their own way back to their old grazing ground. In order to secure continuing access to this land, Hermes came to an agreement with the *mburuvicha*, Felix, paying him to "look after" his animals and ensure no harm came to them in his absence.

Yet this does not appear to have held sway with other men in the community, who took the return of Hermes and his cattle as an affront. The conflict came to a head in 2005, when two young men from Yukiporo beat Hermes up badly. The precise events that led up to this were uncertain from Rómulo's account—perhaps because he was away at the time, doing military service in Tarija. He raced back to the community (in a taxi, with a pistol and without military authorization) after hearing from a relative of Beatriz Vaca that his father had been killed (something it turned out was untrue). He and one of his brothers then rushed to Yukiporo with a view to finding and punishing the assailants themselves. In spite of this violent confrontation, Rómulo claimed that he continues to graze his father's cattle on the disputed piece of land and does so with Yukiporo's permission—although he stressed that this is a personal arrangement and not a privilege that everyone from Tarairí enjoys. How this access was negotiated and whether it involves payments in cash or in kind was not revealed in this brief discussion. What it did reveal is that the conflict with Yukiporo was not only about palm—although Rómulo also referred to the palm conflict, telling me that several years ago, the residents of Yukiporo "burned down all their palm" in an effort to prevent neighboring communities from taking it.

As these examples reveal, in a context where communities' boundaries and resource entitlements are subject to continual dispute and negotiation, the TCO provides an important symbolic and moral resource for competing environmental claims. On the one hand, as an imagined collective space, the TCO provided Tarairí community members with ammunition for their claims to access palm reserves and grazing land adjacent to Yukiporo. On the other hand, for residents of Yukiporo, INRA's fieldwork seemed to verify and make official the boundary between the two communities, a boundary also validated in a written agreement signed by Fausto, which—in an oral culture—seems to mimic a property title. In the context of such symbolic struggles, notions of "traditional" land use are not apolitical but are themselves mobilized toward specific ends. As Pablo declared in a private interview:

> I say to them [Yukiporo]: "Brothers, why do we have to fight over land? Why do we speak of the TCO? What is the organization for?" You see? In that case, there is no border. There is no border. If I want to build my house there in Yukiporo, I can go and build my house. If they want to come and live here, they can come and live here.

Here, it is not just the legal-cartographic status of the TCO but the entire collective Guaraní struggle for territory that appears to be at stake in the dispute over Tarairí's access to the palm reserves. The TCO is thus subject to multiple interpretations, with the fragmentary effects of INRA's measurements—used by some to defend exclusive resource rights—countered by appeals to the communal imaginary underpinning the territory's production. Yet barbed wire fences could not be imagined away. Thus my basic point stands: that land titling contributed toward fixing boundaries that were historically permeable and negotiable, if often disputed.[23] As I now explore, land titling is not the only factor at play here, but articulates with a series of other incentives and pressures for fixing boundaries.

Incentives for Enclosure

Although Felix acknowledged that Yukiporo's fence was partly about protecting palm supplies, this was not the first thing he mentioned when I asked him about the motives behind the new fence. Our discussion took place against the unusual backdrop of a ceremonial distribution of clothing by a group of evangelists who were visiting Tarairí from Santa Cruz in early January 2012. They had been camped out in the health clinic for several days, distributing Spanish language religious materials to a largely illiterate and Guaraní-speaking audience, whom they attracted with regular meals (which sadly included our household goat) and film screenings. On this particular day, as their final act of benevolence, they had collected minibus-loads of people from several nearby communities to participate in the distribution of secondhand clothes of North American origin. The atmosphere was one of festive anticipation, but the event was long drawn out enough to facilitate several interviews with people from other communities.

I began by asking Felix about the land situation in Yukiporo, which he explained was far from satisfactory, and compounded by worsening drought conditions and diminishing fish stocks. Unlike in Itikirenda, which had access to a larger and more fertile area of TCO land, Yukiporo's situation resembled that of Tarairí: the community found itself in an acute land and resource squeeze. Our discussion of livelihood problems and strategies moved naturally to the issue of the new fence, subject to so much controversy in Tarairí. Felix claimed that the main reason for erecting the fence was not to protect the palm reserves but rather to enable Yukiporo to grow pasture for cattle the community had recently acquired. He explained that it was necessary to fence the land to prevent the cattle of neighboring landowners from entering and eating up this pasture:

> Our motive for fencing the land is ... you know that the other side there are the *terceros*, they're there with their cattle, that is, on their property, but they have cattle, so we've fenced so that these cattle don't enter in our area ... because we're in the process of making our little cattle stronger, and all of the work we're doing we have to ... we have to maintain it.

He went on to explain that cattle ranching was part of a necessary shift in livelihood strategies brought about by drought, soil erosion, and declining fish stocks. As noted earlier in this chapter, ecologists suggest that the drought and soil degradation are a result of declining forest cover, extensive ranching practices, and climate change, while declining fish stocks are attributed to overfishing and upstream water contamination from mining around Potosí, as well as the construction of diversion channels in Paraguay and Argentina, which have made the river impassable for some fish.[24] As in Tarairí, these changes have had a doubly devastating effect on traditional fishing and farming livelihoods in Yukiporo—which was part of the reason people viewed cattle ranching as an attractive alternative. According to Felix, the land the community had fenced was no longer suitable for farming and could be used only for pasture: "As the climate has already changed, it's not like it was years ago; now it's drier and crops hardly grow ... The area we have fenced ... it isn't suitable for farming, we're just fencing to grow pasture, and it's only suitable for cattle ranching—for cattle ranching, and there's nothing for anything else."

As this illustrates, deteriorating environmental conditions, combined with land scarcity and population growth, are encouraging new and more intensive forms of land use in Itika Guasu, which present their own incentives for land enclosure. Of course, the palm conflict is also a product of resource competition exacerbated by land scarcity and drought. As noted earlier, such competition is exacerbated by the failure of TCO land titling to resolve problems of racialized land inequality—or to reserve the environmental impacts of *karai* settlement and land use practices. To put it another way, without "territory," Guaraní communities are increasingly forced to appropriate "land as property," using similar productive and exclusionary strategies to those of their *karai* neighbors, but in smaller and less fertile areas. Rather than a Malthusian "tragedy of the commons" (Hardin 1968), in which population growth leads to inevitable conflict and individualization of rights, the dynamics I have described illustrate how indigenous efforts at producing territory are profoundly conditioned by historical and contemporary territorializing processes that structure resource access and availability in ways that are profoundly racialized. Indigenous peoples do not produce territory in conditions of their choosing, even after state recognition of their territorial rights.

As I have suggested, fencing reflects a shift in local *karai* as well as Guaraní land use practices: whereas previously both groups allowed animals to roam freely in search of food, worsening drought conditions mean that pasture must now be grown to ensure their survival. Influenced by environmental conditions (and local authorities' and NGOs' environmental concerns), Itika Guasu is seeing a gradual shift from extensive to semi-extensive forms of cattle ranching. As Felix's remark illustrates, however, this shift is a partial one; the fencing of pasture is itself necessary because private landowners' animals still roam freely, often transgressing unfenced boundaries of TCO land. That they do so echoes historically grounded notions of settler entitlement to indigenous lands, framed as "empty" and unproductive (see chapter 3). This colonial logic of territorial expansion (on which Tarija's cattle ranching sector developed) is now enshrined in the minutiae of the INRA Law, which—despite to some extent fixing ranchers in place—allocates land to them allowing for projected growth of an existing herd.

Paradoxically, it is precisely because the *karai* do *not* contain their livelihood activities within fixed boundaries of private property that the Guaraní are compelled to fence areas of communal land. In that sense, non-human animal geographies present both incentives and disincentives for the fixing of human territorial boundaries.[25] Despite dreams of recovering a pre-colonial life-world, Guaraní communities continue to inhabit an "entangled landscape" in which their geographies are conditioned by those of other human and non-human actors (Moore 2005). Racialized land inequalities, environmental limits, and cattle-based livelihoods contribute toward producing a territorial assemblage in which exclusion and enclosure (Li 2014), rather than free movement and shared use, are increasingly normalized.

These territorial dynamics articulate with shifting geographies and agendas of state and NGO intervention. NGOs and state officials actively promote private land enclosure on conservation grounds; they rightly argue that extensive ranching is a major contributor to deforestation and desertification in the Chaco, as grazing cattle prevent the regeneration of native forest. At the same time, development programs are also giving Guaraní communities opportunities and incentives for fencing. As Felix went on to explain, Yukiporo had obtained both the cattle and the barbed wire from PROSOL, an agricultural subsidy program funded by departmental gas rents,[26] which allows each community to spend an annual budget (calculated according to the number of households) on material resources for rural development—such as animals, barbed wire, machinery, or irrigation infrastructure. The fact that PROSOL, like many state development programs, privileges "community" as a basic unit of geographical and political organization illustrates how networked relations with a *karai*-dominated world undermine the idea of the TCO as a collectively governed indigenous territory and reinforce the importance of community as a scale of territorial governance and rights. Yukiporo was not alone in responding to this confluence of pressures and opportunities by seeking to fix and defend communal boundaries. For all their complaints about Yukiporo's fence, people in Tarairí were engaged in acquiring and putting up barbed wire fences of their own, for similar reasons, as the following vignette illustrates.

The sight of rolls of barbed wire piled in front of Tarairí's crumbling adobe preschool center had become so familiar to me that I'd only recently thought to inquire about it. The barbed wire was, Fausto told me one day in early September 2011, the community's annual allotment from PROSOL. This marked the Guaraní's recent appropriation of the departmental gas-rent-funded direct cash transfer program, which they had initially complained benefited only *campesinos*, sometimes counter to their interests. The community requested a water tank and motorized pump in 2008 but was unable to make a claim at all in 2009 (when the program saw widespread fiscal problems). Its request for 2010 was for barbed wire, which arrived, belatedly, in August 2011, only shortly before the community expected the arrival of some goats, which they had requested for 2011.

In early September, a meeting was called to distribute the barbed wire among households. This distribution corresponded with the logic of the program in that, although a community is expected to agree on a collective demand, funding is calculated on a per household basis. Of course, the program's logic was of little interest to community members, who were more concerned with making their household plots secure from the encroachments of *karai* landowners' and other households' wandering animals, as well as wild pigs. Representatives from each household gradually appeared and gathered in a circle around the stacked barbed wire. Fausto opened the meeting, explaining in Guaraní that the barbed wire had arrived and should be put to good use and that the amount they would receive in future from PROSOL had increased, owing to the recent *campesino* mobilizations. Jimena, one of Fausto's daughters and the oldest literate woman, took charge of distribution, calling out names from a list, after which the relevant household representative would lug a roll of barbed wire from the central stack and place it at his or her side.

I struggled at first to grasp the politics of distribution, as it seemed to me that some people/households ended up with much more barbed wire than others; it soon become clear, however, that some people were collecting on behalf of absent relatives. After the first round of collection, almost half the stack of barbed wire remained in the center of the group. Following a brief discussion, Jimena went through the list once more, and each household acquired an additional roll. At least a dozen rolls still remained, and with no other instruction, some people helped themselves to the left-over rolls, although most people by this stage seemed to have little interest in acquiring even more barbed wire. The scene gave every appearance that the amount of barbed wire available far exceeded the community's immediate needs. By the time I left Tarairí three months later, few households appeared to have used any of their wire; most rolls remained stacked at the back of palm-thatched kitchens, gathering dust.

After the meeting, I visited Fausto at home to inquire about the community's previous engagement with PROSOL and choice of barbed wire this year. He told me that barbed wire was better than wooden fencing, which often blows down in the wind, and that they would use it to fence their household plots and grow pasture for animals, as well as squash, maize, and black beans. In this sense, the barbed wire was merely an upgrade for traditional stick fencing, preferred for its greater reliability, lower labor requirements, and the diminishing supply of suitable wood. As Fausto explained, "There are no more sticks . . . they've already cut them all down"; the construction of wooden fences now required a longer journey to collect sticks, as well as permission from a *karai* landowner—usually Mendez. Yet there were also new incentives for fencing. As Fausto told me, in the past it rained more, and the community had access to more land, so there were sufficient wild plants and fruits for their animals to eat. Animals were allowed to roam freely, and there was no need to sow pasture for them. Now, however, the limited area of land accessible to the community, combined with decreasing rainfall, had made it increasingly necessary to grow pasture, which meant fencing larger areas of land—which is precisely what the people of Yukiporo were doing.

As this illustrates, incentives for land enclosure do not necessarily imply a fixing of boundaries at a *community* level; in Tarairí, people seemed more interested in securing household *potreros*. As already noted, the provision of barbed wire in Tarairí appeared to far outweigh the requirement for it, suggesting that there are limits to how much people want to fence. This example also highlights that fencing is nothing new for the Guaraní; for traditional livelihoods that combine animal husbandry and agriculture, stick fencing has long been an essential part of land management, as well as the staking of temporary land claims.

Nevertheless, this provides further evidence that Guaraní communities in Itika Guasu are experiencing new pressures and opportunities to enclose land, in the context of deteriorating environmental conditions, land scarcity, wandering *karai*-owned cattle, and new gas-funded development programs. While these conditions are not merely a product of TCO land titling, TCO titling has failed to transform, and contributed toward reinforcing, a territorial logic of enclosure—a logic that is more consistent with a history of colonial settlement than it is with either global imaginaries of indigenous territory or Guaraní aspirations of reclaiming territory. In fact, in a context of continuing landowner presence, the TCO is increasingly imagined *like* a private property, as a space from which *karai* are excluded. As Pablo put it during the men's focus group:

> The TCO is ... where, where ... where a landowner ... where a landowner can't sell land, also where other landowners can't come, because it's inside the TCO ... You see? That's what the TCO means. If some *karai* want to come and live here, are we going to let them build their house here in the middle of the soccer field? [To other men,] Are you going to let them? No. That's the TCO. That's the way I understand the TCO.

As discussed in chapter 6, it is in the context of hydrocarbon negotiations that this notion of the TCO as Guaraní property has been most powerfully articulated.

Exclusion's Double Edge

As we have already seen, enclosure is a double-edged process. The desire to exclude *karai* landowners (or other communities) from communal land has to be weighed constantly against the unintended exclusionary effects that fixing boundaries may have for Guaraní community members. The following example is illustrative. One morning, not long after my arrival in Tarairí, I accompanied three women—Fausto's partner and two of his daughters—to let the community's sheep out of their pen to drink water from the Salado River. These hair sheep,[27] recently acquired by the community from a CERDET project, were being kept in a stick-fenced pen a half hour's walk from the community and were looked after by the community's women according to a household rotation (figure 14). This daily task soon became unnecessary; it turned out that the sheep were not eating enough in their pen and they were moved to the community *oka*. Here they roamed freely, grazing on whatever they could find, dodging

FIGURE 14. Fausto's daughter Bertha closes a stick fence erected on part of Simón Mendez's property claim as a pen for the community's hair sheep (photo by author).

missiles hurled and long sticks swished at them by women and children when they strayed into people's private *oka* space.

After returning that day, I sat with the *mburuvicha* in his house, and he told me about some of the community's land problems. He complained that *karai* landowners were letting their cattle graze on *la banda*—the disputed riverbank area traditionally used by the Tarairí community—and should put up fences to keep their animals within property boundaries. (In this case the boundaries were ambiguous, given the unrecognized legal status of Roberto Vaca's property claim.) The next day, I accompanied Armando to Entre Ríos. As we walked the one-and-a-half-hour stretch of road to the bus route, he told me that he planned to return to Tarairí as soon as possible because he wanted to talk to Mendez, who was visiting his property, about his plans for fencing part of his land. Following my recent discussion with Fausto, I initially assumed that Armando wanted the area to be fenced to prevent Mendez's cattle from entering communal land. It turned out, however, that the reverse was true: Armando planned to ask Mendez *not* to fence this land, as doing so would create problems of access for the community.

As noted earlier, a number of the Tarairí households' plots are located within Mendez's property, as was the stick-fenced pen where the hair sheep were initially being kept. As we have seen, this is also an area where the community collects increasingly scarce forest products such as palm and wood. In fact, it was only when I accompanied community members to identify property boundaries with a GPS device that I realized how much of the land they used formed part of Mendez's two property claims—only one of which had been titled by INRA.

These examples illustrate how Guaraní people are frequently faced with what Derek Hall and his coauthors call "exclusion's double edge." They argue that, while global development discourse frames land rights in terms of *inclusion*, in the context of on-the-ground land struggles, the opposite of *exclusion* is not *inclusion* but *access*. Because one person's access is predicated on another's exclusion, "exclusion creates both security and insecurity. From the moment land becomes scarce, the exclusive access to land that is productive for some comes into tension with the fact that others cannot access it" (Hall, Hirsch, and Li 2011: 8). It is precisely this dilemma that Guaraní communities confront.

As we have seen, the Guaraní frequently contest the exclusionary regimes of the *karai* and dream of returning to a lost world of free movement and unrestricted access. Yet it is only by *excluding* the *karai* that such a world seems possible. In a context where the state recognizes landowners' property claims, the best the Guaraní can hope for is to exclude *karai* neighbors from the fragments of TCO land they have rights to. Yet the enforcement of boundaries between communal and private property can also backfire, excluding the Guaraní from accessing resources located within *karai* properties. When we consider relations between Guaraní communities, "exclusion's double edge" becomes more complex still. In a context of growing land and resource scarcity, one community's quest to "reclaim territory"—by asserting its own entitlement to access areas of traditional use—can quickly become a source of exclusion for other communities, which are also feeling the spatial squeeze of *karai* land control, state-funded fencing, population growth, and drought-induced changes in forest cover and soil quality.

To echo the critique of Hall, Hirsch, and Li, TCO titling offered indigenous peoples discursive *inclusion* in the nation-state as bearers of collective rights while leaving unresolved the on-the-ground material question of *access*, with its exclusionary implications. The result is that the thirty-six Guaraní communities of Itika Guasu find themselves sharing (in legal terms) unevenly distributed fragments of TCO land. Not only are the fruits of this inclusion elusive for many communities, but also attempts to secure these fragments against further *karai* encroachments can have the result of excluding either themselves or other Guaraní—which, of course, may be precisely the intention in a context where communities compete for scarce land and resources. These dynamics reveal how the distinction between *property* and *territory* not only is pertinent to the legal-cartographic practices and results of TCO titling—which produced a fragmented legal landscape—but also plays out in the everyday pressures, conflicts, and dilemmas facing Guaraní community members as they seek to sustain precarious livelihoods amidst the material realities of post colonial territory.

Through an ethnographic exploration of the lived realities of land and territory in Tarairí community, this chapter has provided further insights into the limits of state land titling as an instrument of decolonization. I began by describing Tarairí as an "entangled landscape" (Moore 2005), in which Guaraní territorial imaginaries and land use practices coexisted in awkward and asymmetrical articulation with a racialized regime of property rights. Some community members initially saw the TCO claim as a route to overcoming this predicament. They hoped to "reclaim territory" as a space of unrestricted mobility, cultural integrity, and material abundance. Yet the results of TCO titling have failed to live up to such expectations. Instead, the titling process has served to legitimize and consolidate the claims of private landowners. Community members in Tarairí remain hemmed in on all sides by private properties, a reality that creates daily challenges for subsistence farming and other livelihood activities, such as collecting palm for handicrafts or firewood for cooking. While they routinely contested this exclusionary regime of liberal property—through clandestine boundary transgressions and moral critique—they remained conditioned by its effects.

Nevertheless, seen from the perspective of community life, it was not just the failure of TCO titling to redistribute land or property rights that made it an ambivalent instrument for reclaiming territory. As I have revealed, the spatial logics and legal-cartographic knowledges of INRA were fundamentally at odds with how community members viewed and interacted with their territory. Through an examination of the conflict around Yukiporo's new fence, I have shown how the TCO's grounding in abstract Cartesian space (which overlooked communities' differentiated entitlements), combined with the boundary-fixing work of INRA's cadastral practices, resulted in a fixing of previously permeable and negotiable boundaries. The effect was an exacerbation of intercommunal conflicts, in which imaginaries of the TCO as a collective space were pitted against INRA's demarcation of communal boundaries. Yet, as I also argued, such conflicts must be placed as well in the broader context of resource scarcity and degradation in Itika Guasu—a product of climate change and racialized land inequality, problems that TCO titling has failed to resolve.

It is in the context of these multiple pressures toward more intensive forms of land use that the Guaraní are confronted with "exclusion's double edge." While Guaraní community members continue to dream of returning to a world where "you could make your *potrero* wherever you wanted," the land and resource squeeze they face presents increasing incentives for land enclosure. But incentives for excluding others also have the potential to backfire, in a context in which the transgression of established boundaries remains an important strategy for survival. These dilemmas are emblematic of how TCO titling failed to modify, and served to reinforce, a postcolonial logic of *property* that makes alternative imaginaries of territory both invisible and unviable.

As the final two chapters of this book reveal, it was not only in remote communities of Itika Guasu that the postcolonial logic of property was gaining precedence over a lingering vision of a shared ancestral territory. As the Guaraní struggled to respond to a new form of territorial incursion—that of hydrocarbon development—the notion of "territory as property" would eventually come to define the politics of the Guaraní land struggle.

EXTRACTIVE ENCOUNTERS
Struggles over Land and Gas

The oil frontier is a globalized time-space that marks the
instantiation of a new space of accumulation . . . [Q]uestions of
access to and control of property and rents as a prerequisite for
accumulation . . . are integral to its operations and character.

Michael Watts, "Securing Oil," 2015

[Repsol] haven't respected the vision of the Guaraní People of the
use and management of natural resources, neither have they thought
about the sustainability of the Territory, given that for the Guaraní
people our territory is an intrinsic part of our life and we depend
on the existence of our territory and its natural resources. We're
conscious that the national government has given as concessions
large areas of our territory to oil companies, without the consent of
our people and without considering the future of our lives.

APG IG, "Negotiation File," April 24, 2004

With the new governmental administration [of Evo Morales] we had
the hope of a better tomorrow for our children, but up till now we
don't feel a real change in our lives. Even worse, our communities
are threatened by the growing advance of the oil and gas
industry . . . [and] the formation of new elites that take advantage
of the gas rents that come from our territories, without us having
yet been able to achieve the titling of our lands and territories, and
a direct benefit from the resources exploited.

"To the Plurinational State and the Population of Tarija," Third Departmental
Assembly of the Tapiete, Weenhayek, and Guaraní Indigenous Peoples, 2011

As previous chapters have made clear, the legal-cartographic recognition of TCOs
did not reverse or override historical processes of territorialization in the Bolivian Chaco. Rather, indigenous land rights were constrained by, and slotted into, established (post)colonial geographies of private property and state authority.

The final two chapters of this book explore how TCOs intersected with a contemporary territorializing process: a boom in hydrocarbon development in the Bolivian Chaco.

In 1996, the same year the INRA Law created TCOs, the government of Gonzalo Sánchez de Lozada set forth its "energy triangle" policy, consisting of a new Hydrocarbons Law, the capitalization (privatization) of the state hydrocarbon company YPFB, and construction of a natural gas pipeline to Brazil.[1] As a result of these investment-friendly policies, hydrocarbon extraction in Bolivia increased fourfold in the period 1995–2005 (Hindery 2015: 52). This development was concentrated in the Chaco region of Tarija Department (Humphreys Bebbington and Bebbington 2011), where key gas reserves lie beneath indigenous territories—many of which were being claimed as TCOs. By 2008, twenty of Bolivia's eighty-four TCOs were subject to contracts for hydrocarbon exploration or exploitation (Tito, Soto, and Guardia 2008; see figure 15).[2]

These convergent geographies highlight the contradictory effects of an evolving neoliberal development agenda, in which the relentless marketization of land and resources was accompanied by an expanding set of governmental interventions designed to manage the social and environmental fallout (see chapter 1). Against a background of transnational energy investments, the exclusion of subsoil rights from TCOs was a nonnegotiable point during the national debate over the INRA Law. Of course, the separation of soil and subsoil rights was itself nothing new. The hydrocarbon boom of the 1990s was a continuation of Bolivia's historical positioning as a primary resource producer within a global capitalist economy.

In what follows, I examine the implications of the recent hydrocarbon boom for indigenous peoples' struggles for territory.[3] The site of Bolivia's largest gas field, TCO Itika Guasu provides a particularly rich case through which to explore these implications. As noted in previous chapters, the Guaraní saw state recognition of their land rights as a route to achieving territorial control and political autonomy. Hydrocarbon development challenged, and provided a new context for, these aspirations.

The present chapter describes the evolution of a decade-long conflict (2000–2010) over land rights and hydrocarbon governance in TCO Itika Guasu. As will become clear, TCO status failed to guarantee the Guaraní territorial control in the context of hydrocarbon development. Rather, the TCO titling process served to facilitate the resource-accessing claims of transnational capital and the state, in ways that undermined Guaraní land rights and claims to participation in the governance of extraction. Continuing my discussion in chapter 4, I show how competing ideas of "property" and "territory" were mobilized in the context of hydrocarbon negotiations. I also trace how the Guaraní increasingly came to

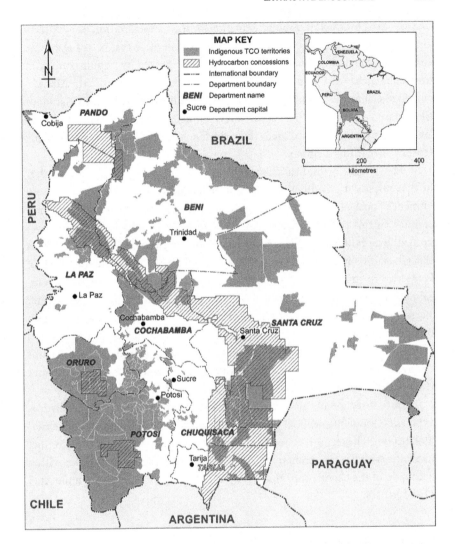

FIGURE 15. Map of Bolivia showing overlap of hydrocarbon concessions and TCOs (elaborated by Cartographic Unit, Department of Geography, University of Cambridge, based on Paye et al. 2010. Previously published in Anthias and Radcliffe 2015)

articulate their territorial demands through a language of "property." This shift is indicative of how hydrocarbon development has, over time, transformed the meaning and context of the Guaraní struggle for territory.

What makes this hydrocarbon conflict particularly illuminating is that it coincided with—and contributed to—a revolutionary period in Bolivian national (hydrocarbon) politics. As noted in the introduction, the 2005 election of Evo

Morales was a product of popular demands for the nationalization of hydrocarbons. The Margarita gas field played a central role in these events, as I elaborate later in this chapter. Bolivia's 2003 "gas war" was sparked by popular outcry at President Sánchez de Lozada's plans to build a new gas pipeline from the Margarita field to California via Bolivia's historic rival Chile. Meanwhile, the Guaraní of Itika Guasu were engaged in their own less publicized "gas war." When the MAS government took power in 2006, their conflict with the Spanish oil company Repsol was reaching a climax.

As we will see, this radical change of government did not immediately alter the dynamics of this conflict. As Guaraní leaders were well aware, the MAS government's "post-neoliberal" project relied on the extraction of gas from their territory. In this context, after several years of failed negotiation with the government over both land rights and hydrocarbon governance, Guaraní leaders in Itika Guasu finally concluded that the state would never complete the titling of their territory. In 2009 they abandoned the TCO titling process to focus on financial negotiations with Repsol, which operates the gas field. In short, this chapter charts how hydrocarbon negotiations came to surpass agrarian law as a terrain for pursuing and defending "territory," and how a transnational hydrocarbon company came to stand in for the state as an audience for and arbiter of claims for territorial recognition. The result was a new vision of territory and autonomy, which is the subject of the next and final chapter.

In the first section of this chapter I examine the articulations between hydrocarbon development and TCO titling in Itika Guasu during the neoliberal period (1997–2006). The second section describes the evolution of this resource conflict under the Morales government (2006–present). The chapter concludes with a discussion of the negotiations that led up to a 2010 agreement between the APG IG and Repsol.

The Neoliberal Slick Alliance

Securing Rights for Capital

On May 14, 1997, following a number of initial mergers and sales, the Spanish company Repsol,[4] along with partners British Gas and Pan American Energy (a subsidiary of BP), signed a contract with the Bolivian state awarding it the Caipipendi concession, which includes the Margarita gas field (now called the Margarita-Huacaya gas field),[5] located within the boundaries of TCO Itika Guasu (see figure 16). An initial phase of seismic testing by Repsol's then subcontractor Maxus revealed the existence of significant gas reserves. In the years that followed (1997–2003), Repsol (via Maxus) drilled four gas wells and constructed a processing plant, airstrip, gas pipelines, and access roads. This development began just months after TCO Itika Guasu had gained official recognition, setting in motion the SAN-TCO titling process. As the former director of INRA Tarija put it: "We arrived at practically the same time. [INRA's fieldwork] began in 2000 and the companies entered the zone in that period. So it was like everything happened in parallel."

This meant that, throughout the course of Repsol's activities, Itika Guasu was in a legal state of "immobilization" for TCO titling. Under this status, all private property claims within a TCO area (even those with title) are subject to legal revision, private land transactions are prohibited, and indigenous land rights are given priority until the titling process has been completed. Regardless of TCO status, ILO Convention 169 (ratified by Bolivia in 1991) stipulates that indigenous peoples have the right to prior and informed consultation, through their representative institutions, on development processes that affect them directly (Articles 15.2 and 7.1). In spite of this, when Repsol began its operations in the TCO, the company did not consult, or even inform, the APG IG of its planned activities. As APG IG leader Angelo put it: "They entered [the TCO] as if they were entering their house. It was as if you're the owner of the house and they pass under your nose, in other words. They didn't even present us with the environmental impact study." In fact, the environmental impact study presented to the Bolivian state made no reference to the fact that Itika Guasu was an indigenous territory. In the early years of its activities, Maxus made ad hoc payments to Guaraní community leaders in the area of the gas field and refused even to recognize the APG IG as a legitimate representative of communities.

In order to avoid negotiating land access with the APG IG, Repsol established its operations within private properties claimed by non-indigenous landowners, signing land use agreements and negotiating compensation payments with these individuals. According to the 1996 Hydrocarbon Law, such agreements—known as Contratos de Servidumbre (Service Contracts)—must be negotiated with the legal owner of the required land. In this case, they were made with third-party claimants within the TCO, whose land rights had not yet been established and who potentially stood to have their properties confiscated or reduced under the TCO titling process, depending on INRA's assessment of their properties' economic social function. In fact, official documentation from INRA's fieldwork (conducted in 2000) shows that several claimants with whom Repsol made land use contracts failed to prove productive use of their properties. At least three properties (those of wells X-3 and X-4 and of the processing plant) were earmarked for reductions (INRA 2008b and 2010). According to Guaraní community members, neither these two properties nor those of gas well X-2 and the airstrip are used productively, since their owners—all from one elite landowning

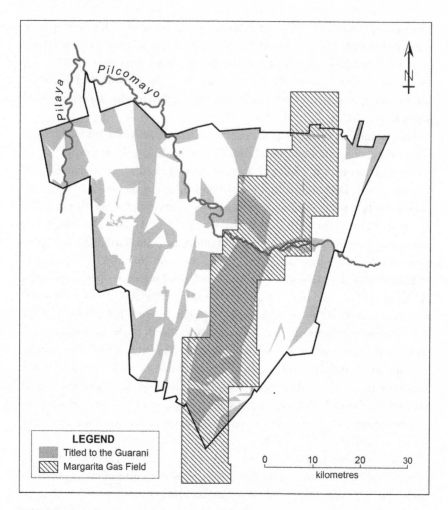

FIGURE 16. Map showing overlap of TCO Itika Guasu and Margarita-Huacaya gas field (elaborated by Cartographic Unit, Department of Geography, University of Cambridge, based on adaptation of figure 7.1 in Anthias 2012a)

family—live in Tarija city, where they own a popular chain of friend chicken restaurants as well as other businesses. These properties previously formed part of the region's largest estate, renowned for its harsh treatment of debt-bound Guaraní workers. The justification of the FES is also ambiguous in the case of the property of gas well X-1, claimed by the brother of landowner Simón Mendez (again, formerly part of a much larger estate), a cattle rancher who was initially due to face a property reduction but contested it before the National Agrarian Tribunal, with no clear result.

Not only did Repsol's land use agreements *preempt* the results of the TCO titling process, but also the company's presence *influenced* these results. In the case of an airstrip, APG IG leaders and NGO staff claimed that infrastructure built by Repsol was used as evidence of productive land use, thereby legitimizing a private claimant's rights to an otherwise unproductive property. This is referred to in a footnote of an environmental monitoring report produced by the APG IG and NGOs in 2005–6, which states that "REPSOL YPF made agreements with and payments to the supposed owners of the properties where they've constructed various installations, thereby legitimizing occupations that still haven't been validated under the terms of the titling process" (APG IG, CEADES and CER-DET 2005: 29). Having heard various reports of INRA's collusion in these land use contracts, I asked the agency's former (2000–2004) director, Jorge Campero, about them directly in 2009. He began by explaining that "land titling helps the transnational companies a lot, because it identifies the property owners with whom the company can make the corresponding contract." When I asked how the owner could be determined, given the unfinished status of the titling process, he replied, somewhat nervously, that the agreements between Repsol and private land claimants had been validated on the basis of titles awarded following the 1953 agrarian reform: "The company looks for information, evaluates it, and the owner emerges. The owner says, 'This is mine,' and proves it with plans, with documents. And later with the titling process [INRA] went about ratifying this."

> PA: So some already had titles?
>
> JC: Yes, in the zone there were already titles. Yes, yes, yes, yes, yes. In the zone there were already titles; in the zone there were already titles. The titling process is the revision of the agrarian reform of '53, so from '53 to '92 there were already titles in Bolivia. So there were already rights.
>
> PA: And does INRA sometimes have to respond to the needs of the company, if there's a situation that isn't very clear—that maybe there is no title, or maybe it's disputed?
>
> JC: INRA is required to inform whoever is the supposed owner, or the owner of this area. We can help to clarify, but INRA doesn't get involved in resolving anything . . . In general INRA certifies who is the owner, and that that property is in the process of titling and isn't going to be confiscated or is going to be consolidated. That helps them a lot.

His use of the future tense "is *going to be* consolidated" gives implicit acknowledgment of the speculative and preemptive nature of INRA's validation of private rights to TCO land pending the completion of fieldwork and the legal technical evaluation.

This might all seem like a rather technical discussion. Yet as we will see, these land use contracts have been at the heart of a decade-long conflict over land rights and hydrocarbon governance in Itika Guasu. They also presaged the Guaraní's eventual abandonment of the TCO titling process. From the Guaraní's perspective, they revealed INRA's readiness to sacrifice indigenous land rights in order to provide legal security for a Spanish oil company. As APG IG president Nestor Borrero retold these events:

> There was the TCO, but inside there was a third party who said, "This is my property: here is your property, here is mine." What Repsol did is enter this property, measured but still without title, entered and said: "I want to work in your property. That is to say, renting a part of your land, I'm going to work here, I want to live here." Repsol settles there, was a tenant . . . INRA legally certified this case [i.e., provided legal accreditation of the claimant's property rights as a basis for a Services Contract with Repsol]. I told them clearly that they were concentrating on conserving the huge interests; INRA knew, loads of people knew, but they preferred not to admit it, and to let [Repsol] settle, give them security of where to live.

From one perspective, this can be read as a local iteration of the neoliberal "slick alliance" between the state and capital (Watts 2001) that was emblematic of Goni's government (Hindery 2013) and generated popular critiques that would eventually overthrow his regime. Yet these events also had a colonial resonance. The existence of old titles to the properties in question (referred to by Jorge Campero) is noteworthy; documentation produced by INRA at the start of the TCO titling process reveals that a minority of non-indigenous land claimants in Itika Guasu possessed formal land titles (INRA 1999). Those that did belonged to the region's longest-standing and most powerful landowning families, who built up their estates on the back of debt-bound indigenous labor and secured property rights at a time when the Guaraní were excluded from citizenship. As APG IG leader Celestino put it, "[Repsol] went to [negotiate] directly . . . with the third parties, and with whoever was the biggest [landowner] and already had [property rights]." It is precisely this racialized geography of rights that the Guaraní sought to contest and transform through TCO titling.

In this context, the land use contracts appeared to the Guaraní less as a neoliberal machination than as the latest link in a chain of historical collusions between the Bolivian state, capitalist resource interests, and non-indigenous landowning elites in this region. As another APG IG leader, Teodoro, commented: "They're all [links] in a chain . . . The manager of the [oil] company is the friend of the cattle rancher; the state official is also a relative . . . They surely made an agreement." In fact, after leaving INRA in 2004, Jorge Campero went on to work as a legal adviser for Repsol, fueling speculation about corrupt dealings between Repsol and INRA during this period. As these events reveal, extractive industry does not just *reterritorialize* the spaces in which it operates but rather maps onto *existing* geographies of property rights. In fact, the security of capital investment *hinges on* the state's monopoly on violence and its ability to enforce property rights (Emel, Huber, and Makene 2011). In Itika Guasu, as on many (post)colonial frontiers, this established geography of rights was predicated on the violent dispossession of indigenous peoples. Capitalist resource extraction thus worked to reinscribe a colonial geography of rights at the very moment when the Guaraní sought to call it into question through their TCO claim.

Property versus Territory

As the social and environmental impacts of hydrocarbon development in the TCO became more apparent,[6] APG IG leaders began to make sustained claims for recognition of their rights. In 2003 they complained about the lack of consultation and demanded land use payments, compensation for social and environmental impacts, and measures to monitor and address these impacts. They articulated these demands with support from CERDET and CEADES (a Bolivian NGO based in Cochabamba, formerly called CEADESC), and with reference to ILO Convention 169.[7] It was at this point that APG IG leaders learned of the land use contracts Repsol had signed with private landowners. Former CERDET employee Hernán Ruíz recalled a meeting between the APG IG and Repsol's subcontractor Maxus in February 2003, in which Guaraní leaders demanded land use payments and Maxus responded:

> "We've sorted it out; we've paid land use payments to the owners." And there the answer was: "There are no owners precisely because all rights are under a process of revision. And the preferential right is with the [Guaraní] people, with the TCO. So if you've paid, you've paid wrong, you've paid before knowing who is the final owner, you've paid wrong." And if in the end [INRA] determines that the owner is different from who [Repsol] paid, the company would have to pay again. Because to pay wrong is to pay double, isn't it?

Maxus flatly rejected this claim in a letter to the APG IG (Maxus 2003a). In late March 2003, another meeting was held, this time between the APG IG, Maxus, and INRA, in which INRA officials were called upon by the APG IG "to explain the situation of the land titling process in Itika Guasu, through which companies should respect the preferential right of the APG and mitigate the environmental impact" (CERDET 2003). In April, following a complaint by the APG IG to the Ministry of Hydrocarbons, Maxus agreed to fund a development plan proposed by the APG IG and to make payments based on the market value of land the company occupied. The agreement was framed as a goodwill gesture, however, and explicitly rejected Guaraní rights to consultation or compensation (Maxus 2003b). These concessions failed to satisfy the APG IG leadership, which, on May 28, 2003, organized a blockade of the Margarita Bridge adjacent to the gas field in zone 3 of the TCO, bringing extractive activity to a halt. Within days, the government had ordered a military division from Villamontes to break up the demonstration (Perreault 2008). This was just the first in a series of Guaraní road blockades that provoked a violent response from the Bolivian state (Gustafson 2009)—events that coincided with national protests demanding a new regime of hydrocarbon governance. In the months that followed, the APG and Maxus reached a compromise over land use payments and signed the final version of the first development plan, which remained a voluntary agreement.

Yet the Guaraní's battle with Maxus and Repsol continued, and the land use agreements continued to resurface as a pretext for defending or contesting other claims. An APG IG environmental monitoring team sent to inspect the four gas wells in 2006 concluded in a report: "This terrain is property of the TCO, for which reason they should have consulted [us], given that it is in a process of land titling and therefore immobilized" (APG IG 2007). Repsol responded by reiterating:

> All the contracts made with proprietors of the zone, called third par-
> ties by the indigenous people, were made following verification of their
> property rights, certified by the same National Institute of Agrarian
> Reform [INRA], so that the air strip, the gas wells, the Margarita plant,
> and other installations are found in properties that will be titled to the
> said third parties. (Repsol 2006)

In the years that followed, Repsol continued to refuse to recognize either the land rights of the Guaraní or their right to consultation and compensation, despite negotiations over a development program (discussed later in this chapter).

It is worth reflecting on the competing imaginaries of "property" and "terri-tory" that underpinned this conflict. Initially, Repsol—reproducing a "resource triumphalist" vision of resource-producing zones as devoid of people and con-flict (Bridge 2001)—simply failed to *see* the Guaraní and their territory. Instead, the company located its operations within the abstract space of the postcolo-nial nation-state, where a separate subsoil property regime (the concessionary model) eclipsed overlapping surface geographies. Once Repsol "landed" in the territory (Li 2014)—and was forced to negotiate land access—its primary focus was on "securing the hole" (Bridge 2013), something achieved through the private land use agreements. When the Guaraní subsequently demanded rights to consultation, Repsol responded that it required only small plots of land for its installations, which were located within private properties. In contrast, the APG IG insisted on its ownership of the *entire* TCO area (APG IG 2007). It demanded that Repsol respect the Guaraní's "integral vision of territory" wherein "the ensemble [*conjunto*] of natural resources that surround them, flora and fauna, rivers, streams, forests, mountains, are all part of territory" (APG IG, CEADES, and CERDET 2005: 32). It pointed to the synergistic impacts of extraction, which caused "impacts on their [the Guaraní's] territory, and not on a few communities" (ibid.). Repsol refused to recognize this vision, telling the Guaraní (in the words of one CERDET employee), "As long as you're not owners of the territory, you can't question the work we're doing."

The meaning of the TCO was at the heart of this dispute. While the Guaraní referred to the TCO as evidence of the spatial reach of their territorial sovereignty, the TCO titling process had ultimately served to bolster an imaginary of "property" over one of "territory." It did so both by fragmenting the space of the TCO (and consolidating private land claims within it), and by vesting the state with ultimate authority to allocate land rights, thereby obscuring the pre-colonial origins of Guaraní sovereignty claims. As Repsol put it, the Guaraní would not be "owners" of the territory until the state legally consolidated their property rights, nor would they ever be the owners of privately titled properties. While the APG IG defended an alternative "integral" vision of territory, they also began to articulate their claims through a language of property, as illustrated in the assertion that "this terrain is property of the TCO." This is indicative of how capitalist processes collude in the production of abstract space (Lefebvre 1991; Brenner and Elden 2009), subordinating other territorial imaginaries—a subordination to which the TCO titling process contributed. As the military's forcible removal of Guaraní protesters in 2003 illustrates, "violence [is] intrinsic to abstraction, and to abstraction's practical use" (Lefebvre 1991: 289).

As we will see, the notion of "territory as property" would continue to gain force in Itika Guasu over the next decade. Yet another important shift had also begun to occur during the course of these tense negotiations. Whereas Guaraní demands for "territory" were initially framed in relation to local landowners and the Bolivian state, hydrocarbon negotiations were now emerging as a key arena for achieving territorial recognition and control. While it was in communities that the effects of extraction were increasingly being felt, it was the Entre Ríos–based APG IG leadership that emerged as the injured party and rights-bearing subject in this dispute.

Scaling Up

The APG IG's bitter dispute with Maxus and Repsol took place against a backdrop of growing international critique of the corporate practices of transnational oil companies. In a context in which negotiations with Maxus had reached a dead end, this provided the Guaraní with an opportunity to scale up their demands to a transnational level. In 2005–6, the APG IG, CERDET, and CEADES collaborated with the Spanish NGO Oxfam Intermón on a campaign titled "Repsol Mata" (Repsol Kills), which aimed to draw attention to the impacts of Repsol's activities on indigenous communities across Latin America. In 2006, APG IG representatives traveled to Madrid to meet with executives at Repsol's head office and to publicize a report based on their independent study of the social, cultural, and environmental impacts of Repsol's activities in TCO Itika Guasu (APG, CEADES, and CERDET 2005). One night in 2009, I missed the final transport from an assembly in zone 3 of the TCO and spent the night outdoors drinking with an APG leader who had taken part in the trip. He talked with great pride and nostalgia about his experience traveling to Madrid on an airplane to confront the powerful directors of Repsol's international headquarters—a journey that few Bolivians would ever make.

While the visit did set in motion a formal process of negotiation—and the exchange of a series of proposals and counterproposals—Repsol's head office proved to be just as eager to circumvent and dilute the Guaraní's rights as their Bolivian counterparts. Under pressure from the negative publicity campaign, the company did eventually agree to make payments of $13.5 million over a twenty-year period for a Guaraní development plan. The company's proposed agreement framed this, however, as part of its corporate social responsibility strategy rather than as compensation for social and environmental damages. Moreover, the proposal contained a series of deleterious conditionalities, including that the APG IG abstain from any public protests for the next twenty years (the duration of the contract), renounce any claims for damages caused by Repsol in the past and for the next two decades, and forfeit any right to direct administration of funds or oversight of projects implemented by Repsol. The company's head office also refused the APG IG's demand to act as a legal guarantor for the contract, insisting this would be between the APG IG and Repsol YPF E&P Bolivia.

While contemplating Repsol's offer, APG IG leaders made contact with two European legal advocacy groups, Sherpa and Equipo Nizkor, which urged them to reject the terms of the agreement and to fight their case directly with the parent company, Repsol YPF S.A. APG IG leaders accepted their advice and offer of further legal assistance, sealing a relationship that would define the next decade. For their part, local NGOs CERDET and CEADES urged the APG IG to accept Repsol's proposed agreement and were unwilling to take their role in the hydrocarbon conflict any further—apparently owing to a financial conflict of interest.[8] In 2007 the APG IG presented Repsol with a proposal for legal guarantees elaborated by lawyers from Nizkor and Sherpa. Repsol, however, failed to provide a written response or to designate a representative from Repsol YPF S.A. to conduct negotiations. This led to the formal breakdown of negotiations in October 2007.

The Limits of "Post-Neoliberalism"

This struggle against neoliberalism is based on four fundamentals: varying forms of democratic expression (community-based, territorial-based, direct, and participatory), the recovery by society of its collective wealth, the reinforcement of the state—subordinated to society— for the sake of international protection, and, lastly, unification of the social movements.

Álvaro García Linera, "Neoliberalism and the New Socialism," 2007

Oil simultaneously elevates and expands the centrality of the nation-state as a vehicle for modernity, progress, civilization, and . . . produces conditions that directly challenge and question these very same, and hallowed, tenets of nationalism and development (the national development project).

Michael Watts, "Petro-violence: Nation, Identity, and Extraction in Nigeria and Ecuador," 2001

Engaging the Plurinational State

As the APG IG scaled up its negotiations with Repsol from a local to a transnational level, the terrain of hydrocarbon governance in Bolivia was radically transforming. The Margarita gas field played a central role in this history. Following the discovery of its abundant gas reserves, in 2001 Repsol YPF and its partners formed the Pacific LNG consortium, which planned to construct a pipeline to export liquid natural gas from the Margarita gas field to California via Chile, Bolivia's historic rival. This project, which foresaw minimal Bolivian state participation in profits, catalyzed the 2003 "gas war" (Hindery 2013; Lazar 2008). Indigenous and peasant groups staged a series of strikes and roadblocks demanding the nationalization of hydrocarbons. Violent police repression of the protests led to calls for the resignation of President Gonzalo Sánchez de Lozada, who was ousted from power in October 2003. This paved the way for the 2005 election of Evo Morales Ayma, Bolivia's first indigenous president, who promised an "end to neoliberalism" and the restoration of "popular resource sovereignty."[9] On assuming office in 2006, Morales passed the Heroes of the Chaco decree, which declared Bolivia's gas fields "national patrimony" and saw them theatrically occupied by the military while contracts with transnational oil companies were renegotiated.[10] Although not a full nationalization (Kaup 2010), this increased state involvement in extraction and greatly expanded the state's share of oil and gas rents—money that has been channeled into a range of social programs targeting poor and marginalized groups. Morales also promised to redress the country's colonial legacy through new forms of representation and rights for indigenous peoples, including the right to autonomous governance of their territories.[11]

Initially the APG IG leadership had high hopes that the new government would support them in their ongoing conflict with Repsol. In 2006, they presented Morales and Repsol with their independent environmental monitoring report (APG IG, CEADES, and CERDET 2005). The same year, they occupied Repsol's national offices in Santa Cruz and conducted a march to the Margarita gas field, calling on the government to uphold their rights to consultation and compensation. Yet their appeals seemed to fall on deaf ears. While Bolivian state agencies did conduct a series of inspections of the gas field, the results were never made public, and the government refused to intervene in the conflict. As APG IG president Nestor Borrero related in 2009:

> To date, [the government] hasn't reached any conclusion about who is right, the APG or the company. They keep telling us: "No, we haven't reached a conclusion." We've already shown them all the documentation, but all the government has done is to remain silent. How can they say they guarantee indigenous rights when there are guilty parties who have committed violations and contamination, social and cultural impacts?

As Angelo explained, APG IG leaders were told by the government that their negotiation with Repsol was between "private parties" and that the state could not get involved: "In negotiations [the government says]: 'You are the people of Itika, you're a private people, it's a negotiation between the oil company and you.' The reply of the organization: 'No, you're the father of the nation; you have to comply with the law, not the oil company.'" In July 2010, APG IG leaders sent a letter to Morales, whom they addressed as "the President of the Plurinational State," expressing their anger at the granting of twenty new environmental licenses to hydrocarbon companies to operate in the TCO, without prior consultation. As in their earlier correspondence with Repsol, the APG IG leaders explicitly grounded their claim to consultation in their territorial rights, accusing the Morales government of "explicitly violat[ing] the property right that corresponds to us as a legally recognized TCO."[12]

These examples reveal how APG IG leaders appealed to the MAS government for support by deploying a discourse of plurinational citizenship, in which indigenous rights were supposed to take precedence over the interests of foreign capital. They also continued to deploy a language of "property," which appeared to hold greater sway than "territory" in the context of hydrocarbon negotiations. Yet their demands as plurinational citizens and property owners met with an intolerant response. In private negotiations, Vice President Álvaro García Linera accused APG IG leaders of being "the single biggest threat to Bolivia's energy development," while Morales publicly dismissed their claims to consultation and compensation as *chantaje* (blackmail).[13] In a context where nationalized gas reserves are portrayed as the basis for national sovereignty and social development, those who contest extraction have increasingly been framed as a threat not only to the state but also to the Bolivian people. For the Guaraní, who have throughout history been placed on the margins of the Bolivian nation-state—as violent savages, untrustworthy allies, unproductive farmers, and unworthy citizens—such accusations were particularly hurtful. In this context, the APG IG leaders sought to defend their position—and membership in the nation—by affirming that they were not against extraction in their territory. As Nestor Borrero emphasized in 2009: "The problem isn't that we want to obstruct the development of the country; we just want legal security to guarantee that whoever comes here from outside will work well ... If a project guarantees, respects indigenous rights, the people are always going to say, 'Go ahead, work!' because it's development for this country."

This did not discourage the APG IG leaders from asserting their right to consultation, for it was precisely in doing so that they reaffirmed their citizenship. As Angelo put it, "If you don't make them comply with the law, no one else will; you as a citizen have to say, '*Compañeros*, I have a law.'" Another Guaraní leader, Román, accused the government of neglecting its responsibilities toward its citizens, arguing that "what the government is doing is as if you had a son and you don't want to defend him." Here, an analogy of denied paternity highlights the gap between the Guaraní's vision of a plurinational state committed to the defense of indigenous rights and the realities of hydrocarbon nationalism. Read together, these statements are illustrative of the tensions between the Guaraní's desire for inclusion in the MAS national-popular project and their continuing experiences of exclusion and dispossession in the context of extraction in their territories—an example of what Michael Watts calls "oil's double movement" (2001: 208). As the following vignette illustrates, their frustration was compounded by the continuing lack of progress on TCO titling.

The Bottleneck Issue

At 3:30 a.m. on November 28, 2008, I set out with CERDET staff from Tarija city along the cliff-edge dirt road to Mokomokal community, where Guaraní community members from throughout zone 1 of TCO Itika Guasu had gathered for a meeting with the director of INRA Tarija. When we arrived, participants were gathered inside a palm-thatched structure, sitting on plastic chairs and makeshift benches. The officials' arrival, also from Tarija city, had been delayed by several hours—reportedly because they didn't have money to purchase gasoline, although I had witnessed them tucking into chicken soup in Entre Ríos market.

The INRA director arrived just after eleven, accompanied by a younger female technician. The first task assigned to the pair was the on-site investigation of a nearby forestry conflict with a private landowner.[14] The officials trudged off reluctantly into the midday heat accompanied by several Guaraní leaders and CERDET staff. While they were gone, participants expressed their frustration about the lack of tangible legal progress, INRA's predictable excuses, and the lack of information about the current legal status of property rights in the TCO. The president of the CCGT noted that the unfinished status of land titling weakened Guaraní claims to prior consultation from oil companies. Community representatives spoke of continuing problems of land scarcity and specific conflicts with non-indigenous private land claimants, who continuing fencing untitled land while allowing their cattle to graze in communal areas. As one leader asked, summing up the general sentiment:

> Why doesn't INRA's departmental office achieve anything? Why doesn't the titling process advance? Why do they continue titling land to third parties? How are we going to move forward? We don't have land! We have to make more demands—they say there are no technicians, there's no money . . . always the same discourse. [Private landowners] are fencing land for projects without taking into account its legal status . . . cutting wood every day in our territory. We have to be like the *karai*—they have their property and no one enters—but that's difficult if we don't even know what is ours.

By the time participants reassembled in the afternoon to listen to INRA's latest progress report, tensions were running high. Many Guaraní viewed the director (Jorge Campero's successor, who was also from a local cattle ranching family) as corrupt and partial to private landowner interests. His speech did little to pacify them. He began by explaining that the titling process had been delayed for "financial reasons" and because of a lack of personnel.[15] He announced that he was unable to meet the APG IG's request for a list of all of private claimants to TCO land and their current legal status of their claims because the files had been sent to INRA's national office "for security reasons."[16] He then proceeded to deliver a report on the history and current status of the TCO titling process in Itika Guasu—a barrage of historical, legal, and technical data that was neither comprehensible nor new. Finally, under pressure from the assembly, he read out a list of the names and locations of the forty-nine properties that had been titled to third parties.

In the discussion that followed, participants expressed frustration with the apparent lack of progress or a plan for overcoming it.

Their angry complaints brought about a noticeable change in the demeanor of INRA's director, who suggested INRA and the APG IG work together to finance and manage the titling process. A follow-up meeting was scheduled for the next week. Although participants agreed to this, they speculated that the land issue would never be resolved by talking to INRA Tarija; rather, they needed to "go further up," to demand a response from the national MAS government.

Yet when the Guaraní and other Chaco indigenous organizations met with INRA's national director in Tarija city several months later, in March 2009, the dynamics were strikingly similar (discussed in the introduction). Ultimately, the Guaraní's hopes that direct appeals to the MAS government would overcome years of legal-bureaucratic inertia at the hands of INRA Tarija were undermined by what APG IG president Nestor Borrero called the "bottleneck issue": "The bottleneck is investment in energy development [to export] abroad—that's the problem of this government. If I were the president, I'd do the same, *compañeros*. Why give them the title if it's going to bring conflicts to fulfill the commitments of energy development to overseas?" By this point, the idea that national hydrocarbon interests were the underlying reason for the lack of progress on TCO titling enjoyed widespread currency in Itika Guasu and other Chaco TCOs. As APG IG leader Teodoro explained the theory:

> If we review the UN declaration, the ILO, the new [i.e., 2009] constitution of the current government, the Hydrocarbons Law 3058, it's clear . . . [that] before the government or someone wants to intervene or exploit those resources, they must go through a process of consultation, because it's inside a TCO. And that is not foreseen in the new [hydrocarbon] contracts . . . The reason why we don't advance with the consolidation of the TCOs is that we are going to directly intervene; we're going to demand that they comply with the norm and go through a consultation process. And if it's going to affect us directly, we can say that we don't agree and they're not going to exploit.

On the one hand, this discourse reflected lessons learned over the previous decade: namely, that transnational companies can gain state collusion to influence the outcomes of land titling in order to weaken indigenous claims to participation in hydrocarbon governance. In that sense, it points to the APG IG leadership's recognition of the *continuity* in state behavior under the Morales government. Yet these statements also highlight the particular, indeed exacerbated, contradictions between indigenous rights and extraction under the Morales government. As Teodoro and Nestor note, indigenous peoples had gained new legal and constitutional support for their rights to prior consultation on extraction in their territories under the 2005 Hydrocarbon Law (passed by Morales's predecessor, the caretaker government of Carlos Mesa), the 2007 UN Declaration on the Rights of Indigenous Peoples (ratified by Bolivia in 2007), and the 2009 Bolivian constitution. These changes were accompanied by the implementation of a new hydrocarbon regime that not only makes the state more dependent than ever on gas revenue but also commits the state to meet the cost of any delay to planned extraction. In this context, the implementation of indigenous rights presents a conflict of interest for the Morales government (see also Hindery 2013).[17]

If this illustrates the MAS government's continuing imbrication in path-dependent relationships with transnational capital (Kaup 2010)—and colonial resource extraction (Galeano 1971)—then the scenario is further complicated by the fact that pressure for extraction increasingly comes from *within* Bolivia, where gas rents are now framed as the basis for social development. As Angelo summarized the government's position in 2009:

> The government gives this excuse for not titling TCO Itika Guasu because there is an interest of its friend in this area. Its friend is the oil company . . . If it doesn't exploit [gas], this government administration could fall. So [the government thinks,] "How am I going to attend to a group of 4,000 little people, knowing that these little Guaraní [occupy] 216,000 hectares, instead of helping a giant, powerful entity that is the oil company, to generate my income and support the 8 million or 9 million Bolivians? That's it.

Here, Angelo captures precisely what is at stake here: a new regime of citizenship in which the "common good"—as defined by the MAS government—has become inextricably wedded to the extraction of hydrocarbon resources located beneath TCOs. In this context, indigenous land rights in gas-rich territories become a sacrifice necessary for the "redemption" of the Bolivian people (Povinelli 2011). APG IG leaders speculated that, without the existence of gas reserves, their land rights would have been consolidated. As the APG IG's vice president noted: "Where are they titling? They're titling in . . . Machareti, Alto Parapetí,

Ingre—where there's no oil the government's titling; in Tarija they're not award-ing any title, they won't do it the next month . . . Obviously the oil companies have fucked with it." Nestor Borrero conjectured that the government had "made some calculations of which TCOs of different peoples to title and which to leave pending . . . There were TCOs with a delay because of the big interest of the Bolivian state . . . and that included almost the majority of the Bolivian Chaco."

I now examine how the APG IG responded to this seemingly intractable situa-tion by forging new territorial strategies built on an explicit recognition, and stra-tegic exploitation, of the links between land rights and hydrocarbon development.

Negotiating Land for Gas

The APG IG's first attempt to link land and gas in negotiations with the state took the form of an ultimatum. In February 2009 (just before the meeting with INRA's national director), the leaders sent a letter to Evo Morales expressing their decision that no type of hydrocarbon operations in Guaraní territory would be allowed until TCO titling was completed. The letter was discussed in a departmental assembly held in April. Although the APG IG received no reply from Morales, it was asserted in the assembly that the letter had delayed the granting of authoriza-tion to two other oil companies for operations in the TCO. On the basis of this achievement, participants reflected on the success of such an approach; as one leader concluded: "It is necessary to reach decision-making political bodies, and finally realize that the hydrocarbon issue is intimately linked to the titling issue."

This statement reflects a shift in APG IG strategy toward seeking reso-lution of the land issue through direct political negotiations with central government—what one participant in the departmental assembly described as "winning on the field as well as at the table." This was an attempt both to circum-vent elite-dominated regional institutions and to capitalize on the links between the land and gas issues. Above all, it was an attempt to assert territorial control in a context of continuing hydrocarbon development in the TCO. Whatever ripples of unease it might have generated, this ultimatum failed either to advance TCO titling or to halt extractive activity.

A few months later, in August 2009, the APG IG wrote to the Vice Minis-try of Land requesting the indefinite suspension of the TCO titling process (APG IG 2009). Ironically, this happened at a time when INRA Tarija had just secured funding to continue with the titling process, following years of fiscal problems. This was the achievement of a longtime Guaraní ally and former CER-DET lawyer, Nolberto Gallado, who had assumed the position of departmental director of INRA in June 2009, following a series of directors who were overtly hostile to indigenous land claims. That the APG IG leadership should demand suspension of the titling process just as progress appeared imminent seemed puzzling. A long interview with a disillusioned Nolberto in early 2011 shed little light on the matter, although it did point to a breakdown in his personal relations with the APG IG leadership. It was only after obtaining a copy of the APG IG letter to the Vice Ministry of Land that I gained further insight into what was at stake in this decision.

The letter begins by criticizing INRA's failure to provide requested information on the status of the SAN-TCO process and expresses familiar complaints about the fragmenting effects of partial titling, affirming the APG IG's demand that "100 percent of the TCO be titled, that is, that the INTEGRITY of the Original Communal Land is maintained." The next passage relates to private property claims in the area of the gas field:

> [The APG demands] the annulment of all the assignments to irregular third parties, that is, those who have violated their resource rights and/or [expressed] opposition to the APG IG, and the priority in this annulment should be all the assignments that coincide with the oil and gas exploitation or transport pipelines that pass through the TCO, making clear that none of the companies that are found operating in the TCO has complied with the rights to prior consultation, nor with the procedures for calculation of damages, for which reason ALL are operating illegally and don't have the corresponding environmental licenses . . . All this demonstrates the total lack of defense of, and permanent violation of, our most elemental rights, including to property. (APG IG 2009: 1)

This passage reveals that the APG IG's decision to annul the land titling process was driven by concern that the TCO titling process would consolidate third-party claims within gas-rich areas of the TCO and, in doing so, weaken the APG IG's claims to consultation, compensation, and "damages" for new hydrocarbon projects and in ongoing negotiations with Repsol. CERDET's lawyer, Hermes Arce, claimed that the APG IG made the decision after being shown a map of the TCO produced by the Vice Ministry of Land. The map, which he showed me a copy of, reveals that a number of large private properties overlying the Margarita gas field were on the verge of being awarded land titles.

The resurgence of this issue—who owns land earmarked for extraction—further illustrates the continuities in resource conflicts under the Morales government. The APG IG's decision can be read as an attempt to preempt a repetition of the experiences of 1997–2003, when Repsol made land use contracts with private claimants and used these to undermine Guaraní claims for consultation. In fact, the 2009 letter makes explicit reference to these past events. Yet the letter also marks an important shift in strategy, based on the possibilities of the political context. Rather than simply waiting in vain for INRA to complete the legal titling process, APG IG leaders believed that they could get faster and surer results by *purchasing* private properties within the TCO. This is made clear by the letter, which states, "In the case of assignments to third parties that can't be annulled for reasons of legal process, [the APG-IG] will make an offer to buy [these properties] that will be 1.75 ... [times] the price of expropriation." The possible terms of negotiations over land purchases remained unclear; while some leaders emphasized that sales by third parties would be voluntary, by 2011 there was a discourse circulating of a "clean territory" free of third parties—a notion that generated fear and uncertainty among the non-indigenous TCO residents. Indeed, this is suggested by the letter, which proposes that "following a period of three years, all those who have not agreed to sell [their properties] will be expropriated and the properties integrated into the TCO."

Of course, the crucial question that arises is: Where would the money come from to purchase these properties? The letter proposes that the money would come from a loan from the national Fund for the Development of Indigenous, Originary, and Peasant Peoples, known as the Indigenous Fund, which would be "underwritten by the nationalized oil companies present in the TCO, that is, Transredes and YPFB." The repayment of this loan, the letter stipulates, "should be *deducted from* the payments that [the companies] should make to the APG IG for environmental licenses and compensation for damages, which will be negotiated directly with the APG IG."

This vision of the APG IG purchasing TCO properties with compensation money from hydrocarbon companies (as well as the Indigenous Fund, financed by the National Hydrocarbon Tax) never materialized and was soon overtaken by other developments (discussed later in this chapter). Land rights in Itika Guasu remain in the frozen and fragmented legal state described in chapter 3. Yet these shifting strategies of land and gas are highly significant. The 2009 letter marks the APG IG's abandonment of the "legal-cartographic strategy" (Wainwright and Bryan 2009) as a means of "reclaiming territory." TCO status had failed to guarantee the Guaraní territorial control in the context of hydrocarbon development. Instead, the state-led titling process had proved itself responsive to hydrocarbon interests, as well as to local landowning power. By purchasing private properties, the APG IG sought to take land redistribution into its own hands. This marked a turning point in the Itika Guasu land struggle, where for two decades an imperfect law had been wielded tirelessly by the APG IG as the only means of extracting territory from a recalcitrant state. Of course, this decision also marked the triumph of a market-based regime of property allocation over a quest for state recognition of indigenous pre-colonial rights to territory.

The 2009 decision and the ultimatum that preceded it also demonstrate how the APG IG sought to gain political and economic leverage from hydrocarbon negotiations to secure territorial rights—a kind of Faustian bargain of "gas for land" that echoed the strategies involved in securing state recognition of Bolivia's first TCOs (see chapter 1). Ironically, despite identifying hydrocarbon development as the single biggest obstacle to the consolidation of its territorial rights, it was increasingly *through* hydrocarbon negotiations that the APG IG sought to advance with the land struggle. This provides an important precursor to the events that followed.

The Agreement of Friendship and Cooperation

On December 29, 2010, the APG IG and Repsol YPF E&P Bolivia signed an Agreement of Friendship and Cooperation which put an end to their decade-long conflict. Among the terms of the agreement was the creation of an Itika Guasu Investment Fund totaling $14.8 million. While this was only slightly more than the "voluntary contribution" Repsol offered in 2006, the APG IG was granted autonomous management of interest on this fund, which sits in a Brazilian bank account. Crucially, from the perspective of APG IG leaders, the agreement provided written recognition of the APG IG's property rights over the *entire* area of TCO Itika Guasu, as well as a series of other rights established in international law. As I was not privy to the secret negotiations that led up to the agreement (which took place between my two substantial periods of fieldwork), it is difficult to say precisely what broke the deadlock in negotiations and persuaded Repsol to meet at least some of the APG IG's demands. Nevertheless, it is notable that the agreement coincided with a substantial new wave of investment in the Margarita gas field.

In 2009, Morales met with Repsol executives and Argentine president Cristina Fernández to discuss a new Margarita-Huacaya Development Plan, which would form the basis for a new hydrocarbon sales agreement between the two countries.[18] With a projected investment of $1.5 billion over a five-year period, this development was projected to increase the volume of gas produced by the field from 2 million to 14 million cubic meters per day by the end of 2013. In March 2010, the MAS government signed a formal agreement with Argentina for the sale of gas. The following year, Repsol YPF E&P Bolivia and its subcontractors initiated a series of new projects in TCO Itika Guasu, including the expansion of the Margarita processing plant, the drilling of several new gas wells, and the construction and widening of gas pipelines and access roads.

Under the post-2006 hydrocarbon regime, it is the Bolivian state via the Ministry of Hydrocarbons and the state oil company YPFB rather than private companies that conducts prior consultation processes—the usual context for negotiating compensation and other benefits. The Ministry of Hydrocarbons established contact with the APG IG in late September 2010 to begin a formal process of consultation and participation over the first of the new projects in the TCO. The process took place in mid-December 2010, when the APG IG declared it was ready to negotiate. According to APG IG leaders, YPFB refused to recognize the APG IG's property rights over the TCO—or even to refer to the organization directly—in the project documents it initially presented. By this time, however, with the help of international lawyers from Sherpa and Nizkor, the APG IG had won a number of concessions and were moving toward an agreement in its private negotiations with Repsol. In this context, APG leaders demanded the presence of a representative from Repsol alongside state representatives in the official consultation process. Following observations by the APG IG and its legal advisers, on December 16, 2010, the APG IG (that is, the eight leaders present at the meeting) reached an agreement with the Bolivian state. Less than two weeks later, they signed an Agreement of Friendship and Cooperation with Repsol. As the final chapter shows, this agreement provided the basis for a new vision of territory and autonomy among the APG IG leadership—a vision that both mimics and competes with the MAS government's resource nationalist project.

GOVERNABLE SPACES

Territory and Autonomy in a Hydrocarbon State

> [Indigenous] territorial citizenship is a moving target, one that
> leaders pursue, members assess, and multiple outsiders attempt to
> grasp and bend to their own political agendas. Territorial leadership
> is also continually reworked as citizens attempt to make the
> government meet their own expectations.
>
> Juliet Erazo, *Governing Indigenous Territories*, 2013

On March 23, 2011, community members from throughout TCO Itika Guasu gathered in the community of Ñaurenda—the birthplace of the APG IG—to celebrate the twenty-second anniversary of the founding of their organization. Celebrations began with an evening "cultural event," in which alternating Guaraní music groups accompanied classes of dancing schoolchildren, interspersed with speeches wishing everyone a happy anniversary and a happy future. The atmosphere was surprisingly flat; most of the audience sat silently through the hours of acts. When at midnight twenty-two fireworks were set off in celebration, the response was muted. Speakers blasted the usual Spanglish version of "Happy Birthday," and the audience was asked to stand and participate, but there was little response. One Guaraní friend contrasted the event nostalgically to the days of Machirope—a leader of the Guaraní land struggle in the 1990s killed in a bus accident en route to La Paz—who had been capable of rousing an audience with his oratory skills and charisma.

The next morning was spent in preparation for the official parade, speeches, and lunch, which had mobilized all the community's women. Throughout the morning's preparations, a rolling announcement prepared by Radio Nizkor blared from loudspeakers,[1] informing people of the terms and achievements of the recent "Agreement of Friendship and Cooperation between the APG IG and Repsol YPF E&P Bolivia S.A." In fact, no one seemed to be listening; those gathered on Ñaurenda's *oka* were more preoccupied with preparations for the speeches and lunch or catching up with friends from other communities than they were with the details of an agreement negotiated by an increasingly distant leadership elite. After peeling a few potatoes, I accompanied some CERDET *técnicos* to pick up slaughtered cows and *chicha* from a nearby community.

When I returned, the speeches had begun. Representatives of the APG IG leadership, CERDET, EAPG, the army, and the municipal, departmental, and provincial governments spoke in turn, each giving his (all were male) personal and political take on the organization's twenty-second anniversary. Also notable in this staged performance of plurinational citizenship was the presence of a community relations representative of Repsol, who sat alongside other speakers and was repeatedly welcomed, although he remained silent. When it was the turn of the APG IG president, Nestor Borrero, to speak, he told the audience that 2011 was a "special year" for the Guaraní of Itika Guasu, who had "cause for celebration." He went on: "On December 29 we signed an agreement with Repsol Bolivia S.A., which put an end to the difficult confrontation that we've maintained for many years. But we signed without renouncing any of our rights and gained full legal recognition of our property over the native community land and of the existence of the APG IG." Among the agreement's achievements, he referred to the creation of an "Itika Guasu Investment Fund" totaling $14.8 million, which he described as "part of our long-term funding strategy, which will permit us to carry forward our own development. This guarantees our real autonomy and that of our children."

This speech reflects the emergence of a new vision of territory and autonomy in Itika Guasu in the wake of the 2010 Agreement of Friendship and Cooperation. In contrast to the notion of territory as a space inhabited by ancestors, or where communities currently live out their lives, territory had come to signify the legal-political jurisdiction of the APG IG, as defined in relation to extraterritorial actors. Territorial recognition was to be achieved through hydrocarbon negotiations rather than land titling, while territorial autonomy was linked to control of gas rents rather than subsistence livelihoods. Conceived amidst a localized struggle against *patrón* power, the TCO had been resituated and resignified in the context of multi-scalar conflicts over the governance of gas. This is not to suggest that community members in Itika Guasu ceased to imagine territory in other terms. In fact, the disjuncture between the APG IG's vision of the TCO as a legal-political entity and community members' imaginaries of territory was a source of growing tension.

In this chapter I interrogate these shifting visions of territory and autonomy, and the conflicts and divisions they have produced. I argue that the APG IG's vision of gas-funded autonomy has to be understood in two key contexts. The first—documented in the previous five chapters—is the exhaustion of a multicultural politics of recognition associated with the TCO titling process. As will become clear, the agreement with Repsol gained meaning in the context of the failure of TCO titling to achieve the Guaraní's vision of "reclaiming territory"—a vision in which recognition was intimately connected to territorial control and autonomy. The second is the emergence of new forms of hydrocarbon citizenship in Bolivia under the MAS government, in which struggles overs recognition, rights, and authority have become intimately linked to the governance of gas. Put simply, APG IG leaders were responding to a national context in which other territorial actors—from departmental and regional elites, to peasant communities, to the MAS government itself—were framing their territorial projects and sovereignty claims around control of gas rents.

Contextualizing the friendship agreement in this way challenges the dichotomy between resistance and cooptation that frames many accounts of indigenous engagements with extractive industry. It highlights the fact that deals with oil companies do not necessarily imply an *abandonment* of indigenous visions of territory, but may reflect indigenous leaders' efforts to exercise agency in constrained circumstances and to position themselves amidst a broader set of political and territorial struggles. It provides further evidence of indigenous peoples' efforts to exceed limited forms of multicultural recognition in defense of more radical claims for resource control (see Postero 2007).

Yet what has emerged from this effort to reclaim the political content of territory is not a rejuvenation of a collective territorial project but rather a process of political fragmentation, the erosion of indigenous governance structures, and the harnessing of political authority to external interests and modes of recognition. By tracing these dynamics, this chapter highlights the profound challenges faced by indigenous peoples in contexts of resource extraction. Despite its defiant framing, the APG IG's new vision of autonomy also signaled a pragmatic acceptance of what could be achieved in the context of a hydrocarbon-based development model: an autonomy within limits. Growing skepticism about whose interests this kind of autonomy really served—and the emergence of alternative modes of hydrocarbon citizenship linked to national forms of gas rent distribution—have given rise to a protracted leadership struggle that has fractured communities and territorial politics in Itika Guasu. As this political conflict has unfolded, communities' responses have also been pragmatic, framed less by lingering dreams of reclaiming territory than by new opportunities for "development" and by the day-to-day challenges of subsistence in a context of worsening drought conditions, diminishing fish stocks, and ongoing problems of land access.

Reimagining Territory in the Age of Gas

Reframing Recognition

In his 2011 anniversary speech, the APG IG president framed territorial recognition as a key achievement of the friendship agreement.[2] Through it, he claimed, the Guaraní of Itika Guasu had "gained full legal recognition of our property [rights] to the native community land and of the existence of the APG IG." This speech could be read simply as an effort to pacify community members, many of whom had become skeptical of the APG IG's opaque negotiations with oil companies—something the event's tense atmosphere reflected. Nevertheless, my informal engagements with APG IG leaders during this period revealed that many of them saw Repsol's recognition of Guaraní property rights as the most significant aspect of the friendship agreement. By "recognition," they referred to the production of a written agreement, elaborated with participation of the APG IG and its legal advisers and signed by Repsol, in which the oil company stated that it recognized the APG IG's ownership of TCO Itika Guasu, as well as the organization's legal existence and rights under international law. As APG IG leader Román put it during a five-hour discussion in Tarija in April 2011, "They don't recognize you if you don't have a written document." Underscoring the connection between recognition and redistribution, he emphasized that recognition was the starting point from which all other negotiations derived: "Once they recognize that you're the owner of this *ivi* [G: territory], then we can discuss [other things]," implicitly compensation. Yet recognition was also important in its own right. If outsiders wanted to extract resources from Guaraní territory, he stipulated, they should say: "'Excuse me brother, I'm going to pass by here.' That makes clear their respect." This "respect"—which he felt the friendship agreement had achieved—gained meaning in the context of Repsol's (and the Bolivian government's) refusal to recognize the Guaraní's territorial rights over the previous decade.

The 2010 friendship agreement is just one example of how agreements over extractive industry development in Itika Guasu have come to *stand in for* state-sanctioned land title as a symbol of territorial recognition. An agreement signed between the APG IG and the former departmental prefect Mario Cossío in 2010 regarding the construction of an Interoceanic Highway through the TCO was described by APG IG leaders as the first time in history that the departmental government had given (to use Román's phrase) "legal recognition that the APG IG is the owner of Itika Guasu."[3] This acknowledgment represented a departure from the resource triumphalist vision underpinning the highway project, which was advertised locally under the slogan, "With projects like this there are no valid borders" (see figure 17). Later the same year, a legal judgment (Sentencia Constitucional; October 25, 2010) issued by the Plurinational Constitutional Tribunal, relating to a conflict between the APG IG and the departmental road-building company—which had leased a workers' camp in the TCO from an oil company without consulting the APG IG—provided such a strong legal endorsement for the APG IG's territorial rights (drawing on national and international legal norms) that it was heralded by the APG IG as worth *more* than a TCO land title.[4]

FIGURE 17. Advertising poster for the Interoceanic Highway project in Tarija. The slogan reads, "With projects like this there are no valid borders." (Photo by author)

As APG IG vice president Fabio (a pseudonym) told me, "We're going to give it to every institution so that they know, so that they too can read it." Such agreements gain meaning in light of the Morales government's failure to recognize Guaraní land rights—either by concluding the TCO titling process or in official hydrocarbon documentation, which APG IG leaders claim consistently evades acknowledging the TCO's existence, referring only to municipal, provincial, and departmental boundaries. As Fabio put it: "The ex-governor of Tarija, Mario Cossio, has already recognized everything, and the company [Repsol] has also recognized the rights of the people, but the only one who doesn't want to recognize [our rights] is the government . . . Abroad, in other countries, the APG is recognized; the only one who hasn't recognized us is the government."

Actualizing Autonomy

Perhaps even more striking than their reframing of territorial recognition was the way in which APG IG leaders reimagined territorial autonomy after the agreement with Repsol. As earlier chapters highlighted, from the early days of the land struggle, the TCO has been associated with regaining autonomy, or becoming *iyambae* (free, without an owner). Grounded in the struggle to break relations of dependency and exploitation with local *patrones*, autonomy was associated with moving freely through territory (uncurtailed by the presence of landowners), and recovering cultural practices that enabled ancestors to "live well" without reliance on outside goods and labor markets (for example, collecting honey rather than buying sugar). As noted in chapter 5, the Morales government has seen the emergence of new tropes for imagining indigenous autonomy, through the creation of autonomously governed indigenous territories within a "plurinational state." In the wake of the friendship agreement, APG IG leaders began to talk about the Itika Guasu Investment Fund as a route to, and a symbol of, indigenous autonomy. The APG IG president's 2011 anniversary speech—in which he referred to the fund as "part of our long-term funding strategy, which will permit us to carry forward our own development [and] guarantees our real autonomy and that of our children"—was indicative of a broader discourse.

Later that year, Román visited me in my small room in Entre Ríos, where we were able to talk out of earshot of other APG IG leaders and *técnicos*. As usual, he'd come armed with piles of papers, relating to the APG IG's numerous ongoing conflicts with private companies and state institutions. After a familiar discussion about the disappointments and insults of the MAS government, the conversation turned to the controversial hydrocarbon projects under way in Aguaragüe, a national park containing the Chaco's primary aquifer, which is co-administered by the Tarija-based CCGT and the state parks agency SERNAP. Román was scathing about this co-management deal, insisting: "Aguaragüe doesn't belong to the Guaraní; it's private property of the state . . . The state has converted itself into another *patrón*; if it pays you, then that's not called autonomy." When I asked, "What is autonomy?" he replied, "Autonomy is knowing how to look after your things." He went on to talk about the official process for establishing indigenous autonomy (under the 2010 Autonomies Law) in the Guaraní municipality of Charagua Norte, which he also dismissed as "not real autonomy" owing to the continuing presence of non-indigenous *campesinos* in local government. When I asked again, "What is *real* autonomy?" he referred to the agreement with Repsol, emphasizing, "We negotiated *on our own* with the company; now we're managing the money *on our own*; we made our development plan for the next twenty years *on our own*."

The fact that the money was from a transnational oil company, negotiated with the help of foreign lawyers, was unimportant. For Román, "on our own" meant independently of *karai*-controlled regional institutions and the MAS government, both of which had sought to contain the Guaraní's quest for territory and autonomy, whether through clientelistic overtures or through outright opposition to their territorial project. Yet "on our own" also had a deeper significance: it framed the agreement as another step in the Guaraní's struggle to break relations of dependency with their former *patrones*. As he went on: "Before you had to work for the *patrón*, [and] he would pay you in coca; if the women wanted to wash the clothes, then first they had to grind maize; you had to work a whole month just to get some sugar for your mate, but now you are working on your own, you're doing things yourself." To emphasize the point further, he compared the fund—the interest from which would pay for APG IG projects in the TCO—to "a donkey that you fatten and breed every year," concluding, "*That is autonomy.*" Imagined in such terms, the Investment Fund had transformed gas—a nonrenewable resource whose extraction requires little direct Guaraní participation—into a sustainable source of subsistence to be owned, nurtured, and exploited by the Guaraní. This discourse furthermore placed recent APG IG success in negotiating with extraterritorial actors over extraction on a continuum with early struggles to gain independence from local *patrones*. But whereas the latter struggle has been grounded in the quest for *material* control of territory—something to be achieved through state-sanctioned land rights—this new notion of autonomy rests less on land control than on the APG IG's ability to capture gas rents.

Somewhat surprisingly, Román did not see this pathway to autonomy as incompatible with an official state-sanctioned route; in fact, he went on to talk about Itika Guasu's future as a TIOC (Indigenous Originary Peasant Territory)— the official title for indigenous autonomous territories under the 2009 constitution and 2010 Autonomies Law—assuring me that "when we're both forty years old [i.e., in 2020], Itika will be autonomous." He looked forward to the day when, as a recognized TIOC, TCO Itika Guasu would have its own Guaraní mayor. Some APG IG leaders took a different view, insisting that indigenous autonomy was neither a distant dream nor the reward for completing a lengthy state-led administrative process, but rather something that has already been achieved. As Fabio proclaimed: "We're already autonomous! Because we're not maintaining ourselves here with [help from] other local institutions, we're not dependent on NGOs, on the [regional government] anymore—all those things." Like Román, Fabio emphasized how the Investment Fund enabled the APG IG to transcend the clientelistic relations with the state and non-indigenous institutions that had marked the first two decades of the land struggle.

My introduction to this discourse came almost a year earlier, when, having recently returned to Bolivia after an absence, I unexpectedly encountered my friend Santiago in an elite café in central Tarija. Previously one of a small number of APG IG–funded university students studying human rights in the departmental capital, Santiago informed me that he had now graduated and been recruited by the APG IG leadership. Following the update on his personal progress, I asked him about the state of affairs in Itika. Santiago's face lit up as he told me, "Finally the moment has come when we will be able to realize all our dreams." It took me a few seconds to understand that he was talking about the recent agreement with Repsol, which I had already learned of from Tarija-based friends. His enthusiasm about what the agreement meant for his people seemed genuine; he referred to aspirations to expand health services, build new schools, and recruit a range of medical professionals to work in the TCO. Perhaps more striking was the sense of pride with which he spoke of the agreement. He claimed that the APG IG had learned from the mistakes of the past and "done everything right this time." The sum of money negotiated would make the state's development programs seem like mere crumbs in comparison, he told me, beaming. More important, the APG IG would be able to administer the money itself, according to its own development priorities and without state interference.

Like Román, Santiago expressed great pride that the APG IG had negotiated the agreement without the involvement or knowledge of the state; indeed, he gleefully imagined the surprise and anger of leading government officials when they learned that "un pueblo chiquito" (a little tiny people) had managed to strike such a beneficial deal with a transnational company behind their backs. In reflecting on the achievement that this represented, Santiago used an interesting analogy. He compared the Guaraní people to a baby that was learning to walk—at first stumbling around uncertainly but then gradually finding a surer footing. This notion of the Guaraní organization growing up and achieving full personhood in the context of a hydrocarbon conflict provides a powerful illustration of how recognition and autonomy—once framed in relation to the state and local *patrones*—are now understood in relation to the governance of gas.

This discourse continued to reign among the APG IG leadership over subsequent years. At the APG IG's 2014 anniversary celebrations—a reportedly lavish event featuring a local rock band—the leadership formally declared Itika Guasu an "autonomous" territory. This came at a moment when many other indigenous organizations in Bolivia were still struggling to meet the requirements of the state-sanctioned autonomy process. The poster advertising the APG IG event (figure 18) provides insight into a vision of gas-funded, TCO-based indigenous autonomy. At the center of the poster, against a backdrop of the Pilcomayo River is the outline of the TCO. Yet rather than bearing the official title "Native Community Land," the outline bears the inscription "Native Community Territory"—an explicit critique of the TCO titling's offer of "land and not territory," and a bold assertion of the *political* nature of the APG IG's territorial project. This assertion of territorial sovereignty is echoed by the streamer above it, which declares the APG IG "owner [*propietaria*] of TCO Itika Guasu"—an assertion that simultaneously reproduces a discourse of property and challenges the state's authority to arbitrate property rights. Below the map outline, five photographs depict the forms of development envisaged from the Itika Guasu Investment Fund: the acquisition of tractors for maize cultivation and the creation of technologically

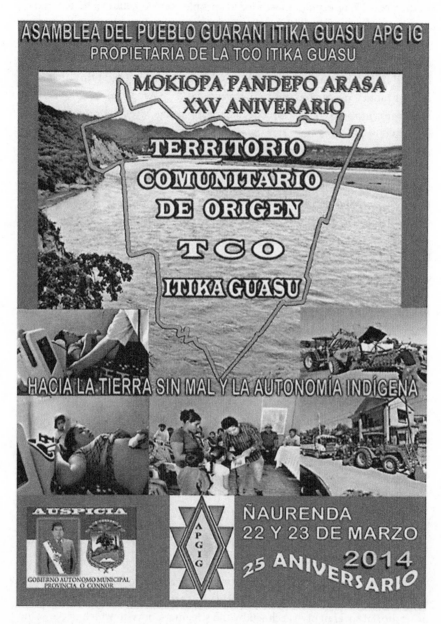

FIGURE 18. Poster produced by APG IG for its twenty-fifth anniversary celebrations, held in Ñaurenda community on March 22–23, 2014 (published on private Facebook page). Courtesy of APG IG.

advanced TCO-wide medical services. Inscribed across these images are the words "Toward the Land without Evil and Indigenous Autonomy"—a slogan that links a pre-colonial Guaraní territorial project (discussed in chapter 1) to a contemporary vision of gas-funded indigenous development.

Hydrocarbon Citizenship

The APG IG is not alone in seeking to gain access to a share of gas rents as a means to implement its vision for indigenous territorial autonomy. In December 2011 the Tarija-based CCGT proposed the creation of a departmental indigenous fund consisting of 15 percent of Tarija's gas rents, which would be used for the implementation of territorial management plans in TCOs. This proposal replicates at a departmental level—and seeks to provide an indigenous-controlled alternative to—the state-managed national Indigenous Fund (discussed earlier), which receives a fixed share of the national direct hydrocarbon tax—rents generated largely by gas operations in indigenous territories of Tarija. In early 2012, I asked CCGT's president Celestino, an Itikeño leader who served as a land promoter in the early stages of TCO titling, how this proposal sat with the official autonomies process under MAS. He responded that it was impossible to think about autonomy without fiscal resources: "First there has to be money." Rather than viewing the proposed departmental fund as a means to *avoid* engagement with state authorities, he saw the fund as a potential starting point for building new (and more symmetrical) alliances with state authorities—as well as foreign NGOs—to implement projects in housing, production, health, and education. Although hopeful that such resources would be accompanied by formal political autonomy, Celestino expressed the familiar concern that the TIOC status would serve as a pretext for the inclusion of non-Guaraní *campesinos* in both TCO rights and development projects.[5] The Guaraní didn't want this, he emphasized, because TCOs were an ancestral demand.

While Celestino complained that the APG IG was "doing nothing about autonomy" and had "thrown everything on the floor" when it came to the land struggle, Román was equally scathing about the CCGT proposal. He suggested that, like its national predecessor, the departmental indigenous fund would be a co-opted space; as he put it, "It might be a Christmas present, but with what conditions?" The idea in any case made little progress, and departmental elites—by 2011 largely aligned with the MAS, following the ousting of the right-wing governor Mario Cossio—seemed unlikely to approve it. Yet when I returned to Tarija in 2014, CCGT leaders were still busy elaborating the proposal, now visualized in a complicated diagram pasted to the wall of the CCGT's building in Tarija—a 2009 present from the MAS, although not for Christmas.

At a national level, too, hydrocarbons were coming to play an increasingly important role in Guaraní visions of autonomy. An interview I conducted in early 2012 with the APG's national autonomies officer in Camiri was particularly illuminating. An educated and articulate leader, he talked excitedly about a proposal for the creation of a national Guaraní oil company to conduct extraction within Guaraní territories, which, he argued, could provide the "economic base" for an autonomous "Guaraní nation." He went on to describe this idea in detail with reference to the experience of some Canadian First Nations with whom the APG had been in contact, suggesting that,

> at least in Itika, you could invest those I don't know how many millions that you've received in damages, in compensation, in an oil company that *you* manage. Where *you're* the owners, the shareholders, when the oil company is going to drill in your territory, *you* provide them services instead of them contracting . . . the services of other companies.

Criticizing the APG IG's isolationist stance, however, this leader emphasized that Guaraní involvement in extractive process should function to benefit the Guaraní at a *national* level:

> The beneficiaries are going to be the Guaraní nation. Now, there are critiques with respect to this: they say, "So you're going to be doing what the state should do." But we can't sit and wait for the state to do it, the central government. We're not going to wait; we too want to do it—that is part of *autonomy*.

As this makes evident, the reframing of indigenous autonomy in relation to gas rents has the potential to create new tensions within indigenous movements, as well as between indigenous movements and the state—dynamics that were echoed in communities of Itika Guasu, as I discuss later in this chapter.

These visions of gas-funded indigenous autonomy must be placed in a context in which indigenous peoples have, under the 2009 constitution and 2010 Autonomies Law, seen their demands for formal indigenous autonomy "domesticated" into a form of "autonomy without resources," which remains largely unachievable in practice (Garcés 2011; Cameron 2013; Tockman 2014).[6] They must also be placed in a national context in which political actors at a variety of scales are framing gas rents control as a basis for their territorial projects and sovereignty claims. Examples include the departmental autonomy movements of 2007–8 (Kohl and Breshanan 2010), the successful bid for regional autonomy in Tarija Department's Gran Chaco province (Humphreys Bebbington and Bebbington 2010; Lizárraga, Vacaflores, and Arostegui 2010), a 2011 interdepartmental conflict over the boundaries of the Margarita gas field (see chapter 5), and *campesino* communities' mobilizations around the gas-funded departmental cash-transfer program PROSOL (see chapter 4).[7] These subnational articulations of hydrocarbon citizenship gain meaning and possibility in relation to the MAS government's resource nationalist project, in which state control of national gas wealth is framed as the basis for popular sovereignty and decolonizing development (Perreault and Valdivia 2010).

Indigenous experiments in hydrocarbon citizenship must be understood in the context of the failure of TCO titling to satisfy the historically grounded demand of indigenous peoples for "reclaiming territory." This was made explicit by the national Guaraní autonomies officer, who situated his proposal for a national Guaraní oil company in the context of broader efforts to recover a *political* vision of indigenous territory, which had underpinned TCO demands but become diluted in the course of the TCO titling process, with its narrow focus on agrarian rights:

> I think it's the result of constant reflection . . . about the fact that, even if we managed to title our land, it turns out that what we've titled is insufficient—even though the initial demand was for our ancestral territory . . . There once existed a territory of the Chiriguano, the Guaraní nation, you see. This territory was the reference point for our demand to the Bolivian state, the titling process, and the process of consolidating land-territory.[8] So now the change [in our vision of territory] is substantial in the sense that we're transitioning from a way of thinking based on agrarian [rights and development], and now we're thinking of land-territory on the level of *political practice* [*ejercicio político*]. And it's there that we talk about *autonomy*. Indigenous autonomy now imagined not just for [agrarian] production—territory just for production—but to practice what we consider to be our vision, our own political project. So there is that substantial change . . . that is, we don't want the consolidation of territory just in agrarian terms but for the exercise of *power*.

By drawing on these broader examples, I do not mean to idealize the shifting territorial visions of the APG IG leadership. Rather, I seek to situate these in relation to the limits of multicultural recognition and the emergent dynamics of hydrocarbon citizenship in Bolivia. Indigenous territorial projects are both historically grounded *and* contemporary; shaped by long historical memories of racialized dispossession and by the processes with which indigenous peoples today find themselves entangled. Yet, the APG IG's autonomy vision was also fraught with ambivalence and contestation. I now return to Itika Guasu to examine some of the tensions and political challenges that it has given rise to.

Territorial Trade-Offs

The Wheel of Power

As already noted, the friendship agreement was not just about money; APG leaders saw it as an affirmation of their sovereignty over, and ownership of, the entire TCO territory—a challenge to regionalist and nationalist resource claims as well as to paternalistic relations with NGOs. In fact, in parallel with the agreement's negotiation, the APG IG began to demand prior consultation on all state and NGO projects undertaken within TCO boundaries. This demand placed them at loggerheads with a range of other local actors, as well as with the MAS government. In this context there was something disingenuous, something uncanny, about the APG IG's 2011 anniversary celebrations. Side by side on a makeshift stage overlooking Ñaurenda's central *oka* sat the departmental governor (a MAS candidate); the provincial governor (the former cattle ranchers' leader Winston Mignolo, also now aligned with MAS); the mayor of Entre Ríos (from a local *karai* landowning family); APG IG leaders; Repsol's community relations person; an army general; and the uninvited Guaraní president of Tarija's Departmental Assembly, Julio Navarro (now aligned with the right-wing parties), all awaiting their turn to comment on the APG IG's anniversary. When the speeches were over, they stepped down from the stage and joined hands with one another and with local Guaraní women—festively dressed in colorful embroidered *mandureta*, their cheeks painted with colored circles—for a traditional *rueda* (wheel) dance, accompanied by flute and drum (see figure 19).

The event captured something unique about this particular political conjuncture in Itika Guasu—and perhaps in Bolivia. In addition to conflict and power struggle, this was a time of shifting alliances, as local and regional actors jostled to find their place within the new "post-neoliberal"/"plurinational" order. Familiar faces appeared in new masks, as in the case of Winston Mignolo, the son of a local *patrón* now adorned in MAS colors, or Itikeño leader and former CCGT president Julio Navarro, who had risen to power within the departmental government as an ally of the MAS before switching allegiance to right-wing parties. If APG IG leaders and state officials cursed each other in private (and sometimes in public), the presence of the former on this new political stage was undeniable. Tensions were palpable but stage-sharing unavoidable.

On Ñaurenda's scrubby *oka*, the different male authorities obligingly allowed themselves to be whisked away by the colorfully-dressed *kuñareta* (Guaraní: women), their plump shirted bodies sweating beneath the Chaco sun. Yet where Guaraní communities fitted in this shifting configuration of political authority

FIGURE 19.   Local authorities join Guaraní women to dance the *rueda* at the APG IG's twenty-second anniversary celebration, March 23, 2011 (photo by author).

remained unclear. If authorities presented themselves at such events as embodying the natural, harmonious, and immutable scalar hierarchy of the state, then in practice the question of *jurisdicciones* (jurisdictions) and *competencias* (competencies) was undecided and viciously disputed. The APG IG's role in mediating community-state relations in this new context was also becoming subject to increasing debate and disagreement in the communities of Itika Guasu—internal conflicts that departmental and national politicians followed with considerable interest.

Autonomy for Whom?

El Departamento Jurídico, no somos muchos pero somos Machos.

[The Legal Department [of the APG IG], there aren't many of us but we're Macho.]

Skype tagline of APG IG leader Román, 2013–14

Even if APG IG leaders believed they had achieved autonomy through their agreement with Repsol, not everyone in Itika Guasu felt included in this vision. During the course of negotiations leading up to the agreement, the APG IG leadership had become increasingly distant from Guaraní communities. An important signal of this was the leadership board's assumption in 2009 of special decision-making powers through a new and unprecedented statute that allowed them to make decisions without authorization from the communities. While APG IG leaders claim that consent for this was given in zonal assemblies, community members dispute this; according to Fausto, the *mburuvicha* of Tarairí, who is himself illiterate, "They made the *mburuvichas* sign without knowing [the contents of the statute]—they don't know how to read." This decision led to an effective end to communal, zonal, and regional assemblies in Itika Guasu, the primary form of Guaraní political participation. Having attended seven multi-day assemblies in Itika Guasu in 2008–9, and missed many more, I was struck in 2011–12 by the dramatic nature of this decline in popular participation. Guaraní community members were particularly critical of the fact that the APG IG leadership's annual evaluation—when communities have the chance to replace ineffective leaders—had also not taken place since 2009. As Felix, the *mburuvicha* of Yukiporo, explained, communication and coordination between different levels of the APG IG leadership has deteriorated in the context of the centralization of decision-making power with a small leadership elite:

> There's no coordination with the communal leaders, the zonal leaders . . . they continue the negotiation with the companies, they continue fighting, but we . . . we're just *here* . . . They never come down to . . . the countryside, and that's what bothers us . . . I think that every year the *capitanes* should have their evaluation and I believe we should start mobilizing, because if not, the *directorio* is sitting there and it doesn't remember us.

This lack of communication and accountability fueled rumors of corruption and fiscal mismanagement by the Entre Rios–based leadership following the friendship agreement. As Felix speculated: "It could be that they're lying. Is it really true that they're doing their work? That's what we want to know." Tensions were exacerbated by the introduction of unregulated "salaries" paid to APG IG leaders after the agreement. The fact that this followed the sudden dismissal of the APG IG's widely respected accountant in 2009 fueled suspicion among communities, NGOs, and other Guaraní *capitanías* about mismanagement of the fund. Critics speculated that the severing of relations with former allies was also an attempt to avoid oversight, and claimed leading members of the APG IG *directorio* had used the Investment Fund to purchase expensive vehicles, private properties within the TCO, and lavish houses in Entre Ríos and other nearby towns. Shortly before I left Bolivia in early 2012, Celestino—then CCGT president and a leading critic of the APG IG leadership—informed me, after switching off my voice recorder, that some communities in Itika Guasu were beginning to organize their own assemblies to discuss the "state of the organization."

In this context, it is easy to see why the APG IG president's celebratory remarks about the 2010 friendship agreement at the anniversary met with a muted response. While some community members were indeed hopeful about the prospects for new projects funded by the Itika Guasu Investment Fund—and certainly wanted to ensure they got their fair share of any such projects—many remained skeptical about whether these funds would ever arrive in communities. As Pablo, the nurse from Tarairí, reflected:

> Money is tempting. If one sees money, the first thing one thinks is to keep it. But now, if the *compañeros* who are at the head, the leadership [of the APG IG], really think about the rest of their brothers who are suffering, [they could say,] "They're suffering so let's do this." But on the other hand, if they think of themselves, they're going to keep everything, and the brothers [in the communities] will end up with nothing.

These tensions came to a head at the APG IG anniversary celebrations in March 2014. According to reports by CERDET staff who attended the event, the APG IG, Repsol, and the municipal government introduced a rock band they'd hired for the occasion at considerable expense. While the performance went on, a group of community members gathered in a nearby house, where they played traditional flute and drum music. Before long the traditional party attracted more participants than the official staged event, to the intense annoyance of the APG IG president, who called in the local police to break up the rival gathering and confiscate the instruments. These competing festivities foreshadowed events that were to follow. Such tensions also manifested themselves *within* communities, where some APG IG community-level representatives—including Armando, the father of my host family in Tarairí—had also begun to receive APG "salaries" funded by the Investment Fund. This sporadic distribution of gas money generated economic inequalities and political divisions in communities of Itika Guasu, as I elaborate later in this chapter.

Environmental Anxieties

The APG IG's management of the Investment Fund was not the only source of concern for community members. In 2011–12, concerns about the environmental and cultural impacts of hydrocarbon development were also widespread in

Itika Guasu. Such concerns were not new; as noted in the previous chapter, these impacts were a central reference point in the APG IG's negotiations with Repsol. They were also the implicit basis for the creation of the Investment Fund, although its title evaded recognition of Repsol's responsibility for any such damages. Of course, financial compensation does not diminish the ecological and social impacts of extraction. Rather, as noted in chapter 5, the 2010 friendship agreement coincided with a new wave of hydrocarbon development in the Margarita-Huacaya gas field. In February 2012, Repsol announced that it would invest $327.4 million in the gas field in 2012 alone, as part of the first phase of the $1.5 billion five-year development plan (Energy Press, February 27, 2012). This included the expansion of the gas processing plant, the construction of a variety of new access roads and gas pipelines, and the drilling of several new gas wells. This new wave of expansion was already under way by the time I left Itika Guasu in early 2012 and was producing visible impacts on the landscape (see figure 20).

In October 2011 I counted more than thirty hydrocarbon companies working in the TCO and was informed that the registered number of gas workers there totaled 1,500.[9] APG IG leaders emphasized that the 2010 agreement made special provisions for their participation in socio-environmental monitoring. Yet the

FIGURE 20. A new gas pipeline requires the diversion of the Pilcomayo River (October 2011, photo by author).

leader responsible for natural resources (one of those who had traveled to Spain in 2005 for the "Repsol Kills" campaign) acknowledged that the APG IG lacked the technical expertise to assess or control the environmental impacts of extraction. As he explained:

> You need a professional who works on environment . . . I could say with my words, or note down, that they haven't done such and such, but . . . I don't know the environmental issue well . . . What you see is outside . . . but I have to see *inside*, I have to *know*. I have to know the subsoil professionally and also outside, and that's difficult to do . . . We're looking at how we can control the environment. It's complicated; all the time the temperature is rising and we can't produce.

This statement highlights the practical challenges involved in exercising indigenous oversight over the extraction of subsoil resources, a process that involves complex, technologically advanced, subterranean processes. Although APG IG leaders spoke of plans to contract European specialists to conduct an environmental audit of the entire TCO, this had not begun by the time I left Tarija in early 2012. Despite this leader's positive framing of the agreement with Repsol (which echoed that of other APG IG leaders, discussed earlier in this chapter), he also expressed deep-seated fears about the environmental and sociocultural impact of hydrocarbon development. As he went on to ask:

> What could happen in zone 1? What could happen in zone 2 in five years? What could happen in ten years in zone 3? What would happen if the oil ran out? What would happen if it didn't rain? What impact will the oil companies have, what damage will they do? What development are we going to lose? What development could we gain, now or later, or will it cause lasting damage? What difficulties will the organization come to have? Will it be empty land? Will it be land you can sow? It's very complicated thinking about all these things.

He also shared his concerns that the younger generation would become so acclimatized to the cultural and environmental changes associated with hydrocarbon development that they would cease to feel its impacts—both corporeal and ontological—in the way that he insisted he did:

> There are some people who know, who feel, feel that they're damaging their TCO, that the oil companies damage the environment. In contrast, now [the younger people] don't know. There are more people who feel weak. But the people like us, I *feel* it . . . My head aches, because this isn't in my blood, this isn't my life, to have to listen to the noise of engines,

of loads of people of different types talking, different people who look
at you and what you're consuming.

As his remarks make clear, despite the defiant discourse of APG IG leaders, they
were aware that their actions involved trade-offs that were potentially dangerous
and only partially understood. It is worth remembering that, as younger men,
these leaders had mobilized to defend a vision of indigenous territory as a space
of cultural preservation, subsistence production, and sustainable environmental
management. Despite their increasingly isolated existence in Entre Ríos, they still
had their homes, fields, and kin in communities of Itika Guasu.

These environmental anxieties were reiterated by community members—
most often through the widely held theory that hydrocarbon development is the
cause of the worsening drought conditions in the TCO. When I asked him one
day about the costs and benefits of hydrocarbon development for communities,
Pablo began by noting the limited number of community members employed
in the Margarita gas field, then referred to communities' environmental crisis:

> What are we suffering now? The drought, it doesn't rain. Why? Because
> not long ago—I don't know if you were here that time—they drilled,
> I don't know where, somewhere nearby, and a fire broke out. A fire
> broke out, even here, it made everything light up—I'm telling you,
> Kuñati, I was afraid, I was afraid! *Clear as day* [*clarito*], *clear as day*, you
> could see the houses, you could see everything! For a while it went out,
> for a while it lit up again. And who knows? But that's already a *contami-
> nation*. It's a worry for us, because I don't know the truth about it, but
> I ask myself this, Kuñati, the people of Puerto Margarita—how will they
> be able to *live*? Being so near, so near, over there in Yuati, over there in
> Camandaroti, and how do they live? And even right here one feels it.

When I visited these and other communities nearest to Repsol's operations in
October 2011, people also speculated that the drought they were suffering could
be linked to hydrocarbon development. They complained of deforestation, a
decline in wild fauna, and air pollution from traffic, and knew nothing about how
environmental impacts were being monitored. Even so, many of those I spoke
to viewed the presence of oil companies positively, owing to the employment
opportunities it offered. Unlike in Tarairí, the majority of men in these communities were employed by Repsol's subcontractors, although generally for menial,
low-paid, and temporary jobs that were likely to disappear once new infrastructure development had been completed. Despite complaining that wages are lower
than what they earn in the fishing season, people noted that oil companies provided a stable source of income in a context where environmental change made

subsistence livelihoods increasingly precarious. Ironically, the drought—which some linked to hydrocarbon development—made extractives-based livelihoods increasingly attractive.

Women had also found employment with hydrocarbon companies; on their own initiative, they had recently begun washing oil workers' clothes—a demand that they proudly told me had been incorporated into the friendship agreement. The five communities nearest the gas field had distributed four hydrocarbon companies among them. When I visited Zapaterambia, the community's women were busy scrubbing away at thick blue overalls belonging to workers of the Kaiser company, which hung on a long clothesline behind us as we talked (see figure 21a). Women valued the fact that they could complete this work in their own homes, alongside their domestic tasks, such as caring for children and animals, and the fact that—unlike handicrafts, their other main source of income—it allowed them to earn wages comparable to those of men. Women have also found work cleaning or cooking at the nearby workers' camps. They emphasized that they have had to fight for this participation in the hydrocarbon labor market but claimed they are "living better now" as a result.

As these examples reveal, economic benefits are weighed against environmental costs of extraction not just at the level of the APG IG leadership. For nearby communities, such benefits include not only employment but also a variety of Repsol-funded development projects, including house improvements, water tanks, health posts, school materials, apiculture, and a handicrafts shop (see figure 21b). Despite the APG IG's emphasis on the importance of a Guaraní-managed Investment Fund, at this writing the projects implemented by Repsol far surpass those initiated by the APG IG. Of course, the latter's impact is highly uneven; while the communities closest to the gas field have seen numerous corporate social responsibility projects in recent years, communities like Itikirenda (across the river from Tarairí) continue living in traditional palm-thatched houses. These projects thus illustrate both the reterritorializing effects of Repsol's presence and the way these effects have served to fragment and undermine the TCO as a collective territorial project and indigenous-governed space.

Community members' analyses of the costs and opportunities of extraction in Itika Guasu resonate with a broader set of trade-offs unfolding in the Bolivian Chaco, where environmental concerns exist but tend to be subordinated to, and aggressively traded with, demands relating to the distribution of economic benefits. To portray Guaraní communities as environmental stewards and the APG IG leadership as rent-seeking and environmentally negligent would misrepresent the complexity of this context. Communities actively sought participation in benefits, including access to the Investment Fund. They also acknowledged that they lacked the scientific evidence to link

FIGURE 21. Extraction's benefits: women in Zapaterambia community wash overalls for the hydrocarbon company Kaiser (a; above); signboard announces Repsol-funded housing project in Zapaterambia (b; below) (photos by author).

their livelihood struggles conclusively to hydrocarbon development. Nevertheless, for leaders and community members alike, environmental change and its possible causes provided a discursive terrain for articulating deeper anxieties regarding the transformative and potentially irreversible impacts of extraction. Unpredictable harvests and unplanned children fathered by oil workers served as powerful symbols of the Guaraní's diminishing control over their ancestral territory, notwithstanding the accumulation of written agreements recognizing the TCO's existence.

The Desire for Development

Communities' concerns about fiscal mismanagement, accountability, and environmental impacts all contributed toward growing tensions in Itika Guasu following the 2010 friendship agreement. Yet it was another issue that eventually came to the fore. Besides doubting whether APG IG projects would ever materialize, community members increasingly felt that they were losing out from other development projects owing to the APG IG's acrimonious relations with state institutions and former NGO allies and their uncompromising demands for prior consultation. These concerns were present to some degree while I lived in Tarairí in 2011–12, although they would surface more forcefully in 2014 (discussed later in this chapter). In general, most people shared Pablo's sentiment that "all institutions, all NGOs that arrive are welcome," regardless of their relations with the APG IG leadership.

While the presence of development actors—both state and non-state—in the TCO was not new, times were changing. As the community's participation in PROSOL demonstrated, the new "post-neoliberal" regime of hydrocarbon governance has produced an unprecedented influx of gas rents into departmental and municipal, as well as central state, coffers. Most of Tarija Department's hefty share remained either unspent or channeled into urban-based vanity projects, such as a series of musical fountains romantically named *aguas danzantes* (dancing waters). However, sustained peasant mobilization had succeeded in directing more of this investment into rural development projects like PROSOL, which were eventually—if unevenly—coming within reach of indigenous communities. In a context of diminishing foreign development funding since the 2008 global financial crisis, local NGOs were also seeking to position themselves within this new scenario; one employee of the EAPG noted that the organization was asking Guaraní communities to contribute resources they received from PROSOL toward EAPG-assisted agricultural projects. CERDET was collaborating with communities on similar hybrid activities.

Communities were also securing state funds through their own initiative. During my time in Tarairí, I was frequently called upon to transcribe letters to the municipal government, the few literate (male) community members being absent from the community for wage labor. Requests included new furniture and supplies for the school, the continuation of a food aid project for pregnant women and young children, and cooking equipment to prepare school meals. I felt a mixture of ambivalence and pride in my letter-writing role, and wondered who would write such letters when I left. At the time, I was volunteering at the school, where I had been assigned to teach extracurricular lessons to four eleven- and twelve-year-olds for what remained of the school term. One day I did an exercise with the children that involved their writing a letter to the municipal government requesting things they wanted for the community—which turned out to be a new soccer ball, soccer clothing, schoolbooks, and improvements to the crumbling preschool center. This was followed by an activity named "Who are our authorities?" in which I asked the children to match up ongoing projects in the community with the name of the responsible authority, and the scale to which each one belonged (TCO, municipality, department, central government). They needed a lot of help. Yet the activity highlighted the multiple and multi-scalar governmental relations in which Tarairí is embedded—relations that were increasingly linked to the distribution of gas rents. It was only afterwards that I reflected that I was schooling the children in a particular brand of hydrocarbon citizenship that was at odds with that of the APG IG leadership.

It was not only hydrocarbon rents but also changing racial attitudes that made possible communities' inclusion in state development projects. Fausto, in his sixties at the time, described how inaccessible local state institutions had been in the past. He prided himself on being a modern *mburuvicha*, adept at capturing development projects from a *karai* state:

> There are *mburuvichas* who are illiterate; they don't know *karaiñee* [Guaraní: Spanish]. Me, I speak Spanish and I get invitations from the municipal government . . . Before, a Guaraní didn't enter the office, not even of the municipality, it was pure *karaireta* [*karai* people], pure *karaireta*. Now one can go and [say]: "I'm a *mburuvicha*" [and] those in the office [say], "Enter!" It's nothing like [in the past].

As will become clear, local state authorities had their own reasons for seeking out such relationships. When I returned to Itika Guasu in the summer of 2014, communities' demands for unmediated inclusion in gas-funded, state-administered development projects had emerged as the central theme—alongside fiscal accountability—of a growing movement in opposition to the APG IG leadership.

Shifting Alignments of Sovereignty

A Leadership under Siege

I left Tarija in early 2012 amidst rumors that communities of Itika Guasu were beginning to hold unofficial meetings to discuss "the state of the organization." By the time I returned in July 2014, these meetings had developed into a full-blown leadership challenge. In the weeks prior to my trip, CERDET's director sent me several news articles proclaiming that a new APG IG *directorio* had taken over. On my arrival, I discovered that the reality was far messier than portrayed by the elite-owned Tarijeño media. In fact, an intense battle over leadership of the territory was under way. The leaders of the "old" APG IG of Nestor Borrero—still supported by both Repsol and Equipo Nizkor—remained holed up in their office (now in a different building) and were publicly denouncing a government-backed conspiracy to overthrow them led by provincial governor Winston Mignolo. In parallel, a rival leadership had installed themselves in other offices in Entre Ríos, supported by NGOs, the provincial and departmental government, the MAS, and some community members.

My first insights into this power struggle came from my old *indigenista* friends in Tarija city. Although they rarely journeyed to Itika Guasu these days, they continued to circulate between government consultancies, NGO jobs, and indigenous organizations, making them an informed, if not impartial, source of news. They reported that the uprising had begun in zone 1 of the TCO—the most productive and farthest from the gas field—and was led by Horacio Tarabuko from Ñaurenda, the birthplace of the APG IG. They told me that Tarabuko was being supported by Winston Mignolo, the governor of O'Connor Province and former president of ASOGAPO (now aligned with MAS). My friend Hernán noted the irony that Mignolo's family had formerly "kicked around" (*pateaba*) Tarabuko's as their slaves.

I witnessed these dynamics at closer range the following week, when I traveled to Entre Ríos. I arrived to unexpectedly cold weather; a freezing fog hung over the town, and I regretted not having dressed more warmly. On top of that, I had a stomachache and mild fever. I spent almost an hour looking for somewhere to stay; the familiar accommodation options (all modest) had been occupied by hydrocarbon firms, their walls papered over with corporate social responsibility posters, their entrances bearing company logos. I finally found a tiny cell-like room in the run-down but friendly family-run hostel on the corner of the plaza. After dumping my backpack, I made a few circuits of the town, refamiliarizing myself with well-known landmarks: Beatriz Vaca's veterinary shop, the central market, stores selling basic supplies for people visiting from the countryside. I passed the (now vacant) old APG IG building and abandoned CERDET office—both victims of the recent contentious hydrocarbon politics. Unsure what else to do, I was soon gratefully occupying my cell, where I slept a solid few hours. I woke up feeling better and decided to venture out. As I was about to descend the stairs, one of the two men who were chatting with the owner in the courtyard caught my eye; I recognized him as an APG IG leader. Before I knew it, I had been loaded into a APG IG 4x4 and brought to a large building on the outskirts of Entre Ríos, to which the APG IG had relocated—apparently to escape the prying eyes of local *karai* and the government.

In the building's central courtyard, one hundred or so leaders and community members had amassed for the next day's meeting. Above them hung a huge banner, which read:

Guaraní People's Assembly of Itika Guasu
Toward the Land without Evil and Indigenous Autonomy
APG IG
Property Owner of TCO Itika Guasu

The leaders took me through the courtyard to a back office, where I was brought before Freddy Gordillo, a former CEADES employee who had left the organization in a bitter dispute over its failure to support the APG IG in its ongoing legal battle with Repsol, and who had emerged as an influential *técnico* within the APG IG and a key advocate of its autonomy vision. Freddy was sitting behind a desk printing out some kind of press release. During our exchange (which was more of a monologue), various leaders either asked for or received instructions from him, demonstrating his power within the organization. Yet his defense of the APG IG's autonomy vision seemed genuine and passionate. He had little time for those (including academics) who refused to recognize its radical power. Charting the organization's continuing success in pursuing its "legal strategy," he described how, in a recent dispute over rights to land used for a gas pipeline, the president of YPFB had signed an agreement respecting the APG IG as the *dueño propietario* (property owner) of the TCO. Furthermore, Evo Morales had officially recognized the APG IG as *propietarios* (property owners) of the TCO during a recent visit to sign an agreement over the construction of the Entre Ríos–Tarija road.

More cynically, he described the euphoria provoked by Evo's visit, when more than two hundred Guaraní community members had lined up to greet and "defend" their president (it was unclear from what). Bizarrely, he claimed that Winston Mignolo had paid one hundred bolivianos to anyone who agreed to dress up in Guaraní costume and join the parade. The idea of a local cattle ranching leader garnering (apparent if not real) Guaraní support for Evo made me raise an eyebrow, but after all, this was an electoral campaign marked by such unlikely alliances and cynical maneuvers. Like governments before it, the MAS understood that doing business with local elites was key to achieving hegemony in the Bolivian lowlands.

Freddy also referred to the APG IG's progress in implementing Repsol-funded development projects, including maize production in Timboy (zone 1) using APG IG seed and tractors, as well as health services. Remembering the empty maize storehouse in Timboy I'd visited in 2009—a remnant of a failed maize cooperative set up by CERDET—I wondered about the APG IG's capacity to assume functions previously performed (not always successfully) by NGOs or government. Despite Freddy's optimism, the precarious state of the APG IG was clear. Not only had the organization relocated its office, but also, he informed me, the almost exclusively male leadership had enlisted Guaraní women to cook their meals for them—apparently so they wouldn't have to risk going out into Entre Ríos. Male leaders took turns guarding the office doors at night. In other words, they were living under siege. The primary threat identified by Freddy was the unlikely trio of the MAS government, Winston Mignolo, and Itikeño leader and then president of Tarija's departmental assembly Julio Navarro, who he claimed were working in tandem to oust them from power.

Despite the chattering crowds of community members, the meeting maintained a measure of this siege mentality. During that day's preparations, it was Armando (my host from Tarairí) who self-importantly assumed the role of gatekeeper for the APG IG building. This proved a frustrating full-time job, owing to the number of people wanting to come and go. Watching him clutching the gate and opening it readily for each familiar face that appeared, I reflected that the Guarani people I knew were not natural gatekeepers, but rather adept at fluid and flexible relationships with both people and space. It was curious how an atmosphere of friendly openness permeated the meeting, and facilitated my presence, even as the organization remained visibly under siege.

As I made my way out of Freddy's office and into the crowd, I found many familiar faces, including friends from Tarairí, who greeted me warmly. I was somewhat surprised by the level of community participation, given the APG IG's isolationist trajectory. The catalyst for the meeting was the existence of a rival APG IG *directorio* gaining increasing support from communities. Rather than a spontaneous "reaching out," this was a belated bid for popular legitimacy by a leadership facing growing opposition from within, as well as from outside, the TCO. In fact, the APG IG was not merely reaching out to community members but had also invited delegates from the APG Nacional, CIDOB, and COICA (Coordinator of Indigenous Organizations of the Amazon Basin), who arrived the next day. The widely publicized outcome was a joint statement expressing solidarity with the APG IG against attempts by the MAS and regional elites to divide the organization, which were compared to parallel MAS interventions in both CIDOB and the highland indigenous organization

CONAMAQ (National Council of Ayllus and Markas of Qullasuyu). Following a period of widespread critique from the broader indigenous movement, it seemed that the bravado of the APG IG's autonomy vision and its embattled plight were gaining interest from other lowland indigenous organizations, which were also losing patience with the clientelistic, divisive, and authoritarian tendencies of the MAS government.

I did not witness the meeting that produced this public expression of support; the next day, when the delegates arrived and the meeting was about to begin, an APG IG leader I didn't know informed me politely but abruptly (I was the only "outsider" present) that it was now time for me to leave, as an "internal meeting" was about to commence. Outside the building in the freezing fog, I saw that the arriving delegates had hung several banners, recycled from the G77+China summit held in Santa Cruz a few weeks previously (June 14–15). One declared, "WE ARE LIVING A NEW IDEOLOGICAL AND POLITICAL COLONIZATION"; another read, "TRANSNATIONALS PUT AT RISK OUR RELATIONSHIP WITH NATURE." I reflected that this discourse sat awkwardly and anachronistically with the APG IG's current model of hydrocarbon citizenship. Yet perhaps indigenous movements' shared marginalization by the MAS—implied in the first statement—would prove a unifying force capable of overcoming even the divisive effects of hydrocarbon development. I spent the rest of the morning back in my cell, huddled under blankets. In the afternoon I heard the sound of drums and went to join a march around Entre Ríos—a brief reversal of the APG IG's voluntary isolation from town life. The barefooted women—dressed in the traditional *mandu* with festive adornments of ribbon—danced resiliently through the freezing drizzle. Katuire, the oldest man from Tarairí, played a skin drum, accompanied by traditional flutes, as the new COICA banners were paraded through the town alongside decades-old faded APG IG cloth banners.

Later that day I was at the bus terminal looking for transport to Tarairí when I ran into a young woman I'd been chatting with at the moment when I was expelled from the meeting. Her mother was Guarani, her father *karai*, and she'd left her community in Itika Guasu at an early age to work, then gone on to study human rights. In the meeting she'd openly (and not especially discreetly) expressed her concerns about the growing authoritarianism of the APG IG *directorio*—particularly the president, Nestor Borrero, whom she accused of intimidating opponents and abusing his power. At the bus terminal, she informed me that she'd been expelled from the meeting shortly after me. As she boarded her bus, she introduced me to a large, mustached man and invited me to Ñaurenda the coming Thursday, where an assembly was being held by Tarabuco's rival leadership (an invitation I did not take up).

I stayed and chatted with the man, who told me he lived in the TCO and had supported the Guaraní in the land struggle in the past, but wasn't a current member of the APG IG. Remembering my conversations with APG-affiliated *campesinos*, but not wanting to assume his origins, I mentioned what I'd learned about this group. He related a similar experience: during the early days of the land struggle, the APG had approached him as someone who, like them, wasn't educated and had to "live off the land." They had invited him to join the organization. Yet, he claimed, the Repsol money was making the APG IG increasingly (racially) closed and *celoso* (jealous), leading it to expel non-Guaraní who had joined the organization earlier on. He complained that no real projects had arrived in communities as a result of the Investment Fund; rather, the APG was giving "little handouts"—distributing sacks of maize and so forth. He also claimed the APG IG leaders had blocked the communities' access to PROSOL, demanding the departmental program be administered exclusively through them.

A Kind of "Super State"

The APG IG leadership's sense of being "under siege" was not mere paranoia. As well as facing rejection and political revolt from some community members, they were the object of sustained derision and hostility from a range of local, regional, and national actors. Regional and national media coverage of developments in Itika Guasu provides insight into what they were up against. Following the friendship agreement, elite-owned Tarijeño newspapers ran numerous articles accusing the APG IG of obstructing regional and national development, denouncing its mismanagement of the Investment Fund, challenging the legitimacy of the friendship agreement, and speculating about Equipo Nizkor's collusion in a foreign imperialist conspiracy to derail Bolivia's national "process of change." On December 9, 2011, the Tarija-based newspaper *El País* ran an article titled "YPFB desconoce existencia de fondo extraterritorial financiado por Repsol a favor de la APG Itika Guasu" (YPFB Does Not Recognize Existence of Extraterritorial Fund Financed by Repsol in Favor of the APG Itika Guasu). It quotes the director of the state oil company YPFB for Tarija Department as saying that the fund "threatened the development of Tarija and Bolivia." The article goes on to note that the fund was being held in a Brazilian bank account and asks:

> Did YPFB know about the existence of the agreement? Did it permit Repsol YPF, a company that according to YPFB is only an "operator," to subscribe agreements related to hydrocarbon activity without YPFB's oversight? What has come of "nationalization" of hydrocarbons and [the related constitutional clauses], which say that YPFB is the only entity qualified to act in this arena?

The writer also expresses concern that YPFB could be obliged to compensate Repsol for this money as "recoverable costs," accuses the APG IG and Equipo Nizkor of violating the constitution by jeopardizing the state's role in hydrocarbon development, and calls for the NGO to be investigated by the Bolivian state.

Another article published in *El País* a few days later (December 16, 2011), titled "ONG Nizkor no da nombres de 'donantes'; los dirigentes de la APG IG se esfuman" (Equipo Nizkor refuses to reveal names of donors; APG IG leaders vanish), expands these warning and questions. The article quotes the ombudsman of Tarija as warning of the emergence in Itika Guasu of "a kind of 'super state' in which really no one can enter; I received a complaint in my area and I couldn't enter without permission from the APG." A named "analyst" is quoted as echoing this statement, warning that "in the coming years there will be confrontations between state authorities and . . . indigenous-originary-peasant nations and peoples, who little by little are forming a 'super state' that, without a doubt, will be a time bomb and a headache for any government." Other, unnamed "analysts" are reported as saying that the 2009 constitution is "a breeding ground [*caldo de cultivo*] used by foreign interests, transnational oil companies, and NGOs in the service of these actors to territorially divide Bolivia." One is quoted as warning, "The risk of balkanization of Bolivia is serious and action should be taken immediately to correct errors of the *carta magna* [the Bolivian constitution]." The article goes on to ask a series of questions about the APG IG's management of the Investment Fund: "Who are the members of the Council of Sages [who manage the fund]? Are they also advised by Nizkor? What have the resources of the Investment Fund . . . been invested in? What are the names of the donors of Nizkor? How much do they receive in donations? Since when?" While the author complains of his failure to engage APG IG leaders in answering these questions, I suspect they would not have known the answer to the last three.

Equipo Nizkor's status and funding sources have been subject to a series of articles in online news media, including two articles authored by Andrés Solíz Rada, who was minister of hydrocarbons from February to September 2006, when the famous "nationalization" decree was passed.[10] In an article published on the Bolivian news site Bolpress in January 2012, the former minister elaborates on the supposed links—some of which are rather tenuous—between Equipo Nizkor, oil giant Exxon Mobil, the Rockefeller Foundation, George Soros's Open Society, and the Ford Foundation (Solíz Rada 2012). Echoing the articles just quoted, he warns that recent victories in international legal cases on indigenous rights could give prior consultation a veto power in ways that would "weaken even further national states . . . like Bolivia, Ecuador, and Peru, accelerating the risk of their disintegration." In another Bolpress article, titled "*Pachamamismo* in the Service of the Oil Companies" (Solíz Rada 2011), Solíz Rada declares: "The oil companies and *pachamámicos* [those defending Pachamama, "Mother Earth" in Aymara and Quechua] want to destroy peripheral nation-states. They advanced with this objective on obtaining constitutional recognition of twenty-six nonexistent indigenous nations in Bolivia. This delayed even further the consolidation of the Indian-mestizo social fabric." Another article from the newspaper *El País* (January 12, 2012) plays a slightly different card, asserting:

> [Equipo] Nizkor doesn't have legal personhood to function in Tarija. In June of last year, the executive secretary of the departmental government [a former right-wing politician now representing MAS] officially confirmed that "Nizkor hasn't been granted any permission to operate in Tarija" ... Nizkor started to operate in Bolivia in 2006, which means it has completed more than seven years of illegal presence in the country.[11]

These examples show how the APG IG-Repsol friendship agreement has been perceived as a threat to the MAS government's resource nationalist project and, more broadly, to the integrity of the Bolivian nation-state. Such fears of the nation's "disintegration" and "balkanization" are reminiscent of the passage quoted in chapter 1, in which former INRA employee Tomy Crespo paraphrased President "Goni" Sánchez de Lozada expressing his fears of Guaraní territorial claims during the mid-1990s: "Isn't there a danger that the country will divide? Because the Guaraní are still going to be down there and what will happen? ... They could end up with the hydrocarbons and make another country."

As this reminds us, the anxieties provoked by the friendship agreement are not new; indeed, as I have argued, they draw on deep-rooted imaginaries that position the Guaraní as a threat to national sovereignty and a constitutive Other to white-mestizo settler identity. The press coverage I have quoted reveals how such fears have gained a new resonance under the Morales government. Whereas U.S.-educated Goni worried about the problems the Guaraní might cause for the neoliberal state, current discourses present the APG IG's agreement with Repsol as a threat to a collective national-popular project, an anti-imperialist, and supposedly decolonizing project waged in the name of "the Bolivian people." The MAS government's insistence in 2009 that the APG IG's conflict with Repsol was "between private parties" turned out to be an augury of—and motive for—strategies that would become deeply threatening to resource nationalist sentiments.

The discourses I have outlined are also illustrative of what Jessica Cattelino describes as "the double-bind of needs-based sovereignty," whereby "American Indian tribal nations (like other polities) require economic resources to exercise sovereignty, and their revenues often derive from their governmental rights; however, once they exercise economic power, the legitimacy of tribal sovereignty and citizenship is challenged in law, public culture, and everyday interactions within settler society" (2010: 235–36). Put simply, it is the APG IG's economic *agency*—a challenge to multicultural discourses of indigeneity—that has made its claims to territorial sovereignty so threatening to national and regional elites. The fact that critiques are directed at Equipo Nizkor in many ways represents an attempt to deny that agency, depicting the APG IG as helpless victims of foreign intervention, in much the same way that private land claimants opposed to the TCO claim portrayed the Guaraní as docile instruments of self-serving NGOs. Underpinning such portrayals of victimhood are regional and national elites' claims to sovereignty over indigenous bodies, territories, and resources.

These critiques notwithstanding, these articles also raise valid questions about the relationship between NGOs like Equipo Nizkor and First Peoples Worldwide (a U.S.-based NGO that also provided funds to the APG IG) and transnational oil companies. Countless hours following digital trails that link the organizations on Soliz Rada's list did not prove conclusive. For NGOs ideologically commit-ted to mediating relations between indigenous groups and oil companies, insti-tutional engagements with transnational companies and corporate foundations (for example, through joint board membership) are not especially surprising. As noted in the previous chapter, local NGOs in Tarija had their own indirect links to hydrocarbon capital, exposed when the Spanish bank Caixa, which had shares in Repsol, pressured Intermón to end its support for local NGOs involved in the "Repsol Kills" campaign. A friend from a La Paz–based NGO in charge of tran-scribing minutes from the COICA G77 meeting (delegates from which arrived at the 2014 APG IG meeting) reported the low-profile presence of the Ford Foun-dation as one of the event's organizers.

But acknowledging the blurred boundaries between the oil complex, the development complex, and indigenous politics does not mean that indigenous peoples are puppets of foreign imperialist interests. As I have argued through-out this book, indigenous struggles for decolonization require strategic naviga-tion of double-edged political spaces; they take place "in the teeth of Empire" (Simpson 2014). Lowland indigenous peoples' struggle for territory in Bolivia has from the outset been waged within, as well as against, the oil complex. It is worth remembering that the first TCOs were recognized in the context of a World Bank–funded hydrocarbon project. The articles I have quoted emerge not from a critique of hydrocarbon-based development, but rather from an ideologi-cal and political defense of the MAS government's claim to be the sole legitimate mediator of relations between transnational capital, hydrocarbons, and Bolivian citizens.

Of course, regional opposition to the APG IG did not play out only through discursive critique. In a context of growing community discontent, political opponents of the APG IG have thrown their weight behind Tarabuco's rival leadership, providing logistical support and the offer of development projects. This does not mean that Tarabuko and his supporters are merely "henchmen" of Winston Mignolo and departmental elites, as Freddy Gordillo and Equipo Nizkor would have it.[12] As should be evident, communities' concerns about the direction of their leadership were real and legitimate. Rather than a grassroots uprising or a top-down governmental intervention, the leadership struggle in Itika Guasu points to the emergence of new sovereign alliances, built around competing modes of hydrocarbon citizenship. Whereas the "old" APG IG's vision of autonomy privileged the TCO as a space of political control and economic distribution—a micro-level replica of (as well as competitor to) the MAS's own resource nationalist, anti-imperialist model—Tarabuko's group sought to facilitate the flow of hydrocarbon capital from outside institutions (state and nongovernmental) to communities—a model more compatible with the MAS government's "post-neoliberal" agenda. As I discovered when I returned to Tarairí after the APG IG meeting, these competing visions were being fought out not only at the level of regional politics but also within communities.

Return to Tarairí

Although I'd planned to accompany Armando and other community members to Tarairí right after the meeting, the cold weather and a resulting head cold forced me to return to Tarija. I made the journey to the community several days later, taking a private taxi from Entre Ríos to make the most of my limited time—an unthinkable expense for most community members (although an increasingly common one for APG IG leaders). Armando was still in Entre Ríos, but I found Sandra at home, doing her usual domestic tasks and keeping a vague eye on her two-year-old twin daughters, born during my absence. One had a clubfoot and struggled to keep up with her sister (although she made an impressive effort) as they toddled barefoot across the community's central *oka*. After catching up with the family, I made my familiar round of *visitas*, beginning with Fausto's large and predominantly female household.

During my previous fieldwork, community life had seemed refreshingly distant from the intense political struggles surrounding the Entre Ríos–based APG IG leadership. Certainly the more connected community members like Pablo had criticized their absence and wondered if they were "really doing their job," while others, like Armando's brother-in-law Hermes, had little faith in APG "politics" to begin with. But views of the leadership had never been an important topic of conversation, or defining of people's relationships with one another. By 2014 this had changed. The tense struggle for leadership of the APG IG had trickled into the very fabric of everyday life in Tarairí. The community was divided, roughly fifty-fifty, between the rival leadership factions, the two sides barely speaking to each other.

The news that I was going to visit Fausto's household provoked vague disapproval from Sandra, although she had long ago abandoned her efforts to influence my movements. When I arrived at Fausto's, the *mburuvicha* was out, but his daughter Mariana—young enough to speak reasonably good Spanish—welcomed me in with the usual offer of mate. We sat on wooden stools sipping the sugary herbal brew and exchanged pleasantries and gossip. The most significant piece of the latter was that in my absence Mariana had had a baby daughter, fathered by a now absent *karai* construction worker from the municipal ecotourism project. The child sat cradled in her lap as we spoke.

In the past, I was usually the one who instigated any discussion of local politics with the community's women, and responses were often cynically detached, if not wholly indifferent. I was surprised, then, by the passion and spontaneity with which Mariana offered me her lengthy analysis of the current leadership struggle. She was damning in her critique of the old APG IG leadership—in particular the president, noting that he "isn't even Guaraní" (a reference to Borrero's mixed parentage). Some of her criticisms were familiar: "Nestor works in the office and we don't have anything, we continue as poor people"; "We just want to see evidence of the accounts [*rendición de cuentas*]"; "Nestor says that he's going to lock up in jail anyone who doesn't support him." But the critique that came to the fore was the way in which the APG IG's attempts to exercise territorial control by demanding prior consultation were jeopardizing the arrival of development projects to the community.

> Nestor says [there must be] consultation, [and that's why] government projects don't come; he doesn't want projects with the government, or with CERDET . . . Nestor asks for a load of paper—consultation—but if the community wants [the project], he shouldn't have to say "consultation." Nestor wouldn't have brought [electric] lights. We have to say, "Yes, we want projects," if someone comes from the municipality, from the [central] government.

She viewed the rival APG IG leadership as the solution, describing how its leader, Tarabuko, was "looking for computers," had "personnel in Entre Ríos supporting him," and was "getting projects for the community." Tarabuko "can accept projects now," she emphasized. "He doesn't ask for consultation; he speaks more Guaraní, he's come here, to talk to Dad [Fausto]." In contrast, "Nestor says, 'Consultation, consultation, first you have to do a consultation.'" She gave the example of the Plan de Empleo—a vote-winning departmentally managed gas-funded public employment scheme that usually focused on road improvements—complaining that Nestor "didn't want it to come," but "the community needs money to buy things, needs money, and he blocks it, says they have to come to the office; that's why we're not working in the Plan de Empleo." She also referred to the fact that the departmental electrification project currently under way—half of Tarairí's houses had been connected to the grid at the time of my visit—had arrived four months late, owing to the APG IG's demand for prior consultation. Summarizing her analysis of the situation, she concluded: "The departmental government supports us with electric light and water tanks; from the municipal government we got the ecotourism [project], we have chicken coops from CERDET, and what have we got from the APG? Well, nothing!" She spoke of the divisions the situation had created in the community, claiming that people on different sides of the leadership battle no longer talked to each other (something I learned was not completely true).

My next visit was to Pablo's house, where the *mburuvicha*, returning from agricultural tasks, soon joined us and interceded in the conversation. Pablo described how communities' demands for oversight of accounts had been a key factor that led them to organize a series of assemblies, in which they elected a new APG IG *directorio*. Fausto interjected that there had been five assemblies to date and that Tarabuko was elected before three hundred community members, confirming his involvement in these events. Like Mariana, Pablo emphasized the lost opportunities for development resulting from the APG IG's hostile relationship with state and non-state entities: "It's cost us a great deal; if there isn't a consultation, there isn't [a project]. There are institutions or NGOs that want to reach the community, and [the APG IG] obstruct them without consulting us." Although he insisted, "I don't get involved in that; I look after my work," he described how the TCO-level struggle over political authority had replicated itself at a community level. He claimed that those affiliated with Nestor's leadership were demanding consultation from public doctors arriving in the community, reporting one doctor's anger when he was barred from entering a house. Pablo complained that the APG IG was also demanding consultation from Health Ministry doctors and expressed his concern that this would jeopardize his ability to manage the community's health needs, insisting, "I need a doctor—I'm not a doctor, I'm a nurse."

Pablo also complained that the APG IG's promised projects for health, education, and employment, financed by the Investment Fund, had failed to materialize: "They should come to see the children—what they need, whether they have books, if they need medicines, if the water pump is working. They always say that they have money—14.8 million [dollars]—but *where is that money? What are they investing it in?* What's more, they've started to divide the people." He answered his own questions with another:

How many workers are there now [in the APG]? Maybe fifty—and all are family. With a salary of more than seven thousand bolivianos—they're not even graduates, they don't even know how to read, they don't even know how to write, and they're occupying top positions. And there are people who are graduates and they don't want them to enter.

Pablo identified the origin of this trajectory as the fateful 2009 statute, which had removed communities' oversight and decision-making power. He described how APG IG leaders were now picked up by taxi—a far cry from the early days of the organization, when leaders would walk hours and sometimes days to garner local support for the land struggle.

Fausto echoed these frustrations, commenting: "There are no projects; 'consultation, consultation, consultation,' they say . . . Itikirenda doesn't have houses like these," a reference to that community's traditional palm-thatched abodes. "The APG was supposed to do that [i.e., build houses], but they haven't done it." Instead, Pablo interjected, the APG leaders had threatened to send a tractor to Tarairí to *flatten* the houses of anyone who opposed them. When critics sought dialogue, they "shut themselves in their office and . . . padlocked the door." Fausto mentioned a meeting he had scheduled with the departmental government regarding a new Plan de Empleo and a second communal *potrero*, making clear that—the continuing presence of the old APG IG *directorio* notwithstanding—a new set of relationships and political alliances was already starting to take effect in communities of Itika Guasu.

My final visit was to Victoria's all-female household, where she had returned after a long absence working in the bustling village of Palos Blancos at the southeastern boundary of the TCO, a key accommodation and transport hub for hydrocarbon companies. Victoria, like Mariana, had had a second daughter in my absence, fathered by an absent *karai* man and, like Sandra's daughter, born with a clubfoot that remained untreated—although she claimed that she was actively seeking treatment, whereas Sandra was not. While I first assumed this was connected to the contentious political struggles around state doctors' visits, Victoria told me that Sandra's child's elderly grandmother had physically removed her to prevent the doctor from treating her.

Back at my old home, I continued to realize that things were more complicated than the picture of polarized relations first presented to me. Over breakfast, building up a fire to boil water for mate, Sandra gazed at the foot of her daughter, who lay cradled in her lap, and—contradicting Victoria's comments—told me the child was going to be operated on soon, something she seemed eager to have happen. I asked where, and she told me the doctor who visited the house had suggested Bermejo or La Paz. "But we also have a doctor here," she added.

I thought she might be referring to the Repsol-funded APG IG doctor, but it turned out she meant the departmental public health service, funded by Tarija's hefty share of the direct hydrocarbons tax. Somewhat surprised, I asked out of curiosity if she was participating in the CERDET chicken project. She said she was too busy with the children but that her daughter Mabel was. Indeed, shortly afterwards Mabel appeared, carrying a plastic bowl containing a dead chicken. Other young women from Fausto's household could be seen scurrying across the community collecting chicks—which they planned to sell in Entre Ríos—in time for the arrival of the *micro*, which now comes twice a week to the community, since the municipally funded road improvements. Sandra informed me proudly that Mabel had been up for much of the night helping the other young women collect chicks.

As this revealed, the complex webs of relationships—of communal labor, development provision, familial care, and traditional knowledge—that constitute Tarairí community had been only partially reconfigured by the divisive politics of the APG leadership struggle. Yet even Sandra positioned herself in this struggle. In the hushed whisper she used for gossip, she told me that Fausto was "with the *gobernación* [departmental government]" and they were making problems, trying to overthrow Nestor. Nestor was planning a project for new houses, she reported optimistically; he had even said they could have two floors. Perhaps imagining the benefits of more space, Sandra told me that her father had recently died and she planned to bring her mother to live with them. The APG had promised to collect her—from a faraway community near Camiri—in their *camionetta* (pickup truck), she said. She seemed impatient for this to happen but powerless to act. I asked how long she'd been waiting. She didn't reply but reflected that the APG delegates who'd come from Camiri to the APG IG meeting could have brought her mother. Clearly, the embattled APG IG leadership had other priorities.

Supervised Sovereignty

When I left Bolivia in August 2014, the leadership struggle remained unresolved, with the two rival APG IG leadership committees claiming authority and pursuing their competing forms of territorial governance. A few months later, on November 10, the Tarijeño newspaper *El País* reported that representatives from Repsol YPF E&P Bolivia had signed an Act of Coordination and Relations with Tarabuko, recognizing his APG IG committee as the legitimate authority of TCO Itika Guasu. The agreement was announced publicly by Guaraní leader Julio Navarro, then president of Tarija's Departmental Assembly. In his address, Navarro described the agreement as "a triumph for the [Guaraní] people." He claimed that management of the Investment Fund had passed to the new *directorio* but pointed to an important change in the fund's administration: "With respect to the administration of economic resources, [under the old leadership] one didn't know how much was spent each day or month . . . That's why we've agreed with Repsol that, from now on, it will be a joint task." Paraphrasing the remainder of Navarro's statement, the article continues:

> He also recognized that it isn't possible that one can make this kind of agreement in an isolated manner outside of the national norm, for which reason he proposed some modifications in the original document, because, as he said, supervision [*fiscalización*] of the administration of the APG IG is necessary, and in this the state could be "an overseer" [*veedor*]. On this last point, he said that control of the management of resources would also pass under the gaze [*bajo los ojos*] of the oil company, because given that it was the oil company that gave the money, it's necessary that it knows what it's being spent on and how they are doing it.

The article quotes a passage from the agreement, which states that "an obligatory meeting will take place every six months . . . as well as a trimestral meeting in TCO Itika Guasu that will be undertaken in zonal meetings, on the request of the leadership of the APG IG."

At first I assumed this would mark the final demise of the APG IG headed by Nestor Borrero and its dream of gas-funded autonomous territorial development, undertaken without state or corporate supervision. Yet Skype communications revealed that Borrero's leadership continued to occupy their offices and Equipo Nizkor continued to publish articles denouncing the MAS and Winston Mignolo's political interventions and "racist attacks" on the APG IG leadership. When I visited Tarija again in April 2016, the two leaderships were engaged in a lengthy legal battle involving a string of complaints, sentences, and demands for legal protection directed at distinct levels of governmental and judicial authority as well as at a broader indigenous movement that was itself deeply divided between pro- and anti-government factions. On October 12, 2016, Borrero's leadership committee published a statement denouncing a new YPFB consultation process with Tarabuko's leadership committee as part of a "merciless legal attack which is aimed . . . at destroying the legal authorities of Guarani communities." When I returned to Tarija in April 2017, the leadership struggle was still ongoing, with reports that Tarabuko's group had travelled to Brazil to access the Investment Fund only to discover that $6.8 million of the $14.8 million was missing. The MAS government continued to negotiate hydrocarbon projects with Tarabuko's (apparently compliant) leadership, while Borrero retained tenuous support from some factions of a broader indigenous movement that was itself deeply divided. The outcome of the leadership struggle in Itika Guasu remains to be seen, as does the future of the MAS government's resource nationalist project. But one thing seems clear: two decades after the INRA Law created TCOs, indigenous territorial politics in the Chaco have become inextricably bound up in a broader set of conflicts around the governance of extraction.

CONCLUSION

This book has traced the evolution of one lowland indigenous people's struggle for territory in Bolivia, from its insurgent origins to its more recent evolution under the MAS government. As I have shown, this struggle for territory emerged in response to a history of colonial dispossession and exclusionary citizenship in the Bolivian lowlands and cannot be understood outside that context. Yet it was also shaped by a particular global conjuncture, which saw new forms of multicultural recognition alongside pro-market reforms that opened up indigenous territories to transnational investment. TCOs were forged at the intersection of these processes, revealing indigenous peoples' ability to insert their historically grounded demands into an evolving and contested development agenda.

Since the 1980s, TCOs have reshaped identities, territories, and politics across Bolivia in ways that have been largely overlooked by academic scholarship. With this book I have sought to address this gap. I have examined to what extent TCO recognition enabled the thirty-six Guaraní communities that make up Itika Guasu to achieve their historic demand for "territory." I have also explored how indigenous visions and strategies of territory are changing, in ways that are informed both by past experiences of struggle and by a changing national context. The MAS government's "process of change" has called into question traditional understandings of citizenship, nation, and the state in Bolivia. Yet it has also seen the continuation of an explosive double movement: an expanding framework of indigenous rights alongside intensifying hydrocarbon extraction in indigenous territories.

When we consider the situation of Guaraní communities of Itika Guasu prior to the construction of a territorial claim—when most remained trapped in relations of debt peonage on *karai* haciendas—the achievements over this period are striking. While this was not all thanks to the TCO, the TCO has served as an agglutinating force and guiding imaginary for a broader decolonial struggle that has transformed Guaraní relations with local landowners, state institutions, and transnational companies. I have tried not to lose sight of these achievements, or of the continuing evolution of the Guaraní struggle for territory.

Yet this book has also exposed the *limits* of TCO mapping and land titling as a route to achieving the Guaraní's agenda of "reclaiming territory." My emphasis on these limits is informed by the profound disillusionment felt by many Guaraní people in Itika Guasu (and other Guaraní TCOs) regarding the outcomes of their TCO claim. It is also informed by the failure of most previous literature on indigenous mapping and land titling to examine the lasting social, political, and material outcomes of these processes in relation to indigenous peoples' territorial aspirations and projects.

I have shown how state knowledges of property and abstract space subordinated Guaraní territorial imaginaries and resource practices; how legal norms were reworked in situ in ways that privileged the interests of non-indigenous land claimants; and how hydrocarbon interests shaped and obstructed the allocation of land rights in TCOs, shoring up a (post)colonial geography of private property predicated on indigenous dispossession.

These dynamics cannot be reduced to the unfolding of a neoliberal governmental project. The Guaraní's ambivalent engagements with a "neoliberal" state were just one iteration of a postcolonial predicament in which subalterns are forced to struggle within the knowledges and institutions of postcolonial society. While such engagements are productive and potentially transformative, the resulting spaces are never free from the power relations surrounding their production. Thus, although TCO claims remapped the Bolivian lowlands, this new geography did not have the power to override state boundaries, private property, or capitalist resource concessions. Nor did it empower indigenous community members or state officials to confront a settler population willing to defend their land with violence. In a context in which mapping and land titling remain central to many indigenous struggles, it is important to reflect on these limits. Nevertheless, this book is not just a story of frustrated aspirations. It is also a story of how indigenous peoples in Bolivia have responded to these limits.

Materializing Recognition

In June 2014 I gave a presentation in Tarija city in which I shared some of the conclusions of my research. The audience was small and consisted largely of NGO staff and activists: urban middle-class intellectuals with a long-standing involvement in local indigenous movements. My presentation took place against the tense backdrop of the APG IG leadership struggle. On one side was Nestor Borrero's leadership, seeking to implement their own contentious vision of indigenous autonomy, based on the implementation of prior consultation and their management of the Repsol-financed Investment Fund. On the other was Horacio Tarabuko's rival group, promising a return of collective decision making and the fast-tracking of a variety of state-funded development projects in the

TCO. Both projects positioned the TCO as a governable (and investible) space within a hydrocarbon economy, something I had begun to think about in terms of hydrocarbon citizenship.

I was still struggling to define my position on these dynamics. I was also keenly aware that members of my audience had personal and institutional stakes in this conflict. Most I knew to be critical of Borrero's leadership. By contextualizing current dynamics, I sought to open space for reflection and dialogue. I didn't expect anyone to defend the APG IG and its Repsol-sponsored vision of autonomy. In this context, the response of Negro, a lawyer and longtime Guaraní ally, surprised me. Throughout my fieldwork, Negro had articulated an idealized vision of indigeneity, based on his concept of *lo indígena puro* (pure indigeneity), a term he associated with a pre-colonial spirituality and philosophy, only traces of which remained in current indigenous people. He'd critiqued Guaraní leaders for having entered a "wheel of power" that required them to speak in inauthentic discourses. I expected him to be a leading critic of the recent trajectory of APG IG politics. Yet, as he explained, participating as a lawyer in recent negotiations between the APG IG and the state oil company YPFB over the construction of a gas pipeline had changed his perspective. As he reflected:

> At the beginning, all of us who worked on the indigenous issue, we approached it with a discourse of autonomy, didn't we? Of selling them [indigenous peoples] "autonomy," "recovering territory," etc., etc. But it was a bit . . . let's say, the discourse was also a bit . . . *idealistic.* But now [the Guaraní] are thinking of a reconceptualization, of having real political concepts, a *real* autonomy.

Drawing on his firsthand observation of APG IG–YPFB negotiations, he argued that by defending the legal right of the Guaraní to prior consultation, the APG IG had found a way of "materializing" (*de concretizar*) a form of "cultural recognition [that], even if it existed before, was not effective." He concluded: "I believe they're achieving a form of territoriality . . . and not just based on the issue of [agricultural] production . . . In the end, [the important thing is] to say, *What control do I have over this territory?*"

In the discussion that followed, other audience members accused Negro of being too "optimistic" about the APG IG's trajectory. As one person commented:

> Even if there's a process of recovering territory, they arrive at a logic that is very extractivist—based on money. An autonomy based on money . . . Despite being indigenous, of having their territory, etc., money con-

vinces us and we continue being extractivist. We continue taking advantage of the gas resources, of the compensation . . . In the end, what it generates is *extractivism*.

Negro's response was, once again, grounded in a critique of the "idealistic" discourses of indigeneity that had marked previous decades, and in a positive assessment of the Guaraní's redeployment of the TCO as a space for exercising indigenous territorial control:

> I'm neither optimistic not pessimistic, but I see that it's more a question of *realism* [*una cuestión más real*]. That is, we've left this idealistic part, of living like the grandparents, the beautiful community . . . It seems that doesn't happen. With the INRA Law, they've achieved—even if it's just a titling of ninety thousand hectares with many third parties inside, which could make you pessimistic—but, as a result of that . . . the Guaraní of Itika Guasu have an *imaginary of territory* . . . They make the departmental government undertake a consultation, and until that happens, [the gas pipeline] doesn't pass.

This discussion highlights an ambivalence at the heart of this book. From a positive perspective, recent developments in TCO Itika Guasu demonstrate indigenous peoples' ability to exceed limited spaces of cultural recognition in pursuit of a historically grounded struggle for territorial control. But they are also illustrative of the entrenchment of an extractivist logic in Bolivia, which produces political division and long-term environmental risks for communities. As the second audience member's slippage from third to first person indicates, this is a dilemma that is shared by other Bolivians, as efforts to build a "plurinational state" unfold in tense articulation with an extractives-based development model.

As I described, the APG IG leadership's efforts at "materializing recognition" were deeply contested in Itika Guasu, as well as within the broader regional context. Yet communities who supported Tarabuko's rival leadership as a means to secure development projects from local state institutions also sought, in their own way, to "materialize recognition." From their point of view, agreements with oil companies seemed like another empty form of recognition, whereas state development projects offered tangible, and material, benefits. As Fausto's pride at being welcomed into the municipal offices as a Guaraní *mburuvicha* with the invitation "Enter!" makes clear, the ability of communities to claim their share of state development projects is—like the APG IG's Investment Fund—symbol and fruit of a historic struggle for recognition.

To summarize, in this book I have argued that these competing Guaraní projects, although extractivist in nature, cannot be understood merely as rent-seeking behavior. Rather, they must be placed in the context of a longer struggle for territorial recognition, sovereignty, and citizenship. This is what my concept of "hydrocarbon citizenship" seeks to capture. Conflicts over the governance of gas are not a generic "resource curse" that emanates from the subsoil independent of history and geography; rather, hydrocarbons act as a conduit for deeper struggles over (post)colonial citizenship—struggles that emerge from regionally specific histories of racialized exclusion and dispossession.

Hydrocarbon citizenship also refers to a particular moment or regime of rule, in which citizen-state relations are increasingly mediated by extraction. Evo Morales was brought to power by the demand "that energy be taken out of the privatized realm of the market and reinserted into the public arena, where the citizenry can participate" (Postero 2007: 17). This has produced forms of gas-funded development patronage, in which citizenship is experienced and rewarded *materially,* through the construction of schools, roads, or soccer fields. It has also led to conflicts over the control of gas rents among different groups and levels of government—struggles in which national, regional, and local identities are mobilized to make competing claims. Guaraní claims for economic compensation and state development projects have to be placed in the context of this changing national setting, in which citizenship and nation have become inextricably tied to the subsoil. While discussions of "neo-extractivism" (Gudynas 2010) and the "commodities consensus" (Svampa 2015) have tended to emphasize the state's relationship to extraction—and local examples of dispossession and resistance—this book shifts attention to how political authority and citizenship are being reconfigured at a variety of scales in relation to the new extraction. Further ethnographic research is needed to examine how this is occurring in different sites, in articulation with sedimented formations of property and power, as well as with indigenous decolonial struggles.

Indigenous Peoples and the New Extraction

The research behind this book began in 2008 in the aftermath of a series of violent clashes between supporters of the MAS government and regional elites who had previously held power in the Bolivian lowlands. To many observers, these events—and the broader power struggle that underpinned them—seemed to confirm the revolutionary nature of the MAS government's "process of change." Scholars and activists were still reflecting on the incredible feat of Morales's electoral victory, which had brought together diverse social movements—peasants, workers, and indigenous organizations—in a successful challenge to "neoliberalism." To many on the left, Bolivia seemed to represent the hope that "another world is possible"—one that rejected the socially devastating prescriptions of a global "neoliberal" development agenda while also transforming a colonial legacy of racialized rule. The 2009 constitution, written with indigenous participation, enshrined this dual agenda of "post-neoliberalism" and "plurinationalism." Elite opposition served to reinforce the sense that the MAS and its diverse social movement bases were united in a struggle for economic justice and decolonization.

When I presented my research at academic conferences in 2009, I felt a responsibility to complicate this picture. What I described—an indigenous leadership at loggerheads with the MAS government over recognition of indigenous territorial rights—didn't seem to fit with prevailing narratives of what was happening in Bolivia. Of course, I was not alone in witnessing these tensions, which soon became the focal point of Bolivianist scholarship, as well as of intellectual and political debate within Bolivia. The 2011 march protesting a proposed highway in the Isiboro Sécure National Park and Indigenous Territory (TIPNIS) served as a catalyst and focus for these discussions. The march brought together indigenous peoples from across the Bolivian lowlands, many of whom were engaged in their own less publicized battles for prior consultation and territorial rights. The Guaraní of Tarija used the event to protest planned hydrocarbon development in Aguaragüe, a national park that lies within their ancestral territory, which is the aquifer for the entire Chaco region.

While the TIPNIS march has played an important role in highlighting conflict between indigenous and state resource sovereignty claims in Bolivia, it has also revealed the limitations of existing framings of the relationship between indigenous peoples and leftist governments. Many critical commentators, both in Bolivia and internationally, interpreted TIPNIS as an example of the conflict between an extractivist development model and indigenous cosmovisions based on notions of *buen vivir* and reciprocal relations with Mother Nature (Escobar 2010). Other leftists dismissed such critiques, pointing to the benefits of Morales's pro-poor social investment policies and the restoration of national resource sovereignty. Some even echoed the MAS government in accusing environmentalists, NGOs, and indigenous movements critiquing extraction of being instruments of foreign imperialist interests and traditional elites (García Linera 2012).

Neither of these perspectives is adequate for understanding a case like Itika Guasu. Analyses that depart from essentialized tropes of indigeneity purge indigenous struggles of their historical context, political dynamism, and heterogeneity. Worse still, they risk effacing and delegitimizing the struggles of many indigenous groups engaged in pragmatic negotiations over extraction (or other capitalist processes), which often spring from necessity rather than choice. For their part, leftist defenses of the "new extraction" rest on a reified notion of the state that overlooks the violent origins and contested nature of the state's territorial sovereignty, as well as the continuing agency of transnational companies and foreign capital investment in shaping "national" territory and politics. Contesting colonial discourses that frame indigenous peoples as guardians of nature, passive beneficiaries of state-led decolonization, or dupes of foreign imperialist interests—and making visible indigenous voices that do so—is a key task of decolonial scholarship.

Most important, neither of the two perspectives just outlined sheds light on the question of how political authority and territorial citizenship are being *reconfigured* in the context of the new extraction. I have addressed this question ethnographically, in a way that makes visible the deep roots and decolonial content of indigenous struggles for territory, but without obscuring indigenous peoples' increasingly intimate—and often ambivalent—relationship with extractivism. I have drawn attention to the dilemmas indigenous peoples face as they are confronted with the offer of inclusion in a gas-funded national development model alongside continuing forms of dispossession, environmental contamination, and the weakening of rights to consultation over extractive industry development in their territories.

It is unclear how long the MAS government will remain in power in Bolivia. In 2016, Morales lost a referendum on a constitutional amendment to allow him to run for a fourth term in office, indicating waning public support. Yet Morales has ignored the referendum result and, for the time being, there is no effective political opposition to the MAS. The government's backing for a rival Guaraní leadership in TCO Itika Guasu is illustrative of the clientelistic tactics it has deployed more widely, which have left many Bolivian social movements weakened and divided.

Whether or not Morales remains president, it is hard to imagine an imminent shift away from a hydrocarbon-based development model in Bolivia. While a recent global slump in commodity prices has generated more vocal critiques of extractivism in the Bolivian Chaco, the resulting shortfall in state funds has only served to exacerbate conflicts over control of gas rents. When I returned to Tarija Department in 2017, hydrocarbon-based autonomy claims seemed to be emerging at every possible site and scale.[1] As in TCO Itika Guasu, these resource claims drew on longstanding critiques of elite rule and lingering dreams of a "plurinational state." As I was repeatedly told by a variety of indigenous and non-indigenous people, "without resources, there is no autonomy."

Meanwhile, the extractive industry frontier continues to expand, including into protected areas.[2] Environmental risks continue to accumulate in specific territories, with potentially devastating long-term impacts on indigenous and peasant livelihoods. The government's intolerant stance on indigenous demands for prior consultation—and recent weakening of the consultation process—is not being taken lightly by groups that have spent decades fighting for such rights.[3] The question of land rights in TCOs and their implications for hydrocarbon governance remains bitterly contested.[4] Despite some advances on formal indigenous autonomy, it seems unlikely that this process will be accessible to, or meet the aspirations of, most indigenous groups.[5] Whatever the future of national electoral politics, indigenous struggles for territory will continue. There is every indication that TCOs—as spaces for imagining and exercising indigenous territorial sovereignty—will remain at the heart of such struggles, even as indigenous peoples seek to transcend the limits of multicultural recognition and agrarian rights.

Notes

NOTE ON PSEUDONYMS

1. The community I call "Tarairí" bears no relationship to the real Guaraní community and ancient mission of Tarairí, located to the north of Villamontes municipality in the Bolivian Chaco.

INTRODUCTION

1. Bolivia's 2009 constitution grants the right to indigenous autonomy in "consolidated indigenous territories [i.e., titled TCOs] and those undergoing that process, once consolidated" (Article 293; see Albó and Romero 2009). There are two alternative routes to indigenous autonomy, at a municipal or regional level. Both, however, require winning an autonomy referendum, which is unviable for most lowland indigenous peoples, who are demographic minorities within their municipalities and regions.

2. The World Bank oversaw and financed legal and institutional reforms relating to TCOs. The Danish International Development Agency (DANIDA) financed the implementation of TCO mapping and titling procedures in eastern Bolivia. The 1996 Ley de Servicio Nacional Reforma Agraria (National Agrarian Reform Service Law, commonly known as the INRA Law) foresaw the conclusion of TCO titling within a decade (1996–2006), a goal that was not met. In Tarija Department, DANIDA funds for TCO titling were diverted to finance other land titling procedures within the department (see chapter 3).

3. The concept of a plurinational state emerged from a dialogue with indigenous and peasant organizations and is set out in Bolivia's 2009 national constitution. It is based on the recognition of collective subjects—"the indigenous originary peasant nations and peoples, and the intercultural and Afro-Bolivian communities"—as constituents of "the Bolivian people," and of these groups' rights to autonomous self-governance (see Postero 2013).

4. During the years leading up to the agreement with Repsol, the Guaraní organization received legal advice from the international human rights advocacy organization Equipo Nizkor (see chapter 6).

5. In some cases, communities lived within hacienda properties; in others, they resided on marginal lands adjacent to private estates.

6. Today "Itika Guasu," the Spanish language adaptation of the TCO's name, is most commonly used, including by Guaraní people. For Guaraní speakers, this is useful in distinguishing the TCO from the Pilcomayo River. It is also emblematic of the "translations" required to make territory visible to the Bolivian state (chapter 2). I refer to the TCO as "TCO Itika Guasu" throughout this book.

7. The Guaraní have been titled roughly one third of the total land area in the TCO, an area that is discontinuous and largely composed of lands that Guaraní communities already occupied.

8. Bryan 2012; Bryan and Wood 2015; Herlihy and Knapp 2003; Offen 2003a, 2003b; Stocks 2003; Gordon, Gurdián, and Hale 2003; Brody 1988; Peluso 1995; Nietschmann 1995; Radcliffe 2011; Chapin, Lamb, and Threlkeld 2005;Harris and Hazen 2006; Herlihy 2003; Coombes, Johnson, and Howitt, 2011; Wainwright and Bryan 2009.

9. Rights and Resources Initiative 2012 and 2015; World Resources Institute 2016; Borras and Franco 2012; FAO 2012; World Bank Group et al. 2010.

10. Political ecologists have shown how local configurations of resource access and property rights are shaped by broader structures of political economy (Peet and Watts 2004; Tsing 2005; Sawyer 2004; Peluso 1992), while postcolonial and decolonial scholarship emphasize the colonial foundations and racialized exclusions of liberal property regimes (Razack 2002; Bhandar 2011; Sparke 2005; Simpson 2014; Moore 2005) as well as the persistent "coloniality of power" in former European colonies (Quijano 2000; Mignolo 2007). My analysis of TCO titling draws heavily on these insights. I pay particular attention to how capitalist processes map onto and reinscribe colonial geographies of rights in ways that curtail indigenous efforts at reclaiming territory through law (see especially chapters 3–5).

11. Hale 2002 and 2006; Bryan 2012; Bryan and Wood 2015.

12. Sparke 2005; Radcliffe 2011; Wainwright and Bryan 2009; Coombes, Johnson, and Howitt 2011; Bhandar 2011, Hodgson and Schroeder 2002.

13. "La CSUTCB exige revisión de las TCO e indígenas rechazan la propuesta," 2010, Erbol. March 29, http://observatorio-ddhh.blogspot.dk/2010/03/la-csutcb-exige-revision-de-las-tco-e.html (accessed January 20, 2017); García Linera 2007.

14. See Postero 2017, 2015, 2013; Gustafson and Fabricant 2011; Almaraz et al. 2012; Escobar 2010; Gudynas 2010; Bebbington 2009; Bebbington and Humphreys Bebbington 2011; Haarstad 2012; Hindery 2013; Cameron 2013; McNeish 2013; Chavez et al. 2010; Viceministerio del Estado Plurinacional de Bolivia y Fundación Boliviana para la Democracia Multipartidaria 2010; Schilling-Vacaflor 2016.

15. In Escobar's view, they are symptomatic of broader processes of political transformation in Latin America, which combine two potentially complementary but also competing and contradictory projects: "alternative modernizations," based on an anti-neoliberal development model, and "decolonial projects," based on communal, indigenous, hybrid, pluriversal, and intercultural practices, oriented toward the construction of "post-liberal" societies.

16. Whereas ethnography traditionally tended focus on a single-site location— embedded in a world system, historical political economies of colonialism, market regimes, state formation, and so on—"multi-sited ethnography" blurs boundaries between the "local" and the "global" by following "connections, associations, and putative relationships" (Marcus 1995: 97).

17. My research outputs for CERDET in 2008–9 included a report, presentation, and digital file. I have continued to share written outputs, presentations, and in-depth conversations with CERDET through my subsequent research progress.

CHAPTER 1. IMAGINING TERRITORY

1. Chiriguanía, a colonial name for the Chaco lands, is taken from the term Chiriguano, given to the Guaraní by the Inca and adopted by the Spanish. The term continued to be used after Bolivia gained formal independence in 1825.

2. See Pifarré 1999; Langer 2009; Saignes 2007; Echazú 1992.

3. I use the term "racialized" in this book to denote how race is socially constructed and historically produced in relation to, and through, other forms of social difference and inequality, including relations of land and labor.

4. For detailed accounts of this history, see Langer 2009; Echazú 1992; Pifarré 1999.

5. The designation of Chaco lands as tierras baldías, subject to unrestricted settlement, occurred under President Aniceto Arce Ruíz de Mendoza (1888–1892), replacing a prior regime whereby the state awarded lands only to those who had contributed military service (Echazú 1992).

6. As the American geographer Isaiah Bowman wrote in 1915: "The mystery of that large blank space on the maps of the Argentine and of Bolivia that represents *El Gran Chaco* is realized by only a few people. There are tracts as large as the state of New York of which we know practically nothing; in others, white settlements are absent for hundreds of square miles; in still other places in the Gran Chaco live Indian tribes of which little more than the name is known. Government enterprise, however, is now opening up the best sections of the Chaco . . . improved means for trade will transform this land of mystery into a settled region" (176). Shortly after writing this, in 1917, Bowman led a massive U.S. intelligence-gathering effort known as "The Inquiry," which laid the foundation for the rise of the United States as a global power and inspired recent military mapping projects—most notably the 2009 "Bowman Expeditions," a controversial project for mapping indigenous lands in Oaxaca funded by the U.S. Army's Foreign Military Studies Office and the American Geographical Society (Bryan and Wood 2015).

7. While Franciscan missions offered Chaco indigenous peoples a potential refuge from the abuses of the republican army and settlers, they were also instrumental to the seating of national sovereignty in the Chaco. As one Franciscan archbishop declared in a letter written to his superior to justify a continuing missionary presence in the Chaco, "In the end, the work of the missionaries is national, it has brought the only sign of possession of the Bolivian deserts and has protected its frontiers with a zeal that, as well as being evangelical, is highly patriotic." Note from archbishop requesting that missionaries remain in charge of Itau, Chimeo, and Yacuiba, document 20, in Calzavarini 2005–6: 538.

8. See VAIO and MACPIO 2000: 30; Gustafson 2009: 101.

9. Non-Bolivian scholars have argued that the war had its roots in social and political turmoil in Bolivia (Klein 1992).

10. The Chaco saw its Guaraní population decrease by an estimated fifteen thousand people, owing to deaths of Guaraní combatants and migration to Argentina and Paraguay (Pifarré 1989).

11. Hydrocarbon development in the Chaco began in 1921, when the Standard Oil Company of New Jersey acquired from the government all concessions for oil exploration in Bolivia, including 2.5 million hectares of concessions in the country's eastern Amazonian and Chaco lowlands (Perreault and Valdivia 2010: 694–95). Development intensified after the Chaco War, following the creation of the state-owned oil company YPFB (1936) and nationalization of hydrocarbon reserves (1937), which led to a period of intense exploration, exploitation, and construction of hydrocarbon infrastructure in the Chaco.

12. See Kay and Urioste 2007; Soruco, Plata, and Medeiros 2008.

13. U.S. aid to Bolivia during the first agrarian reform (1953–1961) superseded that provided to any other country in the world except Israel (Soruco, Plata, and Medeiros 2008), and was contingent upon Bolivia's granting concessions to U.S. oil firms, formalized under the 1956 Hydrocarbons Law (Perreault and Valdivia 2010: 695).

14. A rectangular colored piece of cloth worn traditionally by Guaraní women. The Guaraní term is *mandu*; *tipoy* is the Spanish translation.

15. A traditional Guaraní party where the fermented maize drink *kaguiye* (*chicha* in Bolivian Spanish) is shared by the host community, accompanied by music and dancing.

16. Derogatory colonial terms used to refer to lowland Indians. *Chaguanco* refers to an animal but was used as a racialized insult for Chaco indigenous peoples; *ava* means "man" in Guaraní but was used by the Spanish to mean "savage"; *cumpa* usually means *compadre* (the godparent of one's child) but also refers to Guaraní folk traditions in Argentina and Paraguay.

17. Some landowners were more violent and demanding than others. Moreover, whereas some communities (known as "captive communities") were trapped within the estate of their *patrón*, others maintained some communal space and were able to continue practicing subsistence farming alongside their labor obligations.

18. Postcolonial scholars have explained these liberal exclusions as intrinsic to the construction of the nation as a homogeneous ethnic community, which requires a constant redrawing of geographical and racial boundaries to define who should and should not be included (see Said 1978; Pratt 1992; Larson 2004).

19. See APG IG and EAPG 2013.

20. Documents recovered from CERDET's archives and interviews with those involved confirm the presence of all of the following organizations in early assemblies, alongside CERDET: the Swiss-funded Equipo de Apoyo al Pueblo Guaraní (Aid Team for the Guaraní People, EAPG); the Asamblea Permanente de Derechos Humanos de Tarija (Permanent Human Rights Assembly of Tarija, APDHT); the Instituto de Investigación y Capacitación Campesina (Institute of Peasant Research and Training, IICCA); the Bolivian branch of the United Nations–funded Instituto Indígena (Indigenous Institute); the American Sisters of the Presentation, a group of Catholic nuns based in Entre Ríos; Comunidades en Marcha, a militant project of the peasant organization CSUTCB; and the rural development NGO Fundación ACLO. This list draws on CERDET 2004a; IICCA, undated; IICCA, n.d., ca. 1992; APDHT 1990; CERDET, n.d. 2.

21. See Andolina, Laurie, and Radcliffe 2009; Brysk 2000; Yashar 2005.

22. This model, known as PISET (Production, Infrastructure, Health, Education, Land/Territory), was developed by the Bolivian NGO Centro de Investigación y Promoción del Campesinado (CIPCA).

23. *Empatronamiento* relations continued in some Guaraní territories of the Bolivian Chaco and were the subject of a 2009 mission by the United Nations Permanent Forum on Indigenous Issues, requested by the Morales government.

24. CERDET, n.d. 1.

25. This refers to the quincentennial of Columbus's landing, thereby linking Guaraní resurgence to a national and continental process of indigenous organizing.

26. The "Land without Evil" (Guaraní: *ïvï marae* or *kandire*; Spanish: *tierra sin mal*) refers to the Guaraní myth of a primordial land of material abundance free from suffering, the search for which is thought to have motivated past Guaraní migrations.

27. Other terms used to refer to the relationship between development and culture include "development-with-identity," "alternative development," and "self-development."

28. In 1993 the United Nations Indigenous Special Working Group issued its draft Declaration on the Rights of Indigenous Peoples. Two years later, the UN declared 1995–2004 the International Decade of Indigenous Peoples (Andolina, Laurie, and Radcliffe 2009). In response, in 1996 the World Bank published a report titled "Including the Excluded: Ethnodevelopment in Latin America" (Partridge, Uquillas, and Johns 1996).

29. Canadian indigenous peoples' struggles for legal title and countermapping efforts during the 1970s provided an important precedent for global advocates of indigenous mapping and land titling (see Bryan and Wood 2015: chap. 4).

30. See Hart 2010; Peck and Tickell 2002.

31. This agenda has been characterized variously as "roll-out neoliberalism" (Peck and Tickell 2002), the "post-Washington consensus" (Fine, Lapavitsus, and Pincus 2001), "social neoliberalism" (Andolina, Laurie, and Radcliffe 2009), "pre-emptive" development (Soederberg 2004), and "soft neoliberalism" (Hindery 2013).

32. See Hall and Patrinos 2012: 7; Andolina, Laurie, and Radcliffe 2009: chap. 2.

33. See Stevens 1997; Conklin and Graham 1995; Davis and Wali 1993; Engle 2010.

34. Prior to the 1990s, most conservation projects were predicated on the colonial assumption that saving nature meant excluding people. From the 1980s, academics and activists began to denounce the detrimental effects of exclusionary conservation on indigenous populations, other local resource users, and even the environment (Colchester 2004; Adams and Hutton 2007; Negi and Nautiyal 2003), producing a paradigm shift

toward an approach that saw the development needs of local populations as compatible with, and complementary to, the achievement of conservation goals (Marquette 1996).

35. See Bryan 2010; Wainwright and Bryan 2009; Bryan and Wood 2015.

36. "Legal personhood" is a juridical term that refers to the capability of having legal rights and duties within a certain legal system.

37. See Lehm Ardaya 1999; Paredes and Canedo 2008.

38. Although presidential decrees in theory have the force of law, they have an exceptional status as an expression of the president's final judgment in a particular case. These decrees therefore did not provide any legal guarantee that other indigenous territorial claims would be recognized by the Bolivian state, nor did they establish the general principle of indigenous peoples' territorial rights under Bolivian law.

39. Although this project officially commenced in 1995, project documents affirm that "since 1992, the Bank has maintained an intense policy dialogue on land tenure and administration with the [Bolivian] Government" (World Bank 2001: 3).

40. The Instituto Indigenista Boliviano (Bolivian Indigenist Institute) was established in 1941 as part of the Instituto Indigenista Interamericano (Interamerican Indigenist Institute), a Mexico-based organization created with the objective of coordinating indigenist policies throughout the Americas. Tomy claims that the Instituto Indigenista Boliviano received funding from the United Nations Development Programme (UNDP) during the 1990s and participated in early processes of mapping lowland indigenous territories.

41. See Canedo 2007; Viceministerio de Tierras 2008; Deere and León 2002.

42. This is reflected in the creation of an Agrarian Superintendence, charged with the task of fixing land prices, and the payment of taxes as a precondition for demonstration of productive land use.

43. Under the INRA Law, medium and large properties must demonstrate fulfillment of an economic social function (FES), whereas small properties and peasant plots are deemed to automatically fulfill a social function. Properties within TCOs that do not fulfill the FES are to be reverted to the state and awarded to indigenous TCO claimants. The parameters for defining the FES were subject to continuing debate following the promulgation of the INRA Law.

44. Full text printed in Libermann and Godínez 1992.

45. Hindery (2013) provides details of this project, which involved irregular dealings between oil giants Shell and Enron, and President Sánchez de Lozada, who took office in 1993.

CHAPTER 2. MAPPING TERRITORY

1. See Bryan and Wood 2015: chaps. 4 and 5. An example of indigenous mapping from a cultural ecology perspective is Bernard Nietchmann's (1995) work with Miskito people in eastern Nicaragua.

2. Indigenous place names were an important part of land use and occupancy studies in earlier indigenous mapping efforts in Canada (Brody 1988). Sarela Paz completed a master's in sociology at the Universidad Mayor de San Simón (UMSS) in Cochabamba, Bolivia. She later earned a master's and a doctorate in anthropology at the Mexican university Centro de Investigación y Estudios Superiores en Antropología Social (CIESAS).

3. The use of colonial documents as evidence of ancestral occupation not only undermines assertions of pre-colonial indigenous sovereignty but also presents problems for claimants who are unable to provide such "evidence."

4. In the context of indigenous politics, the term *técnico* usually refers to non-indigenous activists or *asesores* (advisers) working within indigenous organizations, in most cases funded by NGOs, European donors, or the Bolivian state. *Técnico* can also refer to employees of NGOs, private companies, or state institutions. *Técnico* literally means "technician" or "expert."

5. According to *Encyclopedia Britannica, entelequia* literally translates as "entelechy," a philosophical concept referring to "that which realizes or makes actual what is otherwise merely potential." The concept is connected with Aristotle's distinction between matter and form, or the potential and the actual.

6. He refers here to the Instituto Indigenista Boliviano (Bolivian Indigenist Institute, described in chapter 1), which was involved in early processes of indigenous territorial mapping in the Bolivian lowlands.

7. A photocopy of the 1992 map was found attached to an undated document that refers to Itika Guasu as "a Guaraní region of 284,194 hectares"—larger than the 216,000 hectares legally recognized by INRA in 1997 (CERDET, n.d. 2). One secondary source points to the existence of a previous claim for 530,900 hectares (Guzmán et al. 2007). Another CERDET publication states that the first territorial demand presented to the state was just over 300,000 hectares (CERDET 2004b: 79). This was supported by CERDET's longest-tenured employee, Alipio, who specified that in 1993, CERDET and the APG IG elaborated a territorial demand for 310,000 hectares, which they presented in 1994 to the Secretariat of Ethnic Affairs, where it remained with no clear answer until the 1996 march, when a more limited demand was presented to INRA.

8. For a discussion of the role of "indigenous intellectuals" in the early Guaraní movement, see Gustafson 2009: chap. 2.

9. The zones are significant within the APG's organizational structure, with the next level of leadership above community-level *mburuvichas* being the *mburuvichas zonales*.

10. Participants (who included representatives from all households) began by drawing a map depicting the community and its surroundings, which then provided the basis for discussion about territorial boundaries and land use practices. In subsequent activities, people identified frequently visited places beyond the community and discussed how people described the location of their home to different kinds of outsiders. Finally, we talked about legal titling outcomes, at which point I shared maps and information collected during the course of my research.

11. Kuñati is my name in Tarairí. Composed of the noun *kuña* ([Guaraní] woman) and the adjective *ti* (white), it translates as "white (Guaraní) woman."

12. Most communities have at some point experienced focus group–type activities in the context of NGO *capacitaciones* (training) or development projects. These methodologies may thus perpetuate a familiar dynamic of a powerful and knowledgeable outsider imparting knowledge to ignorant and passive Guaraní recipients.

13. For the majority of my stay in Tarairí, I did not talk about the TCO or the legal process beyond discussions with a few community members I knew well; this was to enable me to observe the ways in which people did talk about and inhabit the territory without imposing prior categories on my experiences and exchanges. The examples given here are taken from more structured activities conducted in my final months in Tarairí.

14. While some Guaraní friends (members of the APG IG) stress that *ivi* is a concept closer to "territory," which includes forests, sky, and subsoil, in Tarairí people most often used the term to refer to land used for cultivating maize and other crops.

15. Women added seven other Guaraní communities where they made frequent visits to see family; men depicted the rural haciendas and urban centers where they went for labor migration, which were largely in Tarija Department but stretched as far as Argentina. Both groups depicted Entre Ríos, in the case of women as the location of the nearest hospital.

16. Wendy described how calculations of indigenous income from forest resources were taken directly from commercial data on timber values made by transnational companies operating nearby forestry concessions.

17. Immobilization means that no land within the TCO area can be bought or sold prior to the completion of the TCO titling process—although this did not prevent land sales in practice.

18. The figure projected is 32,377.82 bolivianos (about 4,681.48 U.S. dollars) per family. Based on the categories of land use identified earlier, the study identifies indigenous spatial needs, relating to forestry, agriculture, pastoral farming, and conservation—the first three figures being calculated on the basis of land required to generate the projected minimum family income.

19. For example, the study notes that "the forests in the Guaraní demand of Itika Guasu are in a period of natural regeneration and recuperation; for this reason, forestry activity should be restricted," and recommends the elaboration of community forest management plans toward this end (147).

20. For example, it suggests that agro-forestry projects, sustainable cattle ranching, access to certified seed, and post-harvest storage facilities could help increase Guaraní incomes.

21. See also Hodgson and Schroeder 2002; Wainwright and Bryan 2009.

22. This includes historical evidence used to show that "the area currently demanded by the communities of Itika Guasu corresponds with the historic and traditionally occupied area" (VAIO and MACPIO 2000: 145).

23. The Spanish verb *mezquinar* (as used in the Bolivian Chaco) means to be stingy; to keep something to oneself and deny others access to it. Because there is (interestingly) no direct English translation, I leave the term in Spanish for subsequent uses.

24. *Challa* is a ritual offering to Pachamama (Earth Mother) practiced throughout the southern Andes, in which people offer *chicha* (a fermented drink similar to the Guaraní *kayuiye*), food, alcohol, coca, or cigarettes. The word has Quechua (Inca) origins but is used widely in Bolivia, often in its Españolized verb form *challar*.

25. Spivak 1988; Fanon 1967; Bhandar 2011.

CHAPTER 3. TITLING TERRITORY

1. TCO recognition did not amount to a collective legal title for the Guaraní, but rather signaled the beginning of a complex legal process (SAN-TCO) in which all private property claims within the TCO area would be identified, measured, evaluated, and recognized (i.e., prioritized over indigenous land rights) provided they could demonstrate productive land use.

2. This consists of a first title of 64,758 hectares, awarded in 2002, and a second award of 27,007 hectares, made in January 2008. Although the second award appears in recent INRA data, APG IG leaders and communities claimed they had never received the legal documents for this second award.

3. The chapter draws on over seventy in-depth interviews with actors involved in the titling process; participant observation of nine APG assemblies and two meetings organized by local cattle ranching associations; and analysis of documentation collected from INRA Tarija, the APG IG, and local NGOs.

4. Global development policy accounts of indigenous land titling tend to attribute gaps between objectives and outcomes to weak institutional capacity, procedural shortcomings, or "transactional costs" (Coombes, Johnson, and Howitt 2011). This technocratic view fails to account for power relations embedded within political and institutional contexts and ignores ontological conflicts between indigenous and non-indigenous parties.

5. As Beatriz explained, the reduction of her father's property had removed the most fertile area of the land claim, although he continued to occupy the entire area—land that is coveted by community members from Tarairí.

6. *Colla* is a (usually) derogatory and racialized term used in the Bolivian lowlands to refer to migrants from the Andes. Apparently the term was originally used by the Inca and the Spanish to refer to the Aymara.

7. Under the legal norms of SAN-TCO, medium-sized properties (those between 35 and 350 hectares) and large properties (those over 350 hectares) are required to demonstrate an "economic social function"—that is, to show productive land use—or face property reductions, while small properties (those up to 35 hectares), along with indigenous communities, are classified as automatically fulfilling a "social function."

8. Ranchers lent or rented cattle to one another during INRA's fieldwork for the purpose of demonstrating properties' economic social function, which was based on the calculation that one cow justifies five hectares of land.

9. *Compadre* refers to either the godparent of the speaker's child or the parent of the speaker's godchild. The relationship of *compadrazgo*—a kinship-like bond between the parents and godparents of a child—is a powerful one in Bolivia (see Lazar 2008: 104–6). As Sian Lazar notes, as well as cementing friendships between social equals, it can serve to create bonds of mutual obligation between people of different socioeconomic status. In Itika Guasu, such bonds exist between some Guaraní community members and local mestizo landowners, giving institutionalized form to clientelistic relations predicated on racialized inequality. As Lino's experience shows, *compadrazgo* relationships are also instrumental in perpetuating non-indigenous landowning elites' privileged access to regional state power.

10. Space plays a productive role in the sedimentation and reproduction of these ethnic power inequalities. The fact that Itika Guasu's most powerful landowning families reside in Tarija city—the center of regional power—bears testimony to the historic role of land control and indigenous labor exploitation as a basis for social and spatial mobility. Urban residence in turn presents subsequent generations of these families with educational and professional opportunities—including access to positions and influence in regional state institutions—that perpetuate the historical correlation between race, landownership, spatial mobility, and political power.

11. Studies produced by NGOs working on TCO titling in other parts of the Bolivian lowlands suggest that the role of racialized power inequalities and institutionalized corruption in shaping titling outcomes in Itika Guasu is far from unusual (see Guzmán et al. 2007; Paredes and Canedo 2008; Almaraz 2002).

12. *Ganadero* (cattle rancher) does not necessarily have the elite connotations of *hacendado* (hacienda owner), given that it refers to a livelihood practice and implies closer links to, and sometimes permanent residence in, the countryside. However, in the Chaco the terms are often conflated, given the prevalence of ranching, with both being opposed to the more humble *campesino* category.

13. The INRA Law classifies small farmers (those possessing up to thirty-five hectares) as automatically fulfilling a "social function" and therefore eligible for land title. The only caveat to this is that they must have been resident in the territory for two years prior to the start of the titling process.

14. I located ASOGAPO resolutions dated June, August, and December 2007. Other complaints dating from 2003 were found in INRA Tarija's archives.

15. Officially named the Fund for the Development of Indigenous, Originary, and Peasant Peoples, the Indigenous Fund was a controversial source of funding for TCO titling for two reasons: first, the state was already obliged to title indigenous territories under the INRA Law, and these funds were supposed to be for "indigenous development" initiatives; and second, the fund had been proposed by lowland indigenous organizations

as a resource for indigenous communities directly affected by hydrocarbon extraction, but ended up being created as a national fund shared with *campesino* organizations and governed by a board that includes several MAS ministers, who routinely vetoed indigenous applications for funds. Thus the Indigenous Fund is viewed by many Guaraní as a classic example of co-option and betrayal by the MAS government. The Fund was subsequently frozen due to a corruption scandal.

16. Over time, the APG IG did successfully engage with the TAN, which became less partial to landowners during Morales's first term as president (e.g., in the case of Roberto Vaca's property claim). Yet even where recommended property reductions were upheld in law, they have rarely been implemented in practice, owing to bureaucratic inertia, fiscal shortages, and the continuing lobbying efforts of ASOGAPO.

17. These steps include the election of candidates for positions in municipal and departmental government. Julio Navarro, a Guaraní leader from Itika Guasu, even rose to the position of president of Tarija's Departmental Assembly—although, sadly, he became distanced from the APG IG leadership and communities in the process.

18. A key complaint was that INRA was titling only cultivated land individually, and was titling grazing areas communally, causing confusion and conflict between neighboring ranchers.

19. He used the word *desconocimiento,* which can denote either ignorance (the opposite of *conocimiento,* knowledge) or non-recognition (the opposite of *reconocimiento,* recognition). Given the context and popular usage, I used the latter translation.

20. "Internal land titling" (*saneamiento interno*) is a faster process of land titling applied to conflictive regions and for communities with common areas and small properties. Internal land titling means that community members determine individual and communal areas and resolve boundary disputes through internal consultation, then INRA recognizes and certifies the agreed-upon boundaries. Participants at the meeting complained, however, that INRA was pressuring them to claim individual title only to the land surrounding their houses and designate all grazing areas as "communal"—something that was generating conflict and confusion.

21. Despite these restrictions on local people's land use, the Tariquía park is now subject to a forty-year hydrocarbon contract between the Bolivian state oil company YPFB and the Brazilian state oil company PETROBRAS, a project that peasant communities of Tariquía have strongly resisted.

22. The idea of the social function of property has its origins in John Locke's theory of property as a "natural right" (1690), based on the idea that when one mixes one's labor with nature, one gains a relationship with that part of nature with which the labor is mixed. However, many indigenous land management systems (including the Guaraní's) also link property rights to labor investments (Li 2014).

23. The use of the term *originario* (native) rather than *indígena* (indigenous) here, and in subsequent examples, is significant. *Originario* is a term preferred by many indigenous people in the Bolivian highlands, owing to the pejorative colonial connotations of *indígena.* The wide use of *indígena* in the lowlands emerged from the transnationally articulated process of ethnic resurgence of the 1980s and 1990s. In this example, the use of *originario* can be viewed as a discursive challenge to the historically contingent identity politics underpinning the TCO claim.

24. The notion of "food security" comes from international policy discourse and reflects a neoliberal vision of large-scale, market-based agricultural production. This model is contested by many peasant social movements, which call for a prioritization of "food sovereignty."

25. As noted earlier, during the first decade of TCO titling (1996–2006), the National Agrarian Tribunal systematically favored non-indigenous landowners, who presented

legal complaints against property reductions. Following Morales's 2005 election, the TAN became more accessible to indigenous peoples and sympathetic to their claims. By 2017, however, activists in Tarija reported that the TAN was being politically controlled by the MAS government, and used to contain indigenous territorial claims (and reward political allies) in regions of extraction.

26. This is defined in opposition both to neoliberal resource governance arrangements—which are framed as selling off Bolivia's "national patrimony"—and to the 2006–2008 autonomy movements in gas-producing departments, which were predicated on demands for departmental control of gas rents.

27. APG leaders from Chuquisaca, who had already organized following contact with leaders in Camiri and NGO and church campaigns to end slavery, played a leading role in early ethnic mobilization in Itika Guasu (CERDET 2008).

28. Until the first agrarian reform (1953), Bolivian indigenous peoples were excluded from citizenship rights, while white and mestizo property owners enjoyed the legal right to subject indigenous populations within their lands to forced labor.

29. One list of properties I found (INRA 2008b) claims that roundtable negotiations took place for thirty-four of the 133 private properties in the TCO. In twenty-one of these, the agreement reached concerned an increase in the number of cattle in the legal technical evaluation (ETJ) report. In documentation of the Conciliation Acts themselves, fifteen of twenty-four acts obtained concerned an increase in the number of cattle for the fulfillment of the FES. This is stipulated through statements such as "The quantity of X cattle was agreed between both parties" and affirmation that INRA had modified the ETJ reports accordingly.

30. A 2011 interview with Nolberto Gallado (2009 director of INRA Tarija) shed light on the institutional pressure faced by INRA's departmental office to meet national targets for land titling, defined on a "per hectare" basis with no separate provisions for indigenous land claims.

31. For an account of the massacre, see Miranda 2002.

32. Although some property reductions had been agreed on through the *mesas de concertación*, this involved only landowners whose property claims coincided with Guaraní communal areas (those where communities currently lived), and not those occupying land in other parts of the TCO.

33. There were rumors in Itika Guasu in 2009 that INRA was issuing titles "by community" rather than collectively. Discussions with INRA technicians and lawyers, and documentary analysis, suggest that, in legal terms, all titles issued in Itika Guasu form part of the collective TCO award. Nevertheless, this perception conveys Guaraní frustration at the fragmentary effects of TCO titling, and long-standing anxieties regarding the state's and landowning elites' efforts to "divide" Guaraní territory.

CHAPTER 4. INHABITING TERRITORY

1. Armando's cousin Victoria had become seriously ill with gallstones—a condition suffered by many Guaraní women in Itika Guasu. Fortunately, this coincided with a visit from anthropologist Bret Gustafson, who facilitated Victoria's transfer to a hospital in Tarija. While she was being treated, I met with Armando and Bret in a café in central Tarija to discuss the possibility of my living in Tarairí. Armando's willingness to host me was undoubtedly influenced by the community's positive experience receiving Bret, who completed fieldwork in Tarairí during the 1990s (when Armando was still a teenager) for a study on intercultural bilingual education (Gustafson 2009).

2. This had changed by 2017, when Tarairí was receiving cell phone signal from at least one Bolivian network.

3. In Bolivia this often means in a nuclear rather than an extended family.

4. Meaning white (Guaraní) woman.

5. I lived in Tarairí for six months, from August 2011 to January 2012, although I made various trips to Tarija during this period for treatment of a broken ankle.

6. When I visited Tarairí in July 2014, the bus route had been extended to include the community twice a week. (On the other days the walk was still necessary.)

7. The ninety-six people I counted included one mixed (Guaraní-*karai*) household. According to APG figures, the average community size in Itika Guasu is 95.4 inhabitants (APG 2005).

8. Other households would retreat to the shade of their porches during the day.

9. Except for the one mixed household, made up of a young Guaraní woman and the *karai* son of one of landowner Mendez's *vaqueros* (cowhands).

10. *Mandu* (*tipoy* in Spanish) is the Guaraní word for a rectangular piece of colored cloth pinned at the shoulder, worn traditionally by Guaraní women.

11. This came in the context of distributing seed to community members on September 1, 2011.

12. This had produced a series of brick buildings ("eco-lodges") overlooking the river and transformed a dirt path down to the river into concrete steps, employing a number of the community's men.

13. Chagas' disease is a disease of the heart common throughout rural Bolivia. It is transmitted by a blood-sucking insect called the *vinchuca* (kissing bug), which likes to live in adobe houses.

14. According to Gustafson, some Guaraní were able to maintain subsistence lands in return for seasonal collective labor in salt and limestone outcroppings (2009: 101).

15. While it is the APG IG, and not individual Guaraní communities, that receive title to TCO land, INRA measured Guaraní communities separately—with the participation of APG IG "land promoters" and adjacent private claimants—as part of its initial work of mapping out all land claims within the TCO area.

16. As discussed later in this chapter, four of thirteen households have no plot at all, while some households' plots are located farther from the community and within private properties.

17. A number of informants did not know whether the plots they farmed were located on Mendez's land or on TCO land because of their lack of knowledge about legal boundaries (see chapter 2).

18. On the contamination of the Pilcomayo River, see Smoulders et al. 2002 and Miller et al. 2007; on drought and environmental risk in the Chaco, see Reyes Pando et al. 2012; on climate change and health vulnerability in the Bolivian Chaco, see Aparicio-Effen et al. 2016; on cattle ranching and sustainability in the Bolivian Chaco, see Fundación AGRECOL Andes 2006.

19. In a household survey conducted in January 2012, eleven of thirteen households listed handicrafts as one of the four main sources of household income: for one household it was the primary income source, for four the secondary source, for four the third-most-important source, and for two the fourth-most-important source. While the Guaraní did traditionally make some items (such as sieves) from woven palm, the handicrafts they make today—decorated pots, table mats, and bowls—were learned from the nearby Weenhayek people as part of a project of the NGO EAPG, with CERDET subsequently supporting the planting of palm trees, which are native to the Chaco.

20. Guaraní: people, used to mean "Guaraní people."

21. As we saw in chapter 3, the notion that indigenous communities might be measured *before* private properties was a matter of struggle for the few pro-indigenous technicians within INRA.

22. This is one of several land purchases made by local NGOs in an effort to remediate the continuing land scarcity faced by Guaraní communities following the TCO titling

process. The assumption was that the Guaraní would benefit collectively from acquiring the land adjacent to Itikirenda, which was the site of an EAPG-sponsored cattle ranching cooperative shared among four neighboring communities. The cooperative ultimately failed, in part owing to the difficulties posed by the river crossing for other communities, and their perception that the land (and hence the cooperative) belonged to Itikirenda. Today, the purchased land primarily benefits community members from Itikirenda.

23. According to Albó (1990), the failure to resolve such intercommunal disputes historically resulted in the migration of one community to a different part of the territory—something that is clearly no longer possible.

24. On the crisis of fish stocks in Tarija and local analysis of its causes, see "El Sábalo Está al Borde de Extinción en Tarija," El Deber, May 4, 2016, http://www.eldiario.net/noticias/2016/2016_05/nt160505/nacional.php?n=37&-el-sabalo-esta-al-borde-de-extincion-en-tarija. Citations to scientific analyses of environmental risks in the Bolivian Chaco are provided in a previous note.

25. On non-human animal geographies, see Philo and Wilbert 2000; and Whatmore 2002.

26. PROSOL (Communal Solidarity Program) emerged from *campesino* organizations' demands—via sustained social mobilization—for a share of departmental gas rents, which they complained were concentrated in Tarija's elite-dominated urban centers. Following initial complaints of discrimination, Chaco indigenous communities were included in the program, illustrating their growing efforts to access their fair share of new state development programs funded by hydrocarbon development in their territories (see chapter 6).

27. Hair sheep are sheep that have more hair fibers than wool fibers.

CHAPTER 5. EXTRACTIVE ENCOUNTERS

1. The 1996 Law of Capitalization sold 50 percent of the state industries that had provided 60 percent of all government revenues to multinational corporations (Kohl 2006).

2. This figure includes forty-four hydrocarbon contracts signed by the Bolivian state in April 2007.

3. As chapter 1 details, oil development in the Chaco began in the 1930s, shortly after the end of the Chaco War.

4. The concession is operated by Repsol's Bolivian subsidiary, Repsol E&P S.A., which became Repsol YPF E&P after buying the Argentine oil and gas company YPF S.A. in 1999.

5. In 2011 a controversial technical study concluded that the Margarita gas field (Tarija Department) and neighboring Huacaya gas field (Chuquisaca Department) were continuous and, as such, constituted one "mega-field," Margarita-Huacaya. This was a pretext for the redistribution of rents from the more productive gas wells, located in Tarija Department, to Chuquisaca Department.

6. See APG IG, CEADES, and CERDET 2005, for a description of the social and environmental impacts of this first phase of hydrocarbon development in TCO Itika Guasu, which include noise and air pollution, contamination of ground and surface water, loss of wild fauna, deforestation, unwanted pregnancies, and prostitution.

7. ILO Convention 169 requires governments and companies to consult with the peoples living on the land prior to permitting resource exploitation, and states that the latter should participate in the benefits of such activities and receive "fair compensation" for any damages they sustain as a result of these activities (Articles 6 and 15).

8. Guaraní leaders and some NGO staff argue that the NGOs made this decision to withdraw under pressure from Intermón (a key funder for both CERDET and CEADES in this period), which was itself receiving funds from the Spanish bank Caixa, a major shareholder in Repsol YPF S.A.

9. See Kohl and Farthing 2006; Perreault 2008; Postero 2010; Goodale and Postero 2013.

10. Like other oil companies, Repsol was forced to renegotiate its contracts with the Bolivian state following the 2006 Heroes of the Chaco decree. Repsol's new contract with the state oil company YPFB was signed on October 28, 2006, and entered into effect on May 2, 2007, for a period of twenty-four years.

11. The establishment of indigenous autonomies (seen as the basis for a "plurinational state") was a key demand of the Pacto de Unidad Indígena, Originario y Campesino (Unity Pact of Indigenous, First Peoples and Peasant Organizations), an association of indigenous and peasant organizations that formed as a strategy of collective negotiation in Bolivia's 2006–8 Constituent Assembly (Tapia 2007). This demand was incorporated (in diluted form) into the 2009 constitution and 2010 Autonomy Law, through the establishment of jurisdictions called Indigenous Originary Peasant Peoples' Autonomies (Autonomías Indígena Originaria Campesinas, AIOCs), which can be established at a regional, municipal, or TCO level (Tockman 2014; Garcés 2011; Postero 2017). Related dimensions of indigenous autonomy introduced by the Morales government include intercultural education reforms, special indigenous representation in congress, recognition of indigenous justice systems and healthcare reforms that recognize "traditional" medicine.

12. The letter is quoted in a press release published by Equipo Niskor on June 20, 2010, titled "La APG Itika Guasu reclama al Gobierno por no respetar su derecho a la consulta." http://www.derechos.org/nizkor/bolivia/doc/apgig8.html.

13. "Evo: Consulta a indígenas es un chantaje y una extorsión para las empresas." 2007. Erbol (La Paz). April 27. Reprinted by Equipo Nizkor. http://www.derechos.org/nizkor/bolivia/doc/consulta17.html.

14. Such conflicts were routine, exacerbated by the unfinished status of the land titling process.

15. As noted in chapter 3, fiscal problems stemmed largely from INRA director Jorge Campero's diversion of Danish funds allocated to TCO titling to individual titling processes in the Tarija Department.

16. Many property files from Itika Guasu were sent to La Paz following the discovery, during an internal monitoring exercise, of numerous irregularities in the work of INRA Tarija (see chapter 3).

17. For example, a prior consultation process—which the Ministry of Hydrocarbons and Energy is responsible for implementing—requires the diffusion of detailed information on planned developments to affected communities and indigenous authorities, and a series of meetings, which rely on logistical support, such as transport of people from dispersed and often inaccessible areas. Reaching agreement may require a lengthy process of negotiation. Given the tight timeframes of contracts with transnational oil companies and gas-receiving countries, this process could easily delay the granting of environmental licenses and ultimately jeopardize production and export targets—the cost of which would be borne by the Bolivian state under the rubric of "recoverable costs."

18. Repsol, "El Campo Margarita de Repsol será el mayor proveedor de gas boliviano a Argentina." Press release, March 28, 2009, https://imagenes.repsol.com/es_es/18-Campo%20Margarita_tcm7-562447.pdf.

CHAPTER 6. GOVERNABLE SPACES

1. Radio Nizkor is an Equipo Nizkor Internet-based project dedicated to the dissemination of audio documents on human rights, civil liberties, and peace. See http://www.radionizkor.org/about.html.

2. A full English translation of the speech is available on Equipo Nizkor's website, http://www.derechos.org/nizkor/bolivia/doc/apgig14.html.

3. The construction of the Interoceanic Highway through Itika Guasu was never completed, as shortly afterward Mario Cossio was ousted from power on corruption charges and replaced by a MAS-aligned departmental governor (a new title introduced under the MAS government to replace the position of departmental prefect).

4. This dispute erupted when Tarija Department's road-building service Sedeca signed an agreement with an oil company, Petrosur, for the lease of a workers' camp in TCO Itika Guasu. The APG IG leadership denounced the agreement, claiming they should have been consulted; Sedeca then won a departmental court case against the TCO's president for jeopardizing its "rights of association." In 2008, following an appeal by the APG IG, the case went to the Plurinational Constitutional Tribunal. The constitutional judgement (October 25, 2010) resulting from this case set an important precedent for future negotiations over extractive industry development in the TCO, by affirming the APG IG's right to prior consultation on any development activities in "its territory." Moreover, referencing numerous national and international norms, the judgement orders the Bolivian state (via INRA) to complete the titling of the TCO in favor of Guaraní claimants. The full text of the ruling is available on Equipo Nizkor's website.

5. Indigenous leaders and NGOs in Bolivia have pointed to the significance of the absence of commas in the official category Territorio Indígena Originario Campesino or TIOC, which appears in the 2009 constitution and 2010 Autonomies Law. Indigenous peoples feared that this conflation of the indigenous, originary, and peasant identity categories would be used to challenge the preferential status of indigenous rights within TCOs.

6. Formal indigenous autonomy can be implemented via three routes: in indigenous-titled TCO land (which is in most cases unviable, given the spatially fragmented nature of land rights in many TCOs); at a municipal level, where indigenous peoples must win a majority in a municipal referendum (something that is unachievable for most lowland groups, who represent demographic minorities within their respective municipalities); or at a regional level (composed of multiple municipalities or a province), although in the latter case autonomous powers are limited to planning and administration.

7. On the 2007-8 departmental autonomy movements in the Bolivian lowlands, see Kohl and Breshanan 2010; Soruco 2011. On regional and departmental autonomy projects in Tarija, see Humphreys Bebbington and Bebbington 2010; Lizárraga, Vacaflores, and Arostegui 2010; Gustafson 2011.

8. The phrase "land-territory" (tierra-territorio) has been used by indigenous peoples, activists, and NGOs in Bolivia since the 1990s to emphasize that indigenous peoples' demand for formal land rights forms part of a broader political vision of "territory." It is precisely the erosion of this link between land and territory that this leader laments, and which he seeks to reestablish through his vision of territorial autonomy beyond the TCO titling process.

9. This research was conducted in the context of a one-month consultancy on hydrocarbon regulation in the Margarita gas field, for the Rural Territorial Dynamics Program coordinated by the Chilean NGO Rimisp (Anthias 2012b).

10. Solíz Rada claims to have resigned from his post after eight months because the government backed down on state control of refineries under pressure from Brazil, without consulting him on the decision.

11. "ONG Nizkor no tiene personería jurídica para funcionar en Tarija," El País, January 12, 2012, http://www.elpaisonline.com/index.php/component/k2/item/32058-ong-nizkor-no-tiene-personeria-juridica-para-funcionar-en-tarija.

12. On April 5, 2014, Equipo Nizkor released an online statement in both Spanish and English claiming that "the sectional executive of O'Connor Province has recruited eighteen individuals as henchmen [*capangas*] in order to visit all the communities within the authority of the APG IG, to try and bring about the dismissal of the board and obtain the necessary majority to achieve the [abolition] of the organization's statute . . . To do this, he has also acquired some pickup trucks (approximately ten) to enable these individuals to move around the extensive territory of the Original Community Territory Itika Guasu (TCO IG) with the publicly stated intention of breaking up the organization and effecting its dissolution."

CONCLUSION

1. These included a proposed law to allocate a fixed share of departmental hydrocarbon royalties to non-Chaco rural municipalities in Tarija Department; the institutionalization of regional autonomy in Gran Chaco Province; a rival demand for regional autonomy in O'Connor Province; a proposal for the creation of a new municipality in Palos Blancos, the nearest village to the Margarita gas field; renewed indigenous demands for a fixed share of departmental gas rents to fund development in TCOs; and discussion of pursuing formal autonomy in Itika Guasu through the creation of an indigenous municipality.

2. On May 20, 2015, Morales issued Supreme Decree 2366, opening up Bolivia's national parks—which are protected under the constitution as ecological reserves—to oil and gas extraction. Just two weeks later, Morales proclaimed that his controversial plan to build a highway through the TIPNIS national park and indigenous territory would go ahead (Achtenberg 2015).

3. Supreme Decree 2298, issued in March 2015, provides for a truncated, government-dominated consultation process in the case of proposed hydrocarbon projects, in lieu of one that seeks the "free, prior, and informed consent" of affected communities, according to their norms and procedures, as required by the Bolivian constitution and by international accords to which Bolivia subscribes (Achtenberg 2015).

4. In August 2015, Guaraní leaders from TCO Takovo Mora blocked a road to voice their demand for prior consultation from the state oil company, YPFB. After several days the police intervened violently, detaining twenty-nine of the protesters. In the aftermath, the president of YPFB announced that the Guaraní's demand for consultation was not applicable because gas wells were located inside a private property. See "Guaraníes denuncian violenta represión en Takovo Mora." *Los Tiempos Digital.* August 18, 2015, http://www.lostiempos.com/actualidad/economia/20150818/guaranies-denuncian-violenta-represion-takovo-mora.

5. At the time of writing, only one indigenous group, the Guaraní of Charagua, had succeeded in completing the official process for establishing indigenous autonomy (AIOC) and winning a municipal referendum in favor of autonomy.

Glossary

Word origins are indicated by S (Spanish) or G (Guaraní).

(la) banda S: Strip, band, bank. Used by Tarairí community members to refer to the strip of land on the opposite bank of the Pilcomayo River

campesino S: Peasant farmer

chagas S. Tropical parasitic disease prevalent in the Bolivian countryside, transmitted by *vinchuca* insects that live in adobe houses

challa S (Bolivia): An offering to Pachamama (Mother Earth)

chaqueño/a S: A person from the Chaco region

chicha S (Andes): Fermented maize drink

Chiriguanía S (Bolivia): Territory inhabited by the Chiriguano

Chiriguano S: Colonial name used by the Spanish and mestizos to refer to the Guaraní

compadre S: Co-parent, used to address the person who is godfather to one's child

criollo S: American-born person of Spanish heritage

economic social function The legal classification of productive land use, which land claimants must demonstrate to obtain land rights under the INRA Law

empatronamiento S: System of debt bondage or forced labor, in which indigenous people worked as virtual slaves for mestizo hacienda owners (*patrones*). Referred to elsewhere as *enganche* or *habilito*.

guirapembi G: Cot or bed woven from leather strips

hacienda S: Ranch or faro

i G: Water

indígena S: Indigenous person

Itikeño S: A person from Itika Guasu

ivi G: Land-territory

iya G: Owner; spirit owner of a natural resource

iyambae G: Without an owner; free

kaguiye G: Fermented maize drink (*chicha* in Spanish)

karai G: Non-Guaraní person

kuña mburuvicha G: Female community leader

Kuñati G: White (Guaraní) woman; the name given to me in Tarairí

mburuvicha G: Leader of community or group of communities

mestizo S: Of mixed Spanish and indigenous ancestry

mezquinar S: To be mean or stingy; to keep something to oneself and deny others access to it

mita S (Latin America): Forced labor performed by Indian men under Spanish colonialism, adapted from Inca *mit'a* system of mandatory public service

ñande G: Us/our/ours

ñande reko G: Our way of being

oka G: Courtyard; the shared central area of a community around which houses are placed

originario S: Native, used in the highlands as an alternative to *indígena*

patrón S: Hacienda boss; often denotes exploitative debt-peonage relations

pochi G: Bad-tempered, angry
potrero S: Field; fenced plot of cultivated land
-reta G: Suffix indicating plural
saneamiento S: The official name for land titling; also means sanitizing, cleaning up
Tarijeño S: A person from Tarija
tierras baldías S: Idle lands (state classification)
tipoy S: Clothing traditionally worn by Guaraní women (G: *mandu*)
vaquero S: Cowboy; cattle driver

References

Achtenberg, E. 2015. "Morales Greenlights TIPNIS Road, Oil and Gas Extraction in Bolivia's National Parks." *Rebel Currents* blog, June 15. http://nacla.org/blog/2015/06/15/morales-greenlights-tipnis-road-oil-and-gas-extraction-bolivia%E2%80%99s-national-parks.

Actas de Concertación. 2003. Unpublished document; obtained from CERDET.

Acta de Reunión. 2009. Minutes from APG Departmental Assembly, March 27, 2009. Unpublished document.

Adams, W. M., and J. Hutton. 2007. "People, Parks, and Poverty: Political Ecology and Biodiversity Conservation." *Conservation and Society* 5: 147–83.

Albó, X. 1990. *La comunidad hoy.* Vol. 3 of *Los Guarani-Chiriguano.* La Paz: Centro de Investigacion y Promocion del Campesino.

———. 2012. *La autonomía guaraní en el Chaco: Charagua, Gutiérrez y proyección regional.* La Paz: Centro de Investigación y Promocióndel Campesinado; Ministerio de Autonomías.

Albó, X., and C. Romero 2009. *Autonomías indígenas en la realidad Boliviana y su nueva Constitución.* La Paz: Vicepresidencia del Estado Plurinacional de Bolivia y GTZ/PADEP.

"Al Estado Plurinacional y la Población de Tarija." 2011. Resolution from departmental assembly of Tapiete, Weenhayek y Guaraní indigenous peoples. May 4–6. Unpublished document.

Almaraz, A. 2002. *Tierras Comunitarias de Origen: Saneamiento y titulación: Guía para el patrocinio jurídico.* Santa Cruz, Bolivia: Centro de Estudios Jurídicos e Investigación Social.

Almaraz, A., R. Fernández, O. Olivera, P. Mamani, O. Fernández, G. Soto, P. Regalsky, and J. Komadina. 2012. *La MAScara del poder.* Cochabamba, Bolivia: Textos Rebeldes.

Andolina, R., N. Laurie, and S. A. Radcliffe. 2009. *Indigenous Development in the Andes: Culture, Power, and Transnationalism.* Durham: Duke University Press.

Anthias, P. 2012a. "Territorializing Resource Conflicts in 'Post-neoliberal' Bolivia: Indigenous Land Titling and Hydrocarbon Development in TCO Itika Guasu." In *New Political Spaces in Latin American Natural Resource Governance,* edited by H. Haarstad, 129–54. New York: Palgrave Macmillan.

Anthias, P. 2012b. "Regulación Ambiental de los Hidrocarburos en el Campo Margarita, Tarija." In *Jamas tan cerca arremetió lo lejos: Inversiones extraterritoriales, crisis ambiental y acción colectiva en América Latina,* edited by P. Peralta and P. Hollenstein. Quito, Ecuador: Universidad Andina Simón Bolívar, Rimisp, and Ediciones La Tierra.

Anthias, P., and S. A. Radcliffe. 2015. "The Ethno-Environmental Fix and Its Limits: Indigenous Land Titling and the Production of Not-Quite-Neoliberal Natures in Bolivia." *Geoforum* 64: 257–69.

Aparicio-Effen, M., I. Arana, J. Aparicio, C. Ramallo, N. Bernal, M. Ocampo, and G. J. Nagy. 2016. "Climate Change and Health Vulnerability in Bolivian Chaco Ecosystems." In *Climate Change and Health: Improving Resilience and Reducing*

Risks, edited by Walter Leal Filho, Ulisses M. Azeiteiro, and Fátima Alves, 231–59. Cham, Switzerland: Springer.

Asamblea Permanente de Derechos Humanos de Tarija (APDHT). 1990. "Informe de las actividades de la Comisión Departamental de Pueblos Indígenas de la APDHT." Unpublished document; obtained from CERDET.

Asamblea del Pueblo Guaraní (APG). 2009. To Ministry of Hydrocarbons. "Ref: Solicitud creación unidad de apoyo a iniciativas económicas de empresas hidrocarburíferas de los pueblos indígenas." March 18, 2009. Unpublished document.

Asamblea del Pueblo Guaraní del Itika Guasu (APG IG). 2005. "Plan de Desarrollo Guaraní del Itika Guasu 2005–2015. Unpublished document.

——. 2007. "Inspección in Situ de las Operaciones de Repsol YPF en el Campo Margarita del 11 al 14 de Octubre de 2006: Programa de Vigilancia Socio Ambiental de las Industrias Extractivas." Santa Cruz, Bolivia: CEADES.

——. 2009. To Vice Ministry of Land, August 27. Unpublished document.

Asamblea del Pueblo Guaraní de Itika Guasu (APG IG), CEADES, and CERDET. 2005. *Impactos ambientales, sociales y culturales de REPSOL YPF en territorios indígenas de Bolivia*. Santa Cruz, Bolivia: CEADES.

Asamblea del Pueblo Guaraní de Itika Guasu and Centro de Estudios Regionales para el Desarrollo de Tarija (APG IG and CERDET). 2005. *Nuestra historia: Testimonios guaraníes de Itika Guasu*. Tarija: CERDET.

Asociación de Ganaderos de la Provincia O'Connor (ASOGAPO). 2007–8. Complaints to INRA presented by members of ASOGAPO in 2007–2008. Unpublished; photocopies obtained from CERDET.

Balaban, S.-I., K. A. Hudson-Edwards, and J. R. Miller. 2015. "A GIS-Based Method for Evaluating Sediment Storage and Transport in Large Mining-Affected River Systems." *Environmental Earth Sciences* 74, no. 6: 4685–98.

Bebbington, A. 2009. "The New Extraction: Rewriting the Political Ecology of the Andes?" *NACLA Report on the Americas* 42, no. 5 (September–October): 12–20, 39–40.

Bebbington, A., and D. Humphreys Bebbington. 2011. "An Andean Avatar? Post-Neoliberal and Neoliberal Strategies for Securing the Unobtainable." *New Political Economy* 15, no. 4: 131–45.

Bhabha, H. K. 1994. *The Location of Culture*. New York: Routledge.

Bhandar, B. 2011. "Plasticity and Post-Colonial Recognition: 'Owning, Knowing, and Being.'" *Law Critique* 22: 227–49.

Blaser, M. 2010. *Storytelling Globalization from the Chaco and Beyond*. Durham: Duke University Press.

Blomley, N. 2003. "Law, Property, and the Geography of Violence: The Frontier, the Survey, and the Grid." *Annals of the Association of American Geographers* 93, no. 1: 121–41.

——. 2010. "Cuts, Flows, and the Geographies of Property." *Law, Culture, and the Humanities* 7: 203–16.

Bobrow -Strain, A. 2007. *Intimate Enemies: Landowners, Power, and Violence in Chiapas*. Durham: Duke University Press.

Borras, S. M., and J. C. Franco. 2012. "A 'Land Sovereignty' Alternative? Towards a Peoples' Counter-Enclosure." Agrarian Justice Program Discussion Paper. Hague: Transnational Institute.

Bowman, I. 1915. *South America: A Geography Reader*. Chicago: Rand, McNally & Company.

Brenner, N., and S. Elden. 2009. "Henri Lefebvre on State, Space, Territory." *International Political Sociology* 3: 353–77.

Bridge, G. 2001. "Resource Triumphalism: Postindustrial Narratives of Primary Commodity Production." *Environment and Planning* 33, no. 12: 2149–73.

———. 2013. "The Hole World: Scales and Spaces of Extraction." *New Geographies* 2: 43–48.

Brody, H. 1988. *Maps and Dreams: Indians and the British Columbia Frontier*. 1981. Vancouver: Douglas & McIntyre.

Bryan, J. 2010. "Force Multipliers: Geography, Militarism, and the Bowman Expeditions." *Political Geography* 29, no. 8: 414–16.

———. 2012. "Rethinking Territory: Social Justice and Neoliberalism in Latin America's Territorial Turn." *Geography Compass* 6: 215–26.

Bryan, J., and D. Wood. 2015. *Weaponizing Maps: Indigenous Peoples and Counterinsurgency in the Americas*. New York: Guilford Press.

Brysk, A. 2000. *From Tribal Village to Global Village: Indian Rights and International Relations in Latin America*. Stanford: Stanford University Press.

Calzavarini, L. 2005–6. *Introducción*. Part 3. *Nueva presencia eclesial y franciscana en el Chaco: Reducciones y parroquias a cargo de los Colegios de Tarija y Potosí*. Tarija: Centro Eclesial de Documentación. http://www.franciscanosdetarija.com/pag/documentos/intro_pres_franc/republica/intro_3.pdf.

Cameron, J. D. 2013. "Bolivia's Contentious Politics of 'Normas y Procedimientos Propios.'" *Latin American and Caribbean Ethnic Studies* 8: 179–201.

Canedo, F. C. 2007. *Situación del Pueblo Guaraní: Tierra y territorio*. La Paz: Capítulo Boliviano de Derechos Humanos, Democracia y Desarrollo.

Canessa, A. 2013. *Intimate Indigeneities: Race, Sex, and History in the Small Spaces of Andean Life*. Durham: Duke University Press.

Cattelino, J. R. 2010. "The Double-Bind of American Indian Needs-Based Sovereignty." *Cultural Anthropology* 25, no. 2: 235–62.

Centro de Estudios Regionales para el Desarrollo de Tarija (CERDET). 1989. "Informe del primer encuentro departamental de solidaridad con el pueblo guaraní realizado en Ñaurenda los días 1, 2 y 3 de Diciembre." Unpublished document; in CERDET archive.

———. 1993. "Pueblos Indígenas: Pequeña memoria de un renacer . . ." In *Informe Sur* 23, Year 4 (March–April): 6–9. Tarija: CERDET; copy in CERDET archive.

———. 2000. "Consolidación de un territorio para el pueblo guaraní." Unpublished document; in CERDET digital file.

———. 2003. "Memoria de las negociaciones entre la Asamblea del Pueblo Guaraní y la empresa petrolera Maxus con el asesoramiento de CERDET." Unpublished record of hydrocarbon negotiations between APG IG and Maxus.

———. 2004a. *Memorias de un caminar: Acompañamiento a comunidades indígenas en el Chaco Tarijeño*. Tarija: CERDET.

———. 2004b. *Tierra y Territorio: Estudio de la ocupación territorial en Itika Guasu*. Tarija: CERDET.

———. 2008. To Ángelo Losada. "Ref: Resumen del Proceso de Saneamiento Tierra Comunitaria de Origen del Itika Guasu." November 11. Unpublished document; in CERDET file.

———. N.d. 1. "Solidaridad con el Pueblo Guaraní." Unpublished document; in CERDET archive.

———. N.d. 2. "Tierra y territorio: Una experiencia de los guaraníes de Itika Guasu." Unpublished document; in CERDET archive.

——. N.d. 3. "Resumen de actividades del área jurídica con relación al problema Guaraní." Unpublished document; in CERDET archive.

Chanock, M. 1991. "Paradigms, Policies, and Prosperity: A Review of the Customary Law of Tenure." In *Law in Colonial Africa*, edited by K. Mann and R. Roberts. Portsmouth: Heinemann.

Chapin, M., and B. Threlkeld. 2001. "Indigenous Landscapes: A Study in Ethnocartography." Arlington, Virginia: Center for the Support of Native Lands.

Chapin, M., Z. Lamb, and B. Threlkeld. 2005. "Mapping Indigenous Lands." *Annual Review of Anthropology* 34: 619–38.

Chávez, P., R. Choque, P. Portugal, O. Vega, R. Bautista, J. Samanamud, F. Wanderley, R. Prada, J. Viaña, R. Cortez, S. De Alarcón, L. Tapia. 2010. *Descolonización, estado plurinacional, economía plural, socialismo comunitario: Debate sobre el cambio.* La Paz: Fundación Boliviana para la Democracia Multipartidaria.

Colchester, M. 2004. "Conservation Policy and Indigenous Peoples." *Environmental Science & Policy* 7: 145–53.

Conklin, B. A., and L. R. Graham. 1995. "The Shifting Middle Ground: Amazonian Indians and Eco-Politics." *American Anthropologist* 97: 695–710.

Coombes, B., J. T. Johnson, and R. Howitt. 2011. "Indigenous Geographies I: Mere Resource Conflicts? The Complexities in Indigenous Land and Environmental Claims." *Progress in Human Geography* 36, no. 6: 810–21.

Coronil, F. 1997. *The Magical State: Nature, Money, and Modernity in Venezuela.* Chicago: University of Chicago Press.

Coulthard, G. S. 2014. *Red Skin, White Masks: Rejecting the Colonial Politics of Recognition.* Minneapolis: University of Minnesota Press.

DANIDA. 2005. "Asociación entre Bolivia y Dinamarca: Estrategia de Cooperación para el Desarrollo 2005–2010." Unpublished internal report. http:// netpublikationer.dk/um/AsociacionBoliviaDK/AsociacionBoliviaDK.pdf.

Das, V., and D. Poole. 2004. *Anthropology in the Margins of the State.* Santa Fe: School of American Research Press.

Davis, S. 1993. "The World Bank and Indigenous Peoples." http://www-wds.world bank.org/servlet/WDSContent Server/WDSP/IB/2003/11/14/000012009_2003 1114144132/Rendered/PDF/272050WB0and0Indigenous0Peoples01public1.pdf.

Davis, S., S. Salman, and E. Bermudez. 1998. "Approach Paper on Revision of OD 4.20 on Indigenous Peoples." Unpublished World Bank report; photocopy obtained from Sarah Radcliffe, April 2012.

Davis, S., and A. Wali. 1993. *Indigenous Territories and Tropical Forest Management in Latin America.* Washington, D.C.: World Bank.

Deere, C. D., and M. León. 2002. "Individual versus Collective Land Rights: Tensions between Women's and Indigenous Rights under Neoliberalism." In *The Spaces of Neoliberalism: Land, Place, and Family in Latin America,* edited by J. Chase, 53–86. Bloomfield, Conn.: Kumarian Press.

Echazú, E. A. 1992. *Historia de Tarija.* Tarija, Bolivia: Fundación Cultural del Banco Central de Bolivia.

Eckert, J., B. Donahoe, C. Strümpell, and Z. Ö. Biner. 2012. *Law against the State: Ethnographic Forays into Law's Transformations.* Cambridge: Cambridge University Press.

Emel, J., M. T. Huber, and M. H. Makene. 2011. "Extracting Sovereignty: Capital, Territory, and Gold Mining in Tanzania." *Political Geography* 30: 70–79.

Energy Press. 2012. "Repsol invertirá $US 327,4 millones en el desarrollo de Margarita-Huacaya." http://www.energypress.com.bo/repsol-invertira-us-327 4-millones-en-el-desarrollo-de-margarita-huacaya.

Engle, K. 2010. *The Elusive Promise of Indigenous Development: Rights, Culture, Strategy*. Durham: Duke University Press.

Equipo de Apoyo al Pueblo Guaraní and Asamblea del Pueblo Guaraní Itika Guasu. 2013. *Ñemoesäka Guasu: Reflexión histórica-participativa de la Asamblea del Pueblo Guaraní-Itika Guasu*. Entre Ríos, Tarija, Bolivia: Equipo de Apoyo al Pueblo Guaraní.

Erazo, J. 2013. *Governing Indigenous Territories: Enacting Sovereignty in the Ecuadorian Amazon*. Durham: Duke University Press.

Escobar, A. 2008. *Territories of Difference: Place, Movements, Life, Redes*. Durham: Duke University Press.

——. 2010. "Latin America at a Crossroads: Alternative Modernizations, Post-Liberalism, or Post-Development?" *Cultural Studies* 24: 1–65.

Fabricant, N. 2012. *Mobilizing Bolivia's Displaced: Indigenous Politics and the Struggle over Land*. Chapel Hill: University of North Carolina Press.

Fabricant, N., and B. D. Gustafson, eds. 2011. *Remapping Bolivia: Resources, Territory, and Indigeneity in a Plurinational State*. Santa Fe: School for Advanced Research Press.

Fabricant, N., and N. Postero, eds. 2014. "Performing the 'Wounded Indian': A New Platform of Democracy and Human Rights in Bolivia's Autonomy Movement." Introduction to Special Issue, "Performance Politics: Spectacular Productions of Culture in Contemporary Latin America." *Identities* 21, no. 4: 395–411.

——. 2015. "An End to Indigeneity? Reconceptualizing the Political Uses of Indigeneity in Bolivia Today." Talk delivered at Latin American Studies Association Annual Congress, San Juan, Puerto Rico, May 27–30.

Fanon, F. 1967. *Black Skin, White Masks*. 1952. Translated by Richard Philcox. New York: Grove Press, 1967.

Ferguson, J. 1990. *The Anti-Politics Machine: "Development," Depoliticization, and Bureaucratic Power in Lesotho*. Minneapolis: University of Minnesota Press.

Fine, B., C. Lapavitsas, and J. Pincus, eds. 2001. *Development Policy in the Twenty-First Century: Beyond the Post-Washington Consensus*. London: Routledge.

Food and Agriculture Organization. 2012. *Voluntary Guidelines on the Responsible Governance of Tenure of Land, Fisheries and Forests in the Context of National Food Security*. Rome: Food and Agriculture Organization.

Fortun, K. 2012. "Scaling and Visualising Multi-sited Ethnography." In *Multi-sited Ethnography: Theory, Praxis and Locality in Contemporary Research*, edited by M.-A. Falzon, 73–86. Ashgate.

Fraser, N. 2005. "Reframing Justice in a Globalizing World." *New Left Review* 36, Nov–Dec: 69–88.

Fundación AGRECOL Andes. 2006. *Desarrollo agropecuario sostenible en el Chaco Boliviano: Problemas, tendencias, potenciales y experiencias*. Cochabamba, Bolivia: Fundación AGRECOL Andes.

Fundación TIERRA. 2011. *Territorios Indígena Originario Campesinos en Bolivia: Entre la Loma Santa y la Pachamama*. La Paz: Fundación TIERRA.

Galeano E. 1971. *Las venas abiertas de América Latina*. Buenos Aires: Siglo XXI.

Garcés, F. 2011. "The Domestication of Indigenous Autonomies in Bolivia: From the Pact of Unity to the New Constitution. In *Remapping Bolivia: Resources, Territory, and Indigeneity in a Plurinational State*, edited by B. Gustafson and N. Fabricant, 46–67. Santa Fe: SAR Press.

García Hierro, P. 2005. "Indigenous Territories: Knocking at the Gates of Law." In *The Land Within: Indigenous Territory and the Perception of the Environment*, edited by A. Surrallés and P. García Hierro, 252–80. Copenhagen: IWGIA.

García Linera, A. 2007 "Neo-Liberalism and the New Socialism." Translated by W. T. Whitney Jr. *Political Affairs*. January 15. http://www.politicalaffairs.net/ neo-liberalism-and-the-new-socialism-speech-by-alvaro-garcia-linera (accessed February 9, 2012).

——. 2011. "Las tensiones creativas de la revolución la quinta fase del Proceso de Cambio." Viceministerio del Estado, Presidencia de la Asamblea Legislativa Plurinacional, La Paz. http://rebelion.org/docs/134332.pdf (accessed January 21, 2017).

——. 2012. *Geopolítica de la Amazonía: Poder hacendal-patrimonial y acumulación capitalista*. La Paz: Vicepresidencia del Estado.

Goodale, M., and N. Postero, eds. 2013. *Neoliberalism, Interrupted: Social Change and Contested Governance in Contemporary Latin America*. Stanford: Stanford University Press.

Gordon, E. T., G. C. Gurdián, and C. R. Hale. 2003. "Rights, Resources, and the Social Memory of Struggle: Reflections and Black Community Land Rights on Nicaragua's Atlantic Coast." *Human Organization* 62: 369–81.

Gotkowitz, L. 2007. *A Revolution for Our Rights: Indigenous Struggles for Land and Justice in Bolivia, 1880–1952*. Durham: Duke University Press.

Griffiths, T. 2000. "World Bank Projects and Indigenous Peoples in Ecuador and Bolivia." Paper for the Workshop on Indigenous Peoples, Forests and the World Bank: Policies and Practice Washington, D.C., May 9–10. Forest Peoples Programme and Bank Information Center. http://www.forestpeoples.org/sites/ fpp/ files/publication/2010/08/wbipsecubolivmay00eng.pdf.

Gudynas, E. 2010. "Si eres tan progresista ¿ por qué destruyes la naturaleza? Neoextractivismo, izquierda y alternativas." *Ecuador Debate* 79: 61–81.

Gustafson, B. 2002. "The Paradoxes of Liberal Indigenism: Indigenous Movements, State Processes and Intercultural Reform in Bolivia." In *The Politics of Ethnicity: Indigenous Peoples in Latin America*, edited by D. Maybury-Lewis, 267–306. Cambridge: Harvard University Press.

——. 2009. *New Languages of the State: Indigenous Resurgence and the Politics of Knowledge in Bolivia*. Durham: Duke University Press.

——. 2010. "When States Act Like Movements: Dismantling Local Power and Seating Sovereignty in Post-Neoliberal Bolivia." *Latin American Perspectives* 37: 48–66.

——. 2011. "Flashpoints of Sovereignty: Natural Gas and Spatial Politics in Eastern Bolivia." In *Crude Domination: An Anthropology of Oil,* edited by A. Behrends, S. Reyna, and G. Schlee, 220–42. London: Berghahn.

Guzmán, I., E. Núñez P. Pati, J. Urapotina, M. Valdez, and A. Montecinos, A. 2007. *Saneamiento de la tierra en seis regiones de Bolivia, 1996–2007*. La Paz: Centro de Investigación y Promoción del Campesinado.

Haarstad, H., ed. 2012. *New Political Spaces in Latin American Natural Resource Governance*. New York: Palgrave Macmillan.

Hale, C. R. 2002. "Does Multiculturalism Menace? Governance, Cultural Rights, and the Politics of Identity in Guatemala." *Journal of Latin American Studies* 34: 485–524.

——. 2005. "Neoliberal Multiculturalism: The Remaking of Cultural Rights and Racial Dominance in Central America." *PoLAR: Political and Legal Anthropology Review* 28, no. 1: 10–28.

——. 2006. "Activist Research v. Cultural Critique: Indigenous Land Rights and the Contradictions of Politically Engaged Anthropology." *Cultural Anthropology* 21: 96–120.

——. 2011. "Resistencia para qué? Territory, Autonomy, and Neoliberal Entanglements in the 'Empty Spaces' of Central America." *Economy and Society* 40: 184–210.

Hall, D., P. Hirsch, and T. M. Li. 2011. *Powers of Exclusion: Land Dilemmas in Southeast Asia.* Honolulu: University of Hawaii Press.

Hall, G. H., and H. A. Patrinos. 2012. *Indigenous Peoples, Poverty, and Development.* Cambridge: Cambridge University Press.

Hardin, G. 1968. "The Tragedy of the Commons." *Science* 162, no. 3859: 1243-1248.

Harley, J. B. 1989. "Deconstructing the Map." *Cartographica* 26, no. 2: 1–20.

Harris, L., and H. D. Hazen. 2006. "Power of Maps: (Counter)-Mapping for Conservation." *ACME: International Journal for Critical Geographies* 4: 99–130.

Hart, G. 2010. "D/developments after the Meltdown." *Antipode* 41: 117–41.

Herlihy, P. H. 2003. "Participatory Research Mapping of Indigenous Lands in Darién, Panama." *Human Organization* 62, no. 4: 313–31.

Herlihy, P. H., and G. Knapp. 2003. "Maps of, by, and for the Peoples of Latin America." *Human Organization* 62, no. 4: 315–31.

Hindery, D. 2013. *From Enron to Evo: Pipeline Politics, Global Environmentalism, and Indigenous Rights in Bolivia.* Tucson: University of Arizona Press.

Hodgson, D. L., and R. A. Schroeder. 2002. "Dilemmas of Counter-Mapping Community Resources in Tanzania." *Development and Change* 33: 79–100.

Humphreys Bebbington, D. 2008. "Letter from Tarija: To the Brink and Back Again." *Bolivia Information Forum*, no. 11: 7–9.

Humphrey Bebbington, D., and A. Bebbington. 2010. "Anatomy of a Regional Conflict: Tarija and Resource Grievances in Morales's Bolivia." *Latin American Perspectives* 37, no. 4: 140–60.

——. 2011. "Extraction, Territory, and Inequalities: Gas in the Bolivian Chaco. *Canadian Journal of Development Studies/Revue canadienne d'études du développement* 30, no. 1-2: 259–80.

Instituto de Investigación y Capacitación Campesina (IICCA). 1990. "Propuesta de trabajo de asesoría legal popular con el pueblo Guaraní presentado por IICCA a consideración de la coordinación de solidaridad con el Pueblo Guaraní." July. Unpublished document; in CERDET archive.

——. N.d. (ca.1992). "Propuesta de trabajo interinstitucional con el Pueblo Guaraní." Unpublished document; in CERDET archive.

Instituto Nacional de Reforma Agraria (INRA). N.d. Informe Final de TCO Itika Guasu. Unpublished document from INRA Tarija; photocopy accessed from CERDET.

—— 1999. "Relación de Tenencia de Tierras en la Región del Itika Guasu." Unpublished Excel document. Obtained from INRA Tarija.

——. 2008a. "Cuadro General Itika, 24–11–08." Unpublished Excel document; accessed from INRA Tarija.

——. 2008b. "Lista General TCO Itika Guasu." Unpublished Excel document; accessed from INRA Tarija.

——. 2010. "Revisión preliminar y posibles acciones a seguir: predios ITIKAGUASU—radicados en la UCSS." Unpublished document; accessed from INRA Tarija.

Kaup, B. Z. 2010. "A Neoliberal Nationalization? The Constraints on Natural-Gas-Led Development in Bolivia." *Latin American Perspectives* 37, no. 3: 123–38.

Kay, C., and M. Urioste. 2007. "Bolivia's Unfinished Agrarian Reform: Rural Poverty and Development Policies. In *Land, Poverty and Livelihoods in the Era of Globalization: Perspectives from Developing and Transition Countries*, edited by A. H. Akram-Lodhi, S. M. Borras, and C. Kay, 41–79. London: Routledge.

Keck, M. E., and K. Sikkink. 1998. *Activists beyond Borders: Advocacy Networks in International Politics*. Ithaca: Cornell University Press.

Killick, E. 2008. "Godparents and Trading Partners: Social and Economic Relations in Peruvian Amazonia." *Journal of Latin American Studies* 40, 303–28.

Klein, H. S. 1992. *Bolivia: The Evolution of a Multi-Ethnic Society*. New York: Oxford University Press.

Kohl, B. 2006. "Challenges to Neoliberal Hegemony in Bolivia." *Antipode* 38: 304–26.

Kohl, B., and L. Farthing. 2006. *Impasse in Bolivia: Neoliberal Hegemony and Popular Resistance*. London: Zed Books.

Langer, E. D. 2009. *Expecting Pears from an Elm Tree: Franciscan Missions on the Chiriguano Frontier in the Heart of South America, 1830–1949*. 2nd ed. Durham: Duke University Press.

Larson, B. 2004. *Trials of Nation Making: Liberalism, Race, and Ethnicity in the Andes, 1810–1910*. Cambridge: Cambridge University Press.

Lazar, S. 2008. *El Alto, Rebel City: Self and Citizenship in Andean Bolivia*. Durham: Duke University Press.

Leach, M., R. Mearns, and I. Scoones. 1999. "Environmental Entitlements: Dynamics and Institutions in Community-Based Natural Resource Management." *World Development* 27, no. 2: 225–47.

Lefebvre, H. 1971. *Everyday Life in the Modern World*. Translated by Sacha Rabinovitch. New York: Harper and Row.

——. 1991. *The Production of Space*. Translated by Donald Nicholson-Smith. Oxford: Basil Blackwell.

Lehm Ardaya, Z. 1999. *Milenarismo y movimientos sociales en la Amazonia Boliviana: La búsqueda de la loma santa y la marcha indígena por el territorio y la dignidad*. Santa Cruz, Bolivia: Centro de Investigación y Documentación para el Desarrollo del Beni.

Li, T. M. 2000. "Articulating Indigenous Identity in Indonesia: Resource Politics and the Tribal Slot." *Comparative Studies in Society and History* 42, no.1: 149–79.

——. 2007. *The Will to Improve: Governmentality, Development, and the Practice of Politics*. Durham: Duke University Press.

——. 2010. "Indigeneity, Capitalism, and the Management of Dispossession." *Current Anthropology* 51, no. 3: 385–414.

——. 2014. *Land's End: Capitalist Relations on an Indigenous Frontier*. Durham: Duke University Press.

Libermann, K., and A. Godínez, eds. 1992. *Territorio y dignidad: Pueblos indígenas y medio ambiente en Bolivia*. La Paz: Ildis, Nueva Sociedad.

Lizárraga, P., and C. Vacaflores. 2007. *Cambio y poder en Tarija: La emergencia de la lucha campesina*. La Paz: Plural Editores.

Lizárraga, P., C. Vacaflores, and J. C. Arostegui. 2010. "Dinámicas de reconfiguración política en el departamento de Tarija." https://www.academia.edu/8082917/Din%C3% A1micas_de_reconfiguraci%C3%B3n_pol%C3%ADtica_bn_el_departamento_ de_Tarija._Pilar_Liz%C3%A1rraga_Carlos_Vacaflores_Juan_Carlos_Arostegui.

Lund, C. 2016. "Rule and Rupture: State Formation through the Production of Property and Citizenship." *Development and Change* 47: 1199–228.

Marcus, G. E. 1995. "Ethnography in/of the World System: The Emergence of Multi-sited Ethnography." *Annual Review of Anthropology* 24: 95–117.

Mamdani, M. 1996. *Citizen and Subject: Contemporary Africa and the Legacy of Late Colonialism*. Princeton, NJ: Princeton University Press.

Mansfield, B. 2007. "Privatization: Property and the Remaking of Nature-Society Relations." Introduction to the special issue. *Antipode* 39: 393–405.

Marquette, C. M. 1996. "Indigenous Peoples and Biodiversity in Latin America: A Survey of Current Information." Unpublished World Bank report; copy obtained from Sarah Radcliffe.

Martínez, J. A., ed. 2000. "Atlas territorios indígenas en Bolivia: Situación de las Tierras Comunitarias de Origen y procesos de titulación." Santa Cruz, Bolivia: Confederación de Pueblos Indígenas del Oriente de Bolivia and Centro de Planificación Territorial Indígena.

Maxus. 2003a, To APG IG, May 7, "Re: Responsibilidad Social y Servidumbre en TCO Itika Guasu." Unpublished document; obtained from CERDET.

———. 2003b. "Convenio." Facsimile of corrections to draft agreement between Maxus and APG IG. Unpublished document; obtained from CERDET.

McEwan, C. 2003. "Material Geographies and Postcolonialism." *Singapore Journal of Tropical Geography* 24, no. 3: 340–55

McNeish, J. A. 2013. "Extraction, Protest and Indigeneity in Bolivia: The TIPNIS Effect." *Latin American and Caribbean Ethnic Studies* 8, no. 2: 221–42.

McNeish, J. A., and O. Logan. 2012. *Flammable Societies. Studies on the Socio-economics of Oil and Gas.* London: Pluto Press.

Merry, S. E. 2006. *Human Rights and Gender Violence: Translating International Law into Local Justice.* Chicago: University of Chicago Press.

Miller, J. R., P. J. Lechler, G. Mackin, D. Germanoski, and L. F. Villarroel. 2007. "Evaluation of Particle Dispersal from Mining and Milling Operations Using Lead Isotopic Fingerprinting Techniques, Rio Pilcomayo Basin, Bolivia." *Science of the Total Environment* 384, no. 1–3: 355–73.

Mignolo, W. D. 2007. "Delinking." *Cultural Studies* 21, no. 2: 449–514.

Miranda, H. 2002. "El caso Pananti y el derecho a la tierra en Bolivia: Informe del estudio sobre la violación de los Derechos Económicos, Sociales y Culturales (DESC)." Santa Cruz, Bolivia: Fundación Tierra.

Mitchell, T. 2002. *Rule of Experts: Egypt, Techno-Politics, Modernity.* Berkeley: University of California Press.

———. 2011. *Carbon Democracy: Political Power in the Age of Oil.* London: Verso.

Moore, D. S. 2005. *Suffering for Territory: Race, Place, and Power in Zimbabwe.* Durham: Duke University Press.

Murphey, O. 2009. "The USA's Reaction to the Bolivian Revolution of 1952: Pragmatism and the Inter-American System." *Studies in Ethnicity and Nationalism* 9, no. 2: 252–66.

Negi, C. S., and S. Nautiyal. 2003. "Indigenous Peoples, Biological Diversity, and Protected Area Management: Policy Framework towards Resolving Conflicts." *International Journal of Sustainable Development and World Ecology* 10: 169–80.

Nietschmann, B. 1995. "Defending the Miskito Reefs with Maps and GPS: Mapping with Sail, Scuba, and Satellite." *Cultural Survival Quarterly* 18, vol. 4: 34–37.

Offen, K. H. 2003a. "The Territorial Turn: Making Black Territories in Pacific Colombia." *Journal of Latin American Geography* 2, no. 1: 43–73.

———. 2003b. "Narrating Place and Identity, or Mapping Miskitu Land Claims in Northeastern Nicaragua." *Human Organization* 62: 382–92.

Ostrom, E. 1990. *Governing the Commons: The Evolution of Institutions for Collective Action.* Cambridge: Cambridge University Press.

Paredes, J., and G. Canedo. 2008. *10 Años de SAN-TCO: La lucha por los derechos territoriales indígenas en tierras bajas de Bolivia.* Santa Cruz de la Sierra, Bolivia: La Rosa Editorial.

Partridge, W. L., J. E. Uquillas, and K. Johns. 1996. "Including the Excluded: Ethnodevelopment in Latin America." Paper presented at the Annual World

Bank Conference on Development in Latin America and the Caribbean, Bogotá, Colombia, June 30–July 2. http://documents.worldbank.org/curated/en/981431468770397760/pdf/272020Including0the0Excluded01public1.pdf.

Paye, L., W. Arteaga, N. Ramírez, and E. Ormachea. 2011. *Compendio de espaciomapas de TCO en tierras bajas: Tenencia y aprovechamiento de recursos naturales en territorios indígenas.* La Paz: Centro de Estudios Para el Desarrollo Laboral y Agrario (CEDLA).

Peck, J., and A. Tickell. 2002. "Neoliberalizing Space." *Antipode* 34: 380–404.

Peet, R., and M. Watts, eds. 2004. *Liberation Ecologies: Environment, Development, Social Movements,* 2nd ed. London: Routledge.

Peluso, N. L. 1992. *Rich Forests, Poor People: Resource Control and Resistance in Java.* Berkeley: University of California Press.

——. "Whose Woods Are These? Counter-mapping Forest Territories in Kalimantan, Indonesia." *Antipode* 27: 383–406.

Peluso, N., and C. Lund. 2013. "New Frontiers of Land Control: Introduction." *Journal of Peasant Studies* 38, no.4: 667–81.

Perreault, P. 2008. "Natural Gas, Indigenous Mobilization, and the Bolivian State." Identities, Conflict and Cohesion Programme Paper no. 12, United Nations Research Institute for Social Development (UNRISD).

——. 2014. "Nature and Nation: The Territorial Logics of Hydrocarbon Governance in Bolivia." In *Subterranean Struggles: New Geographies of Extractive Industries in Latin America,* edited by A. Bebbington and J. Bury, 67–90. Austin: University of Texas Press.

Perreault, T., and G. Valdivia. 2010. "Hydrocarbons, Popular Protest, and National Imaginaries: Ecuador and Bolivia in Comparative Context." *Geoforum* 41: 689–99.

Philo, C., and C. Wilbert. 2000. *Animal Spaces, Beastly Places: New Geographies of Human-Animal Relations.* London: Routledge.

Pifarré, F. 1989. *Los Guaraní-Chiriguano: Historia de un pueblo.* La Paz: CIPCA.

Platt, T. 1984. "Liberalism and Ethnocide in the Southern Andes." *History Workshop Journal* 17, no. 1: 3–18

Postero, N. 2007. *Now We Are Citizens: Indigenous Politics in Postmulticultural Bolivia.* Stanford: Stanford University Press.

——. 2010. "Morales's MAS Government: Building Indigenous Popular Hegemony in Bolivia." *Latin American Perspectives* 37, no. 3: 18–34.

——, ed. 2013. "The Politics of Indigeneity in Bolivia, Past and Present." Special Issue of *Latin American and Caribbean Ethnic Studies.*

——. 2015. "'El Pueblo Boliviano, de Composición Plural': A Look at Plurinationalism in Bolivia." In *Power to the People?* edited by C. de la Torre, 398–430. Lexington: University of Kentucky Press.

——. 2017. *The Indigenous State: Race, Politics, and Performance in Plurinational Bolivia.* Oakland: University of California Press

Povinelli, E. A. 2002. *The Cunning of Recognition: Indigenous Alterities and the Making of Australian Multiculturalism.* Durham: Duke University Press.

——. 2011. *Economies of Abandonment: Social Belonging and Endurance in Late Liberalism.* Durham: Duke University Press.

Pratt, M. L. 1992. *Imperial Eyes: Travel Writing and Transculturation.* London: Routledge.

Provincial Deputy of O'Connor Province. 2008. To Vice Minister of Lands. 28 March. Unpublished document; obtained from CERDET.

Quijano, A. 2000. "Coloniality of Power, Eurocentrism, and Latin America." *Nepentla: Views From the South* 1, no. 3: 533–80.

Radcliffe, S. A. 2010. "Re-Mapping the Nation: Cartography, Geographical Knowledge and Ecuadorean Multiculturalism." *Journal of Latin American Studies* 42, no. 2: 293–323.

———. 2011. "Third Space, Abstract Space, and Coloniality: National and Subaltern Cartography in Ecuador." In *Postcolonial Spaces: The Politics of Place in Contemporary Culture*, edited by A. Teverson and S. Upstone, 129–45. London: Palgrave.

Radcliffe, S. A., and S. Westwood. 1996. *Remaking the Nation: Identity and Politics in Latin America*. London: Routledge.

Razack, S., ed. 2002. *Race, Space, and the Law: Unmapping a White Settler Society*. Toronto: Between the Lines.

Repsol YPF. 2006. "Desarrollo socioambiental en el Bloque Caipipendi." Unpublished document; obtained from CERDET.

Reyes Pando, L. R., and A. Lavell. 2012. "Extensive and Every Day Risk in the Bolivian Chaco: Sources of Crisis and Disaster." *Journal of Alpine Research/ Revue de géographie alpine* 100–101: 1–13.

Rights and Resources Initiative. 2012. "Respecting Rights, Delivering Development: Forest Tenure Reform since Rio 1992." http://www.rightsandresources.org/documents/files/doc_4935.pdf.

———. 2015. "Who Owns the World's Land? A Global Baseline of Formally Recognized Indigenous and Community Land Rights." Washington, D.C.: Rights and Resources Initiative.

Rivera Cusicanqui, S. 2010. "The Notion of 'Rights' and the Paradoxes of Postcolonial Modernity: Indigenous Peoples and Women in Bolivia." Translated by M. Geidel. *Qui Parle* 18: 29–54.

———. 2012. "Ch'ixinakax Utxiwa: A Reflection on the Practices and Discourses of Decolonization." *South Atlantic Quarterly* 111, no. 1: 95–109.

Said, E. W. 1978. *Orientalism*. New York: Pantheon.

Saignes, T. 2007. *Historia del Pueblo Chiriguano*. La Paz: Plural Editores.

Sawyer, S. 2004. *Crude Chronicles: Indigenous Politics, Multinational Oil, and Neoliberalism in Ecuador*. Durham: Duke University Press.

Schilling-Vacaflor, A. 2016. "'If the Company Belongs to You, How Can You Be Against It?' Limiting Participation and Taming Dissent in Neo-extractivist Bolivia." *Journal of Peasant Studies* 44, no. 3: 658–76.

Scott, J. C. 1998. *Seeing Like a State: How Certain Schemes to Improve the Human Condition Have Failed*. New Haven: Yale University Press.

Simpson, A. 2014. *Mohawk Interruptus: Political Life across the Borders of Settler States*. Durham: Duke University Press.

Smolders, A. J. P., M. A. Guerrero Hiza, J. G. M. Roelofs, and G. van der Velde. 2002. "Dynamics of Discharge, Sediment Transport, Heavy Metal Pollution, and Sábalo (*Prochilodus lineatus*) Catches in the Lower Pilcomayo River (Bolivia)." *River Research and Applications* 18, no. 5: 415–27.

Soederberg, S. 2004. "American Empire and 'Excluded States': The Millennium Challenge Account and the Shift to Pre-emptive Development." *Third World Quarterly* 25: 279–302.

Soliz Rada, A. 2011. "El pachamamismo al servicio de las petroleras." *Bolpress*. December 26. http://www.bolpress.com/?Cod=2011122610.

———. 2012. "Nizkor, los guaranies, Soros y las petroleras." *Bolpress*. January 5. http://www.bolpress.net/art.php?Cod=2012010506.

Soruco, X. 2011. "El Porvenir, the Future That Is No Longer Possible: Conquest and Autonomy in the Bolivian Oriente." In *Remapping Bolivia: Resources, Territory and Indigeneity in a Plurinational State*, edited by N. Fabricant and B. Gustafson, 68–90. Santa Fe: School for Advanced Research Press.

Soruco, X., W. Plata, and G. Medeiros. 2008. *Los barones del Oriente: El poder en Santa Cruz ayer y hoy.* Santa Cruz, Bolivia: Fundación TIERRA.

Sparke, M. 2005. *In the Space of Theory: Postfoundational Geographies of the Nation-State.* Minneapolis: University of Minnesota Press.

Spivak, G. C. 1988. "Can the Subaltern Speak?" In *Marxism and the Interpretation of Culture*, edited by C. Nelson and L. Grossberg, 271–313. Urbana: University of Illinois Press.

Stevens, S. 1997. *Conservation through Cultural Survival: Indigenous Peoples and Protected Areas.* 1st ed. Washington, D.C.: Island Press.

Stocks, A. 2003. "Mapping Dreams in Nicaragua's Bosawas Reserve." *Human Organization* 62: 344–56.

Sundberg, J. 2008. "Tracing Race, Mapping Environmental Formations." In *Environmental Justice Research in Latin America*, edited by D. Carruthers, 25–47. Cambridge: MIT Press.

Svampa, M. 2015. "Commodities Consensus: Neoextractivism and Enclosure of the Commons in Latin America." *South Atlantic Quarterly* 114, no.1: 65–82.

Tapia, L. 2007. "Una reflexión sobre la idea de Estado plurinacional." *Observatorio Social de América Latina* 8, no. 22: 47–63. http://bibliotecavirtual.clacso.org.ar/ar/libros/osal/osal22/D22Tapia.pdf.

Taylor, L. 2013. "Decolonizing Citizenship: Reflections on the Coloniality of Power in Argentina." *Citizenship Studies* 17: 596–610.

Tito, H., A. Soto, and H. Guardia. *Atlas de contratos petroleros en Tierras Comunitarias de Origen y municipios de Bolivia.* Santa Cruz, Bolivia: CEADESC, 2008.

Toledo, V. 2002. "Indigenous Peoples and Biodiversity." In *Encyclopedia of Biodiversity*, edited by S. Levin et al. San Diego: Academic Press.

Tsing, A. L. 2005. *Friction: An Ethnography of Global Connection.* Princeton: Princeton University Press.

Urioste, M., and D. Pacheco. 1999. *Bolivia: Land Market in a New Context.* La Paz: Fundación TIERRA. http://www.ftierra.org/index.php?option=com_content&view=article &id=889:rair&catid=130:ft&Itemid=188.

Valdivia, G. 2005. "On Indigeneity, Change, and Representation in the Northeastern Ecuadorian Amazon." *Environment and Planning* A 37: 285–303.

———. 2010. "Agrarian Capitalism and the Struggle for Hegemony in the Bolivian Lowlands." *Latin American Perspectives* 37, no. 4: 67–87.

Van de Cott, D. L. 2000. *The Friendly Liquidation of the Past: The Politics of Diversity in Latin America.* Pittsburgh: University of Pittsburgh Press.

Vandergeest, P., and N. Peluso. 1995. "Territorialization and State Power in Thailand." *Theory and Society* 24: 385–426.

Viceministerio de Asuntos Indígenas y Originarios (VAIO) and Ministerio de Asuntos Campesinos y Pueblos Indigenas y Originarios (MACPIO). 2000. *Estudio de Identificación de Necesidades Espaciales del Pueblo Guaraní de Itika Guasu.* La Paz: MACPIO.

Viceministerio del Estado Plurinacional de Bolivia y Fundación Boliviana para la Democracia Multipartidaria. eds. 2010. *Descolonización en Bolivia: Cuatro ejes para comprender el cambio.* La Paz: Vicepresidencia del Estado Plurinacional.

Viceministerio de Tierras. 2008. *La nueva política de tierras: Reconducción comunitaria de la reforma agraria.* La Paz: Viceministerio de Tierras.

Wade, P. 2004. "Los guardianes del poder: Biodiversidad y multiculturalidad en Colombia." In *Conflicto e (in)visibilidad: Retos en los estudios de la gente Negra en Colombia.* Edited by E. Restrepo and A. Rojas, 249–69. Cali, Colombia: Universidad del Cauca.

Wainwright, J. 2008. *Decolonizing Development: Colonial Power and the Maya.* Oxford: Blackwell.

Wainwright, J., and J. Bryan. 2009. "Cartography, Territory, Property: Postcolonial Reflections on Indigenous Counter-Mapping in Nicaragua and Belize." *Cultural Geographies* 16, no. 2: 153–78.

Watts, M. J. 2001. "Petro-Violence: Community, Extraction, and Political Ecology of a Mythic Commodity." In *Violent Environments,* edited by M. J. Watts and N. Peluso, 189–212. Ithaca: Cornell University Press.

——. 2009. "The Rule of Oil: Petro-Politics and the Anatomy of an Insurgency." *Journal of African Development* 11, no. 2: 27–56.

——. 2015. "Securing Oil: Frontiers, Risk, and Spaces of Accumulated Insecurity." In *Subterranean Estates: Life Worlds of Oil and Gas,* edited by H. Appel, A. Mason, and M. Watts. 201–26. Ithaca, NY: Cornell.

Weber, M. 1919. "Politics as a Vocation." http://anthropos-lab.net/wp/wp-content/uploads/2011/12/Weber-Politics-as-a-Vocation.pdf.

Whatmore, S. 2002. *Hybrid Geographies: Natures, Cultures, Spaces.* London: Sage.

Wolford, W. 2005. "Agrarian Moral Economies and Neoliberalism in Brazil: Competing Worldviews and the State in the Struggle for Land." *Environment and Planning A* 37: 241–61.

World Bank. 2001. PID541: "Bolivia–National Land Administration Project." Internal report. http://www-wds.worldbank.org/external/default/WDS ContentServer/WDSP/IB/2001/08/04/000094946_01080304115476/Rendered/PDF/multi0page.pdf.

World Bank Group, Food and Agriculture Organization, International Fund for Agricultural Development, United Nations Conference on Trade and Development. 2010. "Principles for Responsible Agricultural Investment that Respects Rights, Livelihoods and Resources." http://siteresources.worldbank.org/INTARD/214574-1111138388661/22453321/Principles_Extended.pdf.

World Resources Institute. 2016. "Climate Benefits, Tenure Costs: The Economic Case for Securing Indigenous Land Rights in the Amazon." Washington, D.C.: World Resources Initiative. http://www.wri.org/sites/default/files/Climate_Benefits_Tenure_Costs.pdf.

World Resources Institute, World Conservation Union, and United Nations Environment Programme. 1992. *Global Biodiversity Strategy: Policy-Makers' Guide.* Baltimore: WRI Publications.

Yashar, D. J. 2005. *Contesting Citizenship in Latin America: The Rise of Indigenous Movements and the Postliberal Challenge.* New York: Cambridge University Press.

"YPFB desconoce existencia de fondo extraterritorial financiado por Repsol a favor de la APG Itika Guasu." 2011. *El País.* December 9.

Zavaleta Mercado, R. 1967. "Bolivia: El Desarrollo de la Conciencia Nacional." Reprinted in *Rene Zavaleta Mercado: Ensayos 1957-1974.* Edited by Mauricio Souza Crespo, 121–210. La Paz: Plural.

——. 2008. *Lo nacional-popular en Bolivia.* 1986. La Paz: Plural Editores.

Index

Page numbers in italics refer to figures.

abstract space, 49–50, 55, 69, 83, 158, 179, 243; production of, 190–91
access: exclusion and, 178; to information on maps, 68; to land and resources, 79–83, 156–79, 196, 206
activism. *See* indigenous activism
Africa, 38
agency, 129–33, 206, 234
agrarian law, 6, 11, 28; development of, 38–48. *See also* INRA Law
agrarian reform (1952–1953), 4, 22, 24–25, 28, 43, 59
Agrarian Superintendence, 255n42
"Agreement of Friendship and Cooperation between the APG IG and Repsol," 5, 11, 17–18, 48, 202–11, 216, 219, 231–35
agriculture, 6; commercial, 123; gendered division of labor, 153, 156. See also *potreros*; subsistence farming
Aguaragüe national park, 209, 247
Albó, Xavier, 55, 152, 262n23
Alcides (pseud., *mburuvicha* of Itikarenda), 150, 166, 168–69
American Geographical Society, 37
ancestral land rights, 44–45, 76, 78, 191, 202; counterdiscourse of, 126–29; discourse of, 61, 128–29; mapping territory, 52–55. *See also* "reclaiming territory"
Andean migrants, 104, 258n6
Andes, Spanish colonialism in, 38
APG (Asamblea del Pueblo Guaraní), 14; formation of, 26; mapping territory, 58
APG IG (Asamblea del Pueblo Guaraní de Itika Guasu): accountability, 218; agreement with Repsol (*see* Repsol); anniversary celebration, 204–5, 211–13, *212*, 216–17, *217*,

219; capacity-building programs, 97; community views on leadership struggle, 226–31, 235–39; conflicts with state and local actors, 209, 216; consultation on state and NGO development projects, 215, 236–38; criticism of, 231–34; depicted as outsiders, 129–33, 260n26; distance from communities, 218–19; fiscal mismanagement, 218; formation of, 26–27; hydrocarbon negotiations, 189–93, 199–202, 207; informal negotiations with elite landowners, 135–38, 140; leadership struggle, 226–41, 243–44; mapping Itika Guasu, 33, 52–64, 73; non-indigenous members of, 103–6; purchasing private property in TCO, 200–202; TCO title held by, 261n15; TCO titling and, 87, 99, 110, 135–38, 140; territorial counternarratives, 33
Aráoz, Erick (*técnico*, former INRA employee), 99, 103, 110, 137
Arce, Hermes (CERDET lawyer), 200
Armando (father of host family in Tarairí), 79–81, 90, 145–46, 152, 156–58, *157*, 177, 219, 229, 235, 260n1
Asamblea del Pueblo Guaraní. *See* APG
ASOGAPO (Cattle Ranchers' Association of O'Connor Province), 90–91, 93, 101, 106–8, 111–18, *113*, 134, 259n16. *See also* cattle ranchers
assimilationist discourses, 34–35, 46, 71
authority, 8, 80, 206; colonial, 140; community and, 152; government representatives, 226; moral, 36; political, 216–17, 237, 239, 246, 248; state, 10, 134, 141, 181, 191, 211
Autonomies Law, 209, 210, 214, 263n11

CPSIA information can be obtained
at www.ICGtesting.com
Printed in the USA
LVOW03*1950070218

565674LV00007B/22/P